MARXISM AND THE METROPOLIS

Marxism
and the Metropolis

NEW PERSPECTIVES
IN URBAN POLITICAL ECONOMY

Edited by

WILLIAM K. TABB
QUEENS COLLEGE, C.U.N.Y.

and

LARRY SAWERS
AMERICAN UNIVERSITY

NEW YORK · OXFORD UNIVERSITY PRESS · 1978

Copyright © 1978 by Oxford University Press, Inc.

Library of Congress Cataloging in Publication Data

Main entry under title:
Marxism and the metropolis.

  Bibliography: p.
  Includes index.
  1. Urban economics—Addresses, essays, lectures.
2. Marxian economics—Addresses, essays, lectures.
3. Cities and towns—United States—Addresses, essays,
lectures. I. Tabb, William K. II. Sawers,
Larry, 1942-
HT321.M24   330.9'173'2   77-21815
ISBN 0-19-502261-0
ISBN 0-19-502262-9 pbk.

Printed in the United States of America

Preface

At the 1974 summer conference of the Union for Radical Political Economics, after a particularly spirited discussion of the relationship between urban problems and the basic working of the political economy, the editors of the present volume sat under a shady tree and wrote an announcement calling for a conference to be held somewhere in the east coast megalopolis in February 1975. The goal was to contribute to the development of a radical analysis of what is generally called the "urban crisis." The kinds of questions we addressed ourselves to were:

- How do class relations manifest themselves in the city?

- Do we view the city as a part of the superstructure of the society of which it is a part?

- How can we tie urban form and function to the mode of production?

- How, from a class perspective, do we view local taxation, housing markets, and urban transportation?

- How do regional differences in class structure affect the process of urbanization?

- What are the experiences of urban development in socialist countries?

A Conference on Marx and the Megalopolis did indeed take place, in mid-February 1975 in New York City (at the New School for Social

Research). Over its two days, thirteen papers were presented. A sense of intense excitement was generated by the theoretical overlap between speakers and the consistent thread of the questions and the discussion. The efforts of the New York planning group (Bob Cohen, Gary Edelman, Dave Gordon, Joan Hoffman, Jerry Joffe, Al Watkins, and the editors) were richly rewarded. Hundreds of participants came from all parts of North America as well as from Europe. Over the following year, papers were exchanged among authors. Other colleagues were asked to present contributions for possible inclusion, and two previously published articles were invited.

This book is a joint effort of the authors and editors. Both editors read the several drafts through which most of the papers went and collaborated on their suggestions to the authors. Many of the authors read each others' papers and offered comments that proved useful. As editors, we have attempted to reduce duplication of ideas and to integrate the papers into a single perspective. We have been in constant contact by phone and in meetings over the past two years, making all major and most minor decisions jointly.

The authors of these papers all share a heavy debt to the writings of Marx, Engels, and later thinkers in that tradition. Most of the contributors encountered Marxism well on in their academic careers, coming to it out of a dissatisfaction with mainstream methodology and its assumption of pluralistic harmony. Finding conflict where they had been led to believe there would be consensus, and cumulative crisis instead of steady economic growth, radicals have sought alternative explanations of the urban reality. The urban crisis, as indeed all of the crises of the postwar period, was neither predicted nor seriously dealt with by mainstream social scientists; and this has led to a reappraisal of Marxism.

Marxism has been a major and widely accepted methodological orientation in Europe as well as throughout Asia, Africa, and Latin America. In the United States, however, with its legacy of the (Joseph) McCarthy days and the domestic effects of the anti-Communism of the Cold War period, many have confused Marxism as a social science with the Communism of governments of which they do not approve. This is a confusion we cannot afford. The Marxist tradition is too rich in insight and methodological guidance, and disillusionment with existing approaches too profound and widespread, to fail to accord these essays and this tradition a serious hearing.

Contents

MARXISM AND THE METROPOLIS

Editors' Introduction

In the mid-1970s the reality of the urban crisis presses upon us shrilly at every turn. The media recite a dismal litany, repeating endlessly the bleak story of the big cities, the story of the decay of the social and economic fabric of urban life. Acres of housing lie partly abandoned, shared by poor working people, winos, and junkies. The environment is so desecrated that it endangers health. Fear of crime is such that many older citizens hardly dare venture outside their homes. Inner-city school children graduate from high school unable to read a newspaper. Racial uprisings continue, and urban America continues to become even more rigidly divided by race, ethnicity, and class. With the economy in its longest depression since the 1930s, cities reel under the pressure of their shrinking financial base, disastrously high unemployment, and growing poverty. Many of the nation's largest cities are losing jobs, tax revenues, and population. Even in those cities that are seen as stable or even growing (mostly in the South and West), one finds subtle but steady destruction of the sense of community and the spread of feelings of aimlessness and alienation. Unable to connect in a meaningful way with fellow workers, neighbors, or even family— 20 percent of the population moves every year—unable to exert any degree of influence over "their" government, people retreat into private consumerism or the escape found in alcohol and other drugs.

The purported solutions that government has inflicted upon cities have only exacerbated many of these tensions. Urban renewal has worsened the housing shortage and racial tensions. The overpaving of cities with expressways has fouled the air, destroyed communities, taxed our energy resources. The subsidy of housing has enriched builders and bankers but scarcely begins to meet the stated goal: decent, safe, sanitary housing for all. The attempts by government, from the White House to City Hall, to lessen racial antagonism have been so halfheartedly implemented that racist resistance to compliance with the laws of the land is encouraged. Obeisance to the auto has hastened the outflow of jobs and people from the cities and eviscerated existing surface-transit systems, thereby inflaming the crisis rather than contributing to its solution. Recently built mass-transit systems such as San Francisco's BART or Washington's Metro have only exacerbated these trends. The conventional analysis, which argues that the problem could be solved if one would but make the market work a bit better, seems as bankrupt as many of the older cities themselves. Everywhere the cry is heard for a new approach.

This volume offers an explanation for cities in crisis, demonstrates why government as we know it has failed and must fail to end the crisis, and points to some of the fundamental changes in our system that must be made to solve our urban problems. The perspective underlying all the papers included in this collection denies that self-regulating markets are the ideal answer to most problems or that government is either a benevolent guarantor of social justice or an impotent giant. The perspective imbedded in these papers views the struggle between economic classes as the primary determinant of history. It views the government as an instrument ultimately of the economically dominant classes, although the relation is not a simple one.

WHY A MARXIST URBANOLOGY?

The authors of the essays in this book are part of a large and growing group of concerned academics, economists, historians, political scientists, sociologists, and urban planners who, frustrated by the inability of the tools of their individual disciplines to deal adequately with the problems of our cities, have turned for guidance to the writings of Karl Marx, Friedrich Engels, and other Marxists. The rapid increase in the number of Marxist urbanologists is not confined to the United States. In France, England, and elsewhere, important analyses of cities are being carried out in the Marxist tradition.

One may ask why suddenly in the 1960s and 1970s have so many Marxists begun studying cities and so many urbanologists turned to Marx. Indeed, why did not Marxists pay attention to urban problems before the 1960s? Marx's followers prior to the last decade or so have tended to focus on the core relations of capitalism. While cities were often considered to be the site of class struggle, the space itself hardly seemed important or worthy of special study. Marxists focused their attention instead on problems of unemployment, low wages, arbitrary management, and unsafe working conditions. They have worked to build a class-conscious workers' movement on the factory floor, the place where the primary contradiction of capitalism was seen to be most intense.

This changed in the 1960s. The middle-class exodus from the cities and consequent loss of the tax base, the civil-rights movement, and the urban conflagrations all drew attention to the cities. Struggles over urban space intensified as community groups fought for their homes against highways and urban renewal. Many came to see these struggles over "turf" as forms of class struggle. It became evident that the inner-city poor were being relocated not to eradicate the slums but to move the slums, to "reclaim" valuable land now occupied by the poor and convert it to use for luxury housing, office buildings, convention centers, commuter expressways. The poor working class families, who suffered with little compensation the loss of their homes and communities, were excluded from the benefits of this development. Similarly, the class nature of struggles for community control of schools, the police, and other urban services, became apparent. While racism plays a key role, as the chapter by Jim Green and Allen Hunter on the Boston busing situation so clearly shows, this phenomenon too is amenable to a Marxist analysis. In some European countries, such struggles have advanced far beyond the level of class-consciousness and militancy thus far manifest in the United States, as Katharine Coit's description of the Italian case demonstrates.

As the antiwar movement drew to its successful conclusion in the early 1970s, many radicals redirected their attention away from imperialism and to urban problems. By the mid-1970s, the left-right punch of inflation and unemployment had brought several cities to the point of fiscal disaster and pushed many others close to the brink. Marxists, therefore, could no longer ignore the urban crisis, and Marxist urbanology blossomed.

Concern over the fate of U.S. cities was widespread. Yet not surprisingly, the approach of analysts varied with their ideological predilections and prior methodological and political commitments. A conventional wisdom has developed, and within that view a more conservative and a more liberal approach can be distinguished. In the next section these approaches are briefly described and contrasted with the Marxist position.

THE ALTERNATIVE VIEWS

The mainstream viewpoint holds that the urban crisis is the result of the operation of urban land, job, and commodity markets as they satisfy household preferences and react to various outside stimuli. Even though the results of this process are on occasion deplored, at least by the liberal wing of the orthodox school, they are ascribed to consumers' tastes and various inevitable technological and economic forces.

For conservatives, the policy implication that flows from this stance is to do nothing, inasmuch as the urban crisis results from individual maximizing behavior in a market context and therefore is either optimally efficient or so close to it that a corrupt and bungling government could only make matters worse if it tried to improve upon the market. Conservatives tend to see the solution in less government.

Liberals are more likely to acknowledge the undesirable consequences of the market, such as racial polarization, urban blight, pervasive poverty, and the city's fiscal crisis. During "liberal" administrations, government obliges with a panoply of fragmented programs, each designed to ameliorate a specific problem as though it were unrelated to other programs or to the larger system. The results have been disappointing. There is some debate over why this is the case. Is it that we do not know enough, and have only "thrown money at problems"?

The Marxist political economist finds not only liberal solutions but liberal analysis to be inadequate and believes that it will be virtually impossible to remedy urban ills without a fundamental alteration of the political economic system. The liberal reformers' programs are destined to fail not because we do not know enough but because their programs do not address the systemic nature of the problem. The wealthy find it in their interest that the status quo be maintained. While the powerful can by no means always get what they want, they can generally exercise disproportionate influence within broad situational constraints. If their ability to manipulate the state goes unchallenged, they will continue to frustrate liberal intentions. Mainstream social scientists assume in their explanatory models that capitalism is a permanent system; their analysis fails to explain how it changes over time. For the most part they fail to explore the process of its unfolding. Marx saw capitalist growth culminating inevitably in its demise from causes the system itself creates. The Marxist argues that the crisis the city now faces is the symptom of deep-seated tensions lying within capitalist social relations. Even the most liberal of mainstream thinkers, however, take as given the basic contours of the political economy. The specifically capitalist character of production is taken as given and they presume that it must continue to be organized by the owners of capital. Therefore, in their view, the best that can be done is some redistribution or reform—to patch over the most obvious evils of the system. This necessarily limits reforms to redistribution of resources only after the fundamental array of power and income has already taken shape. By so doing they miss, according to Marx, the central problem: that one group of people, the workers, has to sell for a portion of each day their ability to work (their *labor power*, as Marx termed it) to a far smaller group, which controls labor, the product of labor, and the means of producing the goods and services society needs.

In Marx's view, this simple relationship, the sale of labor power by workers and the control of the investible surplus by capitalists, lies at the root of almost all economic and social problems in a capitalist system. We therefore must pause to describe this process more fully, and then we will talk about its significance.

Marxist analysis begins with a perspective that sees all things in a state of continuous change and evolution—nothing is static. Thus it views traditional social science, which attempts to take "snapshots" of society through a focus on equilibrium and harmony, as unable to treat reality in its essential form. The analysis of any society is rooted in material phenomena rather than in the idealistic theories of conventional social science ("it's human nature," "it was a historical accident"). The most essential material base for any society, Marxists argue, lies in the way production is organized. In every society except the most primitive, the bulk of the population is engaged directly in production, while a tiny minority controls their labor and the things they produce. For example, the slave owner or the feudal lord controls the labor and the product of the slave or serf. In a modern free-enterprise economy, the owners of factories, offices, trucks, and so forth—the owners of capital—direct the labor of wage workers and own the fruit of their labor. The arrangements whereby one class controls the labor of another are called the *social relations of production*. This relationship between a ruling class and a subservient one is inherently conflictual; this class conflict becomes the primary source of social change.

A second defining dimension of society relates to the size and skill of the labor force, the level of technology, the instruments or tools of production, and so forth, which are together termed the *forces of production*. Together with the social relations of production, they are known as the *mode of production*. Marxists divide history into several epochs defined by the prevailing mode of production: primitive communist, ancient, feudal, capitalist, and socialist societies. The rest of society—from the legal structure, parts of which are little more than codification of the social relations of production, to the family structure and even the prevailing personality structure—flows ultimately, though not mechanically, from the mode of production. With reference now to the subject of the present volume, the physical and social structure of the city is seen by Marxists as the evolving product of the social forces of production and the class relations they engender.

Since capitalists make decisions based on their desire to make profits, they try in every way possible to pay workers only part of the value their labor produces, an amount just sufficient to sustain life and to reproduce more workers for the next generation. Value produced by workers in excess of what they are given, Marx called *surplus value;* this is the basis for profit and other property income in our society. Even though wages, or the price of labor power, rises—perhaps a better education comes to be required or the automobile becomes necessary to get to work or a higher standard of living is attained through workers' struggles and becomes the socially acceptable norm—only the capitalist accumulates capital. The vast majority must sell their ability to work, must get a job to eat. A tiny minority, by virtue of its ownership of the means of production, the factories and the office buildings where work takes place, directs the labor of the first group and owns what is produced. One group sells labor power and the other decides how production takes place. In the next section, we describe some of the ways that capitalist social relations affect the social and spatial structure of the metropolis.

THE CLASS STRUGGLE AND SPACE

General Motors, General Electric, and all the other generals whose corporate headquarters impressively rise above our large cities were once small companies with a few employees. But because they are able to plow the surplus back into the firm, they could steadily hire more workers and grow larger. Their machines were produced by past generations of workers, and are in this basic sense the embodiment of workers, of "dead labor."

Living labor confronts the power of these corporate giants. The power that stands over them is a power created by workers; yet is seen as belonging to the corporations, to capital. Thus when workers demand higher wages and better working conditions, and the corporate power refuses, relying on its size, financial and political strength, and most of all on its ability to deny the workers a means of living, it has appropriated this strength from the sweat and blood of past workers. When a company moves from a city to a place where it can find labor that will work for less, it takes the productive capacity built by its workers away from them—creating unemployment, eroding the tax base, leading ultimately to the urban crisis. From the firm's point of view, it must do this in order to survive; if other sellers lower their costs and they do not, they will lose out in the competitive struggle. Capitalists have to expand to survive; they must seek new markets, cheaper raw materials, and lower wage labor or die. The large capitalists—at first the merchants, then the railroads and the banks, and later the multinational corporations—spread their dominion over the hinterland in an ever-expanding outward movement until few places in the world are untouched. In short, the inevitable, incessant struggle to maximize profits shapes the fundamental framework within which industrial location and therefore economic geography is formed.

In capitalism, where the class struggle permeates every segment of society, some sectors of the working class find themselves in a position in relation to their employers that is more favorable than other sectors of the working class. This allows the advantaged sectors greater success in their struggles for higher wages and better working conditions. Moreover, the employers also have an interest in paying their workers a range of wages. These wage differentials, by dividing workers and granting nominal rewards for those working within the system, militate against the formation of a strong class-consciousness and working-class militancy. Thus there is a relatively wide range of incomes found within the working class. This income hierarchy within the working class, as well as the much greater differences between the working class and the ruling class, expresses itself in the spatial arrangements of residence within the modern metropolis. Divisions between and among classes are reflected in conflicts between and within political jurisdictions.

A pattern of residential segregation by income exists within capitalist cities and is often identified with the concentric growth patterns modeled by sociologists such as Burgess and Park and by economists such as von Thünen and Alonso. The sociologists note that similar land uses tend to agglomerate, and that zones take on a pattern of homogeneous land use that gird the city's core in a series of belts.

The first ring from the central business district is a zone of transition, of warehouses and the residences of the very poor. Then comes a ring of the more solid working class; then the white-collar professions, with the richest pushing outward to escape the intrusion of the other groups as the city grows. (When the city declines, as many in the Northeast have begun to do, areas of blight spread outward.) Such an analysis is not new. But as presented by mainstream urbanologists it does not tell us much about the social determinants of such a ring pattern of growth. By far the best explanation and description is over a hundred years old and is found in Friedrich Engels's classic study, *The Conditions of the Working Class in England in 1844,* which contains a rich understanding of the process that Burgess was to describe a half century later. It is well worth quoting at length:

> Manchester contains, at its heart, a rather extended commercial district, perhaps half a mile long and about as broad, and consisting almost wholly of offices and warehouses. Nearly the whole district is abandoned by dwellers, and is lonely and deserted at night. . . . The district is cut through by certain main thoroughfares upon which the vast traffic

concentrates, and in which the ground level is lined with brilliant shops. In these streets the upper floors are occupied, here and there, and there is a good deal of life upon them until late at night. With the exception of this commercial district, all Manchester proper, all Salford and Hulme . . . are all unmixed working people's quarters, stretching like a girdle, averaging a mile and a half in breadth, around the commercial district. Outside, beyond this girdle, lives the upper and middle bourgeoisie, the middle bourgeoisie in regularly laid out streets in the vicinity of working quarters . . . the upper bourgeoisie in remoter villas with gardens . . . in free, wholesome country air, in fine, comfortable homes, passed every half or quarter hour by omnibuses going into the city. And the finest part of the arrangement is this, that the members of the money aristocracy can take the shortest road through the middle of all the labouring districts without ever seeing that they are in the midst of the grimy misery that lurks to the right and left. For the thoroughfares leading from the Exchange in all directions out of the city are lined on both sides, with an almost unbroken series of shops, and are so kept in the hands of the middle and lower bourgeoisie . . . [that] they suffice to conceal from the eyes of the wealthy men and women of strong stomachs and weak nerves the misery and grime which form the complement of their wealth. . . . I know very well that this hypocritical plan is more or less common to all great cities; I know, too, that the retail dealers are forced by the nature of their business to take possession of the great highways; I know that there are more good buildings than bad ones upon such streets everywhere, and that the value of land is greater near them than in remote districts; but at the same time, I have never seen so systematic a shutting out of the working class from the thoroughfares, so tender a concealment of everything which might affront the eye and the nerves of the bourgeoisie, as in Manchester. And yet, in other respects, Manchester is less built according to plan after official regulations, is more outgrowth of accident, than any other city; and when I consider in this connection the eager assurances of the middle class, that the working class is doing famously, I cannot help feeling that the liberal manufacturers, the Big Wigs of Manchester, are not so innocent after all, in the matter of this sensitive method of construction (pp. 84–86).

The way in which class distinctions that originate in the production process determine political power in the urban context and lead to predictable social patterns is described by David Gordon in the first essay of the book. The two following essays, those by Patrick Ashton and Ann Markusen, examine the interaction between the hierarchy of income and status on the one hand, and the spatial ordering of the metropolis on the other. They are particularly concerned with the forms of local government that are unique to American capitalism and how they have reinforced the spatial patterning generated by class divisions. One of the more obvious consequences of the ways in which class divisions within capitalist society are reflected in the spatial arrangement of the metropolis is the fiscal crisis of the American city of today. By concentrating poverty in the central city, its fiscal capabilities are overwhelmed.

The crisis of older cities is predicated then on the pattern of capitalist accumulation and the political constraints that development generates. Thus when a full-blown emergency appears, such as the New York City fiscal crisis, the ways it must be solved prove most harmful to members of that city's working class and most beneficial to its bankers and businesses. William K. Tabb, in his essay on that situation, shows that New York City's crisis is real but that its attempted solution seeks to blame and punish the victims of the process of capitalist accumulation. A fair solution would require facing the root causes of the crisis first and then transforming our economic and political institutions so that a planned urban policy evolves, one which makes social costs and benefits its primary concern.

THE FETISHISM OF SPACE

Sociologists and economists have engaged in seemingly endless debate about the precise nature of the spatial dispersion of various income groups. But what difference does it really make whether the income segregation is concentric-zonal, sectoral, or any other particular spatial form? Since the relation is really one between classes or subclasses, and not one between areas, such a discussion obscures what is really at issue. This mis-specification can be termed "the fetishism of space." It mistakes the surface manifestation of social divisions—spatial segregation—for the social division itself.

This stress on surface concepts in traditional approaches to the city is paralleled by a use of language that obfuscates the class nature of urban society and incorporates implicit ethical judgments. For example, the classical urbanologists have adapted the terminology of plant ecology to the urban scene. In 1925 Burgess, in his paper "The Growth of Cities," characterized the "zones of deterioration" encircling the central business districts as containing "submerged regions of poverty, degradation, and disease," with "their underworlds of crime and vice," the "purgatory of lost souls." "The next zone," wrote Burgess, "is also inhabited predominantly by factory and shop workers, but skilled and thrifty." The notion of social control, of socializing the "inferior" immigrant workers—the Italians, the Poles, the Jews—is largely what was on Burgess's mind. He noted: "Where mobility is the greatest, and where in consequence primary controls break down completely, as in the zone of deterioration in the modern city, there develop areas of demoralization, of promiscuity and of vice."

Engels, a half century earlier, had a clearer sense of the cause-and-effect relationships behind the urban concentric configuration. He saw the workers as victims, not as inferior beings. He knew that retail merchants are forced by competition to open their shops along thoroughfares, and that the rich shut the poor away from their sight, cutting large swaths through working-class neighborhoods so that they can more speedily get to the financial district without seeing the "grimy misery that lurks to the right and the left." The self-regulating market leads to such results. The hierarchy of capitalist structure is mirrored in the segregated living arrangements by occupational status of the metropolitan area.

When the subject turns to the racial hierarchy within the working class, the language used is even more explicitly slanted. As we examine the contemporary mainstream literature on race and land use, we find models which speak of "invasion," "conquest," "retreat." Whites are "ejected" as blacks "invade" (see Laurenti). In their discussion of the Boston busing situation, Jim Green and Allen Hunter analyze such events for us in class terms.

In short, the class struggle under capitalism, unfolding in a complex and contradictory fashion, has shaped the nature of urban space. Unlike the mainstream theorists, who see harmony and equilibrium in the allocation of space, Marxists see the class struggle as affecting where corporations build their factories and stores, and where various residential areas are located. In the next part, we detail how "inevitable" urban processes result from the profit-seeking criteria of decision-makers in the market.

PROFITS, COMPETITION, AND CAPITALISM

One of the defining characteristics of capitalism is that business enterprise is motivated by the drive to gain profits. This is not a matter of
choice for the individual capitalist. Unless profits are earned and rein-
vested in the company, it will not grow and thus will fall behind in the
competitive race. Sooner or later it will be gobbled up by the larger
firms, fade away, or if it does survive, become irrelevant because of
its small relative size. The competitive drive for profit affects every
facet of our society, and its impact on spatial organization is profound.
A few examples will illustrate the point.

Artists and other creative people locate in a poor area of town
where rents are low. Soon their needs are met by coffee houses, art
galleries, organic food instead of processed chemicals, and hand-
crafted products instead of plastic ones. As a market is developed, corporate capitalism and the consumer society move in. Chain stores drive
up rents, and the coffee houses where one could sit playing chess over
a cup of coffee are driven out. High-rise structures are built in place
of the small buildings of the previous century, which had stonework,
intricately inlaid woodwork, and handmade glass. What happens to
the way space is consumed is essentially the same as what happens in
other areas of a market economy: production is dominated by profit-
seeking firms.

Another example of the way in which the profit-seeking character
of enterprise has shaped urban geography has to do with the transportation system. The shape of the metropolis is, of course, crucially affected by the nature of the transportation network. The latter has been
formed by profit-seeking businesses. In the 1930s General Motors
formed various subsidiaries whose sole function was to buy up trolley-
car companies, sack the existing rolling stock and other facilities, convert the system to motorbus—GM was already at that time the largest
bus manufacturer—and then sell the franchise to whomsoever would
promise to buy GM bus replacements. By this method GM destroyed
over a hundred trolley systems in forty-five of the nation's largest
cities. Even a federal court conviction on antitrust charges failed to
stop GM from changing the nature of transportation in cities. The bus
is poor competition for the trolley, so this process served to drive
Americans to the automobile; and there too GM stands to profit. To a

very significant extent, then, the very structure of the modern American metropolis has been shaped by one company's relentless search for profits.

An earlier generation of urban transportation was also molded by the profit motive. While trolley lines "made sense," the way they were built did not. The first trolley-car lines were frequently built out from the cities into empty farmland. The trolley companies made their profits in speculating on the land adjacent to the trolley lines. When the land along the trolley lines was sold off, the trolley companies could no longer sustain the nickel fare. Desperate commuters then forced the city government to subsidize the lines or to buy them outright.

General Motors has profited handsomely from its policy of destroying trolleys at the expense of trolley-car owners and urban dwellers. But capitalist competition for profit may lead to results which are harmful not only to the capitalist class as a whole and to the working class, but also to the individual capitalist. If, for example, an area becomes desirable, land values rise, new dense patterns of land use create congestion, and the environmental amenities which attracted economic activity in the first place are destroyed. The process repeats itself, and still newer, more desirable areas are developed—with the same result. The old abandoned areas degenerate still further. At first it was only the seashore resorts, like Coney Island and Miami Beach, where the overbuilding, congestion, pollution, overcrowding, and then decay became noticeable. Then followed the central business districts and the older suburbs, the fringe areas of central cities. Now it is said that there is no hope for the entire industrial Northeast. The principle is the same in all of these cases. The profit motive puts profit before social need.

The competition that dominates the world of business has spread to the public sector; one finds that the competition among governments has a significant impact on the spatial arrangements of the metropolis. While smaller capitalists may still be tied to a single locality, larger ones are not. This means that manufacturers can play off a government in one potential location against another, seeking better terms. Jurisdictions, knowing that their survival depends on attracting new jobs and holding onto old ones, compete against each other in offering costly incentives, rent-free, specially constructed buildings, utilities at below cost, new roads, tax abatement for several years, and help in discouraging trade-union activities.

In a less than full-employment economy, the gains of one city must come at the expense of others. Not only does this lead local governments to offer location incentives with their inevitable costly competitiveness, but also to minimize local taxes to make their location attractive. Repelling low-income immigrants becomes as important as attracting industry with high taxpaying ability and low public-service requirements. Just as attracting high-wage, tax-contributing firms is not a net gain to the nation, so keeping out the poor is not a program without cost in the aggregate view.

When businesses find ways to use the state in their pursuit of profit, they do so. The logic of the market asserts that the best use of resources is measured not by need but by ability to pay. The poor, of course, have the most limited ability to pay and are thus at the end of every queue, and are offered only society's leftovers. Normally, if the well-to-do desire the land that the poor have been allotted, they merely outbid them in the marketplace and the poor are pushed aside. In the last few decades, capitalists engaged in urban redevelopment, construction, and mortgage banking have been impatient with the slow workings of the market and have utilized the government to seize the land from the poor for their own use.

While it took most mainstream economists and liberal policymakers nearly twenty years after the passage of urban-renewal legislation to become disenchanted with the program (for example, see Wilson), Friedrich Engels had already made essentially the same critique a century before. It took prolonged and widespread citizen protests, well documented by social scientists, to educate informed opinion about the harm routinely done by urban-renewal projects. Yet the same systemic abuses continue, as Chester Hartman and Rob Kessler show in their paper. In evaluating such programs it may well be that the radical's tools of analysis are superior to those employed by mainstream investigators. Yet it is also clear why the radical's methodology is a most unwelcome intrusion. By upsetting neoclassical notions of harmony and undermining the hegemony of consensus theories of decision-making, radical political economists provide both an understanding of underlying class relations and a conceptual framework that can be put in the service of movements for social change. They thus help break the hegemony of reformist solutions as the only conceivable type of change possible.

Here too Engels was there first. We might do well to bring these remarks to a close by citing an extensive passage from Engels on the subject of urban renewal (1872):

> In reality the bourgeoisie has only one method of solving the housing question after *its* fashion—that is to say, of solving it in such a way that the solution continually reproduces itself anew. This method is called "Haussmann." . . . By "Haussmann" I mean the practice which has now become general of making breaches in the working class quarters of our big towns, and particularly in areas which are centrally situated, quite apart from whether this is done from considerations of public health and for beautifying the town, or owing to traffic requirements, such as the laying down of railways, streets (which sometimes appear to have the strategic aim of making barricade fighting more difficult). . . . No matter how different the reasons may be, the result is everywhere the same; the scandalous alleys disappear to the accompaniment of lavish self-praise from the bourgeoisie on account of the tremendous success, but they appear again immediately somewhere else and often in the immediate neighborhood! . . . The breeding places of disease, the infamous holes and cellars in which the capitalist mode of production confines our workers night after night, are not abolished; they are merely *shifted elsewhere!* The same economic necessity which produced them in the first place, produces them in the next place also. As long as the capitalist mode of production continues to exist, it is folly to hope for an isolated solution to the housing question or of any other social question affecting the fate of the workers. The solution lies in the abolition of the capitalist mode of production and the appropriation of all the means of life and labour for the working class itself (pp. 71, 73–4).

WHERE DO WE GO FROM HERE?

The various arguments to be found in this book concerning the political economy of housing, urban renewal, spatial patterning and racism do not stand or fall on the acceptance or rejection of capitalism as an economic system. It is possible for readers to agree with much of what is said and still find American capitalism the best possible system, even given all of its problems. Our view is quite different and should be stated clearly: If the urban crisis is a product of capitalism, then the abolition of capitalism should provide the basis for the resolution of the urban crisis. Consider congestion and urban blight. How much less of a central focus might cities have under a decentralized form of workers' management in a planned economy where shops, clinics, and cultural facilities were established at the neighborhood level? How much of current costs of commuting could be made unnecessary? To what extent can neighborhoods of permanence be established that could be relatively self-contained and self-renewing? What are the advantages of limiting size and scale, of preserving history and continuity over generations? To what degree are urban cultural forms and architectural structures manifestations of a consumerist orientation that is itself the unnecessary product of the merchandising efforts of business—i.e., the premium on newness, on differential status, on enjoyment not only through one-upmanship but also through planned obsolescence? The possibilities inherent in such changes are explored in the last part of this book, where socialist cities are discussed by David Barkin and Larry Sawers. They show that in a different mode of production where profits are not paramount and the class struggle takes a different form the urban crisis of the sort we face is not found.

CONCLUSION

A Marxist approach to the study of urban economics offers a fruitful avenue of study because it begins by asking why cities exist in the form they do, what their evolution has been, and what the tendencies embodied in contemporary production forms are. By examining how the productive relations and ownership patterns yield a particular income distribution and how the social divisions are reflected spatially in terms of residence areas and public services, the Marxist approach is able to show how urban economic problems are created, perpetuated, and re-created over time and how their form changes to reflect development in the mode of production and its superstructural relations.

Once one examines the patterned inequality and class nature of oppression, "policy recommending" takes on a very different meaning. The key questions become what works and what does not work in the redistribution of resources and the establishment of a movement capable of compelling further change. In reply to mainstream economists who argue for a value-free social science, radicals see that the research people choose to do and the selection of initial assumptions and methodology are in essence political decisions.

The decay of urban America continues apace. The alienation and cynicism that assert that "nothing can be done" spread. So too do the slums and the poverty. The grief lies untouched by reforms. This book shows why these reforms do not reverse the decay or bring about a regeneration.

What, then, gives the authors of this volume their optimism? It is that their analysis, which shows the key to solution of the crisis of capitalism and its cities, is gaining steadily in influence both in the United States and throughout the world. The ideas in this book are being used as a guide for many who go on to work for fundamental social change. The popular forces for change are building even as the crisis of capitalism deepens. We do not await this "inevitable" occurrence. We put our scholarship at the service of the class forces which will bring about this transition.

REFERENCES

Alonso, William, *Location and Land Use: Toward a General Theory of Land Rent* (Cambridge, Mass.: Harvard University Press, 1964).

Burgess, Ernest W., "The Growth of the City: An Introduction to a Research Project," *Publications of the American Sociological Society*, 1924.

Engels, Friedrich, *The Conditions of the Working Class in England in 1844* (1845; rpt. Moscow: Progress Publishers, 1973).

————, *The Housing Question* (1872; rpt. Moscow: Progress Publishers, 1975).

Park, Robert E. *et al.*, *The City* (Chicago: University of Chicago Press, 1925).

Wilson, James Q., *Urban Renewal: The Record and the Controversy* (Cambridge, Mass.: MIT Press, 1966).

one

FROM
CITY TO METROPOLIS

Why do some cities grow, others decline? Why do some build toward the heavens and others spread out for miles at low densities? Why do some cities have a clearly defined heart with round-the-clock activities while others become abandoned by dinnertime, and still others seem to lack any definite center at all? The answer to these questions of form are to be found in a study of city functions, of their role in the production process and of the ways decisions are made, and fail to be made, when economic base requirements shift with new developments in the forces of production.

David Gordon, a theorist of urban development, offers us an exciting instance of hypothesis construction within a coherent framework and a marshaling of evidence to support the interpretations developed. From a Marxian framework Gordon challenges the conventional view of urban growth which focuses on various technological changes and consumer preferences that have encouraged decentralization. In contrast, Gordon argues that a complete understanding of the process requires an appreciation of the role of class struggle in forming the geographical structure of the modern metropolis. Manufacturers originally located their factories in cities in order to take advantage of the urban environment that helped to give them the upper hand in disputes with their workers, who were isolated from their allies in other classes. By the end of the nineteenth century, however, working-class militants in the cities had grown so powerful that, even without significant allies from the middle class, they were beginning to win battles with the factory owners. Defeating the militant workers required ever-increasing energies. The manufacturers therefore began, around the turn of the century, to build their plants on the outskirts of cities, and the suburbanization process had begun.

Patrick Ashton argues that as manufacturing employment mushroomed in cities during the last third of the nineteenth century, the growing political control of workers functioning through the boss system, the desecration of the urban environment, and the rising tax burdens pushed many of the well-to-do into the first suburbs. By the turn of the century, the more affluent members of the middle class were able to settle around the first trolley-car stops on the periphery of the city in their attempts to escape the problems of the city. In the 1920s and again in the postwar era, successive waves of immigrants to the suburbs appeared, each with progressively lower incomes. The ability of each of these groups to incorporate itself as a separate jurisdictional entity and thus isolate itself from the working-class militance, environmental degradation, poverty, and high taxes is an integral part of this process. Likewise, the industrialists who have located on the periphery of cities seek to protect suburban autonomy for much the same reasons. These fiefdoms of different economic groups and industries prevent the orderly development of the metropolis.

Ann Markusen explores further the nature of these suburban fiefdoms. She traces the history of local government in the United States and shows how the class struggle which has accompanied capitalist development, political traditions from the colonial and federalist eras, and a "town meeting" ideology have served to create a peculiarly American institution: the strong surburban government. The suburban governmental form allows privileged sectors of the population to avoid paying for the services for those who are less well off. Suburbs reflect the class structure on the periphery of the metropolis.

The essays in this part share a common methodological orientation. They are dynamic in approach. They seek to explain what is going on at one point in time with what has preceded. They start with the forces of production, with how economic activity generates the need for certain spatial ordering. They give a central place to class analysis and the power of those who control the production process to shape the urban environment to maximize profits in production, and to protect themselves as consumers of living space from the social costs the production process inflicts. The authors see government as reactive to the needs of the dominant economic interests. While not claiming a simple correspondence between what capital desires and what urban political jurisdictions decide to do, these authors argue that the power of capital and the requirements of inter-class struggle shape urban form.

Capitalist Development and the History of American Cities

DAVID M. GORDON

Capitalism, as a mode of production, is the basic process of most of what we know as the history of country and city. Its abstracted economic drives, its fundamental priorities in social relations, its criteria of growth and of profit and loss, have over several centuries altered our country and created our kinds of city. . . . The division and opposition of city and country, industry and agriculture, in their modern forms are the critical culmination of the division and specialization of labour which, though it did not begin with capitalism, was developed under it to an extraordinary and transforming degree. . . . The symptoms of this division can be found at every point in what is now our common life.

—Raymond Williams (pp. 302–6)

More and more people live in cities as capitalism develops. And it appears that more and more people dislike many aspects of urban life. Many complain about urban chaos and irrationality, about urban inequality and poverty, about urban impersonality and physical confinement.

* This paper draws upon a larger project. Because it has been considerably abridged for this book, it provides neither the historical detail nor the documentation it requires. Further detail and references are provided in Gordon (1978).

More important, most people apparently regard these urban problems as inevitable. People seem to believe that the modern urban form is inexorably required by advanced industrialism. We may not like our lives in cities, but we seem to think that cities must continue to develop as they have if we are to maintain our present standards of living. How can we forget the need for coordination, for economies of scale, for urban agglomerations, for urban amenities?

This fatalism about our cities resembles an analogous fatalism about technology. That view is often called *technological determinism.* It suggests that our dominant technologies are the *only* kinds of machines which will permit our current standard of living. We may not like the alienated, specialized, hierarchical jobs associated with those machines, but we have to accept them as requisites of our current affluence.

Analogously, our views of cities are suffused with a sense of (what I call) *spatial determinism.* This view suggests that there is only one way of organizing economic life across space, generating only one set of community relationships, which is consistent with advanced industrial standards of living. We may not like those urban relationships, but we have to accept them in order to enjoy what we have. Let them eat concrete!

Recent political struggles and social analyses have begun to challenge the technological-determinist position. Research has suggested that modern machinery has not only permitted affluence but has also been conditioned by the particular characteristics of capitalist accumulation.[1] As Harry Braverman has put it:

> These necessities are called "technical needs," "machine characteristics," "the requirements of efficiency," but by and large they are the exigencies of capital and not of technique. For the machine, they are only the expression of that side of its possibilities which capital tends to develop most energetically: the technical ability to separate control from execution. . . . to subordinate the worker ever more decisively to the yoke of the machine (pp. 230, 231).

We must also begin to reconsider the spatial-determinist view. The new view of technology has led us to the conclusion that capitalist machines develop at least partly in order to control us as workers. So may we also conclude, if we look closely enough, that capitalist spatial

forms also develop at least partly to reproduce capitalist control, helping maintain the class relationships prevalent in capitalist societies.

This reconsideration clearly requires direct historical investigation.
If we hypothesize, in the words of the opening quote, that "capitalism,
as a mode of production," has "created our kinds of city," then we must
be able to trace the historical mechanisms through which these spatial
consequences have gradually evolved. We must explicitly examine, in
short, *the historical links between capitalism and urban development.*
This essay explores those ties through a case study of American history.

Orthodox and Marxian Perspectives

In turning toward that history, we quickly confront a conventional wisdom in the orthodox social sciences. Most urban histories treat the
growth of cities as a gradual, evolutionary, and ineluctable process.
The outcomes seem destined. In any developing society, as Kingsley
Davis writes with assurance, "urbanization is a finite process, a cycle
through which nations go in their transition from agrarian to industrial
society" (p. 9). Cities become continuously larger, more complicated,
more specialized, and more interdependent. Hans Blumenfeld describes the determinants of this historical process:

> The division of labor and increased productivity made concentration in
> cities possible, and the required cooperation of labor made it necessary,
> because the new system called for bringing together workers of many
> skills and diverse establishments that had to interchange goods and
> services. The process fed on itself, growth inducing further growth
> (p. 42).

Because the United States has become the prototypical advanced industrial society, orthodox historians view American urban development
as the consummate reflection of this universal process of urbanization.

In the Marxian view, that history must be seen in a different light.
The Marxian analysis of the spatial division of labor suggests that no
particular pattern of urban development is inevitably "destined," some-
how deterministically cast in a general spatial mold. Spatial forms are
conditioned, rather, by the particular mode of production dominating
the society under study; they are shaped by *endogenous* political-
economic forces, not by *exogenous* mechanisms. Marxians also argue

that urban history, like the history of other social institutions, does not advance incrementally, marching step by gradual step along some frictionless path. Urban history advances *discontinuously,* instead of *continuously,* periodically experiencing qualitative transformations of basic form and structure. During the capitalist epoch, in particular, the instability of the accumulation process itself is bound to lead to periodic institutional change. The current economic crisis and its attendant urban crisis, from this perspective, are just another in a long series of these kinds of transformations.

This essay applies the Marxian perspective. According to that view, we have witnessed three main stages of capital accumulation in the advanced capitalist countries: the stages of *commercial* accumulation, *industrial* (or competitive) accumulation, and advanced *corporate* (or monopoly) accumulation. I argue that urban development in the United States has passed through *three corresponding stages*—each conditioned by the dynamics of capital accumulation that characterize that stage. I argue that the process of capital accumulation has been the most important factor structuring the growth of cities; city growth has not flowed from hidden exogenous forces but has been shaped instead by the logic of the underlying economic system. Finally, I argue that the transitions *between* stages of urban development have been predominantly influenced by problems of *class control in production,* problems erupting at the very center of the accumulation process.

This connected set of historical arguments can be separated formally into three main historical hypotheses about the relationships between capitalist development and urban form in the United States:

> *First,* that three principal urban forms have characterized urban development in America, each corresponding to a determinate stage of capital accumulation. In order to emphasize the *logic* of these connections, I give each urban form, defined abstractly, the name of its conditioning stage of capital accumulation, referring respectively to *the Commercial City, the Industrial City,* and *the Corporate City.*

> *Second,* that the changes from one dominant urban form to another were forged in the crucible of capitalist production, determined by the struggles between owners and workers over social relations of production in the capitalist workplace.

Third, combining these first two hypotheses, that the process of capitalist development more generally has created a uniquely capitalist urban form in the United States—that American capitalism has bred the American capitalist city.

I develop this argument in four sections. The first three trace the emergence of these three successive urban forms—the Commercial City, the Industial City, and the Corporate City. The final section applies that historical analysis to explore the current crisis of American cities, arguing briefly that the relationship between capitalist development and urban form in the United States *lies at the roots of the current urban crisis.*

COMMERCIAL ACCUMULATION AND
THE COMMERCIAL CITY

During the final stages of the emergence of capitalism, merchant capitalists sought to increase their capital through *commercial accumulation.* They made profits through the exchange of commodities in the marketplace. Their profits depended on their capacity to "buy cheap and sell dear." Operating in the market, they did not typically intervene in the production process. They counted heavily upon political favors and franchises to strengthen their privileged intermediate positions in the marketplace. Because monopoly power in the market and political franchise through the State played such a critical role in determining the rate of commercial accumulation, tendencies toward uneven development among merchants, companies, cities, regions, or countries often emerged. Increasingly through this stage of "original accumulation," as capitalists' hungry pursuit of commercial profits grew more and more infectious, the dynamics of commercial accumulation became the major source of change in societies experiencing capitalist transformation.

I would propose in general that cities served four kinds of political economic functions in this stage of commercial accumulation:[2]

A *Political Capital* (and colonial control centers) became the site(s) of the mercantilist government, attracting court followers and mercantile lobbyists eager for commercial privileges.

The *Commercial Metropolis* housed the discounting, lending, accounting, and entrepreneurial functions supporting commercial exchange. (Tendencies toward the uneven development of commercial power among merchants were likely to produce an increasingly uneven geographic concentration of these support activities among cities.)

Ports served as Transport Nodes—as centers for the collection and distribution of commodities being supplied from geographically diffuse points in the hinterlands and carried to dispersed markets. (Merchants were able to consolidate their monopoly control over exchange most effectively if there were few and fixed channels for commodity transport; there were strong tendencies, therefore, for an increasingly uneven geographic concentration of transport functions among Transport Nodes.)

Since artisans producing luxury goods usually clustered in cities to gain access to their wealthy merchant and court-following customers, cities also served as *Craft Manufacturing Centers.*

These few simple observations are sufficient to analyze the emergence and crystallization of the Commercial City in the United States. The dynamics of commercial accumulation dominated American economic development from the colonial era through the middle of the nineteenth century. The American Commercial City evolved during those years.

Among Cities

Before Independence, American colonial cities served few economic functions. The first two general functions of Commercial Cities—those of the Political Capital and the Commercial Metropolis—were firmly lodged in London (see Albion; Nettels). Some seaports developed as Transport Nodes. Many artisans gathered in the colonial ports, producing luxuries for colonial merchants and administrators, but this Craft Manufacturing Center function was obviously limited by the slow growth of the indigenous merchant class itself.[3] The Transport Node function therefore dominated the distribution of people and economic activity both between city and country and also among cities.

Because colonial cities were serving such limited functions, the urban population did not grow very rapidly. Although total colonial population increased more than tenfold between 1690 and 1790, the cities' relative share of the colonial population actually declined.[4] Roughly 9 percent of colonial Americans lived in cities and towns in 1690 (Bridenbaugh, 1971, p. 6). One hundred years later, the relative urban share had fallen back to only 5.1 percent. Although the main port cities grew in absolute numbers, urbanization failed to keep pace "with the diffusion of hundreds of thousands of settlers into the back country" (Glaab and Brown, p. 26). There was little to keep them down in the town.[5]

Given the singular importance of the Transport Node functions, there were strong political-economic pressures which not only limited relative urban population growth but also limited the *number* of major cities. From the beginning, the British Crown strictly controlled town charters. The Crown feared that British merchants would be unable to control commercial transport if too many port cities developed. As early as 1680, according to the governor of Virginia, the King was "resolved as soon as storehouse and conveniences be provided, to prohibit ships trading here to land or unload but at certain fixed places" (Glaab and Brown, p. 1). In the North, these early political-economic constraints limited the growth of commercial ports during the colonial period to just four places—Boston, New York, Philadelphia, and, somewhat later, Baltimore. Although these four ports grew from an average size of almost 10,000 to nearly 22,000 between 1720 and 1775, few other cities were able to attain populations of as much as 5,000.[6] The four ports accounted for 66.9 percent of total urban population in 1790, while only 50,000 lived in all other towns combined. The four ports captured 47.5 percent of urban population growth in the thirteen colonies between 1720 and 1790. There was little space in the economic tableau for other towns to develop.[7]

After Independence, the forces affecting urban development shifted. Commercial accumulation still dominated the pace of economic development, but American merchants were able to gain control over a broader range of commercial functions. As domestic and foreign trade expanded, American merchants quickly replaced British merchants in the middle. American cities added the Commercial Metropolis functions to their earlier roles.[8]

As a result, the growth of American ports exploded. The urban population increased from just over 200,000 in 1790 to more than 6 million in 1860. More important, the urban share of total population *reversed* its decline during the colonial period. Relative urban population rose from one-twentieth of the American population in 1790 to one-fifth in 1860.

With trade growing rapidly, urban merchants competed frenetically to gain control over both the Commercial Metropolis and Transport Node functions. Potential commercial monopolists raced against their peers in other leading American ports. "A complex of city imperialisms arose," as Arthur Schlesinger, Sr., put it, "each scheming for dominion, each battling with its rivals for advantage" (p. 28).

During the first decades after Independence, the major ports were evenly matched in the battle for business. Each of the four main Northern cities participated in the urban trade boom, and each was able to grow more or less apace with the others. Between 1790 and 1810, the populations of Philadelphia, New York, Boston, and Baltimore each increased between 180 and 290 percent. Their absolute population growth alone accounted for 45 percent of total city population increase during those first twenty years.[9]

Soon enough, however, tendencies toward uneven development asserted themselves. New York merchants began to gain clear competitive advantage over their rivals. Thanks to the Erie Canal and to other important commercial innovations, New York commercial capitalists began to control more and more of domestic and foreign trade. Between 1800 and 1860, the New York Port's share of total U.S. foreign trade climbed from only 9 percent to 62 percent. Reflecting its growing role as the primary Commercial Metropolis, the city's population soared. By 1860, New York (including Brooklyn) contained over one million people, more than Philadelphia, Boston, and Baltimore combined.[10] Once again, commercial activity was almost exclusively determining the growth of American cities and the distribution of population among them.[11]

Within Cities

The dynamics of commercial accumulation had much less effect on the internal structure of American cities. Because merchant capitalists were not yet intervening directly in production, commercial accumulation was not yet directly affecting the social relations of production.

As a result, the port cities grew within the context of an earlier precapitalist set of social relations. The ports internally retained their precapitalist forms. In precapitalist cities, as Gideon Sjoberg writes, even business was "conducted in a leisurely manner, money not being the only desired end" (p. 8). Daily life, like the entrepôt around which it centered, was "shot through with chance" (Handlin, p. 11).

Within that precapitalist context, commercial accumulation had two simple direct effects which further specified the content of urban life. First, the economic functions of the port cities determined the groups of people who shared in this "random" urban life. The early port populations were dominated by three main occupational clusters: (1) merchants, associated political professionals like lawyers, and the domestic servants of the wealthy; (2) the artisans, journeymen, and apprentices of the craft trades; and (3) the laborers of the transportation sector, like seamen and draymen.[12] Second, the cities tended naturally to center geographically around the wharves, drawn centripetally to the locus of their main political-economic functions.

As the commercial cities grew, therefore, they began to assume a simple and characteristic urban form, laced with residual social relations not yet transformed by the dynamics of capitalist accumulation.

Most families owned their own property and acted as independent economic agents. Most establishments remained small, making it possible for nearly everyone to live and work in the same place. People of many different backgrounds and occupations were interspersed throughout the central city districts, with little obvious socioeconomic residential segregation. In the central port districts, the randomness and intensity of urban life produced jagged, unexpected, random physical patterns. Streets zigged and zagged every which way. Buildings were scattered at odd angles in unexpected combinations. (Even in Philadelphia, where William Penn's original street plan of 1681 had projected regular, spacious, extensive city growth, the intensive growth around the wharf had resulted in the creation of new unplanned streets around the docks.) It appears that a vibrant community life flourished throughout this central area. The cities featured "an informal neighborhood street life," in Sam Bass Warner's words, threaded by the "unity of everyday life, from tavern, to street, to workplace, to housing. . . ."[13]

Only one group failed to share in this central port-district life. Poor itinerants—beggars, casual seamen, propertyless laborers—all lived outside the cities, huddling in shanties and rooming houses. Too poor to establish themselves stably, moving frequently from town to town, they had little relationship to life in the urban center and little impact upon it.

By the beginning of the nineteenth century, in short, each of the major ports increasingly reflected the characteristic structural logic of the Commercial City. Each city was divided into two parts. One part coalesced around the wharf. Within that central district, many different occupational groups, filling the limited economic roles defined by the Commercial City, lived and worked in intimate, intermingling, heterogeneous contiguity. The second part formed a band around the central port district. In it lived the transient, homogeneous poor. This urban form resulted from the simple intersection between precapitalist social relations among independent economic agents and the limited occupational and locational consequences of the dynamics of commercial accumulation.

Once this basic form was established, rapid urban growth took place *within* it as long as the dynamics of commercial accumulation remained dominant. Between 1800 and 1850, trade expanded rapidly but industrialization had not yet dramatically invaded the urban scene: factories were being built in small towns, not in the large port cities. Some new occupational groups began to enter city life, but all of these groups continued to fit into the places and styles of the Commercial City. The wharves continued to act as magnets, containing urban growth within the central port districts. People pushed toward the docks as much as possible. "In the area adjacent to the waterfront," George Rogers Taylor writes, "a greatly increased work force lived under intolerably crowded conditions" (1970, p. 132). Scattered evidence suggests that central-district residential densities probably reached their peaks in the port cities in the 1840s and 1850s. "In some quarters," Pred concludes, they "approached or exceeded those encountered in modern high-rise housing projects" (p. 196).

And still, the central districts retained their heterogeneity. New immigrant groups were rapidly assimilated into the flowing central-city life.[14] Workplace and residence were still connected.[15] Socioeconomic segregation did not increase.[16] The ebb and flow of street life, however much more crowded it had become, seemed to continue.[17]

The poor also remained itinerant and isolated on the outskirts. There is no evidence that the poor had begun to move into the central districts—where we know that they later began to live—through the 1840s and the 1850s.[18]

One major change in the form of the Commercial City did take place, however, but it simply manifested the intensifying effects of the commercial dynamic. After Independence, as city populations began to boom, land speculators cast their covetous eyes on urban property. The randomness of the earlier street and lot plans gave way to the "rationality" of land speculation. Realtors' straightedges took the zigs out of the maps. In Lewis Mumford's words, land speculators "treated the individual lot and the block, the street and the avenue, as abstract units for buying and selling, without respect for historic uses, for topographic conditions, or for social needs" (p. 421).

The map of Manhattan vividly witnesses this sudden turn. Below Houston Street in Manhattan, streets flow in many directions at odd angles. Streets above Houston Street were first plotted in the Commissioners' Map of 1811. "Motivated mainly by narrow considerations of economic gain" (Reps, p. 299), the commissioners laid out rectangular grids all the way up the rest of the island (to 155th Street). As the commissioners themselves explained, "the price of land" made it seem "proper to admit the principles of economy. . . . The effect of these plain and simple reflections was decisive" (Lyman, p. 113). Thus the "spatially determined" birth of the urban grid!

The Contradictions of the Commercial City

Cities grew very rapidly after Independence in the United States, but, despite their increasing size and complexity, they did *not* exhibit several of the ostensibly inevitable consequences of city growth in "modernizing" societies. For instance, American cities did not experience increasing physical separations among economic functions like work and residence. Nor did they exhibit increasing socioeconomic or ethnic residential segregation. Their poor people did not live in their central districts. And community life in the ports did not become demonstrably more impersonal and anomic.

This kind of emphasis, however heuristic for a skeptical reconsideration of spatial determinism, may convey a misleading impression about the quality of life for early American urban residents. In emphasizing the persistence of heterogeneity and the vibrancy of community life, I may appear to be romanticizing the "good old days" in the early American cities. But sharp conflicts did exist in the Commercial City.

Their basic contour developed directly from the central contradiction of the process of commercial accumulation itself.

Commercial accumulation tended to generate uneven development among buyers and sellers. This tended to bring about, among other consequences, increasingly unequal distributions of wealth and income. Because different socioeconomic groups were living and working closely together in the Commercial Cities, these spreading inequalities became more and more physically evident—manifested in the luxury consumption of local merchants.

It appears that this evidence of inequality generated popular protest against it. As inequalities reached their peaks both during the Revolutionary period and during the 1820s and 1830s, popular protests also seemed to intensify. Most of these protests focused on demands for more equality.[19] Because these protests frequently had political effect, they tended to limit opportunities for further commercial accumulation.[20]

The recurrence of these kinds of protests prompts a final point about the Commercial City. Commercial accumulation both generated uneven development and consequently stimulated popular demands for more economic and political equality. This dialectic of uneven development and popular protest reveals a fundamentally *spatial* aspect to the contradictions of the commercial path to capital accumulation. Capitalists sought a mechanism for increasing their profits on the surface of economic life—tracing profitable connections along the sphere of circulation. Their successes, manifested in increasing wealth through persistently visible exchange, could not be hidden. Because the Commercial City retained the precapitalist transparencies of immediate, intimate, and integrated social relationships, commercial capitalist profits could not be masked. The quest for such a disguise—the urgent need for which was so dramatically witnessed in the streets of the Commercial City—played a central role in prompting the turn to a new and ultimately more opaque mode of capital accumulation.

INDUSTRIAL ACCUMULATION AND THE INDUSTRIAL CITY

Commercial Cities were obviously superseded. City life had fundamentally changed by the end of the nineteenth century. Why?

Following our application of the Marxian perspective, we can draw our first clues from the pace and pattern of capital accumulation. In the United States, the years between 1850 and 1870 witnessed a transition from the stage of commercial accumulation to the stage of industrial accumulation. Capitalists turned more and more toward making profits through industrial production itself—through the direct manufacture of the commodities that they exchanged on the market. In the United States, as in England before it, this consolidation of the capitalist mode of production depended on the final development of the factory system.

Industrial accumulation within the factory form depended centrally on two main factors. First, problems of both cost-minimization and labor discipline required the continual *homogenization* of the labor process; craft jobs were compressed into semiskilled operative work and almost all factory workers were subjected to the same discipline of factory control. Second, the system required the continual availability of a *reserve army of the unemployed*—jobless workers, available for immediate employment, whose presence could help discipline those inside the factory gates.

Given these requirements, it hardly seems surprising that cities became the central locus for factory production. Cities provided easy access to markets, facilitating the scale of production necessary to support homogenized labor processes. Cities also provided easy access to pools of reserve workers, much less accessible to employers in the countryside.

But which cities would house those factories? And what would they look like? Our analysis of the links between industrial accumulation and urban form obviously requires further specification before we can adequately answer those questions.

The Transition to Industrial Accumulation

The first major American factories—the textile mills of the 1830s and 1840s—were clustered along the rivers of New England in small cities like Lawrence, Lowell, Waltham, and Lynn. The factories depended on water power and were small by modern standards. As manufacturing production expanded, the factory cities extended along the rivers rather than piling more and more densely around the original centers of industrial production. When coal replaced water as a source

of energy between 1850 and 1870 and when railroads began to knit together the economic countryside, factories were freed from the river-
banks. Where would capitalists pursue their profits?

Huge cities eventually dominated as the loci for factories. Orthodox economic historians have argued that factories concentrated in
large industrial cities for some combination of four main reasons:
(1) they could be near large numbers of workers; (2) they could secure
easy rail and water access to essential raw materials, particularly coal;
(3) they could be near industrial suppliers of machines and other essential intermediate products, including "innovations"; and (4) they
could be near consumer markets for their final goods. All of these
factors are captured by the conventional term from locational economics, "agglomeration economies." In essence, according to this view,
factory owners will continually discover advantages to locating near
other factory owners.[21]

But these hypotheses about agglomeration economies are not sufficient, by themselves, to explain continuing geographic concentration.
Originally proposed as hypotheses about economies of scale, they can
turn just as easily into hypotheses about analogous *dis*economies of
scale. Too many industrialists located in one city can bid up the price
of labor, for instance, superseding accessibility advantages. Dense
concentrations around rail and water depots can cause congestion and
chaos, obliterating longer-haul savings in transport costs. The same
effects of congestion can impede intermediate commodity exchange,
slowing transport within cities among suppliers and final producers.
And too great a concentration of final producers near the same consumer market, finally, can potentially generate competitive, unstable,
and self-destructive battles for market position and market share.

Where is the threshold? When are industrial cities likely to approach the point of diminishing returns to economic agglomeration?
The mainstream view cannot answer this question *a priori*.

The relevance of these questions, posed initially at a theoretical
level, can be dramatized historically. Evidence suggests that the transition to industrial accumulation was witnessing a *diffusion* of the advantages of urban factory location, not a centralization. Employers' access to workers was spreading because workers were becoming so mobile that labor supply fluidly followed demand. The railroad network
expanded so rapidly during the 1860s and 1870s that most medium-
sized cities quickly gained access to the major coal fields and sources

of other raw materials. Major technological innovations were sufficiently simple and widespread by the decade after the Civil War, according to most historical accounts, that industrialists everywhere were equally able to take advantage of them. And access to consumer markets apparently played a minor role after the rail network improved; most major industries, particularly heavy industries, became increasingly concentrated in one or two cities, more and more isolated from their consumer markets around the country.[22]

Conventional arguments about agglomeration economies, in short, are so indeterminate that one cannot directly derive from them a clear projection of increasingly uneven concentration of manufacturing employment in increasingly large industrial cities. From what we have learned thus far, it appears that capitalists could have profited equally from location in factory cities of almost any size.

Indeed, in the early years of transition, this appears to have been the case. In 1850, many cities of different sizes housed burgeoning factory production. As industrial capitalism took hold between 1850 and 1870, many of these cities enjoyed rapidly expanding industrial production regardless of their former size. Between 1860 and 1870, for instance, manufacturing employment in the three largest cities increased by only 53 percent while it increased in the cities ranked 21st through 50th in population by 79.5 percent. There was no significant correlation between rate of employment increase and initial population-rank size.[23] The New Yorks, Chicagos, and Clevelands were growing rapidly, to be sure, but so were cities like Worcester, Jersey City, Indianapolis, and Dayton. Many cities, it seems, had a grip on the golden ring.

As the economy continued to boom after 1870, however, manufacturing began to concentrate in fewer and fewer large cities. By 1900, New York, Philadelphia, and Chicago each housed well over one million people. Manufacturing employment in those three largest cities grew by 245 percent between 1870 and 1900 while the number of industrial wage-earners in the cities ranked 21st through 50th in population grew by only 158 percent. The ten largest industrial areas increased their share of national value-added in manufacturing from under a quarter to almost two-fifths between 1860 and 1900.[24]

How can we account for this rapid centralization of manufacturing employment without resorting to the kinds of relatively indeterminate *ex post* explanations which the agglomeration hypotheses involve?

I hypothesize that a major reason for the concentration of manufacturing in the largest cities flowed from the dynamics of *labor control in production*. At its most general level, the hypothesis proposes that large cities became increasingly dominant as sites for capitalist factories because they provided an environment which more effectively reinforced capitalist control over the production process. Capitalists had to find *qualitatively efficient* locations for their factories—locations, that is, which maximized their control over the process of production and minimized workers' resistance to that domination (see Gordon, 1976). Medium-sized cities did not fully satisfy this imperative. Larger cities satisfied it much better. And so, more and more capitalists built their factories in those large cities.

This hypothesis can best be elaborated through two separable questions: First, what differences between medium-sized cities and large cities account for their differential sustenance of capitalist production? And second, what explains those underlying differences between the two kinds of cities?

The first question is somewhat easier to answer. The problem of labor discipline plagued capitalists continually after they began to institute the factory form of production. Artisans resisted the degradation of work, and wage-laborers from preindustrial backgrounds struggled against the insecure wages and working conditions which factory homogenization continually imposed. Particularly as Civil War prosperity gave way to the stagnation and depression of the 1870s, workers fought to resist layoffs and wage cuts all across the industrial terrain.

In smaller and medium-sized industrial cities, employers had great difficulty suppressing and overcoming these moments of worker resistance.[25] The power of the industrialist, in Gutman's words, "was not yet legitimized and 'taken for granted'" (1963, p. 11). Many middle-class residents, used to earlier, preindustrial relationships, resented the imposition of the relentless, uncompromising, impersonal disciplines of factory life. When workers struck, newspapers, politicians, and the middle classes often supported them. As Gutman elaborates, the non-industrial classes "saw no necessary contradiction between private enterprise and gain on the one hand, and decent, humane social relations between workers and employers on the other" (1963, p. 48). As the Portsmouth, N.H., *Times* explained, "We have very little of the codfish aristocracy, and industrious laborers are looked upon here with as much respect as any class of people" (quoted in Gutman, *loc. cit.*).

In the largest cities, it appears, relationships among the several classes were significantly different. Workers were, in the transitional years at least, no less likely to strike than workers in smaller cities. But the various strata of the middle class were much more hostile to the workers than their peers in smaller cities. Newspapers, politicians, and the middle classes usually opposed workers on strike. Facing such hostility, workers found it more difficult to fight their employers. Because "there was almost no sympathy for the city workers from the middle and upper classes," workers were weakened and "employers in large cities had more freedom of choice than their counterparts in small towns." One of the many results, according to fragmentary evidence, was that "strikes and lockouts in large cities seldom lasted as long as similar disputes outside of these urban centers."[26]

The implications of this hypothesis seem clear. Even if all other economic factors were equal—equalizing the factors of *quantitative efficiency*, or the amount of output employers could generate from given labor inputs—employers in large cities would be able to gain considerable advantage over their competitors in smaller industrial centers. Many workers were resisting the factory system. If employers in large cities were better able to overcome that resistance, they would suffer fewer losses during strikes, achieve greater discipline over their regular factory, and, in general, extract more surplus value from their workers. Even if employers were not particularly conscious of these relative advantages at first, those located in larger cities would be able to grow more rapidly and profit more steadily than their classmates in other locations. That dynamic alone would account for the growing concentration of manufacturing employment in those larger cities. And this explanation by itself, from the Marxian perspective, has precedence over other, more "technical" explanations based on agglomeration hypotheses. Economies of scale are little use to any employer, in the end, if he has not already solved the more basic problems of labor discipline. Factor cost-minimization makes little difference to the capitalist if he can't get his workers to labor diligently in the service of his own profits.

How can we account for these differences in class relationships and social environment between larger and smaller industrial cities?

Superficially, two explanations seem obvious. First, the greater physical segregation and impersonality of the larger cities seem to have isolated the working class and exposed it to community indifference or ostracism. Second, nonindustrial classes in smaller cities seem to have exhibited more militantly preindustrial values than their larger-city cousins.

These superficial differences are more difficult to explain. It appears that they need to be examined in different fashion for two separate groups of large industrial cities. In the Northeast, New York, Philadelphia, Boston, and Baltimore—the four dominant Commercial Cities—became the four leading industrial centers in that region. Two characteristics of their precedent dynamics as the leading Commercial Cities seem to have played an important role in isolating their increasingly numerous industrial workers. First, they had already attained considerable physical scale as port cities and, on balance, had begun to suffer from the increasing impersonality which large scale tends to implant. Second, many of the professionals, politicians, newspapers, and merchants of those ports had begun to acquire—after years of support for commercial accumulation—a growing sympathy for the calculus of profitability.

Across the Appalachian Mountains, the most rapidly growing industrial cities displayed exactly the opposite traits. Those industrial cities, like Chicago, Detroit, and San Francisco, that changed character most quickly were those which *least* exhibited preindustrial community relations. Those Midwestern cities, like Louisville, Cincinnati, Pittsburgh and St. Louis, that had already developed commercial and preindustrial production activities before 1850, were the cities most likely to expose capitalist production to the friction of residual solidarities between workers and the middle classes. Indeed, if one looks at the ten Midwestern cities which were largest in both 1850 and 1900, one finds that those with the *fewest* wage-earners in manufacturing in 1850 were precisely those whose industrial employment grew most rapidly between 1850 and 1900.

In either case, it turned out that the basis for industrial profits was best secured if and when a homogeneous industrial proletariat could be most effectively segregated from the rest of society. Ironically, in the American case, this appears to have been spatially possible in cities where Commercial City life had become either *most* or *least* manifest. Where it had been most manifest, cities had apparently become impersonal enough, and the relentlessness of commercial accumulation had sufficiently infected precapitalist community relations to facilitate this process of isolation. Where Commercial City relations had been least manifest, industrial capitalists were able metaphorically to establish their factories on *tabulae rasae*. In both cases, the transition to the Industrial City pointed in the same directions.

The Form of the Industrial City

As the largest cities became increasingly dominant, the form of the Industrial City crystallized. Its characteristics can be easily summarized.

> *First,* huge factories were concentrated in downtown factory industrial districts, near rail and water outlets. (There were a few small industrial districts on the outskirts of some of the cities.)
>
> *Second,* entirely new segregated working-class housing districts emerged. Located near the factories so that workers could walk to work, the housing was crammed densely together. In New York there were tenements. In Philadelphia there were row houses. In most other big cities there were wooden tenements. Whatever the specific features of the housing, it was typically clustered together in isolation from the middle and upper classes. Although some ethnic segregation by block began to emerge, almost all working-class ethnic groups were contained within the same isolated areas.[27]
>
> *Third,* the middle and upper classes began to escape from the center city as fast and as far as their finances permitted. The wealthy and not-so-wealthy joined in "fleeing from the noise and confusion of the waterfront, the dirt, the stench, and the intolerably crowded conditions of the old central city" (Taylor, 1970, p. 134). Since the wealthy could afford to travel farther to and from work than the middle classes, residential socioeconomic segregation among those groups became more and more pronounced. The middle and upper classes were gradually arrayed in concentric rings moving along the transport spokes radiating from the center.
>
> *Finally,* shopping districts arose in the heart of the city to provide centralized shopping outlets on which the middle and upper classes could converge for their marketing.

Working from this schematic view, we can easily see that the Industrial City represented a clear *reversal* of some of the most important tendencies reflected in the Commercial City form. The central city was now occupied by dependent wage-earners rather than independent property-owners. Producers no longer worked and lived in the same place; there was now a separation between job and residential location. There was no longer residential heterogeneity; instead, the cities had quickly acquired a sharp residential segregation by economic class. In the Commercial Cities, the poor had lived outside the center while everyone else lived inside; now, suddenly, the poor and working classes lived inside while everyone else raced away from the center. In the Commercial Cities, central-city life involved nearly everyone in easy communality; in the Industrial Cities, only the working classes participated in the increasingly intense, impersonal, and assaulting street life, and they had little choice.

Was this new urban form destined by technical and spatial necessities? Apparently not. Other, much smaller, less segregated cities might well have facilitated equally rapid industrial growth. It appears, in other words, that a wide variety of cities was initially meeting the tests of quantitative efficiency in industrial production. But capitalism requires workers' submission to their exploitation. Only in this kind of large Industrial City, it appears, could workers be sufficiently isolated for their resistance to be rubbed smooth. As one foreign observer commented upon surveying the central districts of Pittsburgh in 1884, "There are no classes here except the industrious classes; and no ranks in society save those which have been created by industry."[28]

The Contradictions of the Industrial City

Although the Industrial Cities grew rapidly, their growth did not proceed smoothly for long. As the end of the century approached, certain characteristic contradictions began to erupt. Accumulating friction began to threaten the speed of the industrial machine. These frictions assumed both quantitative and qualitative dimensions.

Quantitatively, some diseconomies of scale began to plague the increasingly crowded central cities. Before the second wave of immigration flooded the Industrial Cities after 1890, demand for labor was piling up more quickly than supply could meet it, and wages were beginning to rise. (The index of money wages rose from 66 in 1880 to 74 in 1890, despite falling prices.)[29] Transportation was getting increasingly clogged in some factory districts, and some manufacturers were beginning to complain about congestion. Increasing concentration was creating some pressure on land prices. And, to the degree that political machines were beginning to take advantage of the political isolation of the working classes, governmental corruption was beginning to affect business-property taxes.[30]

None of these sources of friction, for the time at least, seemed decisive. The flood of immigrants after 1890 reduced wage pressure. The rapid extension of electric trolleys during the 1890s helped relieve some downtown traffic congestion, easing the strain on intermediate goods supply. The urban construction boom of the 1890s increased building supply and eased land prices. And businesses began to handle the tax problem themselves, helping spur the "good government" movement after the turn of the century to gain increasing control from corrupt bosses.[31]

The qualitative contradictions were much more decisive. The latent explosiveness of the concentration of workers became more and more manifest. At first, the impersonality and isolation of the factory and working-class districts had helped subdue the industrial proletariat. Gradually, through the 1880s, the dense concentrations of workers began to have the opposite effects. As spreading mechanization and speedup drove industrial workers to increasing resistance during the 1880s, individual strikes and struggles began to spread, infecting neighboring workers. Isolated moments of resistance took increasingly "political" forms. Strikes bred demonstrations not only at the plants but throughout the downtown districts. As the Wisconsin Commissioner of Labor and Industrial Statistics observed about the growing movement for the eight-hour day in Milwaukee in 1886, "the agitation permeated our entire social atmosphere" (quoted in Brecher, p. 40).

The evidence for this relatively sudden intensification of labor unrest in the largest cities, spilling from one sector to another within the working class, seems reasonably persuasive. During the 1870s, most labor unrest took place in small towns, in the mines, and along the railroads.[32] During the early 1880s, according to Florence Peterson's review of the data, "strikes were comparatively infrequent in the United States" (p. 22). From 1885, the magnitude, intensity and form of strikes changed rapidly (see Peterson, pp. 27ff.). In Table 1, the average annual index of workers involved in strikes is tabulated for five-year periods between 1881–1885 and 1901–1905. (The data series is interrupted in 1905.) The data reveal a sharp increase in the num-

Table 1. Workers Involved in Strikes, 1881–1905

Years	Index of Strikers, 5-Year Averages
1881–1885	56.8
1886–1890	118.6
1891–1895	125.8
1896–1900	124.0
1901–1905	187.4

Note: The index includes all workers involved in strikes for each year, 1927–1929 = 100, averaged over 5-year periods.
Source: Peterson, p. 21, Table 1.

bers of workers engaged in strike activity during the 1880s and a steady quantitative increase after the first five years of the period covered. Data on character and location of the strikers are also suggestive. A rising percentage of strikes focused on disputes over "recognition" and "sympathy." The percentage of strikes "ordered by labor organizations" also rose. Most important, workers seemed to be gaining increasing strength; comparing the period between 1886 and 1890 with the years from 1897 to 1899—two junctures of relatively comparable prosperity— we find that the percentage of strike resolutions which were "unfavorable to workers" fell dramatically from 41.1 percent in the former years to 19.6 percent ten years later. It appears, finally, that many of these spreading and more militant strikes were taking place in the largest industrial cities. Exact data on urban location are not available, but two sources help suggest the general trends. First, strikes between 1881 and 1905 seem to have been concentrated intensely in Illinois, Pennsylvania and New York, the sites of the three major industrial cities; 59.8 percent of workers involved in strikes over that period were located in those three states alone. Second, increasing numbers of the major industrial disputes surveyed in the comprehensive labor histories of Foner (1955) and Commons were concentrated in the largest industrial cities.[33]

As these contradictions began to erupt, in short, it appeared likely that the form of the Industrial City would have to change. Its original structure had been premised on its sustenance of capitalist control over production. The increasing centralization of the industrial proletariat that it promoted, however, was beginning to backfire. Labor control was threatening to dissolve. Something clearly had to give.

CORPORATE ACCUMULATION AND
THE CORPORATE CITY

We now know that the Industrial City was itself short-lived. For about half a century, at least, our cities have been pushed in different directions. A new kind of city form has framed American urban development. Corporate skyscrapers have come to dominate the downtown districts of many cities. Factories have moved away from the central cities. Cities have become politically fragmented.

Once again, our application of the Marxian perspective leads us to begin our analysis of these changes with an examination of the pace and pattern of capital accumulation. Around the turn of the century—between 1898 and 1920—the United States experienced a transition from the stage of industrial accumulation to advanced corporate accumulation. The accumulation process, still grounded in the production and realization of surplus value, was being guided by the decisions of many fewer, much larger economic units. Those economic units—the giant corporations—now had sufficient size to permit a qualitatively new level of rationalization of production and distribution. Their size and scope led them increasingly to search for stability, predictability, and security. That search, I argue, played a central role in shaping the Corporate City.

The Decentralization of Manufacturing

Through the 1890s, as we saw, manufacturing had been concentrating in the largest central cities. Factories had been piling more and more densely into downtown districts. Workers were crowding nearby. And some contradictions of that geographic concentration were beginning to erupt.

Suddenly, around 1898 or 1899, manufacturing started moving out of the central city. In twelve of the thirteen largest industrial districts in the country, a special Census study showed that manufacturing employment began to increase more than twice as fast in the "rings" of the industrial districts as in the central cities. Between 1899 and 1909, central-city manufacturing employment increased by 40.8 percent while ring employment rose by 97.7 percent.[34]

These numbers refer to a real and visible phenomenon noted by

contemporary authors—in Graham Taylor's words, to "the sudden investment of large sums of capital in establishing suburban plants"
(p. 6). Between 1899 and around 1915, corporations began to establish factory districts just beyond the city limits. New suburban manufacturing towns were being built in open space like movie sets. Gary,
Indiana, constructed from 1905 to 1908, is the best-known example.
Other new industrial satellite suburbs included Chicago Heights,
Hammond, East Chicago, and Argo outside Chicago; Lackawanna outside of Buffalo; East St. Louis and Wellston across the river from St.
Louis; Norwood and Oakley beyond the Cincinnati limits; and Chester
and Norristown near Philadelphia.[35]

Orthodox economic historians have conventionally explained the
decentralization of manufacturing in the twentieth century as the
product of technological change. Somebody invented the truck, and
the truck made it more efficient to locate manufacturing outside the central city. Somebody else invented land-intensive automated processing
machinery, they add, which placed a premium on employer's finding
cheap land outside dense central-city manufacturing districts.

But these conventional explanations cannot explain this sudden
explosion of satellite suburbs at the turn of the century. The truck
certainly had nothing to do with the development, since the truck was
not an effective commercial substitute for freight transport until the
late 1920s.[36] There is no obvious evidence that there was a sudden rash
of new inventions prompting a shift to land-intensive technologies;
indeed, there is some evidence that the sudden decentralization took
place *despite* shifts to less land-intensive technology in some industries.[37]

Other "factor price" explanations also provide little help. I can
find no evidence either that land-cost increases had accelerated at the
turn of the century or that these increases were directly linked to the
sudden decentralization. And one can hardly argue that the factories
began to move out to the suburbs because the working class had already begun to leave the central cities for "dormitory suburbs." Workers were still tightly locked in central-city tenement districts, they had
not been moving out to the suburbs, and many continued to live in the
central city even after they had begun to work in the satellite factories.[38]

It appears that conventional economic historians have overlooked
the major reason for the sudden dispersal of central-city factories.

Throughout the late 1880s and 1890s, as we saw above, labor conflict had begun to intensify in the downtown central-city districts. Employers quickly perceived one obvious solution. Move!

In testimony presented before the U.S. Industrial Commission from 1900 to 1902, employer after employer explained the crystallizing calculus. Some examples:[39]

> *The President of Fraser and Chalmers Co.* in Chicago: "Chicago today is the hotbed of trades unionism. . . . If it were not for the high investment [manufacturers] have in their machines and plants, many of them would leave Chicago at once, because of the labor trouble that exists here. . . . In fact, in Chicago, within the last two months we have lost some of the very largest corporations that operated here."

> *Chairman of the New York State Board of Mediation and Arbitration:* "Q: Do you find that isolated plants, away from the great centers of population, are more apt to have non-union shops than in a city? A: Yes. Q: Do you know of cases in the State where they do isolate plants to be free . . . from unionism? A: They have been located with that end in view."

> *President of a contracting firm in Chicago:* ". . . all these controversies and strikes that we have had here for some years have . . . prevented outsiders from coming in here and investing their capital. . . . It has discouraged capital at home. . . . It has drawn the manufacturers away from the city, because they are afraid their men will get into trouble and get into strikes. . . . The result is, all around Chicago for forty or fifty miles, the smaller towns are getting these manufacturing plants. . . ."

Graham Taylor, in his study of the satellite-city movement written in 1915, confirms that employers were particularly concerned about the contagiousness of central-city labor unrest. The language of one of his examples is suggestive:

> In an eastern city which recently experienced the throes of a turbulent street-car strike, the superintendent of a large industrial establishment frankly said that every time the strikers paraded past his plant a veritable fever seemed to spread among the employees in all his workrooms. He thought that if the plants were moved out to the suburbs, the

workingmen would not be so frequently inoculated with infection (p. 23).

When factories did move to the industrial suburbs, Taylor notes (p. 101), workers were automatically more isolated than they had been downtown: "Their contact with workers in other factories, with whom they might compare work conditions, is much less frequent." In general, Taylor concludes the decentralization served its purpose and the unions were much less successful than they had been in the central-city districts (see, e.g., p. 101).

If labor trouble had been burgeoning since the 1880s, why did this movement wait so long and begin so suddenly? I would propose that the abrupt inauguration of industrial dispersal could not have begun until the great merger wave of 1898 to 1903. Movement to the suburbs required huge funds for new capital investment. The small entrepreneurial firms of the nineteenth century could scarcely afford plant expansion, much less wholesale reconstruction. Falling profits and prices in the late 1880s intensified the squeeze on their capital. The depression of 1893–1897 further delayed what was beginning to seem inevitable. Finally, as corporations rapidly centralized capital after 1898, they acquired enough extra investment cash to be able to finance the new satellite-plant construction.[40]

I do not mean to imply that the sudden construction of the satellite cities represented some massively engineered, carefully calibrated classwide conspiracy steered by the new corporate giants. Individual corporations understood the reasons for and the implications of their actions, to be sure. (Taylor concluded that "the industrial exodus . . . is, in its individual parts, a consciously directed movement" [p. 26].) But individual corporations were largely acting on their own, without central coordination or suggestion, perceiving and protecting their own individual interests. There were some examples of collective planning, Taylor notes, but "much more usual, if not so conspicuous, is the shifting of factories one by one to the edge of the city" (p. 71). The individual corporations did not need to be directed in their flight from the central-city labor turmoil. They had little choice.

The great twentieth-century reversal of factory location, in short, began because corporations could no longer control their labor forces in the central cities. As with the transition to the Industrial City, problems of labor control had decisive effects. U.S. Steel's creation of Gary metaphorically expressed the importance of this spatial effect. "The Steel Corporation's triumphs in the economics of production," Taylor concluded, "are only less impressive than its complete command over the army of workers it employs" (p. 227).

The Central Business District

The second major change in the twentieth century was the creation and growth of downtown business districts. What explains this development?

Conventional historians explain the growth of the central business districts with new versions of the same arguments about "agglomeration." Every complex society needs vast administrative organs coordinating its transactions, they argue, and many of these activities are best located near each other to permit "face-to-face" communication. These conventional explanations come close to the mark, but they do not fully reveal the importance of the transition to the Corporate City.

The first major expansion of downtown central business districts occurred in the 1920s. Downtown office space in the ten largest cities increased between 1920 and 1930 by 3,000 percent. Tall skyscrapers suddenly sprouted; by 1929, there were 295 buildings 21 stories or taller in the five largest cities alone.[41] The towers began to dwarf their dominions.

The "face-to-face" explanation is not specific enough to explain this sudden spurt of skyscrapers. Why was there a dramatic increase in the need for close administrative contact during those years and not before? Technical explanations also provide little help. Both elevators and steel-beam construction had been applied since the first decade of the century. If technical innovations are sufficient explanations of tall buildings, why did construction await the twenties?

It appears that central business districts flowered in the 1920s because large corporations were not yet ready for them before then. Huge corporations had not consolidated their monopoly control over their industries until after World War I. Once they gained stable market control, they could begin to organize that control.[42] They were now large enough to separate administrative functions from the production process itself, leaving plant managers to oversee the factories while corporate managers supervised the far-flung empire. Having already spurred the decentralization of many of their production plants, they could now afford to locate their administrative headquarters where it would be most "efficient." They chose downtown locations to be near other headquarters, near banks and law offices, and near advertising agents. The presence of one cluster of administrative services quickly bred a forest of looming neighbors. The uneven centralization of headquarters locations quickly surpassed the concentration of industrial employment at its late nineteenth-century peak. By 1929, according to McKenzie's figures, 56 percent of national corporations had located their headquarters in New York City or Chicago (p. 164).

From this perspective, there is nothing necessarily destined about central business districts and towering skyscrapers with their "face-to-face" communication. Those spatial forms develop as the sites for administrative control functions when *power gets very centralized*. During the stage of corporate accumulation, even in its first decades, economic power became very centralized indeed.

Suburban Fragmentation

The third major change in urban form during the twentieth century involved its political fragmentation. Conventional analysts emphasize the importance of residential decentralization as a source of this political suburbanization. People began to prefer suburban autonomy, in this view, over central-city domination.

Once again, we must be very careful about the timing of events. Up to the end of the nineteenth century, central cities habitually annexed outlying residential districts as people moved beyond the traditional city boundaries. Central cities continued to unify their political jurisdictions as they spread outward. This process of annexation continued steadily until the end of the century.

Then the continuing spread of the Industrial City suddenly slowed. Chicago completed its last major annexation in 1889. New York City did not physically grow after the great incorporation of Brooklyn in 1898. Philadelphia and Boston had discontinued annexation even earlier. Of the twenty largest cities in 1900, thirteen enjoyed their last geographic expansion by 1910.[43]

This rapid deceleration of central-city annexation cannot be explained by some exogenous shift in people's preferences about suburban autonomy. People had been fleeing the central city since the 1860s.[44] From the beginning, the refugees typically preferred autonomy and opposed annexation. Despite their opposition, extending suburban populations were simply reclaimed for the central-city government by legislative *fiat*. They were continually subjected, in Kenneth Jackson's words, to "the local or downtown brand of urban imperialism" (p. 449).[45]

What changed at the end of the century? Residential suburbanization did not accelerate. There was not yet a widespread use of the car. The electric streetcar developed rapidly through the 1890s, permitting somewhat more distant intra-urban travel, but it represented a simple improvement on a long succession of carriages and horse cars dating from the 1840s rather than a qualitative transformation of urban transit.

What changed most dramatically, it appears, was that manufacturers themselves began to move out of the central cities. Obviously they wanted to avoid paying central-city taxes. It was now in their interest to oppose further annexation. Given their influence over state legislatures, they easily satisfied their desires. Earlier residential opposition to annexation had not been strong enough to resist central-city aggrandizement. Now, with manufacturers switching sides, the scales dramatically tilted. After industrialists joined the movement against central-city extension, political fragmentation was the natural consequence.

The Form of the Corporate City

Once this transitional period had culminated in a stable pattern of urban reproduction, American cities had acquired a qualitatively new structure. It is reasonably easy to review the central political-economic features of the Corporate City.

If a city had reached maturity as an Industrial City during the stage of industrial accumulation, its character changed rapidly during the corporate period although its physical structure remained embedded in concrete. Its downtown shopping districts were transformed into downtown central business districts, dominated by skyscrapers. (Because corporate headquarters were more unevenly distributed than nineteenth-century industrial establishments, many Industrial Cities, like Baltimore, St. Louis, and Cincinnati, never captured many of these headquarters.) Surrounding the central business district were emptying manufacturing areas, depressed from the desertion of large plants, barely surviving on the light and competitive industries left behind. Next to those districts were the old working-class districts, often transformed into "ghettos," locked into the cycle of cenral-city manufacturing decline. Outside the central city there were suburban belts of industrial development, linked together by circumferential highways. Scattered around those industrial developments were fragmented working-class and middle-class suburban communities. The wealthy lived farther out. Political fragmentation prevailed beyond the central-city boundaries.

Many other, newer cities—particularly those in the South, Southwest, and West—reached maturity during the stage of corporate accumulation. These became the exemplary Corporate Cities. They shared one thundering advantage over the older Industrial Cities: they had never acquired the fixed physical capital of an earlier era. They could be constructed from scratch to fit the needs of a new period of accumulation in which factory plant and equipment were themselves increasingly predicated upon a decentralized model. (Orthodox historians explain the decentralization of manufacturing as a *result* of this new plant and equipment; I have argued that an eruption of class struggle initially prompted the decentralization and, by implication, that the new plant and equipment developed as a result of that dispersal in order to permit corporations' taking advantage of the new locational facts.) There was consequently no identifiable downtown factory district; manufacturing was scattered throughout the city plane. There were no centralized working-class housing districts (for that was indeed what capitalists had learned to avoid); working-class housing was scattered all over the city around the factories. Automobiles and trucks provided the connecting links, threading together the separate pieces. The Corporate City became, in Robert Fogelson's term, the Fragmented Metropolis. No centers anywhere. Diffuse economic activity everywhere.

These two models help underscore the significance of the *reversals* reflected in the Corporate City form. Manufacturing had been clustering toward the center of the Industrial City; now it was moving anywhere across the urban space. Working-class housing had been packed into dense central zones; now it was scattered around the metropolitan area and increasingly segmented. Central business districts had been dominated by shopping centers; now, in at least some cities, they were dominated by corporate headquarters. (The shopping centers, at least in the newer cities, were scattered everywhere.) The middle and upper classes had been fleeing but were continually reabsorbed; now, in the older cities, they fled more successfully into separate suburbs. Before, the city had crammed around its center; now, the Corporate City sprawled.

Once this new urban form crystallized, of course, many additional influences affected urban growth. Patterns of defense spending, federal housing policies, the power of the auto-energy-construction block, the shifting dynamics of urban-land speculation—these and many other factors contributed to the content of urban America after World War II (see, for example, Mollenkopf). All of these factors had secondary effects, however, in the sense that they tended to reproduce the structure of the Corporate City rather than to change or undermine it. The foundations of that urban form were so strong that simple political influences could not change its basic shape.

With that final observation, our study of the relationship between capitalism and the history of American cities can be brought to a close. I have argued that the Corporate City, like its antecedent urban forms, was premised on the requisites of capital accumulation. If we look up at the Corporate City from within its form, it seems fixed and unyielding. If we view it more critically over a much longer horizon, its form seems much more contingent. The Corporate City emerged as a historical solution to some eruptive crises in capital accumulation at the turn of the century. Its form began increasingly to correspond to the pace and pattern of a new stage of corporate accumulation. If we have learned that the Corporate City emerged historically from the disarray of capitalism in crisis, it seems equally likely that we can best understand the current crises of the Corporate City with the same kind of probing analysis.

THE ROOTS OF THE CURRENT URBAN CRISIS

Some of the current urban crisis can be simply explained as a product of general economic crisis. When the economy plunges into a tailspin, for instance, city finances suffer badly and many in the cities go jobless.

It would be misleading to stop at that point. It turns out that the current urban crisis is not a *general* urban crisis at all. Some cities are suffering crisis, like New York, San Francisco, St. Louis, and Detroit, while others are not. Which ones are being hit the worst?

The preceding historical analysis points directly toward some obvious answers. The analysis of the emergence of the Corporate City suggested that American cities have been dominated during the twentieth century by either of two characteristic structures. Cities that reached maurity before the stage of corporate accumulation acquired what has become a relatively archaic physical structure. We can call them "Old Cities." Cities that reached maturity after the era of corporate accumulation had begun, gradually developed a more "modern" physical shape. We can call them "New Cities."

Though shaped by the same underlying logic, Old Cities and New Cities were bound to develop in different directions. New Cities inevitably captured more and more manufacturing. Even the suburbs of the older central cities could not compete with the more perfectly suited physical environments of the newer cities, and industry has continually moved out of the older metropolitan areas—out of the old Industrial Cities—into the newer regions of the Sunbelt.[46] Because corporate centralization continued, on the other hand, corporate headquarters continued to concentrate in a few central business districts. By 1974, although New Cities had stolen huge chunks of manufacturing employment away from Old Cities, New York and Chicago still hosted nearly one-third of the 500 largest corporations' headquarters. In New Cities, finally, annexation has never stopped. Industrialists had vested interests neither in the "original" central cities nor in the "expanding" suburban areas alone. Their economic interests were more or less equally distributed across the metropolitan plane. And so, given industrialist neutrality, opposition to central-city annexation never developed in the New Cities. The twenty most rapidly growing cities between 1960 and 1970 more than doubled their total land area between 1950 and 1970 (Jackson, p. 441).

Tracing some of those different directions, we can certainly map much of the current urban crisis. Relying on the careful statistical work of Alfred Watkins, we can distinguish between Old Cities and New Cities. Of the fifty largest metropolitan areas in the United States (ranked by 1970 population), twenty-five are Old Cities and twenty-five are New Cities. Since eleven of those cities reached maturity during the transitional decade between 1910 and 1920, their definitive categorization is problematic. For the purposes of this brief discussion, therefore, we can work more easily with thirty-nine cities whose "age" seems less ambiguous. Of these, seventeen are Old Cities and twenty-two are New Cities.

A first measure by which to locate the incidence of urban crisis involves the basic health of metropolitan economies. If employment and the labor force are shrinking, cities may be in trouble when general economic crisis strikes. Between 1960 and 1970, the labor forces of sixteen of these thirty-nine cities declined; fourteen were Old Cities. Counting another way, over 90 percent of the New Cities grew while 80 percent of the Old Cities declined. When crisis struck in the mid-seventies, it seems obvious that Old Cities were destined to suffer the worst.

If metropolitan economies are stagnating, social problems intensify. Richard Nathan has developed an index of social hardship for metropolitan areas by combining indices of several different problems like unemployment, poverty, and welfare. The hardship index compares the magnitude of these problems in central cities and their suburbs. The higher the index of central-city disadvantage, the more severe the social problems faced by central city governments. Ranked by this measure, thirteen of the seventen *most* disadvantaged central cities are Old Cities and thirteen of the sixteen *least* disadvantaged central cities are New Cities.

Social hardship usually means mounting city expenditures. We can compare general municipal expenditures per capita for (at the time of writing) 1972. Within our group of cities, ten of the eleven central cities with the highest municipal expenditures per capita were Old Cities. The average in the Old Cities was 42 percent higher than in the New Cities.

With declining economies and exploding expenditure obligations, finally, we would expect that Old Cities would be more likely to get into serious fiscal trouble. With revenues lagging and expenditures climbing, Old Cities may be forced to short-term borrowing to balance their budgets. Sooner or later, the threat of municipal default or bankruptcy may loom. Municipal debt, in this sense, becomes the lightning rod for more general urban crisis. A comparison of short-term municipal indebtedness per capita dramatically understores the differences between Old Cities and New Cities. In 1973–1974, fourteen of the sixteen most indebted cities were Old Cities. The average municipal short-term indebtedness per capita in the Old Cities was 6300 percent greater than in the New Cities.

This discussion makes clear that the current urban crisis is neither universal nor surprising. It is a crisis of Old Cities in the corporate stage of capital accumulation. Capitalism has decreed that those cities have become archaic as sites for capitalist production. The process of capital accumulation is leaving them behind. Capitalists have found that they can better control their labor forces and make higher profits elsewhere. In the terms of this essay, it seems clear that the current crisis of the Old Cities stems, at its roots, from their increasing failure to sustain capital accumulation *on the capitalists' terms*. Given the more general argument that American capitalism has bred the American capitalist city, it seems clear that we shall continue to suffer urban crisis, trapped by the shifting economic fates of our respective cities, until we cast aside the logic of American capitalism itself.

We might as well begin now. Over the longer term there should be nothing sacrosanct about the physical and institutional structure of *either* Old Cities *or* New Cities. The forms of both were historically determined, in large part, by the needs of capital. Neither affords the basis for decent community life because both forms were historically conditioned by capitalists' efforts to isolate workers and then to divide them spatially. Rather than taking those urban structures for granted, we should begin instead to cast aside capitalist criteria altogether. The time has come to develop our own spatial forms.

NOTES

1. See Braverman; Marglin; Gordon (1976) for this argument.
2. Price makes some comparable points, less abstractly, about American ports in the eighteenth century.
3. As both Tryon and Morris show, most manufacturing took place in rural villages and households.
4. Unless otherwise credited, all references in this paper to absolute and relative urban population and to individual city populations are based on U.S. Bureau of the Census (1939); Bogue; U.S. Bureau of the Census (1976).
5. This argument obviously conflicts with the general view that cities automatically grow continuously alongside "modernization."
6. According to Bridenbaugh, other cities reaching populations of 5,000 or more included New Haven, Norwich, Norfolk, New London, and Salem (1955, pp. 216–17).

7. The fate of Southern cities supports this argument. Southern rivers provided direct access between the plantations and the ocean, so coastal Transport Nodes were not required. As a result, Southern cities scarcely developed at all; in 1790, only 2.3 percent of the South Atlantic population lived in cities while 7.5 and 8.7 percent of the New England and Middle Atlantic populations, respectively, lived in cities.

8. A variety of factors combined to keep the Political Capital functions out of the port cities, lodged in an entirely new city, Washington, D.C., and small inland cities like Albany, N.Y., and Harrisburg, Pa.

9. Because of later developments, one must also note that New York did not even grow most rapidly among the four.

10. On New York's history, see Albion. For the figures on New York's share of trade, see Vernon (pp. 31, 32); Pred (p. 147).

11. Southern urban underdevelopment continues to support the argument. With New York merchants hogging the Commercial Metropolis functions supporting the cotton trade, there was still little role for Southern cities. By 1860, the relative urban share in the South had climbed to only 9.8 percent, while the New England and Middle Atlantic figures had risen to 28.8 percent and 25.5 percent respectively.

12. Price concludes (p. 133) that about one-quarter worked in the artisanal trades, another quarter in the transport occupations, and the remaining half in commercial support.

13. Warner (pp. 61, 21). This summary draws mainly on Bridenbaugh (1955); Warner (Part I); E. Foner (Chap. 2); Kulikoff; Price; Pred (Chap. 4).

14. See Warner (p. 56); Knights (pp. 49ff.); Schnore and Knights (p. 254).

15. See Warner (pp. 55ff.); Pred (pp. 207ff.).

16. See Warner (pp. 57ff.); Pred (pp. 200ff.), Knights.

17. Warner provides some glimpse of this continuity for Philadelphia.

18. Warner (p. 56); Pred (pp. 200ff.); Knights (p. 89).

19. See Maier for the Revolutionary period and Pessen for later.

20. The change in land-grant policy during the Jacksonian period, for instance, severely crimped land speculation in the West.

21. Pred provides the most careful review of most of these hypotheses.

22. See Pred (pp. 69–70) for some examples of this concentration.

23. These calculations are based on data from U.S. Bureau of the Census (1850, 1860, and 1870).

24. These data are based on U.S. Bureau of Census (1870 and 1900); Pred (p. 20).

25. The following paragraphs rely heavily on Gutman (1963, 1976).

26. Gutman (1963, p. 41). His conclusions are qualitative and cannot, however strong the evidence, be turned, it appears, into numbers.

27. For some particularly interesting evidence for Philadelphia, see Hershberg et al.

28. Quoted in Glaab (p. 236). This kind of Industrial City was not new. In England, Manchester had already pioneered its form in the first half of the nineteenth century, and Friedrich Engels had already perceived the essential social functions which that singular form was serving. See, for instance, Engels (p. 84).

29. Millis and Montgomery (p. 83).

30. For some discussion of these factors, see Pred (p. 43); Taylor (pp. 271, 311).
31. See Millis and Montgomery; Taylor (1970); Hays.
32. See Commons; Foner (1947).
33. These impressions cannot be precisely tabulated because the Foner and Commons presentations do not lend themselves to quantification. But the qualitative histories support the point.
34. See U.S. Bureau of the Census (1905 and 1910).
35. The maps in U.S. Bureau of the Census (1910) are instructive.
36. See McKenzie (p. 93); Tunnard and Reed (p. 238).
37. In the steel industry, for instance, open-hearth furnaces were used more frequently in the Gary plants than in the central-city plants, but those furnaces required smaller plant units, rather than larger ones, when installed within the factories. See Clark (p. 68).
38. Graham Taylor reports (p. 97), for instance, that only 31.3 percent of the workers in the Cincinnati satellite factories actually lived outside the central cities and that almost all the remainder lived in the traditional central-city working-class housing districts.
39. These examples are taken from U.S. Industrial Commission (Vol. VIII, pp. 10; Vol. VII, p. 878; and Vol. VIII, p. 415) respectively.
40. I have not yet systematically investigated this hypothesis, but contemporary accounts do seem to suggest that only large corporations participated in the exodus.
41. See McKenzie (pp. 164, 222).
42. See Edwards; Chandler.
43. See Jackson (p. 443).
44. See Schnore.
45. More detail is provided in Jackson; McKenzie.
46. As Watkins concludes, "the suburban economy has proved too feeble a base from which the old metropolitan areas can regain their lost competitive advantage" (Chap. 2). His statistical analyses support those conclusions.

REFERENCES

Albion, Robert G., *The Rise of the New York Port, 1815–1860* (New York: Charles Scribner's Sons, 1939).

Blumenfeld, Hans, "The Modern Metropolis," in *Cities*, A Scientific American Book (New York: Alfred A. Knopf, 1965).

Bogue, Donald, *The Population of the United States* (Glencoe, Ill.: Free Press, 1959).

Braverman, Harry, *Labor and Monopoly Capital* (New York: Monthly Review Press, 1974).

Brecher, Jeremy, *Strike!* (San Francisco: Straight Arrow Books, 1972).

Brindenbaugh, Carl, *Cities in the Wilderness* (New York: Oxford University Press, 1971).

———, *Cities in Revolt* (New York: Oxford University Press, 1955).

Chandler, Alfred D., Jr., *Strategy and Structure* (Cambridge, Mass.: MIT Press, 1962).

Clark, Victor S., *History of Manufactures in the United States*, Vol. III (Washington, D.C.: Carnegie Institution, 1929).

Commons, John R., *History of Labor in the United States*, Vol. II (New York: Macmillan Company, 1918).

Davis, Kingsley, "The Urbanization of the Human Population," in *Cities*, A Scientific American Book (New York: Alfred A. Knopf, 1965).

Edwards, Richard C., "Corporate Stability and the Risks of Corporate Failure," *Journal of Economic History*, June 1975.

Engels, Friedrich, *The Condition of the Working Class in England* (Moscow: Progress Publishers, 1973).

Fogelson, Robert M., *The Fragmented Metropolis* (Cambridge, Mass.: Harvard University Press, 1967).

Foner, Eric, *Tom Paine and the American Revolution* (New York: Oxford University Press, 1976).

Foner, Philip S., *History of the Labor Movement in the United States*, Vol. 1 (New York: International Publishers, 1947).

————, *History of the Labor Movement in the United States*, Vol. 2 (New York: International Publishers, 1955).

Glaab, Charles N., ed., *The American City: A Documentary History* (Homewood, Ill.: Dorsey Press, 1963).

————, and A. Theodore Brown, *A History of Urban America* (New York: Macmillan Company, 1967).

Gordon, David M., "Capitalist Efficiency and Socialist Efficiency," *Monthly Review*, July–August 1976.

————, "Toward a Critique of CAPITALopolis: Capitalism and Urban Development in the United States" (forthcoming 1978).

Gutman, Herbert G., "The Worker's Search for Power: Labor in the Gilded Age," in H. Wayne Morgan, ed., *The Gilded Age: A Reappraisal* (Syracuse: Syracuse University Press, 1963).

————, *Work, Culture, and Society in Industrializing America* (New York: Alfred A. Knopf, 1976).

Handlin, Oscar, "The Modern City as a Field of Historical Study," in A. B. Callow, Jr., ed., *American Urban History* (New York: Oxford University Press, 1969).

Hays, Samuel P., "The Politics of Reform in Municipal Government in the Progressive Era," *Pacific Northwest Quarterly*, October 1964.

Hershberg, Theodore, *et al.*, "The 'Journey-to-Work': An Empirical Investigation of Work, Residence, and Transportation, Philadelphia, 1850 and 1880" (Unpublished paper, 1974).

Jackson, Kenneth T., "Metropolitan Government versus Political Autonomy," in K. T. Jackson and S. K. Schultz, eds., *Cities in American History* (New York: Alfred A. Knopf, 1972).

Knights, Peter R., *The Plain People of Boston, 1830–1860* (New York: Oxford University Press, 1971).

Kulikoff, Allan, "The Progress of Inequality in Revolutionary Boston," *William and Mary Quarterly*, July 1971.

Lyman, Susan E., *The Story of New York* (New York: Crown Publishers, 1964).

McKenzie, R. D., *The Metropolitan Community* (New York: McGraw-Hill Book Co., 1933).

Maier, Pauline, "Popular Uprisings and Civil Authority in Eighteenth-Century America," *William and Mary Quarterly*, January 1970.

Marglin, Stephen A., "What Do Bosses Do?" *Review of Radical Political Economics*, Summer 1974.

Millis, Harry A., and Royal E. Montgomery, *Labor's Progress and Some Basic Labor Problems* (New York: McGraw-Hill Book Co., 1938).

Mollenkopf, John H., "The Postwar Politics of Urban Development," this volume.

Morris, Richard B., *Government and Labor in Early America* (New York: Columbia University Press, 1946).

Mumford, Lewis, *The City in History* (New York: Harcourt, Brace and World, 1961).

Nathan, Richard P., and Charles Adams, "Understanding Central City Hardship," *Political Science Quarterly*, Spring 1976.

Nettels, Curtis P., "British Mercantilism and the Economic Development of the Thirteen Colonies," *Journal of Economic History*, Spring 1952.

Pessen, Edward, "The Egalitarian Myth and the American Social Reality: Wealth, Mobility and Equality in the 'Era of the Common Man,'" *American Historical Review*, October 1971.

Peterson, Florence, *Strikes in the United States, 1880–1936* (Washington, D.C.: U.S. Government Printing Office, 1938).

Pred, Allan R., *The Spatial Dynamics of U.S. Urban-Industrial Growth, 1800–1914* (Cambridge, Mass.: Harvard University Press, 1966).

Price, Jacob M., "Economic Function and the Growth of American Port Towns in the Eighteenth Century," *Perspectives in American History* 8, 1974.

Reps, John W., *The Making of Urban America: A History of City Planning in the United States* (Princeton: Princeton University Press, 1965).

Schlesinger, Arthur M., Sr., "The City in American History," in P. Kramer and F. L. Holborn, eds., *The City in American Life* (New York: G. P. Putnam's Sons, 1970).

Schnore, Leo F., "Urban Structure and Suburban Selectivity," *Demography* 1, 1964.

———, and Peter R. Knights, "Residence and Social Structure: Boston in the Ante-Bellum Period," in S. Thernstrom and R. Sennett, eds., *Nineteenth-Century Cities* (New Haven: Yale University Press, 1969).

Sjoberg, Gideon, "The Origin and Evolution of Cities," in *Cities, A Scientific American Book* (New York: Alfred A. Knopf, 1965).

Taylor, George Rogers, *The Transportation Revolution, 1815–1860* (New York: Rinehart and Co., 1951).

———, "Building an Intra-Urban Transportation System," in A. M. Wakstein, ed., *The Urbanization of America* (Boston: Houghton Mifflin, 1970).

Taylor, Graham Romeyn, *Satellite Cities: A Study of Industrial Suburbs* (New York: D. Appleton, and Co., 1915).

Tryon, Rolla M., *Household Manufactures in the United States, 1640–1860* (Chicago: University of Chicago Press, 1917).

Tunnard, Christopher, and Henry Hope Reed, *American Skyline: The Growth and Form of Our Cities and Towns* (Boston: Houghton Mifflin, 1955).

U.S. Bureau of the Census, *Seventh Census* (Washington, D.C.: U.S. Government Printing Office, 1850).

————, *Eighth Census* (Washington, D.C.: U.S. Government Printing Office, 1860).

————, *Compendium of the Ninth Census* (Washington, D.C.: U.S. Government Printing Office, 1870).

————, *Twelfth Census*, "Manufactures," (Washington, D.C.: U.S. Government Printing Office, 1900).

————, "Industrial Districts: 1905," *Bulletin* No. 101 (Washington, D.C.: U.S. Government Printing Office, 1909).

————, *Thirteenth Census*, Volume 10 (Washington, D.C.: U.S. Government Printing Office, 1910).

————, *Urban Population in the U.S. from the First Census to the Fifteenth Census* (Washington, D.C.: U.S. Government Printing Office, 1939).

————, *Historical Statistics of the United States*, rev. ed. (Washington, D.C.: U.S. Government Printing Office, 1976).

U.S. Industrial Commission, *Reports* (Washington, D.C.: U.S. Government Printing Office, 1900–1902).

Vernon, Raymond, *Metropolis 1985* (Garden City, N.Y.: Anchor Books, 1963).

Warner, Sam Bass, *The Private City* (Philadelphia: University of Pennsylvania Press, 1968).

Watkins, Alfred, "Urban Development in the U.S. System of Cities" (Ph.D. dissertation, New School for Social Research, 1977).

Williams, Raymond, *The Country and the City* (New York: Oxford University Press, 1973).

The Political Economy of Suburban Development

PATRICK J. ASHTON

One of the most striking and significant social phenomena of the twentieth century has been the growth and proliferation of suburbs around large cities in the United States. From a limited and relatively rare social form at the beginning of this century, suburbs have developed into major growth poles for industrial and commercial investment, and suburbanism has become a way of life for more than eighty million Americans—a plurality of the population. The purpose of this article is to show how this historical development is rooted in the dynamics of the capitalist mode of production and to demonstrate how the specific evolution of suburbs both reflects and contributes to more general contradictions within the economic system.

THE NATURE OF SUBURBS

Suburbs may be defined as politically independent municipalities located outside the corporate boundaries of large central cities but within an economically interdependent metropolitan area. While several different types of suburbs may be distinguished (e.g., bedroom, industrial, commercial), they all share two important characteristics:

political independence and a relatively small scale. As forms of the state,[1] suburbs enjoy a number of independent powers, most significant of which are the ability to make and enforce laws and to levy taxes. The small scale of the suburb is made possible by its dependence primarily upon the large central city and secondarily upon other units within the metropolitan area. An individual suburb need not contain all necessary or desirable services and facilities since they can be obtained elsewhere. This smaller scale makes the suburb much more amenable to domination by a single interest group (or coalition of interest groups) than a large heterogeneous city. And the political independence of the suburb provides a vehicle for protecting and extending a particular group's self-interest.

Suburbs are thus potential conduits for power. But power is not distributed evenly in capitalist society. Its distribution is determined by the nature of capitalist class relations, which are in turn influenced by the level of development of the forces and the social relations of production. The political fragmentation of the modern metropolis is thus a reflection of the hierarchical stratification and uneven development of the capitalist mode of production. In the pages that follow I will attempt to trace the political-economic developments which have led to the current proliferation of suburbs.

PREMETROPOLITAN URBAN FORM

American society underwent a substantial transformation in the middle third of the nineteenth century. A predominantly agrarian, frontier society was recast as an urban industrial one. "The main elements in the new urban complex," observes historian Lewis Mumford, "were the factory, the railroad and the slum. . . . The factory became the nucleus of the new organism. Every other detail of life was subordinate to it" (p. 458). But the factory did not occupy this position of dominance on technical merits alone. Historical experience had taught capitalists that the factory was the most *profitable*, if not the most efficient and humane, method of organizing production.[2] Thus the basis for the evolution of the factory was a political-economic one. Nevertheless, once chosen, the factory had ramifications that were social as well as physical, geographical as well as technological.

The most important implication of the use of factories as production sites in nineteenth-century U.S. cities was *centralization*. Centralization of the actual physical plant, of productive facilities, of workers, of political control.

First of all, the architecture of the factory was dictated by the major source of available energy: steam. Since every piece of machinery had to be connected to a central steam engine by means of belts or shafts, it was most efficient to put the machinery as close as possible to the source of power. Thus factories were built as compact, multistory units.

Second, the primary modes of commercial transportation limited locational flexibility. Since waterways and railroads—the only viable means of shipping large amounts of raw materials and finished goods— were relatively fixed in space, they demanded that production and distribution facilities be grouped around them. In addition, the organization of the factory required a relatively large number of workers producing under one roof. Given the limitations of the existing transportation system, these workers needed to live in close proximity to their place of work. And since they could not outbid more powerful and wealthy groups in the market for space in the city, the development of overcrowded slum housing was all but assured.

The rapid and continued growth of factories and industry swelled the urban population and further crowded the slums. Thousands of people left the countryside and streamed into the cities. Doubtless some were attracted by the excitement of city life or the promise of better wages. But many had no choice. Expanding urban land use pushed farmers off the land. And the uneven development characteristic of the capitalist market process resulted in the destruction of many small regional centers of trade and finance. Rural entrepreneurs as well as farmers increasingly became part of the urban proletariat.

The social relations of the factory came to dominate political life also. Most of the original investment in industrial infrastructure—roads, water mains, power systems, etc.—had been made by the entrepreneurs themselves. But, faced with the rapidly increasing scale and complexity of production, capitalists sought ways to socialize these mounting costs. They quickly realized the value of the state in this regard. For the fiscal powers of the state could be used to generate revenue for infrastructural investments, which would be politically defined as "public goods." To ensure this happening, capitalists attempted to consolidate their control of state and local government.[3]

As the industrial economy spread into the countryside in the mid-nineteenth century, political control was not far behind. Urban capitalists developed a policy of annexing the expanding fringes of the city. Not only did this extend urban administrative control, it increased the tax base of the city. Sometimes this policy was carried out at the local level, but more often it was implemented by state legislatures dominated by urban capitalists. The Pennsylvania state assembly, for example, voted in 1854 to increase the size of the city of Philadelphia from 2 to more than 129 square miles, effectively annexing twenty-eight separate boroughs, towns, and townships in the area.

In addition, annexation was also used to destroy or weaken urban rivals. Brooklyn, New York, for example, was itself an industrial city and annexed many surrounding towns and villages on Long Island. By 1898 it had grown to be the fifth largest city in the United States and represented a powerful rival to neighboring New York City. And so in 1898 the New York state legislature stripped Brooklyn of its political autonomy and awarded it to the city of New York. This completed New York City's annexation of over 250 square miles of its hinterland.[4]

Thus the policy of annexation greatly expanded the size and scale of the industrial cities—in social as well as physical terms. While political and economic control remained centralized in the old central districts—now called "downtown"—new needs, conditions, and interest groups were being created in these sprawling cities. The very process of expansion and development set in motion forces antagonistic to itself. These forces would bring a virtual halt to annexation by the beginning of the twentieth century.

EARLY UPPER-CLASS SUBURBS

As early as the middle of the nineteenth century, small upper-class communities began springing up in the countryside around the large industrial cities. The motivation for the creation of these communities was social, economic, and political.

First of all, rapid industrial development within the anarchic framework of the capitalist market had radically altered the quality of life in the cities. Factories belched smoke and cinders over the entire city, noxious chemicals filled the air, the rivers and canals were open sewers, and garbage and other forms of waste littered the streets.

Workers, crowded into dismal, suffocating slums, suffered the most. But even the living quarters of the rich did not escape contamination.

Second, the city government faced constantly mounting financial demands during this period. On the one hand, there was the increasing demand for investment in the industrial infrastructure, as capitalists fought to socialize their costs. On the other hand, the tremendous influx of population from the countryside into the cities generated a huge new demand for services. Sewers, water, police, firefighters, libraries, and so forth were required in amounts previously unimaginable.[5] Moreover, the proletarianization of artisans, craftsmen and farmers frequently meant their pauperization. Thus the need for public welfare programs. This need was enlarged and exacerbated by continually escalating foreign immigration. While not all immigrants remained in the cities, those who did were predominantly poor. For example, in 1852 more than half of those requiring public assistance in eastern cities were Irish and German. In 1860, 86 percent of the paupers in New York City were of foreign birth (Glaab and Brown, pp. 94–95).

While the tax burden did not fall predominantly on the rich, its sheer size and rate of growth presented them with an economic threat. Furthermore, two major depressions and a general deflation in the economy in the last third of the nineteenth century made tax dollars harder to come by. But tax revenues were only one of the budgetary problems the cities encountered. Faced with spiraling demands for services and investments which constantly outran revenues, most cities borrowed heavily. In the decade after the Civil War, for example, the fifteen largest cities in the United States experienced a population increase of 70 percent; however, their municipal debts increased 271 percent (Glaab and Brown, p. 181). The mounting interest payments on this expanding debt represented an inelastic burden on the municipal budget.

The changing nature of the city politics provided a third motivation for the exodus of the wealthy from the city. Urban capitalists were never a large percentage of the population. But in the early part of the nineteenth century, their control over city government was relatively unchallenged. However, the population boom in midcentury, occasioned by internal migration and immigration, made control more problematic. First there was the fact of sheer numbers. With even a modicum of democracy, capitalists stood the chance of being outvoted on important issues by the rapidly increasing urban proletariat. Second, there was the fact of widespread corruption. This was largely due to the institutionalization of the boss system, which had as its base the masses of newly arrived immigrants. Bribery, graft, embezzlement, and kickbacks became a way of life in city government. This proved to be more than the wealthy were willing to tolerate.

So, motivated by a deteriorating quality of life, mounting taxes, and a loss of political control, the capitalist elite moved their residences out of the city and formed suburbs. Here in the countryside the small scale and political independence of the suburban municipality allowed them to reassert control over their environment. But it would be wrong to assume that, because capitalists had removed their residences from the cities, they had abdicated power in city government. On the contrary. Because of the level of development of production technology, it was still necessary to locate industrial plants in the central cities. Thus capitalists still had a prime stake in the politics of the city, and they did their best to see that their economic interests were protected.

The upper class was not the only group for whom residence in the city was unattractive. The deteriorating quality of life and mounting tax burden were a source of concern to all urban residents. The difference was that the wealthy were generally the only ones who could afford the time and commuting costs engendered by a residence in the suburbs. Initially, the only means of travel to these communities was horse and carriage—a luxury out of the financial reach of most urban residents. With the development of railroads in the last third of the nineteenth century, railstop suburbs began springing up in the countryside. But again, it was only the well-to-do who could afford the time and money to commute.

The appearance of the electric trolley in the late 1880s involved real estate and land interests in the active promotion of suburbs and offered the upper middle classes their first chance to escape the city. Entrepreneurs built tracks out into the countryside, buying up the surrounding property as they went. Then, with fares set artificially low to encourage ridership, they offered the land for sale. Any losses they sustained from the operation of the trolley line were more than offset by their monopoly profits from the sale of the real estate. The majority of workers, barely able to scrape by financially in the urban slums, could not possibly outbid small businessmen and professionals for this new property.

However, these "streetcar suburbs" were often short-lived as independent communities. After they had sold off all the available land, the real estate entrepreneurs often let the trolley lines deteriorate. The new middle-class suburbanites, who were totally dependent upon these lines, frequently succeeded in getting the central city to annex their area and provide public subsidies for the trolley lines.

The development of upper-class residential retreats and upper-middle-class streetcar suburbs during the nineteenth century did not represent a significant shift in the population. Most urban residents lived only a short distance from their sites of work. And since the existing level of productive and distributive technology decreed that these sites be centralized in the city, most urban residents lived in large cities. The widespread development of suburbs as social forms would flow from sweeping changes in the forces and social relations of production that began to manifest themselves near the turn of the century.

THE DECENTRALIZATION OF INDUSTRY

The most important causal factor for the widespread development of suburbs in the early twentieth century was the movement of industry out of the large cities. This decentralization process is discussed by Gordon in the previous article in this book, so great detail is not necessary here. But it should be emphasized that this movement derived its origin and shape from the nature of the developing forces and social relations of capitalist production. The conditions that motivated capitalists to move their industrial facilities out of the central city were both technical and social. On the one hand, the despoliation of the city's physical environment, for which the industrialists themselves were largely responsible—and which, ironically, had forced them to remove their own residences—began to create added costs which the capitalists could not always successfully socialize. Furthermore, the growing tax burden of many cities threatened to cut into profits.

On the other hand, the escalating hostility of urban class relations provided capitalists with an even stronger motivation for getting out, as Gordon has indicated. First of all, the swelling size of the urban proletariat had had a profound effect on city politics, as noted in the previous section. But more importantly, the growing organization and militancy of urban workers challenged capitalist prerogatives and threatened capitalist profits. Capitalists perceived that by moving their industrial facilities to suburban communities they could reassert both economic and political control.[6] At first some industrialists tried to set up company towns; however, the disastrous strike at Pullman in 1894 generally dissuaded them from this approach. Capitalists became content to use the small scale of the suburb and their own position of economic dominance within it (as "big fish in little ponds") as a less direct and less politically offensive means of ensuring that their own interests were satisfied.[7]

Despite capitalists' strong motivations to leave the city, however, the decentralization of industry would not have been possible without facilitating developments in the forces of production. The development of electric power provided tremendous flexibility in site location. At the same time, it allowed for the introduction of the assembly line, by which capitalists gained complete control over the pace of work. But assembly-line production required sprawling one- and two-story plants, not compact multistory ones like those in the city. Since land was cheaper on the city's periphery, decentralization seemed an obvious choice. And the development of truck transport made it a feasible one.

Thus, the immediate effect of the aforementioned developments was the beginning of the decentralization of industrial capital. And, given the strong motivations capitalists had for leaving the city, it is not surprising that they were quick to do so when the opportunity presented itself. Indeed, census data for the decade 1899–1909 shows that industrial employment in twelve of the thirteen largest industrial districts was already increasing more than 100 percent faster in the outlying zones than in the central cities (Taylor, p. 4).

An important political result of this decentralization process was a virtual end to the policy of annexation. Upper-class residential communities had been resisting annexation by central cities with varying success almost since the Civil War. It was the large-scale migration of industrial capital to the suburbs at the beginning of this century, however, which decisively killed annexation. Not only was escape from the city and its social context the primary motive behind decentralization, but the industrial capitalists possessed the economic and political clout in both the new local governments and in state legislatures to assure that the political independence of the suburbs would be maintained.[8]

THE SUBURBAN BOOM

As industry moved out of the city, many workers followed to be near their jobs. When relatively inexpensive automobiles became widely available, even more workers were able to move out beyond the reaches of urban mass transit. At the same time, capitalists became more flexible in locating their decentralized production facilities, confident that a newly mobile labor force could follow them almost anywhere. As more and more people moved to the suburbs, commercial capital decentralized to take advantage of new or shifting markets. And more industrial capital moved out to make use of growing suburban labor markets.

In the suburbs, both capital and labor demanded more and better roads. As they were constructed, decentralization became more and more feasible. And as the auto, rubber, oil, and construction industries grew in size and power, they acquired the economic and political clout to force the building of still more roads—which not only encouraged suburban migration, but tended to make the automobile an economic and social necessity for each new resident.

The development of suburbs, then, was an interactive, snowballing process. Each element both nourished and fed off of the others. Together they generated an economic boom which profoundly altered the social, political, and geographical character of urban America. On the economic front, suburban development made a significant contribution to the ongoing stability of American capitalism. Baran and Sweezy (pp. 218–38) argue that capital investment in the automobile and all its spinoffs (including suburbs), though largely unanticipated and unplanned, rescued the U.S. economy from a period of growing stagnation and underwrote the economic boom of the 1920s. Indeed, in 1900, when there were only about 14,000 autos in the entire country, roughly 10 percent of the U.S. population lived in suburbs. In 1915, with 2.5 million autos registered, new nonfarm residential construction totalled $950 million and there were 414,000 urban-dwelling-unit starts—most of them in the suburbs. Reflecting this, the growth rate of suburbs exceeded that of cities for the first time in 1920. In 1925, new nonfarm residential construction jumped to $4.5 billion and urban-dwelling-unit starts totalled 752,000. From 1926 to 1929, outstanding mortgage loans annually exceeded $5 billion. At the time of the collapse in 1929 there were more than 26 million autos on the road, and the population of suburbs was growing twice as fast as that of central cities.[9]

The Great Depression of the 1930s reined in suburban development dramatically. The suburbs registered only a slight gain in population during the stagnant decade (though the central cities, by contrast, actually lost population). Economic activity in the suburbs, as elsewhere, was sporadic and fitful at best. In its attempt to revive the sagging U.S. economy, the federal government enacted various legislative measures during the 1930s which had a significant impact on suburbs. For the overall effect of the federal legislation was to create subsidies for low-density, detached, owner-occupied single-family housing, to the virtual exclusion of other types of dwelling units. And since space was generally lacking in the central cities, the federal government was effectively subsidizing the development of suburbs.

In 1932, for example, the Federal Savings and Loan Insurance Corporation (FSLIC) was formed. It guaranteed deposits in savings and loan associations, which were granted preferential interest rates to enable them to attract savings with which to finance owner-occupied housing. In 1934, the Federal Housing Authority (FHA) was created. This agency provided guaranteed, self-liquidating mortgages for newly constructed homes. Furthermore, it required low down payments and set up amortization rates which were realistic for middle-class incomes.[10]

These measures did not have an immediate effect, however. The generally pervasive economic stagnation of the 1930s held back suburban development, despite the existence of incentives. The advent of World War II got the economy moving again, but the growth of suburbs was held in check as the country focused its productive resources on war materiel. During the war period, however, the federal government once again engaged in activities which would later represent a massive subsidy of suburbanization. Between 1939 and 1946, the federal government built an average of over $2.5 billion worth of industrial buildings every year. This was more than twice the average of private industry for the same years (Kain, pp. 7–10). Lacking adequate space in the cities, most of these plants were constructed in the suburbs. When the war ended, these production facilities were turned over to private industry, often at nominal cost.

Thus did the state subsidize the exodus of both jobs and households to the suburbs. By the 1960s the decentralization of jobs had increased to the point where the central cities were actually suffering net losses in employment. Between 1954 and 1963, for instance, in the twenty-four metropolitan areas with populations greater than 1 million, the central cities lost more than 500,000 jobs while the suburbs were gaining over 1.5 million (Masotti and Hadden, p. 9). And when wartime construction curbs were lifted, the decentralization of urban households was every bit as dramatic. By 1950, the population of suburbs was growing ten times as fast as that of central cities; nearly one in four Americans was a suburbanite. Sixty-four percent of the nation's total population increase in the 1960s took place in the suburbs. By 1970, 76 million Americans lived in suburbs. They represented 57 percent of the total metropolitan population and a plurality (37.6 percent) of the population of the nation as a whole.

Once again, state subsidy was crucial to this process. In addition to expanded support for low-density single-family homes (through the creation of Veterans Administration [VA] guaranteed mortgages), the federal government embarked on a massive program of highway construction. The effect of the new interstate freeway system in cities was the destruction of many neighborhoods and the creation of a convenient means of access to central-city jobs for suburban residents. And the creation of the Federal Highway Trust Fund ensured that freeways would be self-propagating. For as more freeways were built, more automobile travel was encouraged. The consequently increased revenue from the gasoline tax swelled the coffers of the Highway Fund. And strict controls dictated that its burgeoning budget be used only for more highways—effectively diminishing alternative modes of transportation.

THE SELECTIVITY OF POPULATION DECENTRALIZATION

The unprecedented prosperity of the decades following World War II was largely built upon the phenomenon of suburban development. The real estate, auto, and construction industries boomed as Americans moved to the suburbs in record numbers. But behind this massive migration is an important and often overlooked fact. The urban population did not simply move out of the city into the countryside. Rather, various groups within it moved into specific suburbs.[11] The logic of this process flowed from the very nature of the capitalist mode of production. As monopoly capitalism has developed in this country, it has created an increasing number of distinctions among workers. These distinctions are based on an evolving system of relative privilege for certain groups of workers at the expense of other workers. And, given the highly competitive and individualistic nature of capitalist labor markets, more-privileged workers have generally sought to maximize these distinctions as a means of protecting their own (short-run) self-interest.

But though these distinctions are rooted in capitalist relations of *production,* they become most socially salient and open to manipulation in the sphere of *consumption.* In a commodity-dominated society like ours where "you are what you buy," specific patterns of consumption identify and delineate lifestyles associated with various status groups. In addition, conscious direction of consumption expenditures becomes the basis for any attempt to gain, protect, or expand privileged characteristics derived from the workplace.

The suburb has been an important vehicle for these specialized consumption expenditures. Its small scale and political independence has offered suburban residents a measure of control over their social and economic environment which was impossible to achieve in the city. For in these communities, specific groups of workers could generate and consume the goods and services and build the institutions that would tend to reproduce their own particular status characteristics and thus protect and/or expand their competitive advantages over time.

But in order to make this system work, the new suburban residents sought to establish and maintain a certain degree of homogeneity within the community in order to ensure consensual agreement about major priorities. A number of mechanisms, both formal and informal, have been developed to deal with this problem. Conscious manipulation of the suburb's independent legislative powers is perhaps the most important. A community can carefully control overall development, for example, through selective municipal expenditures on roads, sewers, drains, schools, and so forth. The cost of land and construction can be raised by large-lot zoning. Building costs can be further inflated by specifying minimum quality standards for construction materials that are significantly higher than industry minimums. Finally, the volume, type, and size of dwelling units can be closely regulated.

This ability to zone is a two-edged sword. Not only can various groups be excluded from a municipality, but investment capital can be lured by the prospect of special developments and services (e.g., industrial parks with all utilities) and property-tax breaks. Even with special reductions, though, corporate taxes provide a major source of revenue to suburban municipalities. If enough capital can be recruited, individual property taxes can remain low while still assuring the residents that the level and quality of services will reproduce their privilege.[12]

Residential covenants provide another mechanism for maintaining the "character" of suburban communities. These agreements are often contracts that homeowners must sign as part of their deed. Formerly these protective covenants explicitly limited residents in the type of people to whom they could sell their house. Although overt discrimination of this type has now been outlawed, this kind of arrangement is still perpetuated on an informal basis. Other types of agreements dictate the ways in which residents can use and develop their property. All of these types of protective covenants have been consistently upheld by the courts.

The foregoing conceptualization of suburbs does not mean to imply, however, that *all* suburban communities are the result of conscious decisions by particular groups to organize and incorporate for the purpose of protecting some privileges or perceived advantages in the workplace. Rather, I would argue, the promise of the ability to achieve a measure of control over the social and economic environment has served as the primary attraction of suburban living and exerted a major influence over the specific pattern of population decentralization.

Furthermore, I would not suggest that all or even some suburbs are completely homogeneous by class or status group. Communities can actually tolerate a rather large amount of internal diversity while maintaining a dominant ethos. It is the *possibility* of realizing and/or imposing their own values and mores that has impelled various groups to seek out suburbs as vehicles for the protection of competitive advantages.

Finally, it must be noted that the desire of certain groups to use suburbs for the protection of privilege is not always directly realized.

Rather, endeavors to this effect are translated spatially through real estate, land-development and banking interests. These interests share one common overriding motivation: profitability. It happens, however, that historically it has been highly profitable to construct relatively homogeneous communities. Thus we have the tract homes of the 1920s and 1950s, the sprawling single-family subdivisions of the 1960s, and the elaborate townhouse and condominium developments of the 1970s.

DIVISIONS WITHIN THE WORKING CLASS

Social and economic divisions among workers in this country have grown up simultaneously with the development of the capitalist mode of production. They are part and parcel of the very logic of the system. Capital investment according to the sole criterion of profitability produces a pattern of uneven development throughout the society. Workers reflect this as some of their number are paid better, work under more desirable conditions, receive more education or training, have better fringe benefits, and so forth according to the general location, specific needs, and overall profitability of their employees. In addition, social and cultural divisions among workers not directly produced by the economic system have nevertheless been exploited and enlarged by capitalists in order to dilute the power of the working class. At various points in time, workers have overcome these divisions and achieved class solidarity. But it is also true that short-run rational self-interest has forced workers in more privileged positions to spend a great deal of time and effort attempting to maintain or expand their advantages at the expense of other workers.

One of the earliest and most enduring divisions within the working class was along ethnic lines. When industrial capitalism got its start in the United States along the northeastern seaboard during the first half of the nineteenth century, it drew its labor force from the predominantly Northern European stock of the region. In addition, the flow of immigration during this period was mainly from these same Northern European countries—nations whose historical experience of industrial development was already quite extensive. Thus these workers tended to possess the craft skills and social expectations which were extremely important in early industrialization (the peasant immigrants from Ireland being a notable exception to this rule). A chronic labor shortage coupled with a still-primitive technology of production dictated that these Northern European workers perform skilled tasks in the production process.

As the industrial system moved into high gear after the Civil War, immigrants began to arrive in ever-increasing numbers from Southern and Eastern Europe. These new immigrants were generally destitute, unskilled, and desperate for any kind of work at any wage. Capitalists were only too happy to use this fact to threaten and discipline the entrenched Northern European workers. Responding to this situation and acting in their own rational self-interest, the latter group of workers moved to protect their more advantageous position in the labor market by creating a system of stratification by ethnicity in the workplace. According to this hierarchy, workers of Northern European origin monopolized the skilled jobs with better pay and working conditions while workers from Southern and Eastern Europe and various other countries were confined to low-paying unskilled work.[13]

Centrally important to the consolidation of this ethnic hierarchy was the emerging role of the unions. The leaders as well as the principal beneficiaries of labor-organizing struggles were almost universally skilled workers of Northern European origin. And their control of the unions was institutionalized through devices like separate seniority lists, job classifications, and wage differentials, and separate elections and contract ratification procedures for skilled workers—all codified in the union contract.

When blacks were forced off the land in the South and into Northern cities in this century, the ethnic hierarchy was further refined. Workers of Southern and Eastern European origin moved up into semiskilled jobs and blacks were incorporated at the bottom. But not, however, without considerable struggle and bloodshed. For in addition to the virulent racism which was part of the national heritage, blacks faced manipulation by capitalists that exacerbated racial hostility and further divided the working class. Economically desperate, blacks were often forced to accept recruitment as strikebreakers. Indeed, a great deal of the racial violence so prominent in Northern cities at the beginning of this century can be directly linked to the use of blacks as scabs. And competition and conflict over jobs remains a central feature of urban racial and ethnic violence today.[14]

Another important set of divisions within the working class has been created by the increasing differentiation of the capitalist mode of production. The activity of production and the employment of the labor force have become divided among three major sectors of the economy: monopoly, competitive, and state.[15] The increasing bifurcation of private industry into monopoly and competitive sectors has produced a similar division among workers. Capital intensity, high labor productivity, high public visibility, and the stability produced by concentration and high profit levels have created the structural conditions enabling workers in the monopoly sector to demand and receive significantly higher wages than workers in the competitive sector. On the other hand, high labor intensity, low productivity and profit margins, and market competition have constrained competitive-sector firms from paying high wages. And generally low public visibility has lessened the pressure on them to do so. In addition jobs in the monopoly sector tend to have greater security, better working conditions, institutionalized grievance procedures, and better fringe benefits than jobs in the competitive sector—a condition due almost solely to the higher level of unionization of monopoly-sector workers.

The state sector has experienced rapid growth in size and importance since World War II, especially at the local level. There are two major subdivisions within this sector: production of goods and services organized by the state (e.g., education, health, and welfare) and production organized by private industries under state contract (e.g., highway construction, military and aeronautical equipment). State-organized production tends to have the structural features of the competitive sector. It is labor-intensive; expansion of production depends upon expansion of employment. State-contracted production is organized along monopoly-sector lines. It is capital-intensive and highly concentrated. High profits are guaranteed through cost-plus contracts. Productivity, however, tends to be low because the unique nature of many state products militates against economies of mass production and because the guaranteed-profit plan lacks incentive.

Wage levels in both subgroups of the state sector have tended to be relatively high. This is partly due to the high level of unionization at the federal level and increasing unionization at the state and local levels. But more importantly, wage levels in this sector reflect the political process. Because of its high public visibility and formal democratic creed, workers in the state sector have achieved a stronger bargaining position than in either of the other two sectors.

The division of the economy into monopoly, competitive, and state sectors has created significant variation in the desirability of jobs. But the social composition of the labor force in each sector shows that access to the more desirable jobs is not distributed evenly among workers. The very old and the very young, women, blacks, chicanos, and other minorities are concentrated in the competitive sector. The more privileged jobs in the monopoly sector are disproportionately dominated by white males. The state sector tends to be more heterogeneous. Political agitation for equal opportunity and the high public visibility of government have combined to provide a significant number of jobs for minorities in this sector. These minorities tend to be concentrated in the lower-level service jobs, however, while white males dominate positions of authority and power.

The unequal access of various groups of workers to the more privileged jobs is governed by the operation of dual labor markets.[16] A primary labor market channels white males into jobs in the monopoly sector and the upper levels of the state sector. A secondary labor market confines certain minority groups to employment in the competitive sector and the lower levels of the state sector. The overlap between these two labor markets is not great, and movement between them is rare.

In addition to classification of workers on the basis of demographic and behavioral characteristics, access to labor markets is governed by access to institutions that provide training and certification. The growing emphasis on credentials in the primary labor market has increased the importance of the educational system as a determinant of employment. And it is here that the suburb has played a crucial role. For the promise of control inherent in the small scale and political independence of the suburban municipality offers an unparalleled opportunity to workers with access to the primary labor market. An educational system can be developed, along with various supportive services, that effectively reproduces competitive advantages in the next generation.

Still another important source of divisions within the working class has been the proliferation of status distinctions among workers.[17] These distinctions, rooted in the labor process, have developed for a number of reasons. First of all, as Braverman brilliantly shows, capitalists have increasingly tried to rationalize, routinize, and otherwise objectify the labor process. The result is that workers have been systematically robbed of skills, knowledge, and control over their work. Head work and hand work have been almost completely separated.

The overall degradation of work has stripped it of most intrinsic motivation and exacerbated the problem of alienation. Capitalists have been increasingly compelled to use status distinctions as external motivations for work. The proliferation of job titles and relatively meaningless job trees serves to create the illusion of mobility among workers and keeps them on the treadmill, more or less. These status distinctions have the added benefit (to capital) of helping to keep the working class divided.

In addition, the systematic degradation of physical labor has necessitated the creation of a large white-collar bureaucracy which replicates the process of production on paper before, during, and after it takes place in physical form. Bureaucratic methods of production, however, have tended to undermine the formerly clear relationship between wages, productivity, and manifest labor skill. And as white-collar work itself becomes increasingly routinized and degraded, a growing system of status distinctions takes on even more importance. Finally, increasing reliance upon educational requirements as hiring standards has intensified stratification by status in the labor force.

The implication of the growing importance of status distinctions is this: as they become more and more significant in the labor market, workers possessing desired characteristics will move to consolidate, protect, and reproduce these distinctions over time. The move to the suburbs—not just any suburb, but one whose residents possess the appropriate status characteristics—is a way of accomplishing this. In their chosen suburb, status groups can engage in the types of lifestyles and consumption patterns which reinforce their status. And they can use the educational system to ensure that their own particular attributes are reproduced in their children.

THE CONTRADICTIONS OF SUBURBAN DEVELOPMENT

The growth of suburbs in the United States, like other processes of capitalist development, is a process laced with contradictions. These contradictions represent the juxtaposition of fundamentally opposed social forces within the mode of production. At various times the problematic manifestations of these tensions have been suppressed. But they have always emerged later, albeit in different forms. Furthermore, the very solutions that have succeeded in suppressing contradictions in one era have often become the most salient points of structural tension and conflict at a later point in time.

As we saw earlier, the development of suburbs, with all its accompanying spinoffs and spillovers, has played a key role in the historical development of capitalism in the United States. The unprecedented American prosperity of the last three decades has largely been built upon automobiles and suburbs. But the ongoing stability of this system, in both an economic and a social sense, is heavily dependent upon the continued vitality of suburban growth.[18] However, this growth appears to be seriously threatened today. The contradiction lies in the fact that the barriers to continued growth are the very same elements that served as its earlier basis.

The free market for space in the metropolis has produced a pattern of suburban sprawl. While this pattern has successfully fostered large-scale consumption and thereby prosperity in the past, it may be reaching its limits today. The urban fringe may have been pushed out farther than workers are willing and/or able to commute. The skyrocketing costs of owning and operating private automobiles, coupled with the nearly universal inadequacy of mass-transit options, almost insures this. In addition, the anarchy of suburban sprawl has generated externalities like uneven development, pollution, and the irrational use of space, which increasingly impinge upon the lives of metropolitan residents. Furthermore, the continuing economic crisis has exacerbated fiscal crises that threaten to bankrupt many suburbs—not to mention central cities!

But the rationalization of the metropolis for the purpose of orderly, planned development is blocked by the same force that helped generate it: the political independence of the suburbs. As we have seen, these suburbs are part and parcel of the logic of capitalist development. On the one hand, they are a spatial manifestation of the many social divisions created by capitalist society. On the other hand, they have resulted from the differential ability of various groups to organize themselves to protect competitive advantages. And, again, given the logic of competition within capitalism, those groups using suburbs to protect certain advantages are forced to jealously guard these privileges. They cannot afford to abdicate clear-cut short-run advantages for more ambiguous long-run gains. Thus metropoliswide transportation and land-use planning is extremely difficult, if not impossible, to implement. Yet without it the continued profitability and stability of the metropolis and all of capitalist society is threatened.

The contradiction between the need for capitalist planning on the one hand and the inability to achieve it on the other is not limited to suburbs. Monopoly capitalists have huge fixed investments in the decaying central cities. The size and scale of these investments dictates that they cannot be abandoned as easily as the elite and certain elements of the working class have abandoned their homes there. Capitalists must find ways to reverse the trend of decay in order to revive and guarantee the profitability of their investments. To do this, they need huge investments by the state in services and infrastructure. But the hard-pressed central cities have nowhere near adequate resources to do the job. In fact, their tax bases are declining as capital and middle-class households continue to flee to the suburbs.

Here capital is confronted with a contradiction of its own making. For it was the decentralization of production and distribution facilities which began the movement of resources out of the city. And the political needs and power of capital ensured that the city would not annex these new areas. The central city's tax base has been further eroded by various nontaxable infrastructural investments (e.g., highways, public research facilities) demanded by capital. To overcome this contradiction and ensure the continued profitability of their central-city investments, capitalists must rationalize the metropolis. They must appropriate the resources of the suburbs and plow them back into the central city. But to do this means that they must break the power of the suburbs. Capital must destroy the political fragmentation which it helped create and which it has exploited so profitably. Whether or not this can be accomplished remains an open question. But the attempt will certainly be difficult.

The nature and form of suburban development present capital with still another contradiction. Capitalists have been very successful in using the political fragmentation of the metropolis to their advantage. They have used the competition for capital among suburbs to extort tax breaks, special services and investments, and other highly profitable arrangements from the privileged suburbs in which they have located their investments. But, as we have seen, the residents of these communities often attempt to keep other groups of workers from moving in, in order to protect their own competitive advantages. The result is that the location of production has increasingly become divorced from the residences of the workers.

This has the effect of raising the costs of reproducing the labor force and thus cutting into profits. For as workers face ever-increasing commuting costs, they demand higher wages in compensation. In addition, the costs of commuting to work, coupled with the growing congestion of the metropolis, make it difficult or impossible for many workers to get to their jobs. Thus capitalists are confronted with problems of absenteeism and labor turnover which hurt production schedules as well as profits. Capitalists have tried to exert pressure on the suburbs to build more housing suitable for production workers. So far they have largely been unsuccessful. And their failure is not surprising. For although capitalists were a major force in the creation of the political fragmentation of the metropolis, they do not control the process completely. Thus suburbs now confront capital as a contradiction.

The process of suburban development has also created contradictions for workers. For lower-income workers, the home ownership encouraged by government policy has never been a good investment. Other forms of savings offer greater liquidity and fewer ancillary costs. Yet to the extent that this group of workers has been forced into suburban home ownership in order to remain competitive in the labor market, they have been placed in a precarious financial position. The continuing economic crisis only exacerbates this squeeze.

Furthermore, home ownership is becoming financially problematic even for those workers for whom it once was a sound investment. The rising proportion of residential indebtedness to disposable income means that homeowners are experiencing increased pressure in meeting their financial obligations. The simultaneous expansion of commercial credit and consumer debt has increasingly locked workers onto a debt treadmill. And inflation, recession, and growing insecurity about employment serve to worsen the dilemma for many workers.

The political fragmentation of the metropolis has quite successfully served the short-run interests of some elements of the working class. These groups have been able to maintain and even to expand their competitive advantages through the vehicle of the suburb. But the anarchy, unevenness, and stratification of capitalist development—which are both the cause and the effect of the spatial distribution of privilege—have come to haunt even relatively privileged workers. For, as the residents of older suburbs are rapidly finding out, the marriage between capital and any given suburb is really only a temporary affair. Short-run gains have often become long-run losses as capital has discarded some suburbs for other, more profitable ones. Since the small scale of suburbs make them extremely sensitive to even minor shifts in investment, the continuing migration of capital has spelled economic disaster for some suburbs.

In addition, workers cannot always leapfrog across the metropolis in hot pursuit of capital. Rapidly rising indebtedness limits their financial flexibility. And the increasing costs of construction and residential finance along with ballooning fuel costs further limit their options. Thus the irrationality of suburban development is brought home to workers.

This irrationality is also expressed in the alienation that is part of everyday suburban life. As we have seen, suburbs have become the most important vehicles of consumption in American society. And the process of consumption is an alienated one. For in capitalist society, consumption is recognized as an end in itself. The emphasis is on *having* certain traits or characteristics through *possession of certain commodities* as opposed to *developing* these characteristics through various *modes of being*. Thus humans become alienated from their own physical, mental, and social capacities as well as from the world around them. Nowhere is this alienated lifestyle more developed than in suburbia. Goods must be consumed to "keep up with the Joneses"; personal worth and status are measured by the amount and type of possessions owned in relation to one's neighbors. Lawns, gardens, and "living" rooms are more for show than for recreation and pleasure.

Furthermore, capitalist consumption alienates humans from each other. This process of consumption is individual and privatized; it emphasizes competition over cooperation. And it is in the suburb that this alienated consumption receives perhaps its quintessential expression. For here each family is isolated within its own private home, separated from the neighbors by an expanse of lawn. Neighbor vies with neighbor to achieve the most status through house, yard, and automobile. Appliances and tools are unnecessarily duplicated within each house. Neighbors communicate only about the weather or external threats to the community. There is no collective responsibility for housework or childcare. Thus women, whose lot it generally is to perform these tasks in capitalist society, suffer a particularly oppressive form of alienation.

All suburbanites, however, are alienated to some degree by their consumerist lifestyles.[19]

Finally, the spatial distribution of privilege represented by suburbanization is contradictory to the long-run interests of the working class as a whole. There have always been certain groups of workers who did not benefit from suburban development. Some of these workers have been unable to mobilize themselves to protect whatever competitive advantages they might possess. The majority have simply lacked advantages altogether. The exclusion of these workers from social, economic, and political resources by those who find themselves in more advantageous positions represents a continuing barrier to working-class solidarity. It is an obstacle which must be overcome in order to build an egalitarian, democratic society.

The contradictions of suburban development are becoming increasingly apparent. These contradictions cannot fail to compel changes in the present social arrangements. The important issue is the direction of these changes. Capitalists will attempt to bring about changes that will support their prerogatives and strengthen the capitalist system. The interest of the working class, however, does not lie with propping up capitalism. In the long run, workers must struggle to transform it. A thorough understanding of the origin and historical dynamics of the various forms of capitalist contradictions can only aid in this struggle.

NOTES

1. Following O'Connor, *state* is used here as a generic term referring to government at all levels. The generic is justified by the fact that all levels of government share a common relationship to the mode of production. The functions of the capitalist state are (1) to ensure profitable private capital accumulation and (2) to maintain social harmony. The capitalist state contributes directly to corporate profitability through projects and services that increase the rate of profit (e.g., highways, education). It contributes indirectly to corporate profitability through projects and services that lower the reproduction cost of labor (e.g., urban renewal, unemployment insurance). The state legitimates the capitalist system through projects and services which maintain social order (e.g., welfare, police). The state at all levels is subject to political pressure and manipulation—but more especially so at the local level where its smaller scale makes it more accessible to a greater variety of interest groups. See the following article in this book by Markusen for an excellent discussion of the state at the local level.

2. Marglin points out that the factory system as a method of organizing

production was not historically or technologically inevitable. Rather it was developed by capital because it offered the greatest amount of control over labor and therefore was the most profitable form of organization.

3. Glaab and Brown (pp. 25–51) document numerous examples of state subsidy of capital improvements which maintained or increased the profitability of the manufacturing sector in the mid–nineteenth century.

4. For more details and statistics on this process of annexation, see Kotler (pp. 1–26) and Wood (p. 77).

5. For an excellent discussion and good documentation of the increasing demand for city services, see Glaab and Brown (pp. 52–187). The present discussion owes much to this work.

6. Writing in 1915, Graham Taylor furnished this contemporary account of capitalists' thinking:

> Some company officials act on the belief that by removing workingmen from a large city it is possible to get them away from the influences which foment discontent and labor disturbances. The satellite city is looked to as a sort of isolation hospital for the cure of chronic "trouble." In an eastern city which recently experienced the throes of a turbulent streetcar strike, the superintendent of a large industrial establishment said that every time workers paraded past his plant a veritable fever seemed to spread among the employees in all his work-rooms. He thought that if the plants were moved out to the suburbs, the workingmen should not be so frequently inoculated with infection (p. 23).

7. One of the earliest and most obvious examples of this approach was the development of Gary, Indiana, by U.S. Steel in 1905. The corporation formed a subsidiary land-development company which laid out and developed the community. The town was then incorporated and formal political control put in the hands of its residents. As both the largest employer and largest taxpayer in town, however, U.S. Steel retained effective control. Greer provides a good illustration of the continuing dominance of U.S. Steel in the municipal politics of Gary.

8. See Markusen's more detailed discussion of this point in the next article.

9. For documentation of the growth of suburbs see Wood (pp. 54–87), Glaab and Brown (pp. 281–85) and Masotti and Hadden (p. 7).

10. For more on the development of the U.S. financial structure and suburbanization, see Harvey.

11. Conventional social-science literature on suburbs almost totally neglects this fact. First of all, most discussion and data is presented in terms of central cities and "suburban rings" (see, for example, Schnore; Birch). On the one hand, this position ignores the variation in both the form and the composition of suburbs. On the other hand, it mystifies class relations by setting up a geographical contradiction as the basis for inequality rather than an economic one. For, although classes clearly have different spatial locations, they are primarily defined by their relationship to the economy. Second, suburbs are often described as the outcome of some "natural" market process. This conceptualization ignores the political

component of suburbanization. Muth, for instance, argues that suburbs have been generated by essentially the same market forces as the central city. Furthermore, he argues that the distribution of income and resources among suburbs is largely what it would be if there were no political fragmentation. In my view, however, it is *precisely* this political fragmentation which explains the inequality in resources among suburbs.

12. Of course, not all suburbs compete for industry. The residents of certain middle- and upper-class residential communities militantly oppose the introduction of industry into their municipalities. This opposition has two motivations: (1) a desire to keep local service costs down, and (2) a desire to increase the property values of the already highly valued large-lot, single-family dwellings. Both of these drives have the effect of keeping the tax rate low in these communities.

13. Stanley Aronowitz (pp. 172–83) provides a lucid discussion of this ethnic hierarchy. The present analysis owes much to his work.

14. For the history of urban racial violence see Connery; Geschwender.

15. This distinction and the discussion that follows are based on O'Connor, which I consider to be a pathbreaking work in its analysis of the structure of the U.S. economy and its current conflicts and contradictions.

16. For an excellent short analysis of dual labor markets see Piore.

17. The following discussion is based largely on Braverman; Gordon (pp. 63–66).

18. Larry Sawers (p. 56) calculates that over one-quarter of annual GNP is currently dependent upon roads, cars, and trucks. When all related goods and services (e.g., building construction, duplication of consumer durables and municipal services, local bureaucracies) are factored in, it is reasonable to assume that well over half of the annual GNP of the United States is directly or indirectly tied to suburbs and suburbanization. The truth of this assertion is made painfully obvious by the sensitive and central position occupied by the automobile and construction industries in the ongoing economic crisis.

19. The pervasive consumerism of suburbia was one of the first and has been one of the most consistently recognized features of suburban life. The authors of *Crestwood Heights*, one of the first social-science studies of the suburban phenomenon, were struck by the way in which suburban children were instructed very early on in the value of constant acquisition and the overwhelming importance of the *appearance* of success through consumption (Seeley, Sim, and Loosley). The precise nature of suburban consumption later became the central issue in the debate over the "myth of suburbia." A more extensive discussion of the historical treatment of suburbs in social-science literature was the subject of my Master's thesis; see References.

REFERENCES

Aronowitz, Stanley, *False Promises: The Shaping of American Working Class Consciousness* (New York: McGraw-Hill Book Co., 1973).

Ashton, Patrick J., "Toward a Political Economy of Metropolitan Areas" (Master's thesis, Michigan State University, 1975).

Baran, Paul A. and Paul M. Sweezy, *Monopoly Capital: An Essay on the American Economic and Social Order* (New York: Monthly Review Press, 1966).

Birch, David, *The Economic Future of City and Suburb* (New York: Committee for Economic Development, 1970).

Braverman, Harry, *Labor and Monopoly Capital: The Degradation of Work in the Twentieth Century* (New York: Monthly Review Press, 1974).

Connery, Robert, *Urban Riots* (New York: Vintage Books, 1969).

Geschwender, James, *The Black Revolt* (Englewood Cliffs, N.J.: Prentice-Hall, 1971).

Glaab, Charles N., and A. Theodore Brown, *A History of Urban America* (New York: Macmillan Company, 1967).

Gordon, David M., ed., *Problems in Political Economy: An Urban Perspective* (Lexington, Mass.: D. C. Heath and Co., 1971).

Greer, Edward, "U.S. Steel and Gary, Indiana: The Structural Basis of Racism in an Industrial City, 1906–1974" (Paper presented at the Conference on Urban Political Economy, New York City, Feb. 1975).

Harvey, David, "The Political Economy of Urbanization in Advanced Capitalist Societies—The Case of the United States" (Paper presented at the Conference on Urban Political Economy, New York City, Feb. 1975).

Kain, John F. "The Distribution and Movement of Jobs and Industry," in James Q. Wilson, ed., *The Metropolitan Enigma: Inquiries into the Nature and Dimensions of America's "Urban Crisis"* (Cambridge, Mass.: Harvard University Press, 1968).

Kotler, Milton, *Neighborhood Government: The Local Foundations of Political Life* (Indianapolis: Bobbs-Merrill Co., 1969).

Marglin, Stephen A., "What Do Bosses Do? The Origins and Functions of Hierarchy in Capitalist Production," *Review of Radical Political Economics*, Summer 1974.

Masotti, Louis H., and Jeffrey K. Hadden, eds., *Suburbia in Transition* (New York: New Viewpoints, 1974).

Mumford, Lewis, *The City in History* (New York: Harcourt, Brace and World, 1961).

Muth, Richard R., "The Distribution of Population within Urban Areas," in Robert Ferher, ed., *Determinants of Investment Behavior* (New York: National Bureau of Economic Research, 1967).

O'Connor, James R., *The Fiscal Crisis of the State* (New York: St. Martin's Press, 1973).

Piore, Michael, "The Dual Labor Market: Theory and Implications," in David M. Gordon, ed., *Problems in Political Economy: An Urban Perspective* (Lexington, Mass.: D. C. Heath and Co., 1971).

Sawers, Larry, "Urban Form and the Mode of Production," *Review of Radical Political Economics*, Spring 1975.

Schnore, Leo F., *The Urban Scene* (New York: Free Press, 1965).

Seeley, John R.; R. Alexander Sim; and Elizabeth W. Loosley, *Crestwood Heights: The Culture of Suburban Life* (New York: Basic Books, 1956).

Taylor, Graham, R., *Satellite Cities: A Study of Industrial Suburbs* (New York and London: D. Appleton and Co., 1915).

Wood, Robert C., *Suburbia: Its People and Their Politics* (Boston: Houghton Mifflin, 1958).

Class and Urban
Social Expenditure:
A Marxist Theory
of Metropolitan Government

ANN R. MARKUSEN

An incisive analysis of the fiscal crisis of older U.S. central cities in the 1970s requires an understanding of the Marxist theory of the state. This paper seeks to explain, from a Marxist perspective, the dynamics of the state at the local level. In place of conventional social-science models of pluralism (political science) and competition (economics), the Marxist model used here builds on the concepts of class conflict and the historical development of political form under U.S. capitalism. The contribution of this paper is its elaboration of the Marxist theory of the state, heretofore applied almost exclusively to national government, to include an analysis of a unique American phenomenon: the fragmented urban governmental structure.

The impetus to undertake this investigation was the desire to comprehend why cities like New York and Detroit presently confront serious fiscal crises. Since the same brink-of-bankruptcy condition does not characterize European city governments, it is most probable that the specific form of the government at the local level in the United

* This is an extended treatment of ideas presented at the Conference on Urban Political Economy, at the New School for Social Research, New York City, February 16, 1975, and included in *Kapitalistate: Working Papers on the Capitalist State*, No. 4/5, Summer, 1976.

States is a very powerful force in exacerbating urban fiscal crisis. An inquiry into the origins of this form reveals that it has evolved from the resolution of past class conflicts, each of which in turn was shaped by existing political form. This history provides a means of strengthening the Marxist theory of the state, by illuminating the relationship between state structure and class conflict.

HOW MAINSTREAM SOCIAL SCIENCE EXPLAINS U.S. METROPOLITAN POLITICAL FRAGMENTATION

The class homogeneity and political autonomy of suburban development challenge mainstream social science because they undermine an approach which celebrates pluralism in the political process. Suburbs confront even the casual observer with the class character of U.S. society.

Political scientists and economists alike attempt to explain and applaud the existence of fragmented, autonomous local governments in metropolitan areas. Political scientists herald the structure as a successful solution to the corruption and bureaucratic unresponsiveness of big-city government, and as a nostalgic movement back toward rural living and New England town-hall politics (Wood; Warren). This idyllic model describes only suburban governments and ignores central-city political conflicts. Furthermore, it cannot explain why successive groups of recent migrants to cities fail to gain access to suburban democracy. The lack of a historical perspective that carefully documents the emergence of separate political units cripples the strength of such an analysis.

Empirical evidence indicates that this view focuses on a trivial (and most likely fictitious) aspect of suburban political structure. Residents of suburbia, paradoxically, treat with apathy and indifference the political apparatus which appears to be so accessible. Political scientists, despite their pluralist theory, document the uniformity and dullness of suburban politics and ascribe it to the homogeneity of populations (Keats; Wood).

Conventional economists' approval of the multiplicity of independent metropolitan local governments echoes the political scientists' emphasis on choice and pluralism. During the 1940s and early 1950s, public finance theorists could find no mechanism equivalent to the market with which to model resource allocation in the public sector (Samuelson). The marketplace tool kit was salvaged in part, however, when Tiebout pointed out that such pessimism was not warranted on the local level (Tiebout). The existence of multiple local governments, he claimed, introduces competition into the consumption and production of local public services. Customers (residents) express their preference for a particular package of public services by voting with their feet, i.e., moving to the utility-maximizing suburban location. In Tiebout's view, local governments act as firms, forced to produce efficiently the optimum level and mix of output by threat of resident out-migration.

The empirical evidence shows such arguments to be supple acrobatics indeed. If Tiebout's view were correct, suburban political units would exhibit a wide variety of public-service packages, available to residents of every income and ethnic group. In fact, the most striking characteristics of suburban units are their homogeneity, exclusion of other income and ethnic groups, and nearly identical public-service mixes, with quality of service rising quite consistently with class composition of residents (Newton). A hierarchy of suburbs, ranked by class characteristics, can be identified in all U.S. metropolitan areas. In this political atmosphere, the local government does not act like a firm, as Tiebout proposes, responding to areawide market forces of supply and demand. Rather, it behaves as a conscious constructor of its own local market through influence on the cost and demand features of its constituency (Markusen). Marxist analysis, with its focus on historical and materialist methods, can illuminate the logic beyond such observed outcomes. A Marxist model bests mainstream explanations by replacing the concept of individual with the concept of class.

THE MARXIST THEORY OF THE STATE

Simply put, the Marxist theory of the state sees the political structure of any society as a derivative of its economic system. In its early, simple form, the government represents the views and needs of the dominant economic class and legitimizes its economic power over other people (Lenin). Under capitalism, the state legalizes property rights, protects them with constabulary or military force, and thereby guarantees the expropriation of labor's product. Marxists today criticize the oversimplification of this model (Wright). With the elaboration of the concept of class, more recent Marxist models view the state as the crucible for conflicts among members of the dominant economic class as well as conflicts between classes and subclasses (Milliband; Bates).

In the United States, Marxists use the theory of the state to explain the growing size of the national government, its entry into the production sphere itself, and its continuing crises. Both imperialism and domestic recessions, fueled by intensifying monopolization of the private sector, evoke demands on the state from both capitalist and working-class groups: for subsidies, particular macroeconomic policies, state regulation, direct state production, and so on (O'Connor; Esping-Andersen, et al.). The state responds to these conflicts in ways that produce additional state structures, which become the immediate arena for future conflicts.

This paper attempts to use the elements of this analysis, particularly the concepts of class conflict, and contradiction, to develop an explicitly Marxist theory of the operation of the state at the local level in the United States. It begins by illustrating how class conflict in mercantilist and industrial-capitalist stages of U.S. development shaped the present *form* of the state at the local level.

THE CORPORATE TOWN: INHERITANCE
FROM MERCANTILISM

The United States federal system is unique among capitalist nations. Few other capitalist countries grant states or localities such extensive political autonomy. In Europe, local and regional officers are generally directly subordinate and responsible to the centralized national state. The peculiar American hybrid grew from European, mainly British, colonial policies and the political exigencies surrounding nation-building.

Local public corporate bodies date back to early feudal towns. On the European continent, the rising capitalist nation-states swept away urban self-governance, but in Britain and the United States, the emerging states' strength was, oddly enough, based on local partial autonomy. In England, forces of the developing nation-state manipulated the antagonism between the nascent trading town and the feudal manor. After the Norman invasion of 1066, the crown granted charters to towns in order to secure their independence from local landed gentry and their fealty to the new regime. These charters set up either an oligarchical municipal corporation or a hierarchical structure administered by a justice of the peace appointed by the crown (Harris).

English mercantile capitalists transplanted this corporate form of the city government to colonial America. They deliberately planned and chartered towns as agencies for English control over profits from mercantilist trade. Town charters forbade settlers from engaging in enterprise in competition with the British (e.g., privateering) and banned intracolonial mobility of immigrant labor to ensure a work force for local mercantilist shipping activity. Entire towns, highly socially stratified and tightly controlled, operated as market centers and military and administrative command posts for the colonial empire. From these bases, the English trading elite appropriated land and resources from the native Americans, extracted agricultural and forest products from the outlying areas (especially furs, wheat, and cotton), sold British manufactured goods, African slaves, and West Indian rum, and secured a profitable monopoly over trade (Glaab and Brown, pp. 1–6).

By the American Revolution, sixteen such corporate entities existed on the seaboard with charters originally granted under the authority of the English crown. The American Revolution linked these diverse communities and their hinterlands against a common enemy. Each had begun independently as a peripheral outpost of the dominant culture and had, over the space of 150 years, developed its own aspiring local elite and often a distinct political character. The founders of the new American state, in order to secure the allegiance of numerous emerging native capitalists who viewed each other and any state with suspicion, made substantial concessions to decentralized political structure, resulting in the federal system. The new federal system not only incorporated the existing charters, but vested state legislatures with the power to issue new city charters. Subsequently, state constitutions set up explicit provisions subordinating cities and towns to the state machinery but preserving the form and notion of the corporate town. The administration of local government passed from colonial governors to the emerging native merchant and capitalist classes.

FRAGMENTED METROPOLITAN GOVERNMENT: THE LEGACY OF U.S. INDUSTRIAL CAPITALISM

During the nineteenth century, industrial capitalism produced new class interests, which battled over the control of local government. The product of the various struggles is the contemporary maze of municipal local governments that are the institutional context for the present fiscal crisis of central cities. Cumulatively, the manifestations of this process begin with the push for city public services and municipal home rule, followed by the curtailment of outward extension of city political boundaries, the arrangements for easy incorporation of new political units on the periphery, and the separation of tax and expenditure domains between state and local levels. The forces underlying these developments are examined in turn below.

Growing City Budgets

After 1850, vigorously expanding industrial production triggered rapid development of U.S. cities. It imposed a tremendous need for physical infrastructure to enhance capital accumulation and to accommodate the swelling populations, most of which was immigrant labor. The responsibility for providing some of the power, water, and road needs for factory production was assumed by the local government. It was clearly in the interests of factory owners and merchants to disperse the cost of such infrastructure across the entire population rather than bear it as an internal cost of production.

At the same time, since capitalist production separated the worker from control over the means of production, unemployment emerged as a persistent phenomenon, along with mushrooming poverty, crime, and disease. When these reached levels that threatened the viability of cities, civic leaders (members of the merchant and capitalist classes) demanded that the city undertake programs for public health, sewage treatment, and police and fire protection. Urban education systems, produced and paid for at the local level, taught future workers skills needed in capitalist production and promulgated the ideology of individualism.

Conflict over Land Speculation and City Contracts

Because rapid urban development enriched those with political control, state legislatures became breeding grounds for special-interest legislation, granting lucrative public-sector contracts to private political entrepreneurs. In 1870, for example, three-fourths of the pages of acts passed by the New York State legislature related to cities and villages. A representative of the 1867–1868 New York State Constitutional Convention pointed out that "seven-eighths of all revenues are disbursed by those who hold state appointments and are in no way responsible to the people of the city. . . ." (McBain, p. 40). The Evarts Commission, set up in 1877 to investigate graft in New York City, concluded that

> Cities were compelled by legislation to buy lands for parks and places because the owners wished to sell them; compelled to grade, pave and sewer streets without inhabitants and for no other purpose than to award corrupt contracts for the work (McBain, p. 9).

Capitalist class representatives who did not share in the spoils but had to pay for them through property taxation complained bitterly about such graft and provided the political base for the municipal "home rule" movement (1865–1900). Up until 1900 their efforts resulted in little more than state provisions (statutory and constitutional) limiting in small ways the absolute control by state legislatures and providing for the election of some local officials. The ideological impact of their call for home rule, couched in terms of Jeffersonian democracy and self-determination, had greater consequences. In the 1880s, a Harvard academic, John Fiske, traveled the country popularizing local rights and "delighting audiences by tracing back the town meeting of New England to the village assemblies of the early Aryans, making federalism that began with these local units the key to heaven and earth" (Wickman, p. 70). The appeal of the issue tended to obscure whose interests the movement served. But the prinicple of home rule took root, especially in rural areas.

Interest in home rule among urban capitalist interests faded around the turn of the century and was replaced by politics aimed at defeating Tammany Hall and similar regimes. However, home rule had become a universal state constitutional feature, creating a political structure which was to impede metropolitan political integration in the future. The home-rule arrangement originated in class conflict over control of the state versus local levels of government but created a precedent which would shape twentieth-century urban class conflict by permitting proliferation of semiautonomous local units of government.

Residential Segregation

Long before the first peripheral independent suburb appeared, urban residences began to segregate spatially. Horse-drawn cars and then electric trolleys permitted decentralization of residence in place of an older urban pattern where classes lived in close proximity. Land speculators and trolley-line owners promoted new class neighborhoods in order to receive large capital gains on the land along the trolley lines. Warner documents neighborhood segregation in Boston from the mid–nineteenth century on. (English industrial towns developed similarly [Engels].) There, contractors built housing on the periphery for members of the merchant, capitalist, and professional classes because they could afford the construction of larger houses and because the transportation system favored the location of the more leisured and occupationally stable groups on the periphery while requiring a central location of the poor and occupationally mobile working class.

Elsewhere in this volume, Gordon and Ashton investigate the dynamics of continued out-migration of both workplace and workers over the last century. What is relevant for the present purpose of tracing political proliferation is the tendency for this pattern of residential segregation by class to repeat itself continually, marking neighborhoods in fine degrees of differentiation and providing the spatial basis for independent political incorporation. This differentiation proceeded at a hectic pace, since population burgeoned and no old housing stock existed to absorb it or soften segregation with the inertia of tradition.

Class-segregated neighborhoods thus became the spatial context for class-segregated suburbs. *Class* here refers not only to the basic division between capitalist and worker, fundamental to Marxist analysis of the operation of capitalist production, but to the subclasses within each class. Ashton, above, describes the divisions within the U.S. working class and their importance for the developing spatial array of suburbs. If this separation of residences had not taken place, it is unlikely that political independence and insulation would have been advan-

tageous. Instead, other methods of organizing the public sector would
have emerged.

Conflict over Access to City Government

The potential accessibility of local government machinery to working-
class populations also explains its unique structure in the United
States. Remoteness and scale of the national government allow capitalist interests to construct and manipulate it easily. For national politics, Marx's famous quip about democracy—that it is the political system where once every four years the working class is allowed to vote
for one or two members of the ruling class—is appropriate. But at the
local level, relatively smaller size and geographical proximity render
government power more accessible and potentially responsive to the
working population. In fact, many cities in the late–nineteenth and
twentieth centuries were ruled by political organizations solidly rooted
in the immigrants who were flowing into Eastern cities. There is some
evidence that earlier (mid–nineteenth century) political forces in
favor of annexation and consolidated urban political structure were
capitalists eager to enlist aid against Tammany Hall–type governments
(Feshbach; Kotler, pp. 14–20). However, efforts to dilute the political
power of pro-working-class groups by expanding the jurisdiction of
the city did not succeed. The incorporation of the five boroughs that
now make up New York City did not lessen Tammany's control, as its
architects had hoped.

Progressive mayors, such as New York's Fiorello LaGuardia, ex-
emplified the best of worker-based city regimes within the larger capitalist structure. During the 1930s, LaGuardia pushed for large numbers
of public-service jobs, wiped out the $31,000,000 deficit of the city
with business and public-utility taxes, and expanded city relief to include clothing, subsidized milk distribution, and health care. La-
Guardia's proposals were accompanied by statements such as "If the
right to live interferes with profits, profits must necessarily give way
to that right," and "The economic principles of yesterday are as obso-
lete as the oxcart" (Franklin, p. 99). Despite such intentions, "left"
city-government control merely demonstrated the difficulty that political units face when they attempt major reforms within the larger
capitalist economy. Even when in firm control, worker-oriented re-

gimes could not radically reorganize the city budget, because workers' jobs depended on the health of the private sector. Business emigration threatened any local government attempting to cut back on social-infrastructure expenditures, to transfer the burden for them back on business beneficiaries, or to raise business taxes for expanded social services.

Class Conflict over City Tax Burden

Struggle among classes and subclasses over distribution of the tax burden of growing city budgets provided the ultimate impetus to fragmented local government. At the national level, the growth of social expenses and social accumulation can be financed by deficit spending, so the burden does not cut directly into the operating capital of the private sector nor into consumption funds of the capitalist class. While diversion of funds from the private sector to the public sector does take place, it is voluntarily transferred by capitalist institutions and owners via the bond market. This procedure is welcomed by capitalist interests, because they are guaranteed a return on this loan of their capital.

At the local level, governments are legally forbidden to finance growing operating budgets with deficit spending. Deficit financing by state and local governments resulted in frequent bankruptcy in the early nineteenth century, so state constitutions limited debt to capital expenditure only. In addition, state and local government deficits would hinder the national attempt to pursue a stabilizing fiscal policy. Since World War II, hard-pressed city regimes and their corporate backers have lobbied successfully for substantial federal and state revenue-sharing, accounting for up to 40 percent of big-city budgets today, and have collaborated in the surreptitious financing of operating costs by burying them in capital accounts. During the era critical for the establishment of independent suburban entities, however, local expenditures for social accumulation and social expenses had come principally from sources within the constituency.

Within the local political jurisdiction, the bases for such taxes were the capital funds of business entities and the consumption funds of the capitalist and working classes. The latter include amounts spent on class reproduction. Because taxes affect disposable income, the conflict over who should pay local taxes is an extension of the struggle between profits and wages. If the capitalist interests can arrange for the transfer of various costs of production to the city budget and escape the tax bill for them, they successfully enhance profits at the expense of wage-earners. This appears to be a fight over consumption funds, rather than over the returns to production, but is essentially the same conflict. Instead of occurring in the workplace, this conflict takes place in the local political arena. Given the features of city government detailed above, capitalist interests did not directly control the public means of production. City governments were, and in some cases still are, arenas where classes and subclasses, less unevenly matched in power, fought to secure the benefits of social production and expenses while escaping the costs. The construction of independent local-government production units insulated capitalist-class production and consumption funds from the risk of losing this battle and at the same time created a powerful weapon, exit, to tame working-class-oriented regimes.

Denouement: Suburban Autonomy and Proliferation

These class conflicts accompanying capitalist development in the United States and contemporary political exigencies, from inherited colonial and federalist structure to home-rule ideology, have resulted in a political configuration unique among capitalist countries: strong separate suburban government units that serve class-based neighborhoods but avoid production-associated costs that central cities incur. The first well-documented appearance of an independent political suburban government is that of Brookline, Massachusetts, in 1873. Warner, in his account of outward suburban expansion around Boston in the latter half of the nineteenth century, notes that the change from the tradition of central-city annexation of residential areas on its periphery to independent suburban incorporation occurs abruptly when state-level provisions for independent utilities ends suburban dependence on the city for basic public services such as water and sewers. Brookline was the first suburb to insist upon its independence:

> By the 1880's, with but one exception, no suburban town ever again seriously considered annexation. . . . It was already apparent in the 1880's that to join Boston was to assume all the burdens and conflicts of a modern industrial metropolis. To remain apart was to escape, at least for a time, some of these problems (Warner, p. 164).

The political fragmentation that followed the emergence of class-bound residential neighborhoods takes place only after new jurisdictions can get public services from a source independent of the central city.

In the same era, states adopted constitutions and laws that established uniform treatment of local government structure, instead of individually chartering each city. These laws facilitated the proliferation of independent suburbs by making it easy to incorporate as an independent "home-rule" political entity and difficult for the larger central city to absorb peripheral growth through annexation or consolidation (Markusen, Chap. 7). While there is little historical evidence available on the sources of organized support for such provisions, it probably came from groups wishing to protect local autonomy, like the residents of Brookline. Even without such explicit support, the American tradition of democracy and localism, shored up by the legal principle of home rule, would be sufficient explanation for the evolution of these institutional arrangements. By 1930, every state legislature in the country had adopted some form of legislation accomplishing this. In general, it put the decision to join or not to join the central city in the hands of the residents of the annexable area, leaving the parent who had spawned the child helpless to participate in determining their joint future. Thus, the home-rule movement, which aimed to strengthen the central city against state manipulation, culminated ironically in the weakening of the city by engendering suburban parasites.

The enabling legislation that fostered independent suburban political structure was not a historical accident nor was it prompted by a nostalgia for the town meeting. The latter was merely the ideology accompanying the development. Passage of such legislation lay with the historical strength of suburban-rural coalitions in state legislatures, and their motives were material rather than ideological.

The politically independent suburb first appeared about 1870 on the East Coast and established itself as a prototype for metropolitan structure across the country. Decade after decade, political struggles culminated in the repetition of this pattern in major cities. Detroit had no politically independent suburbs until World War I, but then developed forty-odd such entities in the next forty years. Suburb-ringing is still occurring, particularly in the West, although a few cities like Oklahoma City, Dallas, Houston, and Phoenix are attempting to avoid ringing by massive early annexations. Consolidation, the joining of previously independent local governments, has succeeded only where racist motives are suspectable (e.g., Jacksonville, Richmond).

THE CONTRADICTORY FUNCTIONS OF
METROPOLITAN POLITICAL FRAGMENTATION

This fragmented political apparatus, the inherited product of past conflicts, continues to shape class conflict. Its role in directing the placement and intensity of the present fiscal crisis of the cities cannot be understated. A simple Marxist theory of the operation of the state at the local level can be stated as follows.

The fundamental force in shaping political life is the conflict of class interests associated with the contemporary mode of production. This conflict often takes place within the shell of institutions remaining from previous conflicts and which are important in the specific form of the present conflict. In the United States today, class structure under monopoly capitalism encompasses important subclasses which obscure the unity within a class, create intraclass conflicts, and diminish class consciousness while breeding subclass identification. Suburban geographical and political isolation nurtures subclass consciousness, and diffuses the public-sector struggle between capital and labor over a multiplicity of groups.

In the current urban fiscal crisis, the salient function of suburban governments is to insulate class consumption and capital from the costs of social accumulation and social expenses in the central city, thereby forcing the poor to finance their own oppressive police force and welfare system. The suburban government actually constructs its own public-service market by employing policy tools such as zoning in which class aims for levels and types of social consumption and class reproduction can be achieved by excluding high-cost residents and attracting those with ample resources. At the same time, the independence of the suburban government allows it to use these same exclusionary tools to enhance the private-sector functions of suburbia—the class assimilation of children by restricting their playmates and experience, the removal of class conflict from living situations, and the preservation of asset value of housing. But it also jeopardizes central-city finances and the rational use of metropolitan space.

An example will illustrate the argument. Public safety, meaning primarily the safety of private property, is a social expense necessary under capitalist production relations. It accounts for an average of one-third of all municipal expenditures (excluding schools). Originally a private expense, this function shifted to the state sector (although there are still large numbers of private guards). Construction of separate political units responsible for public safety involved a substantial shift of the burden of this cost. The benefiting classes could escape the costs of public safety that the city provided to their industrial and mercantile properties in the central city, thus leaving the working class and the reserve army of unemployed (precisely the groups from whom such property was to be protected) to pay for the safety of their oppressors' property. Furthermore, non-property-crime control and other poverty-related safety expenses would also be paid for by the same class.

Suburban insularity in turn diminished the costs of policing class conflict by segregating classes spatially and developing locally controlled police forces. In early U.S. cities, the rich and the poor lived quite close together, creating a potential for violence. When political autonomy followed residential segregation, the local police force became controllable via consensus and therefore dependable in any violent situation (Silver).

In addition to escaping the tax burden for social expenses like public safety, health, and welfare, suburban residents have also been able to help themselves to any number of city-financed services without contributing tax support (Neenan). Some of these services are associated with the daytime presence of commuters to the central city—street maintenance, traffic control, waste and pollution control, and water systems. Others are the extensive culture and recreational facilities that the central city provides to all metropolitan residents—parks, zoos, concerts, parade facilities, libraries, and museums—which are only occasionally compensated for by payment of fees.

As independent suburban governments increased in number, their differentiation from the central city grew apace. Autonomous local budgets not only allowed suburban class interests to escape the social expenditures of the central city while enjoying the benefits; it also allowed them to enjoy levels of social consumption and reproduction far above those of city residents by pooling parts of their consumption fund to produce high-quality public service for a limited group of recipients. It is not only an insular high income level that creates this opportunity; it is also the ability of local governments to exclude high-cost populations who would affect its production of local public services. This is most significant in education systems where excluding working-class and minority children from the constituency lowers the cost of providing a "good" education; no special education or compensatory programs are required. Class reproduction through the public education system is important to most suburban residents, from the professional subclass on down. These groups fight jealously to keep their tax dollars out of the unproductive sectors like welfare and in class-reproduction and -consumption sectors like education.

Similarly, excluding "crime-prone" populations and escaping aging physical structures lowers the cost of providing public safety—police and fire services. Even changes in technology, such as the substitution of the police cruiser for the cop on the beat, put a premium on suburban locations; it's cheaper to operate cruisers in suburbia than in the central city. Exclusion of high-cost populations and low-income residents is achieved by using policy tools such as exclusionary zoning and building codes to manipulate both the supply and demand features of local markets for social output. In this sense, the local government attempts to *create* its own market for public-sector output.

Far from acting as an impersonal firm trying to attract a population with an efficiently produced public-service package, the local government acts in class interests to fashion the very market it serves. It is strongly partisan, for instance, about who its customers are, as opposed to the disinterested firm of neoclassical theory, which is interested only in its customer's ability to pay the price. Even if families are willing to pay, the local government tries to exclude them if they are poor (because then they will be apt to get a larger portion of the public output than they pay for under most local tax systems) and if they are apt to raise the costs of production. Regressive taxation, large-lot zoning, strict building codes, discriminatory public-service distribution schemes, and urban renewal all contribute to the ability of local governments to shut out other classes and protect the public-sector class-consumption and -reproduction aims of its constituents.

All suburban governments thus try to attract residents better, not worse, off than current residents. Since better-off residents can always be wooed elsewhere, the result is a tendency for rather strict internal homogeneity to develop within each suburb. This development relegates the poorest and least mobile people to the central city, which is then left with the residents least able to pay and most dependent upon public-sector services. Since they must pay for their own city services, the arrangement ensures that the local public sector, despite its redistributive posture, will not significantly alter the division between wages and profits, nor end the unemployment that keeps wages down.

The growing participation of land speculators and construction interests accompanied the construction of these separate and disparate markets. The gains from insular social consumption in the suburbs can accrue to developers and landlords through their ability to capitalize the value of public-sector differentials into housing price and rent (Oates). Beginning in the 1920s it became profitable to extend the privileges of suburban public- and private-sector insularity to the better-paid members of the working class, but at premium rents (Harvey, pp. 169–70). The expansion of home ownership also meant that housing, including the tax and service value capitalized, became the only asset and chief means of economic security for working people who could afford it. Therefore, it became increasingly difficult for any group to stay in the central city because of the high level of public-sector taxes and low level of benefits, not only because of their effect on current consumption, but their devaluation of this asset as well. With few exceptions, only those who cannot escape, do not. Working-class suburbanization has contributed to the public-sector fragmentation of local government, often militantly defending it, and thus to the construction of a complicated network of class-stratified public-service units surrounding the metropolitan area. A detailed study of Detroit and forty-seven of its suburbs shows remarkable internal homogeneity within suburbs (measured by deviation from mean per capita income) and strong statistical relationships between high social-cost measures (educational background, poverty populations), low wealth status, and public-service levels across the metropolitan area (Markusen, Chap. 7).

The movement of industrial and mercantile establishments to suburban jurisdictions is largely a response to private-sector gains, as Gordon argues elsewhere in this volume, but taxes and public services do play an important role. Many corporations leave in the central city those portions of their operations which require extensive public-investment outlays while removing to suburban locations those which do not. To avoid paying for the social-consumption expenditures of their own work force in these suburban locations, they cooperate with

local class-consumption interests to exclude their lower-paid workers
from living in the same jurisdiction in which the plant pays property
taxes. The existence of fragmented political units allows corporations
to play off one jurisdiction against the other to secure preferential tax
and expenditure arrangements in what public-finance theorists call tax-
base competition (Harrison).

Progressive city administrations continue to face frustration in
their attempts to end public-sector fealty to corporations. Detroit's progressive black mayor, Coleman Young, recently offered Chrysler Corporation a long-run property-tax break if it would simply continue to
run its city assembly lines. A Michigan study confirms that intraurban
tax differentials do make a significant difference in location decisions of
businesses (Survey Research Center). In the recent New York City crisis, corporate hegemony reveals its ultimate power. Because the corporate and banking sectors hold the bonds that the city cannot pay, they
can legally manipulate the city budget to cut back social expenses, require harsh measures against public-sector labor, preserve social infrastructural outlays that enhance corporate activities, and rule out
substantial business-tax increases as a way of solving the fiscal crisis.

Although suburban dispersion would have proceeded outward in
stratified neighborhoods regardless of the state-sector conflict, it is
clear that public-sector forces exacerbate the outward movement and
add to the degeneration of metropolitan cohesiveness. The process is
thus self-reinforcing; the existence of class neighborhoods makes possible the creation of independent political units, and these in turn encourage the creation of class-segregated suburbs. The consequences for
central-city fiscal crisis are obvious. The deformed local version of the
state, therefore, adds a spatial dimension to the capitalist crisis, since
anarchy of production in the public sector weakens the fabric of the
entire community. The drive outward results in the waste of public-
sector facilities already built and fails to incorporate public-sector
economies that would be emphasized in a rational, planned system.

THE FUTURE OF THE STATE AT THE LOCAL LEVEL

What will happen in the future? The phenomenon investigated here is
not a static political condition. The present plethora of political units

is the result of one hundred years of class interests constructing and maintaining separate public-service sectors. In the future, it is possible that new class interests generated by monopoly capitalism will produce still different pressures on local political structure.

Corporate reliance on elaborate administrative, financial, and control functions continues to tie them to the agglomeration of facilities downtown. Certain operations, particularly actual production facilities and warehousing, will continue to locate in suburbia, but large numbers of corporate jobs will remain in the central city. Thus the corporate sector seeks new ways to control the local public sector in addition to its threat to emigrate. Corporate interests have used the New York City fiscal crisis to secure for themselves a legitimate, direct, and dominant position in the budgetary process. To the extent that this domination succeeds and is replicated across the country, the corporate sector has less need for the maintenance of independent suburban political jurisdictions.

At the same time, the existence of fragmented political units encumbers the coordination and administration of national and multinational corporations. Local governments can be a big nuisance in planning expansion and location decisions. Dealings with suburban units to secure zoning changes and infrastructural commitments are often unpredictable and time-consuming. Some corporate leaders complain about the lack of metropolitan regional planning and appear to be increasingly in favor of regionalized political structure. Thus a struggle may ensue between suburban subclasses militant in their desire to preserve their local public-sector autonomy and large capitalist interests pushing for planned, rationalized, metropolis-wide government.

A third change is itself the result of class segregation in suburban areas: the ascendancy by black urban populations to political power in some of the larger cities. This development appears to have different results for urban structure among different regions. In the South, urban areas like Richmond, Dade County (Miami), and Jacksonville have quickly consolidated the preexisting political units to prevent minority hegemony in the central city. In the North, the dominant class interests apparently feel that black central-city governments can be dealt with satisfactorily because of their dependence on private-sector jobs and taxes. No structural change appears to be imminent.

A final change is an increasingly parochial and defensive attitude on the part of suburban and exurban residents, who are beginning to oppose growth in their communities because of high infrastructural costs associated with it, potential overuse of facilities they enjoy, and subtle fear of incursions by other groups who might ultimately undermine the "fabric" of the community and erode property values. Despite liberal efforts to throw out the property tax as the main financial base for municipal and educational expenditures, to force busing across district lines, and to disperse low-income housing into otherwise homogeneous neighborhoods, the subclass interests in suburbia seem to be solidly arrayed against erosion of their preferential status.

The outcome of all this is likely to be a further hybrid: special districts for planning urban land use and constructing urban infrastructure in the interests of the business community, and the maintenance of separate political units for some local public-consumption and class-reproduction functions, particularly public safety, education, and welfare. Maintenance of separate units for the latter will mollify suburban residents for their loss of control over land use and planning.

The last fifteen years have been ones of almost unremitting urban crisis. Clearly the urban public sector is one of the important receptacles for the display of capitalist crisis. The growing pressures on the urban public sector generated by infrastructural demands of the private sector and the growing costs of labor and community pacification are exacerbated in the United States by the structural arrangements that make local governments responsible for them, limit the financial resources available for these purposes, and badly maldistribute the burdens across the political units within an urban area.

The urban crisis is not congenial for corporate capitalism, as evidenced by the regular presence of local capitalist interests on committees concerned with urban problems, e.g., Henry Ford's membership on the Detroit Renaissance Committee. But capitalist interests have made efforts to turn the crisis to their ends, culminating in the recent attempts to control the actual city budget-making process itself through formally established organs. This is a two-edged knife, however. The attempt to cut urban social expenses like welfare may heighten the class conflict within the city. Similarly, the attempt to stop wage and benefit gains by public-sector workers may heighten the visibility of the struggle between capital and labor even as it affects workers in this sector. Some temporary resolution of these conflicts will occur, most likely via greater federal financing of social expenses, continuing a trend begun in the 1930s, and increased regulation of labor disputes in the public sector by ostensibly publicly minded arbitration boards. Nevertheless, there is not likely to be a satisfactory outcome to the basic urban crisis, structural or other. In fact, urban political units may become explicit mouthpieces for class interests and arenas for class conflict, a development which argues in favor of considering community organizing as part of a revolutionary strategy. While there is no possibility of "solving" the urban structural problem under capitalism, community organizations' struggles within the United States and the experience of existing socialist states undoubtedly suggest many steps forward—for example, the neighborhood courts and housing micro-brigades in Cuba.

SUMMARY

Democracy in the United States is subverted at the local level by a unique development—the cordoning off of various subclasses into political units populated by their own kind wherein constituents equally escape the costs that might be imposed by participation of those worse off. Central-city populations are left the privilege of voting to impose the costs of social-capital and class-containment expenses upon themselves. This is simply, in different form, democracy for the rich, although it involves minor gains for subsets of the working class. Real class differences under capitalism are obscured by a subdifferentiation of class enhanced by segregated residence and by the particular consumption and class-reproduction activities that accompany that residence.

Insular suburbia has been a salient feature of urban America for a hundred years, and an important contributor to central-city problems in the last thirty. This investigation has traced its relation to the capitalist mode of production and reflected on its likely fortunes in the future. If nothing else, perhaps it will stimulate further Marxist analysis of local political structure, under both socialist and capitalist modes of production, which might produce a full-bodied analysis and a strategy for urban action.

REFERENCES

Bates, Timothy, *Economic Man As Politician: Neoclassical and Marxist Theories of Government Behavior* (Morristown, N.J.: General Learning Press, 1976).

Engels, Friedrich, *The Condition of the Working Class in England in 1844,* (London: Swan Sonneschein & Co., 1892).

Esping-Andersen, Gosta; Roger Friedland; and Erik Olin Wright, "Modes of Class Struggle and the Capitalist State," *Kapitalistate,* Summer 1976.

Feshbach, Dan, "Notes on Annexation" (Mimeographed, 1974). Library of City and Regional Planning Department, University of California, Berkeley.

Franklin, Jay, *LaGuardia* (New York: Modern Age Books, 1937).

Gitlin, Todd, "Local Pluralism as Theory and Ideology," *Studies on the Left,* October 1965, pp. 21–45.

Glaab, Charles, and A. Theodore Brown, *A History of Urban America* (New York: Macmillan Company, 1967).

Harris, George, *Comparative Local Government* (London: Hutchinson University Library, 1948).

Harrison, Bennett, and Sandra Kanter, "The Great State Robbery," *Working Papers for a New Society,* Spring 1976.

Harvey, David, *Social Justice and the City* (Baltimore: Johns Hopkins Press, 1973).

Keats, John, *The Crack in the Picture Window* (Boston: Houghton Mifflin, 1957).

Kotler, Milton, *Neighborhood Government: The Local Foundations of Political Life* (Indianapolis: Bobbs-Merrill Co., 1969).

Lenin, Nikolai, "The State and Revolution," in Arthur Mendel, eds., *The Essential Works of Marxism* (New York: Bantam Books, 1961).

McBain, Howard Lee, *The Law and the Practice of Municipal Home Rule* (New York: Columbia University Press, 1916).

Markusen, Ann, "The Economics of Social Class and Metropolitan Local Government" (Ph.D. Thesis, Michigan State University, 1974).

Miliband, Ralph, *The State in Capitalist Society* (New York: Basic Books, 1969).

Neenan, William, "Suburban–Central City Exploitation Thesis: One City's Tale," *National Tax Journal,* June 1970.

Newton, Kenneth, "American Urban Politics: Social Class, Political Structure and Public Goods," *Urban Affairs Quarterly,* Dec. 1975.

Oates, Wallace, "The Effects of Property Taxes and Local Public Spending on Property Values: An Empirical Study of Tax Capitalization and the Tiebout Hypothesis," *Journal of Political Economy,* Nov.–Dec. 1969.

O'Connor, James R., *The Fiscal Crisis of the State* (New York: St. Martin's Press, 1973).

Samuelson, Paul A., "The Pure Theory of Public Expenditures," *Review of Economics and Statistics,* Nov. 1954.

Sawers, Larry, "Urban Form and the Mode of Production," *Review of Radical Political Economy,* Spring 1975.

Silver, Allan, "The Demand for Order in Civil Society: A Review of Some

Themes in the History of Urban Crime, Police, and Riot," in David Bordua, ed., *The Police: Six Sociological Essays* (New York: John Wiley and Sons,, 1967).

Survey Research Center, *Location Decisions and Industrial Mobility in Michigan* (Ann Arbor: University of Michigan Press, 1961).

Tiebout, Charles, "A Pure Theory of Local Expenditures," *Journal of Political Economy*, Oct. 1956.

Warner, Sam Bass, *Streetcar Suburbs: The Process of Growth in Boston, 1880–1900* (New York: Atheneum, 1973).

Warren, Robert, "A Municipal Services Market Model of Metropolitan Organization," *Journal of the American Institute of Planners*, Aug. 1964.

Wickman, W. Hardy, *The Political Theory of Local Government* (Columbia: University of South Carolina Press, 1970).

Wood, Robert, *Suburbia: Its People and Their Politics* (Boston: Houghton Mifflin, 1958).

Wright, Eric Olin, "To Control or to Smash Bureaucracy: Weber and Lenin on Politics, the State and Bureaucracy," *Berkeley Journal of Sociology*, 1974–75.

two

CONSTRUCTION
AND DESTRUCTION—
URBAN
REDEVELOPMENT

The first two papers in this part deal with the political economy of urban redevelopment. John Mollenkopf argues that a coalition of central-city politicians, bureaucrats, corporation executives, central-business-district real estate and commercial interests, and construction-union leaders began pushing in the 1950s for downtown redevelopment. This was seen as a remedy for the crisis of the central cities, triggered by the twin processes of suburbanization and central city-decline analyzed in Part I. Policies of this *pro-growth coalition* imposed tremendous costs on central-city residents by disrupting stable communities, exacerbating racial tensions, imposing heavy tax burdens, and increasing congestion and pollution. Protests by those adversely affected by the redevelopment policies during the 1960s have stalled programs in some cities and slowed and altered those in other cities. Indeed, it is hardly too much to say that the way urban problems were "solved" in the 1960s created the basis of the accelerated deterioration of these same older cities in the 1970s. Two types of costs are involved in the failure of U.S. urban policies. First is the social cost engendered in urban blight and abandonment, coupled with congestion and pollution. Billions of dollars of social infrastructure are written off on the one hand and billions more invested to create a pattern of development that serves a small part of the city's population and imposes a redistributional cost on taxpayers generally, and particularly on those forced to relocate. There have been benefits of renewal policies but they have accrued to the members of the pro-growth coalition.

Rob Kessler and Chester Hartman have described in painstaking detail how this process has unfolded in one city, San Francisco. Their paper shows how the pro-growth coalition developed plans for the commercial redevelopment of a central-city neighborhood without input from residents of the area, how they used distortion if not outright illegal means to veil the true costs of the redevelopment, and have employed administrative sleight-of-hand to prevent voters from having the chance to veto the project. Not only were the costs of the project underestimated and revenues exaggerated, but the cost fell importantly on working-class residents of the renewal area and the benefits largely went to members of the pro-growth coalition.

115

Urban redevelopment as it is now practiced in the United States is largely a program to destroy housing available to low-income people. Michael Stone examines federal government policies which have encouraged the construction of housing and discusses the extent to which they have helped meet the need for decent housing in a suitable environment. He argues that there is an insoluble contradiction in capitalism between the limits to consumption, including housing consumption, of the broad masses of the workers and the structure of the housing market, which requires that housing be very expensive. Government policies which have tried to resolve this contradiction have failed, though in the meantime they have bestowed considerable largess on capitalists involved in the housing industry.

The burden of the argument found in all of the papers in this part is that the existence of poor housing, the spread of urban blight and the inability, perhaps even more strongly the unwillingness, of public policy-makers to reverse these effects of market operation are integral to the way the political economy operates. Policies are not so much mistaken as caught in an insoluble contradiction. By placing prime reliance on the private sector, federal legislation has enriched the pro-growth coalition. The lack of a coherent urban policy to serve the mass of city residents results from the impossibility of consensus in this realm, where redistribution toward one class comes at the expense of the other.

The Postwar Politics
of
Urban Development

JOHN H. MOLLENKOPF

During the 1960s, a dual political crisis unfolded in America's big cities. Across the country, neighborhood groups campaigned to halt urban renewal, provide decent housing for themselves, and reclaim public institutions that influence urban life. These groups squatted in vacant housing, stormed public hearings, mobilized thousands for marches and mass meetings, sat in front of bulldozers, and generally made life miserable for public officials. Starting in 1964, a series of ghetto rebellions swept from Cleveland, Watts, Newark, Detroit, and Washington to dozens of other cities, generalizing this community-based political crisis. These neighborhood revolts became an important part of a widespread though ill-defined political culture of insurgency.

Though such waves of protest were not enough by themselves to undermine City Hall, internal political divisions also weakened the mayoral coalitions which had structured urban politics since the mid-1950s. Increasingly organized and independent civil servants pressed for higher pay and better working conditions. Neighborhood property-owners insisted on improved services for less taxes, igniting what some saw as a "taxpayer's revolt." Reformist critics from professions like law

* Copyright © October 1, 1975 by John H. Mollenkopf.

and planning meanwhile took well-aimed potshots at the customary
ways of doing city business, and mayors found their habitual solutions
to such conflicts—increased federal funding, increased taxes, reduced
services, and stimulated economic growth—to no avail, for these were
the very practices being bitterly attacked. Together with external attacks, these internal difficulties fractured many pro-growth political
coalitions, and caused some to crumble. In 1969 alone, such prominent
mayors as Lee (New Haven), Cavanagh (Detroit), Naftalin (Minneapolis), and Allen (Atlanta) left office. By the time the 1960s had
ended, it was clear that growing instability was a fact of city politics.

Why did these two developments—external attack and internal division—take place? What is their significance? Were they merely summer lightning? The social scientists who studied urban violence and
protest generated volumes of "instant research" but few convincing answers to these questions. In the main, prevailing arguments involved
notions about the influence of the civil-rights movement, OEO's "stir-
ring up trouble," and the like. Riot analysts resorted to "alienation,"
"frustrated expectations," "pervasive racism," and similar unsatisfying
attitudinal arguments about why people rioted. And the destabilization
of city political coalitions was, by and large, attributed to white ethnic
reaction to black neighborhoods' transgressions of tacit boundary lines.[1]
Such explanations obviously beg the question: Why did people have
such attitudes, anyway?

An adequate analysis must be based on a larger causal context.
This paper argues that the dual political breakdown of the 1960s was
part of a larger dialectic between the state's attempt to solve a central-
city land-value and revenue crisis, and its striving to manage the unanticipated, but nevertheless sharp, political consequences of the "solution" chosen. In short, the crisis grew out of a class-based political
struggle over the nature of urban development. It is argued here that
politics and the activities of local government in particular played a
central role in determining the outcome of this struggle, and have been
in turn both shaped and destabilized by it.

A FRAMEWORK FOR UNDERSTANDING
URBAN POLITICS

First and foremost, cities must be analyzed as the main physical, and
more importantly social and political, setting in which production, dis-

tribution, and the accumulation of wealth take place. Cities mobilize the economy's basic ingredients. They are the places in which basic infrastructural investments (public and private) are located, and in which an organized labor force is concentrated. Above all, cities are a social and political device for creating the cohesive, ordered environment necessary for combining labor and capital effectively. Many urban institutions were created specifically for this "productive" or "economic" purpose, and the rest are colored by it to varying degrees. Even nineteenth-century religious movements, for example, played an important part in disciplining workers and conveying moral authority on the factory hierarchy.

The relationship between the economy and urban institutions should not, however, be construed as one of simple determinism. Indeed, the opposite is more nearly true: the economy itself could not function without an adequate and cohesive set of social and political institutions to concentrate and mobilize human and physical capital. Power is not merely a fixed quantity to be distributed and redistributed, but a variable whose presence or absence can determine the rate and nature of economic development; it has been cities in which modern forms of power have grown up. Resistance of nineteenth-century landed elites in Europe, for example, often retarded capitalist development, and where, as in England, a strong, capitalist-oriented political coalition enjoyed power, development occurred most rapidly. In the United States, urban political coalitions and local governments played a particularly strong role in influencing growth and development. Federalist decentralization, the widely spread but surprisingly strong nature of local economic elites, and the peculiar weakness of the U.S. national government have made local politics historically of crucial importance to overall economic development. If cities, then, are the main vehicle by which the economy grows, politics provide the fuel.

But cities are more than networks of streets, sidewalks, factories, and office buildings designed to return maximum profits. The people who live in them inevitably express their human needs and pleasures in culturally, socially, and geographically distinct ways. By using their environments for human as well as economic ends, they develop a sense of communal enjoyment of "their" city which, however fragmented, usually holds great sway. Such communal feelings frequently collide with the demands of production. The nineteenth-century neighborhood saloon, for example, with its time-honored rowdiness, clashed with the sober work habits desired in the factory, and was a frequent target of reform efforts. Nowhere was this conflict more evident than in city politics. In return for the right to organize economic life with a free hand, capitalist entrepreneurs gave up the juridical right, which the old aristocracies enjoyed, to organize political life. Instead, they had to organize it in indirect and hidden ways. Politics, and the very structure of urban government, were thus not merely an easily manipulable tool for capitalist elites, but also an arena of competition open to other communal influences as well. The political system (in other words, the state in its various manifestations) thus played a dual role: it made possible and promoted both production and accumulation, but at the same time it responded to noneconomic, communal demand in order to establish legitimacy and political cohesion.

These basic ways of looking at the economy, the city, and urban politics, allow us to isolate three main historical phases in U.S. urban development. In the nineteenth century, urban politics was strongly influenced by the initial establishment of capitalism, with its factory form of organization and newly created urban industrial working class. The industrial revolution not only drastically changed the organization of work, it also magnified the urban character of the society itself. Most of the institutions that seem so familiar and important in urban life today were created during this period: street systems, mass transportation, schools, police forces, and the like. Various historical studies have shown the important, if usually conflicting and contradictory, contribution these institutions made to rapid economic development. Nineteenth-century machine politics in particular enhanced rapid growth through public-works investments and the control of ebullient and sometimes explosive aspects of urban life. The machines exerted this control through saloons, fraternal organizations, the straw-boss work system, and even criminal activities, among others.[2] Yet machine politics never operated smoothly nor with complete effect. Protest movements and lower-class radicalism made growth more costly and less simple. Indeed, some scholars have viewed the more "responsible" political reform movements of the late nineteenth and early twentieth centuries as attempts by business interests to reduce these costs and gain more complete control over the governmental and political environment of production.[3]

The second phase, beginning with the Progressive Era and running to World War II, witnessed the "modernization" or "maturation" of the institutional structure of both economy and government. The rise of organizationally complex and diverse corporations and government agencies, the development of professional strata in each, and the successful elite struggle to take the politics out of government through nonpartisanship, professional administration, decentralization, etc., profoundly changed the nature of urban politics. Parallel to the fragmented and depoliticized nature of government was an increasing fragmentation within the class structure. Each, in its own way, was a method by which nineteenth-century constraints on further capitalist growth could be overcome. On the political side, opposition movements were rendered more difficult and state activities crucial to the economy more efficient and more insulated from political demands. On the social and economic side, growing segmentation of the working class enhanced capitalist control of the production process and made united organization among workers a much more difficult affair.

The period after 1945 marks the full fruition of these trends, but also the emergence of serious difficulties implied in them. As with earlier periods, the "solutions" of one era slowly but surely became the problems of the next. The full development of late, or "postindustrial," capitalism not only changed the nature of urban life and politics, it also undermined the political coalitions that had provided the basis for its very growth. In particular, the economy of the largest central cities has shifted from a factory basis of organization to one of office-based command and control functions (Cohen). Productive activities have been decentralized not only to suburbs and less-developed parts of the United States, but often outside the country itself. "Suburbanization," a cover term for a host of related trends, reshaped the urban political arena, stimulated new political conflicts, and posed unexpected difficulties for coordinated metropolitan development (Harvey, 1973, pp. 261–74).

In particular, the emergence of the postindustrial city has measurably complicated the structure of economic interests and rendered the crucial task of constructing urban political alliances that much more difficult. Where the nineteenth-century city had two basic interests, those of capital and of labor, in the contemporary city each of these has become much more complex. Following O'Connor's distinction between monopoly, competitive, and state sectors within the economy, it can be seen (especially if one examines the conflict between labor and management in each) that different sectors have distinct interest with respect to government policy and the nature of urban growth (O'Connor). In the nineteenth century, capital wanted an efficient organization of urban space, rapid emplacement of necessary public investments and services, and a ruly workforce. It largely secured these through corrupting the political system and the trade unions, though it paid the price of inefficiencies, waste, and city administrations commanded by occasionally unresponsive ethnic working-class leaders. In the postindustrial city, the major headquarters firms wants certain things for their city, and for cities in general, which will appear to competitive-sector capital as excessively expensive and sometimes downright confiscatory (urban renewal, it should be remembered, destroyed many small businesses at the same time that it displaced many thousands of families). The rapid suburbanization that large corporations favored as a means for transforming cities into more efficient vehicles for consumption and production was not always viewed with equanimity by central-city small businessmen. From the labor point of view, monopoly-sector workers who made up the social basis for suburbanization did not favor large welfare and social-service expenditures for the central city, which tended to put them in opposition to the growing class of competitive-sector workers in the central city. The latter—typically service workers who are members of a third-world minority group, and much less likely to be unionized—obviously rely heavily on public goods and services. In this context, workers in the large and growing state bureaucracy also take on their own distinct interests.

Many of these interests, it is clear, can be united around big capital's program of expansion of the suburban periphery and reorganization and more intense development of the urban core. Major corporate interests, financial institutions, the larger commercial and real estate firms, the construction trades, certain government agencies, and, where social-service spending expands, even competitive-sector labor can be brought behind these goals. But it is equally clear that major lines of conflict run through this potential alliance, and that several alternative types of alliance are quite possible. It is this paper's thesis that the nature of postindustrial urban development accounts not only for the nature of mobilization *against* big-city governments, but also for the inherent instability *within* them.

To summarize the argument that follows, this paper will try to show that local government's role in stimulating central-city development contradicted its role as the guarantor of social peace and political cohesion. To put the matter sequentially:

1. National changes in the accumulation process, changes in the spatial structure of economic activities, and federal policies aimed at converting the city from a device for production to one of consumption precipitated a crisis in central-city real estate values shortly after World War II. This was, of course, a period of suburban boom. This crisis involved what was then called "the cancerous effect of the slums"[4] on the central business district, relatively and even absolutely declining property values, and hence a central-city fiscal crisis.

2. This development set the stage for an alliance of central-city politicians, a new breed of bureaucrats, large corporations, central-business-district real estate and merchant interests, and the construction trades. This pro-growth coalition pushed nationally for a strong urban-renewal and highway program, and locally for downtown redevelopment. Strong, innovative mayors like Richard Daley, Richard Lee, Keven White, and Joseph Alioto, and equally strong, not to say dictatorial, renewal administrators like Robert Moses, Edward Logue, and M. Justin Herman forged sufficiently strong local coalitions to change the skylines of every major city.

3. Unfortunately for these political leaders, success undermined their own position. By doing its part to reinforce the command and control functions of the central city over the metropolitan area, the surrounding region, and even overseas territories, the pro-growth coalition imposed tremendous costs on central-city residents. Growth generally and state intervention specifically displaced stable communities, exacerbated racial tensions, imposed heavy taxes on those least able to pay, and proliferated burdens like commuting time, congestion, and pollution. It is thus to the local consequences of growth that the dual crisis of the 1960s can be traced.

4. At present, the situation remains undecided. In some cities the pro-growth coalition has obscured conflict through the generous application of jobs, program money, and other desirable incentives. Others have skillfully exploited social divisions. But where conflicts have forced mayors to choose between support from traditional bureaucracies and support from minority neighborhoods, or between growth beneficiaries and growth sufferers (taxpayers, displacees, transitional neighborhoods), alternative but usually transitory coalitions have sometimes emerged. The diversity of those opposed to growth has ham-

pered the forging of an alternative program, particularly one which includes rank-and-file workers in city bureaucracies. While the current crisis has diverted attention towards survival, and has exacerbated social cleavages, it has also cut deeply into central-city neighborhoods, and may yet provide the basis for an alternative.

THE CENTRAL CITY FROM 1940 TO 1956: CRISIS AND RESPONSE

The Crisis

Nothing so neatly illustrates the rise and subsequent destablization of growth-oriented urban politics as the changing meaning of the term "urban crisis." In 1950, the term included the central city's loss of population to the suburbs, its growing minority population, expanding black slums, and threatened property values. It was generally conceived as a crisis. By 1970, the term covered not only social problems like racism, poverty, crime, and poor housing, but seeming political chaos and growing doubts about whether cities could overcome "negative externalities" like traffic congestion, pollution, and real estate disinvestment. It was, in short, a crisis not of revenues but of political *demands*. Having once reflected mainly the economic travails of the central business district, the term came to cover the whole society's social and political conflicts.

Central-city property values—and tax rolls—generally reached a peak about 1930, only to be knocked down during the Depression. Total local revenues declined considerably between 1930 and 1934, but picked up with greater economic activity and higher tax rates during World War II. Nevertheless, central-city mayors, the bond-holding institutions which had narrowly averted total defaults during the Depression by forcing city expenditure cutbacks, and downtown business interests were sorely worried about the postwar future of the central city.[5] They had ample reason.

During the 1940s and 1950s, central cities experienced a growing expenditure-revenue gap. A 1952 study of New York City's prospects concluded that, given then current trends in revenues and expenditures, a $165 million gap would develop by 1953, burgeoning to $300 million by 1955.[6] This was a period, one must remember, before the advent of urban renewal and other substantial state and federal transfers of funds to central cities. Mayors of other big cities faced similar problems. In Boston, for example, to finance moderately rising expenditures for existing services and compensate for a declining tax base, the city administration boosted assessment rates on commercial and industrial property to "the unheard-of rates of 100 percent of true value and the tax rate reached $86 per $1000," a point at which the business community could complain with some justice that an increase much "beyond this level will spell disaster" (Wood, p. 72).

The Federal Response

According to contemporary analyses, the causes of this crisis in finances and central-city property values were twofold: On the one hand, the metropolitan dispersion of economic activity meant that central-city revenues were declining relative to suburban fiscal capacity. On the other, growing poor black and other minority neighborhoods required expenditures above their revenue contributions and "threatened" neighboring property values.[7] Contributing to the problem were increases in tax-exempt land (e.g., for new highways), limited tax mechanisms, and difficulties in raising public-sector productivity. The appropriate policy seemed clear: eliminate "blighting" slums, stimulate investment in the central business district, and provide the transportation infrastructure necessary to keep the CBD "viable." And the only funding source for this policy, it seemed equally clear, was the federal government.

The result of this consensus was pressure for federally assisted efforts at slum clearance and urban renewal, culminating first in passage of the 1949 Housing Act and then in 1954 amendments which increased its central-city impact. Litigation, the Korean War, and defects in the legislation, together with long planning lead times, prevented urban renewal from having a substantial impact before about 1960, but when it arrived, it did so with great clamor on all sides. As Table 1 suggests, the investment in urban-renewal areas burgeoned rapidly after 1960. As a matter of comparison, total residential mortgages outstanding in 1970 were $334 billion, and in 1970 $26.5 billion was raised on *all* commercial property mortgages and corporate and foreign bonds (Harvey, 1976, Tables 6 and 7). Urban renewal, at a $4 billion annual rate, thus involved an important part of all nonresidential urban investment.

Table 1. Yearly Preliminary Loans for Urban Renewal
(*in millions of dollars*)

1970	$3,833
1968	2,812
1966	1,806
1964	1,474
1962	1,118
1960	706
1958	239
1956	94
1954	44

Source: The Bond Buyer, "Statistics on State and Local Government Finance," May, 1971, p. 17. Total of outstanding notes, 1954–1970, was $22.547 billion.

In his testimony before the House Banking and Currency Committee on the 1949 Act, Housing and Home Finance Agency Director Raymond Moley clearly stated the reason urban renewal should be enacted:

> The mayors and other city officials daily face the problem of heavy municipal expenditures for essential municipal services in slum areas which far exceed the taxes derived from those areas. As new building is forced to the periphery of cities and the tax base in the central city areas decreases, they face the problem of constantly increasing municipal outlays for capital improvements and additions required to serve the newly developed areas. They do not have access to the financial resources required to absorb the full costs of the necessary write down in anything approaching the volume that is required for effective slum clearance operation.[8]

Urban renewal was to throw a wall around a creeping "blight," that is, the growing social problem of the minority urban poor, in order to preserve and enhance central city land values and contain poor neighborhoods' influence. It was no wonder that the program was executed with frequent racist overtones.

A somewhat different coalition forged the second principal link in the national urban policy chain. Late in September, 1954, President Eisenhower appointed a five-person Advisory Committee on a National Highway Program. The Committee included Lucius Clay, a former army general, then chairman of Continental Can's board of directors (who had also been associated with Goldman, Sachs, and with Marine

Midland Trust); David Beck, then Teamsters president; S. Sloan Coalt, Bankers Trust Company president and Morgan Bank director; William Roberts, president of Allis-Chalmers, road-equipment manufacturer; and Stephen D. Bechtel, president of Bechtel Engineering, father of the Bay Area Rapid Transit District, and builder of numerous public-works projects. Their report, "A Ten-Year National Highway Program," led to the passage of the $56 billion Interstate and National Defense Highway Act in 1956, and set in place the second basic instrument for transforming urban space.

THE DEEPER ROOTS OF THE POSTWAR URBAN CRISIS

The underlying causes of the central-city land-value fiscal crisis go far beyond the negative externalities and public-expenditure requirements of urban slums. At least four factors played a part: (1) the national shift from an industrial economy to one based on the service sector and office activities; (2) strong metropolitan dispersion trends (driven by political and labor-capital struggles as well as economic and technological considerations); (3) an associated internal migration; and (4) the contradictory roles of local government and its general fragmentation and weakness.

National Economic Trends and the Central City

In the immediate postwar years, a major economic tide had shifted against the central cities. By the end of the 1950s, definitive academic studies had clearly established the parameters of this change. As Raymond Vernon reported in 1959, "Office activities . . . will continue to expand. This activity aside, one sees only a growing obsolescence in the rest of the central city beyond its central business district" (pp. 22–23). Vernon was supported by John Kain, and most other leading urban economists, in reaching this conclusion.

These analysts give principally technological and market-oriented reasons for central-city decline: improved transportation, the growing suburban retail market, the cheapness of suburban land, new production technologies requiring linear organization of work, and the piling up of "agglomeration diseconomies" like inner-city congestion. And no doubt these factors worked towards making central cities a less important locus of manufacturing and retailing.

The positive side of this analysis stressed the continuing role of the central business district, if not the central city, as a home for corporate headquarters and related service activities. The hearts of big cities provide an "unduplicatable resource for firms requiring quick and efficient communication in persons as well as minimization of transportation of their supplies and output."[9] As such, they were still a natural location for markets of information, capital, and expertise, and for corporate decision-making.

Table 2 suggests that central-city employment markets conformed quite closely in the 1958–1963 period to Vernon's and Kain's predictions of absolute losses, while the more recent period does not. Benjamin Cohen and James have both suggested that the more recent central city gains were due to the overheated war economy of the mid-1960s. Indeed, by the mid-1970s, recession and widespread political opposition had slowed the office-building boom. Nevertheless, it must be admitted that service, government, real estate, finance, and similar office functions showed unpredicted strength during the 1960s and remain strong in many cities today (B. Cohen; James; Harrison, Chap. 2). These gains and the previously noted improvement in central-city tax bases, both of which are quite real, must be traced to factors over and above strictly economic conditions: namely, the pro-growth coalition.

Boston and San Francisco, for example, are older central cities, long developed. Cities of this type were hit hardest by the national shift from production to services, and severely suffered from the loss of construction, manufacturing, and transportation during the 1950s. But Boston and San Francisco are also major capital markets, and each continued to provide a home for numerous large corporations, banks, and insurance companies. The national economy's shift thus made possible strong employment gains in clerical work, government, and professional occupations, as well as in finance and real estate. This was especially true in the 1960s. Again these trends were not accidental: such gains were quite deliberately focused, as we shall see, in the central cities through the plans of the pro-growth coalitions.

Table 2. Job Location Trends, 1958–1967 (11 Largest SMSAs)

	(net gain or loss of jobs, in thousands)			(percentage gain or loss)			(total jobs, in thousands)	
	Central City	Suburbs	Metro	Central City	Suburbs	Metro	Central City	Suburbs
	1958–1963			*1958–1963*			*1958 Base*	
Manufacturing	−125	130	5	−7.9%	12.2%	0.3%	1,952	1,178
Trade (R & W)	−30	216	186	−1.8%	22.6%	16.6%	1,704	710
Finance and RE	56	42	98	8.1%	32.6%	12.9%	686	129
Services	133	215	348	10.8%	37.7%	19.3%	1,230	570
Government	76	138	214	6.4%	29.7%	12.9%	1,191	466
Total*	84	806	890	1.1%	22.5%	11.3%	7,826	3,578
	1963–1967			*1963–1967*			*1967 Endpoint*	
Manufacturing	−23	129	106	−1.3%	9.9%	3.3%	1,804	1,473
Trade (R & W)	51	236	287	3.1%	33.2%	11.0%	1,725	1,162
Finance and RE	38	28	66	5.1%	12.2%	7.2%	780	199
Services	175	201	376	12.8%	25.6%	17.4%	1,538	986
Government	175	178	353	13.8%	29.5%	18.9%	1,442	782
Total*	430	840	1270	5.5%	19.2%	10.3%	8,340	5,224

* Includes miscellaneous uncategorized jobs.

Source: Alexander Ganz, *Our Large Cities: New Light on Their Recent Transformation* (Cambridge: MIT Lab for Environmental Studies, 1972), Table II-8 and Appendix Table II-1.

Metropolitan Dispersion

The Vernon-Kain view, often repeated by Chambers of Commerce, holds, as has been pointed out, that purely technological and transportation forces dictated suburban development. Urban historians, making the same argument, have traced the forces of suburbanization to streetcar-line extensions, speculative home building, and the decline of annexations in the late nineteenth century.

These forces are undoubtedly real, but the Vernon-Kain analysis has serious shortcomings because it fails to show why and how technological changes, such as improved transportation, were introduced. This innovation process, as Marx originally argued, grows out of struggles over production and profit. It is driven not only by the firm's search for comparative advantage over its competitors, but by its owners' search for comparative advantage over its workers and their milieu (Marglin; Stone). In the urban context, the rise of suburban housing developments, relocation of manufacturing establishments outside the tense and dangerous central city, and the development of politically autonomous suburban communities can all be traced back to the capitalist struggle to control the productive process (Gordon; Weiss and Gellen). This fact has evidently characterized metropolitan dispersion since the mid–nineteenth century, but it seems to have accelerated in the period after World War II. By failing to see this relationship, the standard analysis also fails to see that technologies are inherently political.

While the evidence is at best fragmentary and the issue sorely needs further research, it seems that suburban housing and suburban production facilities answered a dual problem sharply posed during World War II. On the one hand, without something to absorb the productive capacity developed during the war, many business commentators and policy-makers evidently feared a return to the Depression. On the other, the black migration to such war-industry cities as Detroit had created very serious labor problems. Some aspects are well known—overcrowded housing, pent-up housing demand, racial antagonisms—but others were equally sharp. The vulnerable location of large manufacturing establishments in the midst of working-class neighborhoods, themselves beset by all manner of problems, evidently spurred corporations to set up new small plants in safer suburban locations. By doing so, corporations could solve both problems at once: stimulate demand (through the suburban military-industrial and auto-oil-highway complexes), and restore social control to the production environment.

That the latter was a serious factor in postwar suburban expansion is suggested by a 1948 report of a meeting published by San Francisco's Commonwealth Club, a businessman's association. Chaired by a community developer and ex-president of the National Association of Home Builders, this session discussed the reasons for urban decentralization. While technological explanations were given, labor considerations were important, as the vice president of the American Trust Company stated:

> Labor developments in the last decade may well be the chief contributing factor in speeding regional dispersion of industry, and have an important part in the nationwide tendency toward industrial decentralization. In this period good employee relations have become a number one goal. Labor costs have expanded markedly. Conditions under which employees live, as well as work, vitally influence management-labor relations. Generally, large aggregations of labor in one big [central city] plant are more subject to outside disrupting influences, and have less happy relations with management, than in smaller [suburban] plants.[10]

The report goes on to quote the California State Reconstruction and Re-employment Commission's 1946 report, *New Factories for California Communities:* "Workers could own their own homes and enjoy contentment, leisure, lower living costs, and better health. . . . The managers of many large and small plants which have located in Santa Clara County testify that their employees are more loyal, more cooperative, and more productive workers than those they have had in the big cities."

The Commonwealth Club session cited Santa Clara manufacturers with similar urban and suburban plants, who claimed that the suburban locations had lower turnover rates, less absenteeism, fewer disputes, and more productivity. Another manufacturer said even five hundred employees was too many to have in one place. "We are going to get away from tenements, traffic jams, high taxes, crowded streetcars, and transient labor, with all the economic waste and irritation those things involve." The session concluded with a vote of 101 to 2 that dispersal improved workers' health and 51 to 37 that dispersal, in general, increased profits.

Boston metropolitan development responded to similar pressures after the war. Although it does not seem to have been planned with public sponsorship in quite the same way as the San Francisco Peninsula's electronics and aircraft industries, the Cabot, Cabot and Forbes development firm quite effectively stimulated development of the electronics industry along Boston's peripheral Route 128. The nature of interlocking directorates, financing, and the presence of old Brahmin families in some of these firms suggests this development was quite clearly a goal of Boston's corporate establishment (*Fortune*). In other words, dispersion resulted not just from the imperatives of competition, but also from a reasonably clear understanding of the social-control aspects of plant location.

Internal Migration

Americans have always been an extremely mobile people geographically, if not economically. A national sample in 1968 showed that about half the population had made a substantial move, including one-fifth who had moved from the countryside to the large metropolitan areas. Of the 40 million people living in the larger cities, fully half were born in small towns or rural areas. For nonwhites, this relationship was even more striking (U.S. Census Bureau, p. 87).

The changing nature of the national economy since 1940 was accompanied by an equally significant internal migration. It was triggered partly by the very development of wartime productive capacity in large cities, and partly by the capitalization of agriculture and other aspects of uneven development in the rural South, Puerto Rico, and Mexico. Black migration to the urban North began during World War I, with the forced abatement of European migration. By 1968, blacks were more urbanized than whites and formed an increasingly large component, along with other minority populations, of the central-city citizenry.

During the 1940s, 1.6 million blacks migrated cityward, more than the total of the previous thirty years, in response to wartime labor demands. Then in the 1950s, mechanized agriculture forced even more blacks towards the North. Between 1949 and 1952 alone, the demand for unskilled agricultural labor in the Mississippi Delta counties dropped by 72 percent.

The 1940s migration first inserted blacks into the Northern urban economy, and then, in the postwar period, steadily deprived them of jobs and housing as veterans returned. The 1950s were thus a time when Northern urban blacks struggled to establish a sense of community, to elaborate communal institutions, and to carve out an economic niche. This effort, as we have seen, was viewed by whites as a menacing, "blighting" development. Other minority ethnic groups have followed similar patterns.

Recent arrivals joined already established black neighborhoods in each of these cities, and by the 1960s their number was expanding more by natural increase than by migration. By the time the influence of pro-growth policies was most devastatingly felt, these black communities had passed a generation at least from its conservative Southern roots, and had begun to establish a more independent, community-based leadership.

The Central-City Political Vacuum and Contradictory Demands on City Government

A final factor also underlay the central-city land-value and fiscal crisis: the absence of strong leadership with a clear program. As Raymond Wolfinger has rightly pointed out, the only way we really know that machine politics is really dead is because we have killed it so often (Wolfinger, 1972; 1974, Chap. 4). The years immediately after World War II provided one such demise, and perhaps one of the more spectacular ones. In 1949, Mayor James Michael Curley of Boston failed to win reelection, and the Hague Machine in Jersey City also suffered a severe electoral setback. In Chicago, the regular party organization entered a period of relative decline, from which Richard Daley later resurrected it with years of careful work. Elsewhere, though machine politics remained alive and well (in cities like Philadelphia, Pittsburgh, New Haven, Providence, and St. Louis), it was bereft of any winning program. Nor did potential allies find regular machine mayors attractive as a way to address the central-city property-value and fiscal crisis. In short, local government did not seem likely to live up to the demands being placed on it. Instead, big cities seemed dominated by haphazardly corrupt, functionally isolated bureaucracies with no particular goal except muddling through the deepening crisis. The stage was thus fully set for a new turn in city politics.

THE RISE OF THE PRO-GROWTH COALITIONS, 1955-1970

At different rates and in numerous local variants, big-city politicians and businessmen forged a new alliance around central-city development in the years between 1955 and 1970. In an important but not widely discussed 1964 article, Robert Salisbury argued that a "new convergence of power" was developing in city politics, based on "an executive-centered coalition" of businessmen, progressive mayors, and planning-oriented technocrats (Salisbury).

Sometimes this coalition was led by a bureaucratically based machine mayor, albeit one with reform overtones like Chicago's Daley or Pittsburgh's Lawrence. Sometimes it stood apart, in uneasy coexistence with machine organizations, as in Newark. And sometimes it defeated a machine organization and stood in an essentially antagonistic relationship to mainline city bureaucracies, at least at the outset, as in Boston under Collins. Certain dimensions, however, seem present in almost every situation.

One element proved to be strong leadership from renewal executives, who learned how to use the urban-renewal program like a political Panzer Division, massing forces in secret and then launching attacks on the chosen territory. Robert Moses, as Robert Caro's widely heralded biography shows, invented the basic techniques in this process—the independent authority, secret planning, well-timed deadline manipulation, and good Washington contacts (Caro). Edward Logue, first renewal director under Lee in New Haven, then under Collins in Boston, and finally director of New York's Urban Development Corporation, refined most of these techniques and endowed them with political sophistication. In the process he trained a bevy of administrators who went on to direct renewal in such other cities such as Washington, D.C., Miami, New York, and Cleveland, or to work for such corporations as James Scheuer (a developer), R. H. Macy, and the United Nations Development Corporation. At the same time, large new bureaucracies commanding money, technical expertise, and large manpower pools were developed to back up these leaders.

A second element involves more or less direct corporate sponsorship of the renewal process. As Roger Friedland has shown, nearly every major city developed, during the fifties, a corporate-based planning body interested in urban development. More often than not, these groups included high executives in the city's largest corporations; many were able to raise sufficient funds to hire staff members and conduct studies of "proper" urban-development patterns (Friedland; Edel). Their activities essentially fit the mold outlined in studies of corporate liberalism by Kolko, Weinstein, and Domhoff; that is, these business planning groups first developed their ideas *in camera*, subsequently developed a wider business consensus around them, and then ultimately promoted them by various political means, most especially including connections with growth-oriented mayors. Even where the corporations designated to finance or undertake redevelopment were outsiders to a given city, they seem to have had strong local backers or partners. (This is an area, however, where further research would be well repaid.)

Pittsburgh provides a classic example of how high-level corporate interests developed and implemented renewal plans. R. K. Mellon—heir to a fortune that included Koppers, Pittsburgh Consolidation Coal, the Mellon Bank, and Gulf Oil—established the Allegheny Conference on Community Development (ACCD) in 1943 because, it seemed, Pittsburgh was "on the brink of disaster" (Lubove). Mellon pulled together a group of young, innovative executives (many of whom he had appointed), hired an executive director, and proceeded to develop plans for what became the Golden Triangle, Pittsburgh's new central business district. The ACCD also developed plans to reduce steel- and coal-related pollution, in order to make Pittsburgh a less unattractive place to live.

In what one commentator called a "reverse welfare state," Mellon, the ACCD, and its corporate cohorts forged an alliance with David Lawrence and the city's Democratic machine, and proceeded to reshape Pittsburgh. It did so, of course, in part because it could create a wide consensus around this program. Because Lawrence and his organization could unite Republican corporate leaders, merchant and real estate interests, the construction trades, and the Democratic party around the divisible benefits so plentifully derived from renewal, the corporate program became what was for a long while an unstoppable public program (Hawkins, Auerbach).

The third element in this alliance proved to be a new generation of growth-oriented mayors. Daley was first elected mayor of Chicago in 1955, after the weak, interim Kennelly administration. Though firmly in control of the Cook County Democratic Party, Daley was stung by charges of bossism and set out to recruit backing from the Chicago business community. Also, as Mike Royko points out, "the fastest way to show people that something is happening is to build things" (p. 97). And build Daley did. By the mid-1960s, he had the solid backing of Chicago's business and real estate communities (Royko, pp. 96–106).

Similarly, New Haven's Mayor Lee was elected in 1953 on a campaign of modernizing the city. He too succeeded a relatively weak mayor, and managed to forge decent working relations with the city's Democratic organization. Lee, a former Yale and Chamber of Commerce public-relations officer, subsequently piled up larger election margins upon putting renewal into action (Wolfinger, 1974, pp. 157–79; Domhoff). Similarly in numerous other cities, innovative, growth-minded mayors, with strong professional and business backing, reached office in the period between 1955 and 1965. Among the best known are those mentioned earlier, such as Lindsay, Alioto, Collins, White, Cavanagh, and Uhlman.

Though no careful, comparative survey of these mayors has been done, it appears that they share certain characteristics. They generally have a liberal, technocratic outlook, come from professional careers, and have strong ties to the local business community. Yet at the same time they also tend to come from ethnic backgrounds, and to one degree or another can replicate the appeal upon which ethnic machine candidates usually bank. Almost without exception they are Democrats, and if they begin their careers without the support of old-line city bureaucracies and regular party organizations, they have usually been able, toward the maturity of their careers, to build ties with them. In general, they have been management-oriented, introducing new techniques like program budgeting, program planning, and computerized management systems. They have skillfully shaken the federal money tree for free resources with which to build their own parallel bureaucracies, often outside of city civil service, as a political base.[11]

There are other elements within this coalition too: city labor councils and construction-trades councils, regular party organizations, realty interests, good government groups, and others. Their participation, however, was both more variable and of less decisive importance. Of more significance was the fact that, in the late 1950s and early 1960s, at least, a growth platform could be touted as a panacea. Since the negative consequences had not yet fully emerged, attention could be focused on prospective rising tax bases, construction jobs and contracts, new housing, expanded central-city institutions, and the like. While neighborhoods were not aware of the consequences for them, local business could see clearly the wide range of benefits which would accrue. Renewal, therefore, for a time commanded a working if not general consensus.

Boston's first pro-growth mayor was John Hynes, who defeated James Michael Curley in 1951 with the aid of the New Boston Committee, a business-based reform group. Faced with a deepening fiscal crisis, Hynes attempted in 1957 to secure loans for city operations, and city bankers forced him to cut back city employees by 5 percent in eighteen months. In an attempt to reverse tax-base declines, Hynes initiated the now-infamous West End Project, one of the first massive slum-clearance projects in the country. It displaced over 2,600 families. He also put together the Prudential Center project—he compared it to the rolling away of the stone in front of Jesus' tomb—with support from George Oakes, a Brahmin vice president of R. M. Bradley, one of Boston's leading real estate firms; Cardinal Cushing; and Charles Coolidge, Brahmin partner in Ropes and Gray, perhaps Boston's most prestigious law firm.

In 1959, a second important election occurred. One candidate, machine Democrat John E. Powers, appeared to be in the lead and threatened, if elected, to declare city bankruptcy in order to get the city out of its fiscal jam. This naturally threw shivers down the spines of the city's Brahmin bondholders, and a business group, soon dubbed "the Vault," organized to put John Collins into the mayoralty. Originally conceived as receiver should the city default on its obligations, the group raised a substantial amount of money to back Irish Democrat Collins. He won.

Among the Vault's members were Gerald Blakely (prime mover behind Route 128 for Cabot, Cabot and Forbes), Coolidge, Ralph Lowell (retired chairman of the Boston Safety Deposit and Trust Co. and director of numerous Boston corporations), Carl Gilbert (chairman of Gillette and director of Raytheon), Lloyd Brace (chairman of the First National Bank of Boston), and various other Brahmin retailers, bankers, and executives of insurance and utility companies. With their backing, Collins improved city administration, used their money to hire consultants, and trimmed 1,200 more employees from the payroll. But most of all, he hired Edward Logue as redevelopment direc-

tor and initiated the "New Boston" renewal program that ultimately
subjected 10 percent of the city's land area to redevelopment.

San Francisco's Mayor Joseph Alioto was a comparatively late
arrival, first elected in 1967, but he had done duty as chairman of the
redevelopment agency in the late 1950s. Alioto put together a political
coalition based on big labor, big real estate, and big corporations, with
substantial minority neighborhood support for good measure. This
alliance gave strong backing to renewal during the mid-1960s, but it is
necessary to go back much further to establish the essentially nonpartisan sources of San Francisco's pro-growth coalition.

In 1945, leaders of the region's major corporations founded the
Bay Area Council; membership was open only to chief executives, including those of the Bank of America, American Trust Company,
Standard Oil of California, Pacific Gas and Electric. The BAC concentrated primarily on two issues: regional transportation, which had been
in a shambles during World War II, and industrial location, including
urban renewal. It issued a number of important studies, and developed
business consensus most importantly for the development of the Bay
Area Rapid Transit District, or BART. BART's impact on the Bay Area
is itself a complex story of government action at corporate behest.
BART's $1.6 billion dollar capital investment alone will influence Bay
Area development for decades, and strongly reinforces the San Francisco central business district.

Some of its San Francisco members founded a second committee
in 1956, the Blythe-Zellerbach Committee, to back urban renewal. It in
turn set up a broader group, S.F. Planning and Urban Renewal Association (SPUR), to build support largely among the city's professionals for urban renewal. In the late 1950s, B–Z gave money for renewal-
related studies to the City Planning Department, and in the early
1960s, SPUR was designated the official citizen-participation unit for
renewal in San Francisco.

As a result of these business initiatives and the resulting alliance
they forged with Mayor Alioto and his two predecessors, San Francisco,
like Boston and Cambridge, launched into massive urban-renewal efforts. During all three administrations, M. Justin Herman—an official
of the Housing and Home Finance Agency previously responsible for
overseeing renewal in the western region—provided strong leadership
for renewal. Indeed, community spokesmen often berated him as a dic-
tator, a charge Herman's usual response did little to disprove. With

backing from B–Z, SPUR, major city property owners, and most trade unions, and subsequently from Alioto and his organized strength, Herman undertook to redevelop such large areas adjacent to the central business district as the city's produce market, its Japanese neighborhood, its major black neighborhood, and a variety of other sites. Though community opposition in 1967 prevented entry into the Mission District, San Francisco's Latino neighborhood, these other projects seem destined for ultimate completion.[12]

These cases suggest certain basic themes. One is the rather clear corporate planning initiative, which develops the basic renewal scheme, often with corporate resources, and then sells it to the right bureaucratic and political figures. It may even recruit the executives to operate the renewal program. The second theme is the emergence of growth-oriented mayors, who seize the corporate-inspired development plan as a program on which they can create a strong organization. The developers and central business-district interests who benefited most directly from urban renewal proved to be the largest campaign contributors to the growth-oriented politicians in each city. But more was involved than a simple graft relationship—pro-growth mayors were able, as long as the costs remained confined, to build a much broader base of support for their regimes. Renewal provided manpower, benefits, resources, and latent political support, for any mayor audacious enough to reach for them.

The initiative for the pro-growth coalition thus came from two sides: corporate planning interests on the one, dynamic and aggressive politicians on the other. The extent to which these two jelled in a coalition determined how massively a city moved into renewal. The leading cities in per-capita resewal funds, particularly older eastern cities, were also cities where this coalition was particularly strong.

THE CHICKENS COME HOME TO ROOST: URBAN STRUGGLES AGAINST THE CONSEQUENCES OF GROWTH, 1965–1975

The Consequences of the Pro-Growth Coalition

As time passed, the seamy side of urban development started to peep out from under its glossy covering of rationalization. As a sign on the side of a vacant lot created by renewal in Cambridge said,

No War Declared,
No Storm Had Flared
No Sudden Bomb So Cruel,
Just a Need for Land,
A Greedy Hand
 And a Sign
 That Said,
"Urban Renewal."
(Goodman, p. 62)

Though Boston's West End residents failed to mobilize against that city's first massive clearance, they banded together afterward and became symbols, in the many neighborhoods to which they were displaced, of the destruction that renewal portended for working-class neighborhoods. It was a pattern that was to recur in most places where the pro-growth coalition was strong.

The pro-growth coalition engineered a massive allocation of private and social resources. Since 1949, the federal government has committed over $8.2 billion in direct outlays and more than $22.5 billion in bonded debt. By 1968, private investors had sunk an estimated additional $34.3 billion into 524 renewal projects across the country. In addition, some $70 billion has been expended on interstate highways, a substantial portion of which went to high-cost urban areas. As a result of these investments, more than a quarter of a million families have been displaced each year. They have received only $34.8 million in relocation payments, or less than 1 percent of the direct federal outlay! (U.S. Department of *HUD*) Even those who defend the renewal program on other grounds admit that it is upwardly redistributive.

Displacement of this kind carries many costs: out-of-pocket expenses, higher rents, psychic trauma, sundered friendships, more crowding in low-rent housing, and on and on. Downs identified twenty-two separate costs borne by those displaced, though he believes only ten should be wholly or partly compensated (others are important, he argues, but impossible to price) (pp. 192–229). For those costs he is willing to estimate, he believes renewal imposes (and he underestimates substantially the number displaced), "unfair . . . costs of at least $156 to $232 million per year upon approximately 237,000 displaced persons and at least another 237,000 non-displaced persons." In other words renewal costs displaced families, who average $4,000 a year in income, fully $1,000!

Equally important to consider are the reuses to which the cleared land was put. While no careful comparative studies of this question appear to have been done, the evidence of the cities under consideration suggest that reuses were by and large in direct service to the central business district and dominant government and educational institutions.

This shift of territorial organization triggered a whole chain of disruptive consequences for the central city, most of which fell upon poor neighborhoods or pitted newer minority areas against older ethnic communities. Thus not only did growth mobilize those directly and adversely affected, but it also stimulated racial antagonisms as displacees sought housing in other areas. As minority neighborhoods became more influential, this racial turf battle extended to city bureaucracies and other politically sensitive employment areas as well.

The Neighborhood Response

Though one would not learn it from the existing literature on community mobilization, in almost every instance the roots of mobilization may be found in struggles over growth. Most of the community turbulence of the 1960s was firmly directed against urban renewal, highway construction, the declining availability of decent inexpensive housing, expansion of dominant institutions, and city bureaucracies tightly dominated by ethnic groups being displaced in the urban population by minority newcomers.

The four cities demonstrate the importance of struggles over growth quite clearly. In Boston, for example, major community protests occurred against urban renewal, construction of the Inner Belt highway, the inadequacy of housing, hospital expansion, and rent control. In Cambridge, the issues were largely the same, coupled with opposition to Harvard's and MIT's expansion. In San Francisco, protests emerged against urban renewal in the Western Addition and the Mission, against poor housing, in favor of community control over housing development, and against racism in the education and law enforcement bureaucracies and in various firms' hiring practices.

Some of the same basic causes contributed to the wave of riots across urban America between 1964 and 1968. Virtually all of the riot areas were sites of major renewal efforts; quite frequently struggles over the nature of renewal lurked behind the riots as an implicit issue, as in the case of Newark's planned new medical school. On a city-by-city basis, the simple correlation between city expenditures in total dollars spent for renewal and how many riots that occurred between 1964–1968 for 100 large cities was 0.352. While this is an admittedly crude measurement, since other factors might lessen or strengthen this relationship, it is nonetheless suggestive.

One of the outstanding characteristics of these movements, which I have described elsewhere (forthcoming), is their alternative conception of how urban development might occur, at least within their neighborhoods. Although this conception never completely jelled, either within any given neighborhood or nationally, it always tended to have the same elements. Opposition to market allocation of private housing, opposition to planning for businesses rather than people, desire for community control of major government services, calls for rent control and government-subsidized housing, and experimentation with local self-development were repeated in all the cities examined. In the process of battling development, new neighborhood-oriented institutions like tenant unions, advocacy planning bodies, tenant self-management corporations, and social-service-advocacy organizations grew up. Though many of these institutions failed or were drawn into the mechanics of traditional city bureaucracies, many retained an important role in the neighborhood and modestly yet obviously pointed toward ways that a whole society might be organized along alternative lines.

The Breakdown of the Pro-Growth Coalitions

The second part of the dual political crisis of the mid-1960s, namely the internal breakdown of the pro-growth coalition's network of alliances, is a complex matter with three basic parts. First, neighborhood mobilization slowed down government decision-making and threatened to have electoral consequences. In response, mayors, realizing they needed a more sophisticated approach, began to allow groups a mostly symbolic part of the policy process (Lipsky; Olson and Lasky), and to set up parallel but for the most part powerless bureaucracies like Model Cities. This introduced discordant elements into City Hall. Worse, they were well-paid discordant elements, and their example suggested to other city employees (especially uniformed services and craft workers) that only by growing more uncooperative would their own rewards be maximized. The growing external pressure on the coalition made this strategy all the more effective (Piven).

Second, as the costs of growth became apparent, constituencies that had previously supported growth began to swing into opposition. Fiscally conservative elected officials urged that commuters be taxed more fully for the costs of growth, while urban upper-middle-class professionals opposed the transformation of "their" cities and mixed neighborhoods. The climate of public opinion, formerly unified, became divided. Middle-class blacks in Boston, Harvard liberals in Cambridge, and ecology-oriented activist professionals in Berkeley and San Francisco all mounted anti-growth campaigns.

Finally, both business and labor drew back from full-scale support from the pro-growth coalition because both disfavor, and to some extent fear, the politicization of their activities. Neither wished to accept the forms of public control—ranging from hearings to environmental-impact reports, from neighborhood vetoes to affirmative-action programs—which were emerging from the battles against growth.

Overlaying this set of frictions was a central-city fiscal and social crisis that was, as has been argued, deepened not only by growth policies but also by the growing distances between workplace and dwelling place, by low-productivity central-city service functions, and by suburban tax protection. The political fight against growth, the burgeoning central-city fiscal needs, and the international plight of American empire joined together to throw old policies and political alliances into question. It did so not only on the electoral level, but on the level of policy adequacy or viability. At a national level, as we shall see, policy changed toward austerity and retrenchment in social spending (which further undermined local mayoral efforts to hide the differences between growth beneficiaries and growth sufferers under a plush patronage carpet), and towards a policy of growth without constraint from labor or neighborhoods. In all, conservative policy-makers had decided that the old approaches to growth had simply become too costly.

From 1969 onward, these forces clearly sapped local pro-growth electoral coalitions. In general, the latter have survived only where the negative consequences were relatively slight (perhaps because development was more sophisticated) and when mayors used their political skills and the urban fiscal crisis to divide growth opponents.

Simply to mention some of the more famous cases, "cop" mayors took over in Minneapolis, St. Paul, and Philadelphia, and law-and-order candidates came close to winning in Newark (Anthony Imperiale), Boston (Louise Day Hicks), and New York (Mario Procaccino), to name a few. In a number of cases these candidates either beat or lost narrowly to black candidates. Blacks, of course, managed to win office in Gary, Cleveland, Newark, and most recently in Los Angeles and Atlanta. Shrewd pro-growth mayors, particularly Alioto in San Francisco, White in Boston, Uhlman in Seattle, and Landrieu in New Orleans, managed to reconcile opposing sides and avert losses to either blacks, middle-class anti-growth exponents, or law-and-order advocates, but they often did so by the skin of their teeth. Uhlman, for example, was faced with recall when he adopted a hard stand against pay increases for Seattle firemen, but he won it decisively.

In a few cities, particularly university towns like Berkeley and Madison, an alliance of poor neighborhoods, radical students, and middle-class ecologists opposing growth, was formed to elect "radical" mayors and city councilors. This form of anti-growth coalition has less to hold it together than the pre-growth coalition, and its fate is far from bright.

Another interesting variant includes New Haven and Pittsburgh, veritable progenitors of the pro-growth coalition. In these cities, candidates strongly oriented towards white ethnic neighborhoods (Bart Guida in New Haven, Peter Flaherty in Pittsburgh) won mayoral elections. Both are conservative Democrats who have been relative mavericks as far as the local party organizations were concerned, although Guida received support from New Haven Democratic leader Barbieri. Both, finally, have cut city payrolls, taxes, and opposed renewal efforts.

What are the consequences of this declining potency of the pro-growth coalition? Aside from the fact that city politics has been opened up to all manner of electoral ventures, and that opportunist politicians have had a field day in exploiting sometimes legitimate grievances in a thoroughly racist manner, the main consequence has been to throw up barriers against growth.

In response to neighborhood protest in the mid-1960s, federal policy and local practice with respect to renewal changed substantially. Relocation rights were strengthened, neighborhood advisory committees were required, the amount of subsidized housing was increased, affirmative-action hiring was propounded, and many renewal projects were delayed, restructured, or killed altogether. New zoning and other impediments to development were thrown up in various neighborhoods in the cities under consideration. To summarize the matter, quite real and serious obstacles were developed to thwart some of the worst consequences of growth. While many of them were designed simply to "buy off" neighborhood opposition and allow the realization of corporate ends, others have proven to be substantial impediments. It is in this light that recent federal policy towards the cities can be understood, as it has attempted to remove such obstacles to growth and throw community movements on the defensive.

TENDENCIES WITHIN THE CURRENT POLITICAL INSTABILITY

The conditions pushing pro-growth coalitions towards breakdown—neighborhood protest, constraints on the growth process, loss of mass legitimacy, independence of public employees, and serious divisions among growth supporters—have not operated uniformly in all cities. Nor have they, for given classes of cities, led consistently to an alternative political coalition for the future. Nevertheless, some broad patterns can be discerned.

The Strength of Growth

The pro-growth coalition took on its most public role in cities where state action was most necessary to promote the large-scale urban changes that have occurred since World War II. These cities are primarily large, old, and highly ethnic and blue-collar, with large but worn capital investments which needed to be replaced. Heterogeneity provides one of the hallmarks for such cities, thus making a well-worked-out political-alliance network all the more necessary.

By contrast, newer, fast-growing cities of the South and Southwest, and smaller cities generally, could undertake most of the needed investments on a purely private basis. No outmoded environment (in both the social and physical senses) needed to be dismantled. Counter-tendencies to corporate strength, such as unions and well-organized minorities, proved infrequent. Without such requirements for political action, the standard devices of zoning and public works proved sufficient for a rapid spurt of growth over the last several decades. In cities such as Phoenix, Houston, Los Angeles, and San Jose, and to a lesser extent Dallas/Ft. Worth and Atlanta, growth interests needed only an efficient, business-minded city government, and not even a particularly powerful one at that. Alliances among major corporations, banks, and developers proved in the main to be all that was needed, and they could operate largely outside public scrutiny. In these cities, then, growth-oriented mayors tended to survive much more easily than their Northeastern colleagues.

In the cities where pressures against growth exerted themselves most severely, a variety of equally temporary outcomes seems to have appeared. In some cities, mayors managed, through political adroitness, to paper over some of the divisions between growth proponents, neighborhoods suffering from growth, and unruly public workers. Mayors like Alioto, White, Cavanagh, Allen, and Landrieu had good connections with business and development interests, provided professionally oriented and innovative leadership, and at the same time drew minority support on the basis of large-scale "citizen participation" and social-welfare-oriented programs. To varying degrees, each was successful in exerting enough political control over civil-service employees to mount a strong campaign apparatus, perhaps the principal fact in accounting for Daley's strength in Chicago. Yet each of these mayors found their grip on public office surely less certain than in the past.

Yet none of the alternative tendencies in city politics have established a hammerlock on the future. Law-and-order regimes have been discredited (Rizzo and police corruption) or undercut by pro-growth coalitions anxious to get back in business (Minneapolis and St. Paul). Black mayors appear to be holding their own, by and large, but in the end may not turn out to be much other than pro-growth coalitions simply manned by black people. This seems particularly likely given the ideology of institution-building and patronage accumulation current within the black community. Finally, none of the "radical" coalitions have distinguished themselves either by being particularly principled (backsliding has been endemic in both Berkeley and Cambridge) or by developing a hold outside student strongholds. In short, the situation remains unsettled. While the current economic crisis and market-oriented federal austerity policies may rekindle pro-growth policies for a time, it seems unlikely that they will be able to overcome permanently the opposition which is sure to arise.

CONCLUSIONS AND SPECULATIONS

Orthodox political science and economics have attempted to explain metropolitan decentralization and the content of urban politics with what are in essence market models. For both economists and political scientists, departure for the suburbs simply constituted a choice individuals made about lifestyles, given a range of means and opportunities. For Edward Banfield, growing personal incomes, improved transportation technology, rising populations, and internal migrations lead "naturally" to suburbanization. For economist Charles Tiebout, the number of metropolitan political jurisdictions and the various political outcomes in each reflect merely a market competition among governments selling different public-policy packages for different tax prices. For the urban economics literature as a whole, transportation and production techniques, and the way they exert their influence through competition, determined not only metropolitan dispersion but land-use intensities within the central city. One firm discovers the truck and the space-extensive suburban plant layout, and by its newfound efficiency forces all others to adopt the same methods. Within the city, an entrepreneur captures benefits from the general urban growth by finding better uses for a given piece of land; if previous social patterns are disrupted, only the market is to blame.

Economists have great difficulty in analyzing and evaluating the content of urban policy, and tend to think markets would do a better job (alas, if they could only be introduced!). Political scientists understand more clearly that public policies must be marketed through bureaucratic and electoral mechanisms which utilize the divisible nature of policy *inputs* for strength, not their collective and uncontrollable outputs. But even here they employ market notions of political competition.

This paper has rejected such views on two counts: first, market explanations remain essentially circular unless the context in which the market operates is specified. In this case, markets function in the midst of a basic conflict over the direction and purpose of urban life, namely the conflict between urban form for human purposes and urban form for efficient capitalist production. New transportation technologies or plant locations are introduced not merely to reduce marginal marketing costs, but to increase production's social control over the

entire environment of work. The upgrading of inner-city neighborhoods occurs not simply because young lawyers and business people
find them quaint, but because the city economic system as a whole is
predicated on concentrating the command functions in the central
city and making it possible for a work force to have ready access to it.

Second, market explanations deny or obscure the central yet contradictory role of the state. Of all the contextual factors that structure
markets, the state is the most important. Land-use patterns are inherently collective, public matters. They cannot be set up without government actions ranging from roads and sewers to police and fire protection to government constraints on how owners use their property. As a
result, land-use questions (always subject to the fundamental tension
described above) inevitably tend to become political. How the politics
of land use are organized, and therefore contained, provides perhaps
the central theme of U.S. urban political history.

The view presented here holds that urban land-use policies are at
the center of a vortex of forces. In order to promote growth of land
values and central-city revenues (problems that were themselves in
part the result of other government policies), business, government,
and to a lesser extent organized labor forged a pro-growth alliance.
The consequence of this alliance was an important class-based transformation of land uses, which in turn triggered severe tensions both
within and outside the growth alliance. The consequent political breakdown allowed community movements to impose increased costs and
impediments on growth which the Federal government is presently
attempting, without a great deal of success, to throw off. Federal cutbacks have thus shifted some aspects of the battle over land use into
a battle over the composition of city budgets, but the situation remains
fluid.

The current situation provides an important opening within city
politics, for a new, more progressive coalition, although it has as yet not
materialized. During the dual political breakdown of the 1960s, neighborhoods and city workers tended to ignore each other when not being
downright antagonistic. Both failed to work for an alliance based on a
positive alternative vision for the city, but merely reacted against relatively obvious "targets." For both parties, this was a shortsighted, if
unsurprising, course. Neighborhoods made their greatest gains when
they gathered support from within city bureaucracies, while conservative political forces can isolate public employees with ease if they fail

to build strong constituencies within neighborhoods and client groups. But on what grounds could such an alliance be effected?

The missing link, to this point, has been a political movement explicitly based on putting in place new city spending priorities and land-use patterns rather than merely redistributing patronage. Such a party on public-service producers and consumers would develop means to make them directly responsive to each other rather than insulated by a layer of brokerage-oriented politics. It would seek to change the framework of decision-making and the values implicit within it rather than simply reducing police expenditures here and increasing welfare expenditures there. Whether such an alliance can emerge remains to be seen, but when all is said and done, this remains the task of city dwellers who would like to live in a truly humane city (Mollenkopf, 1977).

NOTES

1. See Moynihan for explanations of this type about community mobilization and city politics. On riots, see the *Report of the National Advisory Commission on Civil Disorders*, especially pp. 1–2, 8–11. Political science failed to anticipate the riots, failed to anticipate their winding down, and despite the fact that significant urban rioting continues, has failed to pay it much attention. Evidently the subject is no longer "policy-relevant." On political destabilization see Wilson and Wilde.
2. Among the most vivid portrayals of this phenomenon in the literature on machine politics are those of Steffens and Sinclair. Karson describes the Catholic Church's influence.
3. This view has been most boldly stated by David Gordon in his as yet unpublished work on urban history. See also Hayes; Katznelson (1976).
4. In this period, slums as a whole were declining in population. Black and other minority ghettos were growing, however, and the term thus has distinctly racist overtones.
5. Revenue figures may be found in "Statistics on State and Local Government Finance," *The Bond Buyer* (May, 1971), p. 40. Ludeman discusses the history of municipal finances, the defaults of the 1930s, and the current prospects for defaults.
6. The report was *Financial Problems of New York*, reported in Shoup, pp. 218–26.
7. Wood, pp. 71–72. Wood reports that slums occupied 20 percent of Boston's nonbusiness land, required 45 percent of its expenditures, but contributed only 6 percent of its revenue. Similar figures were widely reported by mayors of other cities in testimony favoring passage of the 1949 Housing and Urban Renewal Act. See also "Downtown Woes," *Business Week* (October 2, 1954), p. 64, which reports the first meet-

ing of executives from twenty-seven downtown associations "to discuss ways of combatting the threat to downtown property values and store sales." They decided to push for improved downtown parking, freeways, better mass transit, and "improvement projects to reduce blight areas." *Public Management,* the *National Municipal Review,* and *American City,* carried frequent articles on this general subject. In his forthcoming study, Domhoff gives a close analysis of the 1949 Act and the role of the American Council to Improve Our Neighborhoods (ACTION), a corporate-financed body to promote renewal during the early 1950s.

8. Raymond Moley, testimony to the House Banking and Currency Committee Hearings on the 1949 Housing Act, p. 26. Baltimore mayor D'Alesandro echoed these sentiments (pp. 528–30). He claimed that locally financed efforts had proven insufficient for renewal, and that assessments in Baltimore's growing slums had declined over $10 million between 1938 and 1948. He also filed several dozen letters from other big-city mayors making claims of the same general type.

9. House Subcommittee on Urban Affairs, p. 24. Duncan and Lieberson give evidence based on banking transactions to show how central cities not only maintained but enhanced their financial dominance over subordinate regional cities. Although they do not argue the point, this trend clearly includes investments overseas as well as U.S. in the hinterland.

10. "Should-Must Cities Decentralize?" *The Commonwealth* (May 31, 1948). Previously the report stated that technology now allowed smaller plants. But instead of relying on a naive determinism, it states, "This fact makes possible small factories in suburban or rural areas, where some of the problems attendant upon production is congested urban centers are less apparent or even non-existent. These related directly or indirectly to labor" (p. 13).

11. Admittedly this collective portrait is impressionistic and undoubtedly fails to account for important variations among pro-growth mayors. Nevertheless, I believe it touches the important themes, particularly with respect to the use of federal money and the attendant technicians as a political base. Logue, for example, was a key factor in setting up community-action agencies in New Haven and Boston, and the latter agency, together with the Little City Hall Program, provided Mayor White with electoral manpower and expertise.

12. *The National Journal,* September 18, 1971, quoted one HUD official as saying Herman was "one of the men responsible for getting urban renewal named 'the federal bulldozer' and 'negro removal.'"

REFERENCES

Auerbach, Arnold, "Power and Progress in Pittsburgh," *Trans-Action,* Sept.-Oct., 1965.

Caro, Robert, *The Power Broker: Robert Moses and the Fall of New York* (New York: Alfred A. Knopf, 1974).

Cohen, Benjamin, "Trends in Negro Employment within Large Metropolitan Areas," *Public Policy,* Fall 1971.

Cohen, Robert, "Urban Effects of the Internationalization of Capital and

Labor" (Unpublished paper, Human Resources Project, Columbia University, 1975).

Domhoff, G. William, *Who Really Rules New Haven?* (New Brunswick: Transaction Books, 1977).

Downs, Anthony, "Losses Imposed on Urban Households by Uncompensated Highway and Renewal Costs," in Downs, *Urban Problems and Prospects* (Chicago: Markham Publishing Co., 1970).

Duncan, Beverly, and Stanley Lieberson, *Metropolis and Region in Transition* (Beverly Hills: Sage Publications, 1970).

Edel, Matthew, "Urban Renewal and Land Use Conflicts," *Review of Radical Political Economy,* Summer 1971.

Fortune, "After the Cabots—Jerry Blakely," Nov. 1960.

Friedland, Roger, "Class Power and the Central City," (Ph.D. dissertation, University of Wisconsin, 1976).

Goodman, Robert, *After the Planners* (New York: Simon and Schuster, 1971).

Gordon, David M., "Capitalist Development and the History of American Cities," in this volume.

Harrison, Bennett, *Urban Economic Development* (Washington, D.C.: Urban Institute, 1974).

Harvey, David, *Social Justice in the City* (Baltimore: Johns Hopkins University Press, 1973).

———, "The Political Economy of Urbanization in Advanced Capitalist Societies—The Case of the United States," in Gary Geppert and Harold M. Rose, eds., *The Social Economy of Cities.* Sage Urban Affairs Annual Review, Vol. 9 (Beverly Hills: Sage Publications, 1975).

Hawkins, Frank, "Lawrence of Pittsburgh: Boss of the Mellon Patch," *Harper's Magazine,* Aug. 1956.

Hays, Samuel P., "The Politics of Reform in Municipal Government in the Progressive Era," in Daniel Gordon, ed., *Social Change and Urban Politics* (Englewood Cliffs, N.J.: Prentice-Hall, 1973).

James, Franklin, "The City Sandbox, Reservation, or Dynamo?—A Reply," *Public Policy,* Fall 1971.

Karson, Marc, *American Labor Unions and Politics* (Carbondale: Southern Illinois University Press, 1958).

Katznelson, Ira, "The Crisis of the Capitalist City," in Willis Hawley and Michael Lipsky, eds., *Theoretical Perspectives on Urban Politics* (Englewood Cliffs, N.J.: Prentice-Hall, 1976).

Lipsky, Michael, "Protest as a Political Resource," *American Political Science Review,* Dec. 1968.

Lubove, Roy, *Twentieth Century Pittsburgh: Government, Business, and Environmental Change* (New York: John Wiley and Sons, 1969).

Ludeman, Douglas, *The Investment Merits of Big City Bonds* (Boston: Financial Publishing Co., 1973).

Marglin, Steven, "What Do Bosses Do?" *Review of Radical Political Economics,* Summer 1974.

Mollenkopf, John, "The Fragile Giant," in Roger E. Alcaly and David Mermelstein, eds., *The Fiscal Crisis of America's Cities* (New York: Random House/Vintage Books, 1977).

———, *Growth Defied: Community Organization and Political Conflict over Urban Development,* (forthcoming)

Moynihan, Daniel P., *Maximum Feasible Misunderstanding* (New York: Free Press, 1969).

O'Connor, James R., *The Fiscal Crisis of the State* (New York: St. Martin's Press, 1973).

Olson, David, and Michael Lipsky, *Riot Commission Politics* (New Brunswick, N.J.: Transaction Books, 1975).

Piven, Frances Fox, "The Urban Crisis: Who Got What and Why," in Robert P. Wolff, ed., *1984 Revisited* (New York: Alfred A. Knopf, 1973).

Report of the National Advisory Commission on Civil Disorders (New York: Bantam Books, 1968).

Salisbury, Robert, "Urban Politics: The New Convergence of Power," *Journal of Politics*, Nov. 1964.

Shoup, Carl, "New York City's Financial Situation and the Transit Fare," *National Tax Journal*, Sept. 1952.

Sinclair, Upton, *The Jungle* (New York: Harper and Row, 1951).

Steffens, Lincoln, *Autobiography* (New York: Harcourt, Brace and Co., 1931).

Stone, Kathy, "The Origins of Job Structures in the Steel Industry," *Review of Radical Political Economics*, Summer 1974.

U.S. Bureau of the Census, *Current Population Reports*, Series P-23, No. 25, "Lifetime Migration Histories of the American People," 1973.

U.S. Department of Housing and Urban Development, *Urban Renewal Directory*, June 30, 1971.

U.S. House of Representatives Subcommittee on Urban Affairs, "Central City Problem and Urban Renewal Policy," (93rd Cong., February, 1973).

Vernon, Raymond, "The Changing Economic Function of the Central City," in James Q. Wilson, ed., *Urban Renewal: The Record and the Controversy* (Cambridge, Mass.: MIT Press, 1967).

Weiss, Marc, and Marty Gellen, "The Rise and Fall of the Cold War Consensus," in Judith Carnoy and Marc Weiss, eds., *A House Divided* (Boston: Little, Brown and Co., 1973).

Wilson, James Q., and Harold Wilde, "The Urban Mood," *Commentary*, Oct. 1969.

Wolfinger, Raymond, *The Politics of Progress* (Englewood Cliffs, N.J.: Prentice-Hall, 1974).

———, "Why Political Machines Have Not Withered Away and Other Revisionist Thoughts," *Journal of Politics*, May 1972.

Wood, Robert, *Suburbia* (Boston: Houghton Mifflin, 1958).

The Illusion and Reality of Urban Renewal: San Francisco's Yerba Buena Center

CHESTER HARTMAN and ROB KESSLER

As John Mollenkopf points out elsewhere in this volume, the urban crisis of the 1960s to a large extent "grew out of a class-based political struggle over the nature of urban development." In city after city, local redevelopment agencies acted to take land away from one group of users who were using it "inefficiently" and turned it over to others for what was described as "higher and better use."[1] The land involved was generally large, centrally located sites. The occupants were low-income residents, some 70 percent of whom were nonwhite, and small businesses. The new land uses generally were office buildings, retail stores, and public and semipublic facility complexes (civic centers, pedestrian malls, sports arenas, convention halls, etc.).

San Francisco's Yerba Buena Center (YBC) offers a classic case study both of the urban redevelopment forces of the 1960s and the effects of the more recent breakdown in the pro-growth coalition of big business, labor, City Hall, and the media that provided the political impetus for that kind of legalized, government-subsidized land-grabbing. Yerba Buena Center got caught midproject in these larger political shifts, as its changing fortunes well reflect.

* An earlier version of this article, based on the original Yerba Buena plan only, appeared in *Land Economics*, November, 1973 (© 1973 by the Board of Regents of the University of Wisconsin System), pp. 440–53.

YBC represented an attempt by the region's ruling forces to expand the city's downtown office-headquarters district out of its small and constricted boundaries, across 120-foot-wide Market Street into the South of Market area, traditionally a low-prestige, low-rent area housing blue-collar workers and lower-income residents. The city's increasing role during and after World War II as corporate and financial headquarters for the western United States and Pacific Basin created the demand for more office space, and the urban renewal program, with its land write-down subsidies and powers of eminent domain, was the state apparatus designed to accomplish such ends. The idea was to carry out a massive development, with various public and quasi-public facilities, that would spur related development in the surrounding neighborhood and definitively transform the South of Market area into part of the city's central office district.

Formal planning for the eighty-seven-acre site began in 1961 (although the basic outline of the idea dates from the mid-1950s), and the city's governing Board of Supervisors approved the final project in 1966. The plan included as its centerpiece a new convention center and exhibition hall, an indoor sports arena, and a lavish pedestrian concourse. Also included were a luxury hotel, an airlines terminal, a theater, garage, apparel mart, retail space, and about seven million square feet of new office space.

Opposition to the project on the part of displaced residents—some four thousand in number—led to a federal injunction in 1969 against demolition and relocation activities. That suit, a landmark in protection of displacees' rights, handled by Neighborhood Legal Services attorneys, ended with an agreement by the San Francisco Redevelopment Agency to rehabilitate 1,500 to 1,800 low-rent housing units and later to construct 400 additional low rent replacement units. Subsequent litigation, brought first in 1972, and again in 1975 by other plaintiffs, challenged the city's proposed financing plan for YBC. Those lawsuits, and the delays and public controversy they engendered, led the city's new administration to call a halt to the project and give replanning over to a seventeen-person Mayor's Select Committee on Yerba Buena Center. Almost all land clearance had taken place, but almost no construction, leaving a vast wasteland-parking-lot smack in the middle of downtown. The situation—stopping a major downtown renewal project in midexecution for reconsideration a full ten years after its formal beginning—is unique in the country. The Mayor's Select

Committee, after several months of work and public hearings, approved a "new" YBC plan, different in some ways from the old plan but in substance unchanged. The new mayor, George Moscone, placed on the November, 1976, ballot a nonbinding voter policy statement on the new plan, which passed by a 3-2 margin. The project probably will have to come before the electorate again for specific approval of the bonds, in light of passage of another measure subjecting bond devices of the type planned for YBC to voter approval. Whether the voters will authorize actual expenditure of money is unclear. Thus, the future of YBC is anyone's guess: it could be smooth sailing, with Center construction completed by the mid-1980s—two and a half decades after the Redevelopment Agency received its original federal planning grant for the project—or it could be further controversy, litigation, delay, and plan changes.

A detailed political history of the entire Yerba Buena project and the struggle against it appears elsewhere.[2] In this article we wish to probe the economic rationale and data used to support YBC, and by extension the underpinnings of downtown urban renewal in U.S. cities. (Our discussion will include elements of the original Redevelopment Agency plan and elements of the substitute plan.) The central question is: how are the putative benefits of this process to be distributed—i.e., higher efficiency for whom? This threshold question probes the integrity of the efficiency calculation itself: how accurate and complete are the estimates of costs and benefits from which the assessment of efficiency is derived? Based on our Yerba Buena research, we have found that urban renewal has concentrated solely on narrowly defined potential aggregate benefits which accrue only to a small private sector, rather than on distributive effects, and has been supported by a very partial and one-sided recitation of the possible costs and benefits.

FINANCING THE PROJECT

The project originally was divided into a "public facilities" portion (the convention center, sports arena, pedestrian mall, garage, and heating plant) and a "private facilities" portion (the office and commercial space). The federal urban renewal grant subsidy—through 1974, $38 million for planning, administration, and writing down the price of the land, plus $8 million for relocation of site occupants—supports both the private and public portions. That money essentially brings the original area to its cleared state, ready for disposition to redevelopers (public and private). While the sites to be redeveloped privately require no further direct public subsidy, the public facilities must be financed publicly. As passed by the Board of Supervisors in March, 1972, these were to be paid for through a local bond issue of up to $225 million.

The plan called for the San Francisco Redevelopment Agency to issue lease-revenue bonds to pay for construction and other development costs. Once the public facilities were completed, the Redevelopment Agency would lease the sites and facilities to the city for a rent sufficient to amortize the bonds and to "cover any additional expenses which may be incurred by the Agency" ("Yerba Buena Center," 1972, Exhibit I, p. 9). When the bonds were paid off, after thirty-five years, title to the public facilities would be vested in the city. The financing agreement between the city and the Redevelopment Agency would have obligated the city to pay the stipulated rent (i.e., the full debt-servicing costs) and any other unexpected costs, regardless of whether revenue from the facilities met the amount of the rent.

Actual construction cost of the public facilities was at the time estimated at $219 million. Taking into account the interest payments on the bonds, the total long-term cost of the public facilities in Yerba Buena Center would have been approximately $500 million, well over double the announced cost of the project.

The original financing plan rested on some very tenuous income estimates. These estimates were based on the assumption that the bonds could be sold at a 6 percent interest rate, with an annual debt service of $14.5 million. On the other hand, a memo from the city's budget analyst suggested that a 7 percent to 7.5 percent interest rate was more likely. Income for the city to cover its rental obligation, and hence to pay off the bond issue, was to have come from four sources: (1) Private land rents: the amount the private developer would have paid annually for the rights to develop and sublease the private sites in the central blocks. (2) Income from the public facilities: about half of this amount was expected to come from the 1,850-car public parking garage, while one-fourth was projected from the sports arena and one-fourth from a ticket tax on all public events. The exhibit hall was projected to produce no excess of revenues over costs. (3) Hotel tax allocation: 36 percent of the revenue from the (then) 5.5 percent citywide hotel tax was by ordinance assigned to Yerba Buena Center development. (4) Increased property taxes from privately owned land in Yerba Buena Center, within and outside of the central blocks: all property tax revenue above a 1965 base figure (the tax increment) was to be placed in a special fund to pay off the Yerba Buena bonds.

The total amount of income projected from all four sources for 1976 (the date projected for completion of the sports arena and exhibit hall at the time the Supervisors passed the financing plan) and 1982 (when the entire project was slated for completion) was as follows:[3]

Annual Income Projection

	1976	1982
Private Land Rents	$ 0.5 million	$ 0.6 million
Public Facilities Income	3.6 million	3.6 million
Hotel Tax	1.8 million	2.0 million
Property Tax Increment	6.8 million	10.3 million
TOTAL	$12.7 million	$16.5 million

These were the income projections to cover the projected annual $14.5 million debt payments. Thus, the Center was planned to run at a deficit for the first few years of its operation, and not until its third or fourth year did it project an increase in revenue over debt-service needs. (Later analysis, based on U.S. Department of Housing and Urban Development data, indicated that this deficit period would last five years and that the monies needed from the city's general fund to cover this deficit would exceed $20 million. See Memorandum to George Moscone, p. 11.) Had the interest rate turned out to be 7 percent, as the city's budget analyst minimally predicted, the required annual payments would have been $16.6 million and the projected income would never have been sufficient to meet debt-service needs.

A closer look at the projected revenues from the public facilities shows how shaky were the grounds on which the original Yerba Buena Center financing plan stood and how costly the project would have been (and still may be) to the public. The 350,000-square-foot exhibition hall and convention center was projected to produce no net revenue at all. Based on the experience of convention centers in other large cities, it is likely that the center would show an operating *loss*. Almost all large-city convention centers operate at a substantial loss. San Francisco's current convention facilities in the Civic Auditorium and Brooks Hall currently operate at a net loss of about $200,000 per year.

The Cow Palace, a state-owned convention and sports facility, runs at an annual deficit of some $300,000.[4] In the competitive world of convention business, rents on facilities cannot be raised beyond the prevailing rate or the city risks losing the convention altogether; if other cities are losing money on the operation of their convention facilities, it seems likely that this will be so in San Francisco. And within San Francisco the Yerba Buena Center convention facilities will be competing with the Cow Palace and the Civic Auditorium–Brooks Hall complex, neither of which is presently used to capacity. There will clearly be excess capacity in the city, and in this highly competitive situation rental charges will be driven down.

The sports arena was projected to bring in an annual revenue in excess of operating costs amounting to $817,000, which would have been used to pay debt-service costs. These figures were based on the assumption that the Bay Area's professional basketball and hockey teams (the Golden State Warriors and the California Golden Seals) would have played almost all of their home games in the new arena.[5] Both teams at the time were playing their home games in the Oakland Arena, a new but slightly smaller facility (12,000 capacity, compared with 14,000 planned for YBC). Neither team had made a commitment to move to San Francisco, and based on phone interviews with club officials and patterns of other professional sports teams, it seemed likely that if such a move had been made at all it would have been for only half the home games, with both teams sharing Oakland and San Francisco as their "home city."

Any shortfalls in the projected use of the arena and convention center would have had multiplier effects, compounding the risky assumptions on which the entire financing plan was based. Thus, the arena was scheduled to produce another $843,000 in ticket taxes (over and above profits from rental fees and concessions), and these city tax revenues were also earmarked for debt financing. If the arena had not been used according to projections, the amount of ticket-tax revenue would also have been curtailed. The parking garage was supposed to bring in $1.9 million annually in net revenue, all of which would be earmarked to pay off the bonds. If the arena had not been used to the extent projected, these revenues, too, would have fallen. And finally, revenues from the 1,850-car public garage were based on an intensity of usage equal to that of a nearby 2,000-stall public garage, even though the proposed hourly parking rate for the Yerba Buena Center garage would have been twice as high as, and the monthly rate two-thirds higher than, those of the neighboring garage (which was not operating at full capacity).

The central component of the 1972 financing plan—accounting for three-fifths of all projected revenue—was the property-tax increment. The Agency's fiscal projections assumed an 840 percent increase in assessments between 1975 and 1978, a figure backed by little hard evidence and one that struck many knowledgeable observers as highly optimistic. Just a year earlier, the Redevelopment Agency had claimed property-tax revenues in the area would rise only 757 percent.[6] The tax-increment projections assumed that all eighteen private sites would have been developed on schedule, even though only three of the sites had been sold and developers are known for their fickleness, particularly given litigation and other delays. Had delays ensued, tax revenues would have been less than projected and the deficit already planned would have lasted beyond three to four years. Nor did the tax-increment calculation take account of the costs of increased city services (police and fire protection, street-cleaning, etc.) that the convention center, sports arena, and other YBC facilities would have required.[7]

In sum, revenue projections for the public facilities were risky and highly inflated. And the nature of the city's backup agreement for the Redevelopment Agency bonds meant that the bill would have been picked up via some other tax. These realities were sharply at variance with the claim consistently made to the public by advocates of the Center that it "will not cost the taxpayers of this city one cent." Leaving the taxpayers holding the bill for huge projects of this sort which fall short of the promises made about them is a common phenomenon, moreover. A 1973 *Fortune* study of stadium complexes concluded that "most . . . are financed with bonds issued by state, county, or city governments that are supposed to be paid off by revenue derived from the project but in practice these revenue bonds almost always turn out to load an open-ended general obligation upon the taxpayer" (Burck, p. 105).

INCREASED TAX REVENUES OR HIGHER TAXES?

Use of tax-increment financing as the principal source of revenue to pay for the public facilities would seem to destroy one of the basic

economic justifications given for Yerba Buena Center: that it will increase the city's tax base and thereby provide the aggregate public
benefit of more revenue for the city. If all tax-revenue increase on
Yerba Buena Center properties had been fed back into the project to
pay for the project, then nothing would have been available to the city
to pay for other needed services or to permit a reduction in the tax
rate. Until the 1972 arrangements were made public it was steadfastly
claimed that Yerba Buena Center would be financed without resort to
property-tax revenues.

Use of tax-increment financing to pay off the Yerba Buena Center
bonds would have been even more damaging to the city's economy
than was apparent at first glance, for a great deal of the economic activity that would locate in the project area would have occurred elsewhere in the city had there been no project. In fact the environmental
impact report (EIR) for the project, done in 1973, calculated that office
space to be provided in Yerba Buena Center "is expected to absorb 80
percent of estimated annual demand over the next decade, [but] these
developments will represent a shift in location from the Financial district and other areas rather than a net increase in economic activity
and building ("Yerba Buena Center," 1973, p. v). Thus, the renewal
project's original financing plan actually would have siphoned off from
the city's general fund tax revenues that otherwise would accrue from
future development. Even using some very generous assumptions,[8] the
EIR computed that by 1985 only $4.3 million annually in new property-
tax receipts would have resulted from the original Yerba Buena Center
(only two-fifths of the "tax-increment" fund the Redevelopment
Agency and Supervisors had assigned to pay off the Yerba Buena Center bonds).

Rather than deriving any benefits from the Yerba Buena Center
development for its general fund, the city would have lost substantial
sums of money. The city's general fund would have lost in perpetuity
(or at least until the next round of redevelopment of this area, which
cannot occur until the bonds have been retired, some thirty-five years
hence) the annual property-tax revenue it would have received from
the land in the Yerba Buena area above the 1965 level, which would
have increased annually as both assessed values and the tax-rate climb
in coming years. And the tax roll for property in the area, and hence
the tax revenue, decreased markedly after 1965, when the Redevelopment Agency began acquiring and clearing the land. This "fallow"

period between the clearance of the project area and completion of construction, which was to have lasted at least until 1976, and now will last at least until 1982, has cost the city millions of dollars in foregone tax revenues. For the twelve-year period 1965–1976, the difference between actual tax revenue from land in the Yerba Buena area and estimated revenue from this land had there been no Yerba Buena project amounts to $5.6 million.[9] The true extent of this loss shows up as even greater when the yearly loss is compounded to account for the interest the city would have earned had it received the lost revenues. Using a 6.5 percent interest rate, the present value of the estimated tax loss from the Yerba Buena area is $7.8 million.

(A further issue in tax-increment financing is that public schools and other taxing districts are robbed of needed revenues. Over a third of the property-tax rate is imposed by and goes to the public schools and community colleges, while smaller amounts go to the Bay Area Pollution Control District and the Bay Area Rapid Transit District. The YBC financing plan sequestered all tax revenues produced by this land; public schools, transit, and air pollution control would have been shut off from needed revenue sources, which would have been shunted off to pay for convention and sports facilities.)

Relatedly, the city also will incur losses to the extent that whatever is built in YBC pulls business away from present locations. For example, the EIR projected that the YBC convention hall would have taken away two-thirds of the 1977–1980 bookings scheduled for Brooks Hall–Civic Auditorium, a city-owned and -operated facility.[10] That complex now has an annual deficit of about $200,000, an amount likely to double as a result of such a shift in bookings. These losses are covered by the city's general fund. And in the private sector it can be assumed that the addition of several million square feet of office space will begin a chain of moves that will produce vacancies in older buildings in other parts of the city.[11] (The relocation of the apparel industry into the new apparel mart is a prime example of this process.) This will impose public costs on the city treasury, which will lose tax revenues from the vacated structures, as well as private costs on the owners of these buildings.

THE LEGAL CHALLENGE

Publication of the city's plan for financing the YBC public facilities brought forth two taxpayers' suits in early 1972. The central claim of the plaintiffs was that the "lease-revenue" form of bond financing in fact was a general-obligation bond issue in disguise, and that the sole purpose of this more expensive financing device was to circumvent the voters (the California Constitution requires two-thirds voter approval for general-obligation bonds while until recent voter passage of a local ordinance, lease-revenue bonds did not have to come before the voters at all). The city's obligation to meet its "rent payments" (that is, the amount needed to amortize the bond issue) regardless of whether project revenues were sufficient to cover these payments in effect constituted pledge of the city's full faith and credit, the plaintiffs argued. (Calling things like the hotel-tax subsidy and property-tax increases "project revenues" was another form of attempted fiscal legerdemain, they pointed out.) The two lawsuits were in essence settled in late 1974 (the city, for reasons still unclear, did not bother to answer them or enter into settlement negotiations for nearly two years—during which time the bond sale obviously could not proceed). The principal items of that settlement called for putting a $210 million limit on the bond issue and eliminating the sports arena as a public facility.

While on the surface a fairly innocuous denouement (the plaintiffs were said to be tired of fighting the project and willing to settle on terms which provided some substantial concessions, even though the principal challenge was not met), the settlement turned out to have serious unintended consequences for the city. When the scaled-down public-facilities portion of the project (minus sports arena) went out for bid in early 1975, the lowest bid came in some $17 million above the construction amount that a $210 million bond issue would yield. (A lease-revenue bond issue requires substantial set-asides for funded interest and reserves, and the bond issue also had to include sums for architectural, legal, and engineering fees, land purchase, insurance, etc.) Attempting to fashion a quick solution, the Redevelopment Agency got the Department of Housing and Urban Development to agree to postpone for five years the $14 million payment for the public facilities' site, which, with a few other adjustments, would have gotten costs down to the $210 million ceiling. (When asked how the city would pay back the $14 million—which, with interest, would be closer to $20 million—Mayor Joseph Alioto said the money would come from the project's property-tax increments, blithely ignoring the fact that every penny of projected increased property tax revenues already was assigned to bond-retirement payments.)

This new example of fiscal fudging, combined with the wording of the city's new leasing and bond-repayment agreement with the Redevelopment Agency, was too much for yet other taxpayers. By this time the city's annual "facilities rent" had climbed to the $18.6 million needed for bond repayments, according to latest calculations—$558 million over the thirty-year life of the bonds—and the leasing agreement now called for the city also to pick up insurance costs for the project and all of the Redevelopment Agency's administrative costs related to YBC. In April, 1975, a group of sixty-six plaintiffs filed a taxpayers' suit, based on the same charges that had motivated the two 1972 suits: violation of constitutional protections regarding general-obligation bonds. That suit effectively killed the project in the original form: the time taken by the trial caused the construction bid to expire, and inflationary rises in building costs make it no longer possible to build those facilities within the $210 million limit.[12] By the fall of 1975 the leading mayoral candidate was promising to reconsider YBC in its entirety, and shortly after he took office, as noted above, he appointed his Select Committee to carry out the replanning.

MAKING SPORT WITH THE TAXPAYERS' MONEY

It is instructive to follow the fate of the sports arena, following the 1974 settlement of the initial financing litigation. In late 1975, Melvin Swig, owner of the California Golden Seals National Hockey League team and son of one of the city's big-time real estate men and Democratic Party bigwigs, brought forth a proposal for a "private, nonprofit" sports arena on the YBC site. The deal was as follows: rather than Swig's financing the arena privately, the city would form a nonprofit corporation to sell $20 million in tax-exempt bonds to construct the arena. Once built, it would be leased to Swig at no charge, and Swig would run it, paying all costs, including bond retirement. Beyond the lower interest rate made possible by the public nonprofit-corporation bonds, Swig's proposal also involved exempting his new arena from property taxes (he would pay a possessory-interest tax instead, amounting to 15–20 percent of what his property taxes would have been); the value of this exemption would have been $900,000 a year, $22.5 million over the twenty-five-year life of the bonds and lease agreement. And the land for the arena would have been sold to Swig for $8 a square foot, about one-third the going price. In an act of civic beneficence, Swig offered to give the arena to the city outright at the end of the twenty-five-year period.

Swig's financial projections for the arena were ludicrous. He assumed that the Warriors would move to his new arena, even though they had just signed a ten-year contract to continue playing at the Oakland Arena. He assumed playoff dates for the Seals (a bad joke for local hockey fans, used to seeing their team reside in or very close to the league cellar). He included nonexistent events in his use of projections (pro volleyball, which doesn't exist in Northern California; roller derby, which recently went bankrupt). He projected wildly exaggerated attendance figures (4,000 average gate for pro tennis, whereas present attendance averages 800 to 1,200; 10,000 average for his Seals, which were drawing 5,000 to 6,000 in Oakland). He based his revenue projection on rents calculated as 12 percent of gross receipts, whereas competing arenas in the Bay Area charge 10 percent, with an 8 percent rate for preferred customers like the Seals and Warriors. Overall, his estimate of $3.7 million annual revenue for the sports arena was half a million dollars more than the entire Oakland Coliseum complex (arena, exhibition hall, and stadium for the A's baseball and Raiders football teams) grossed the previous year. Had Swig gone through with his plan, he probably would have declared bankruptcy in a few years, leaving the city with a white elephant to eat up more tax revenues, while Swig and his group would have cleaned up on "front end" profits: developers', architects', and lawyers' fees, tax shelters, etc. Default would also have had an adverse impact on future city bond issues.

Swig's plan did not go through, even though the Board of Supervisors gave it their initial approval, ignoring the wild projections and the costs to the taxpayers. Opposition by citizens groups and later by the Mayor's Select Committee, plus Swig's receipt of a better offer to move his team elsewhere, prevailed. His California Seals are now the Cleveland Barons and will play in a suburban arena that formerly was home to the World Hockey League Cleveland Crusaders, who in turn just picked up and moved to Hollywood, Florida. An aspect of this vignette in the YBC saga is the way in which cities seek to accommodate and placate owners of professional sports teams, often entering into long-term bond repayment commitments, while the team owners feel free at any time to seek greener pastures elsewhere.[13]

THE REVISED PLAN

The 1976 revised Yerba Buena plan by the Mayor's Select Committee retains the convention center, although in a somewhat smaller, less luxurious and expensive version (250,000 to 300,000 square feet versus 350,000; $55 million versus $78 million construction cost). The Committee's financing plan reveals weaknesses similar to those of the old plan, however. Instead of financing the bond issue by pouring back into bond repayments the increased property-tax revenues from privately developed sites, the new plan relies on the city's hotel-room tax. That tax, now 6 percent, with 2 percent earmarked for YBC, would be raised to 8 percent, with all of that additional revenue also designated to repay the $85 million in YBC bonds needed. The 4 percent portion of the hotel tax would, it is estimated, just cover the $6.18 million annual debt repayments needed on this bond issue.

The Mayor's Committee thus treats hotel-tax revenues as something like a special fund, different from other revenue sources—a position buttressed by the hotel industry, which regards that tax (paid by its guests as part of their bills, not by the hotels) as something that can be raised only with its acquiescence and spent only to benefit the hotel and convention industry. (The rest of the tax is allocated as follows: 0.5 percent to pay for renovation of Candlestick Park, the city's football-baseball stadium; 0.5 percent to subsidize the replacement housing mandated in the final settlement of the displacees' lawsuit; 3 percent to the city's "Publicity and Advertising Fund," which goes to support entertainment and cultural events and promote tourism—with by far the largest single amount, slightly over $1 million in 1975–1976, going to the industry's promotional group, the Convention and Visitors Bureau, which has been the principal promoter of YBC in recent years.) The hotel tax is an attractive source of revenue—paid for the most part by well-to-do out-of-towners—but fiscally it is no different from sales- or property-tax revenues. A dollar of hotel-tax revenue used to support YBC (and to date $12 million in such funds have been expended for design and administrative work on the project) is a dollar not used to support the city's transit system, health facilities, day-care, libraries, and other public services. The Select Committee's stance seems to be that it has "convinced" the hotel owners to "allow" an increase in the hotel tax from 6 percent to 8 percent, in order to build the convention center and other YBC "public" facilities, and that the center therefore will cost the taxpayers nothing. (The campaign to convince the voters to pass the policy statement approving the convention center in the November, 1976, elections was centered on this theme. The cover of the campaign literature proclaimed, "No Cost to Taxpayers, Homeowners or Renters.")

RUNNING THE LEASE-REVENUE BOND GAME

The Select Committee also retained the device of lease-revenue bonds for financing the new YBC public facilities plan. According to current estimates, these would bear a 7 percent interest rate, compared with 6.25 percent for general-obligation bonds. And because, unlike general-obligation bonds, they have heavy reserve and funded-interest requirements, lease-revenue bonds yield far less construction money for a given amount raised. Positing a $56 million net construction figure (for illustration), a general-obligation bond issue of $60 million would have to be floated to net that amount, while under lease-revenue financing an $80 million issue would be required to net a similar amount. Together with its higher interest rates, the larger lease-revenue issue would require annual payments of $6.9 million, while under a general-obligation issue annual payments would be only $4.8 million. Over the twenty-five-year life of the bonds, total payments would equal $188 million versus $124 million—a $64 million difference.

The reason the Select Committee chose lease-revenue bonds apparently is the same as the one used by the Redevelopment Agency for the last decade: the voters would not approve so large a bond issue for the convention facility and other YBC elements. The upshot is that an end run around the taxpayers is once again being tried, and if it's successful they'll have to pay an additional $64 million because of the maneuver. Public resistance to the lease-revenue bond game led the President of San Francisco's Board of Supervisors to sponsor the successful ballot measure that calls for most future lease-revenue bonds to receive voter approval (although only a simple majority, rather than the two-thirds majority general-obligation bonds require). The YBC bonds may escape this new protective law under a grandfather clause, but this remains to be seen.

A further cost of the YBC financing plan has to do with the effect that bond issues (whatever their type) of this magnitude have on the city's overall credit rating and bonding capacity. At the same time the new YBC plan is being pushed forward, the city is floating $240 million in sewer-reconstruction bonds. With the city very close to its bonded-indebtedness limit, the huge YBC bond issue may make it impossible to issue future bonds for other purposes, and may also lead to higher interest for future issues—the New York City disease.

THE ISSUE OF JOBS

One of the big selling points for Yerba Buena Center has always been that it means jobs—temporary jobs for construction workers as well as permanent employment. The Redevelopment Agency, Convention and Visitors Bureau, and other project boosters have been prodigious in their claims: the number usually bandied about was somewhere between 30,000 and 36,000 jobs. Not until the state and federal environmental impact reports appeared was it clear how many *new* jobs might be involved: the vast majority of all YBC employment would be in office buildings, and official reports acknowledged that YBC office construction merely would absorb construction that otherwise would occur in other parts of the city; therefore none of that employment could be considered to have been generated by YBC. Similarly, much of the employment—the apparel mart, for example—was merely shifting existing jobs from one location to another. The EIR estimated that the original plan would directly create only 3,600 new jobs, with another 5,100 indirectly created.[14] Research carried out for the Mayor's Select Committee pared these figures down even further, and their substitute plan, designed to maximize job creation, estimates only 4,600 new jobs citywide, generated indirectly as well as directly. The principal facilities are the least valuable in terms of job generation: most notably, the convention center, the largest, most expensive element of YBC, would directly create a mere 281 jobs.

The claims and discussions about job creation have uniformly ignored the jobs and businesses that had been lost as a result of YBC.
Some 723 businesses and 7,600 jobs were displaced from the Yerba
Buena Center site. That work force consisted primarily of small pro-
prietors and skilled, semiskilled, and unskilled workers in diversified
light manufacturing, specialized printing, warehousing, transient hotels, and service institutions. The average age of the businesses was
twenty years, and at the time of a 1963 Redevelopment Agency survey,
fully 90 percent of all businesses stated they planned to remain at
their location.[15] The advantages of the area were central location, access to freeways, ties to the local market and pedestrian traffic, and low
rent.

No official data are available on what has happened to these businesses and jobs. A sample survey indicates that the pattern found in
other cities with respect to business relocation was true for Yerba
Buena.[16] The larger businesses with regional markets and some risk
capital were able to survive the move and often improve their conditions. Marginal and highly localized businesses, frequently operated by
elderly or minority-group owners, rarely survived the move. They had
neither the time nor resources to search for another site, lacked the
ability to build up another business, and were dependent on familiar
customers and the goodwill they had built up over the years. Perhaps
the hardest for these persons was the five-to-ten-year period of uncertainty and reduced business, as the neighborhood deteriorated and
their clientele moved out. Many businesses that did relocate report
lower incomes and higher rents, and not in all cases were all costs of
moving reimbursed. Several of the larger businesses that relocated
moved out of the city altogether. Clearly, the project has meant the loss
of many blue-collar jobs and businesses owned by persons with low
incomes and few alternative resources.

Important questions also have to be raised about the kinds of jobs
and economic base which Yerba Buena Center is helping to create.
White-collar office jobs will go primarily to white, middle-class, suburban commuters. In the years 1963–1968 the number of jobs held by
commuters in the central business district rose by 28 percent while the
number of jobs held by San Franciscans in the same area rose by 1 percent. Well over 90 percent of all new white-collar jobs in San Francisco
are going to commuters.[17] Convention-center and related hotel jobs
would go primarily to the city's Black, Chicano, and Asian population,

as busboys, bellhops, maintenance personnel, and the other tasks associated with servicing and cleaning up after conventioneers and visitors. Although three-fifths of the hotel and restaurant jobs in the city are now held by minority workers, the higher-paying and more prestigious jobs—waiters, headwaiters, bartenders, etc.—are held almost exclusively by whites.[18] The project thus will maintain and perpetuate the existing patterns of occupational hierarchy by race. The short-term construction jobs will go largely to out-of-towners; these jobs rarely provide new opportunities for the unemployed working class who suffer from the exodus of manufacturing and trade jobs. Nonwhites also will find few opportunities for construction employment save in the lower occupational levels, for instance as laborers and hod-carriers. An extensive visual survey of downtown construction sites in San Francisco undertaken recently indicated that fewer than 10 percent of construction jobs are held by minority workers.

Taken in conjunction with the nature of jobs and businesses destroyed, the pattern of job creation in Yerba Buena Center underscores the project's role in hastening the drain of blue-collar employment from the city and bringing about the conversion of the city into the administrative headquarters of the West and the Pacific Basin. In the process, the city's poor, unemployed, and nonwhites—an ever-increasing proportion of the population—find themselves pushed out and around to make room for these new activities and derive little benefit from the employment that is thereby created.

CONVENTION CITY?

A related issue is the wisdom of the city's increasing reliance on the tourism, convention, and entertainment business to buttress its economy. "Tourism is San Francisco's largest industry," as the Convention and Visitors Bureau proclaims. It is unclear how much *new* convention business Yerba Buena Center will bring to the city (and how much existing business that otherwise would leave the city will be retained by virtue of the new facility). The EIR notes that ". . . a significant portion of the convention and show activity which will utilize Yerba Buena will be conventions and shows which could have utilized the existing Brooks Hall facility" ("Yerba Buena Center," 1973, p. III-4). The only figures available are given out by the Convention and Visitors Bureau, an outspoken partisan in the fight for the Center, and not surprisingly these figures tend to be highly exaggerated. The EIR (p. V-A-80) observes that "it is very difficult to estimate the net new conventions and consumer shows that would come to San Francisco as a result of YBC's existence. To date, a thoroughgoing market analysis concerning San Francisco's market share of the tourism and convention industry in the United States has not been completed." A recent memo to the mayor from the director of the city's Office of Community Development noted: "Convention business in San Francisco could double or decrease in the coming years based on a number of variables" (Memorandum to George Moscone, p. 10).

In order to reach their roseate projections showing how much the city needs the new convention hall, the Convention and Visitors Bureau and the Redevelopment Agency's consultants assumed that the average annual rate of growth in San Francisco's convention industry during the 1960s—6 percent—would continue through 1985, producing an increase in the number of conventions from 397 in 1960, to 646 in 1970, to 950 in 1975, to 1,250 in 1980, to 1,550 in 1985! No basis was given for these assumptions, and the fact that from 1966 to 1970 the number of conventions coming to San Francisco actually dropped from 688 to 646 was totally disregarded in this averaging and projection game.

But to whatever extent convention business is increased because of the new facilities, it must also be recognized that this form of economic activity is susceptible to fluctuation according to the up's and down's of the general economy. The sharp fall-off of both convention and tourist activity in 1969 was a powerful reminder of this vulnerability (S.F. Convention and Visitors Bureau). A new source of instability and uncertainty to the tourist trade is limitations on travel that might ensue from what is loosely referred to as "the energy crisis." The February 19, 1974, *San Francisco Chronicle* quoted one travel organization executive as follows: "Quite simply, without adequate transportation, the tourism industry is stopped dead in its tracks." A major impact of Yerba Buena Center may be to weaken the city's economic base by decreasing the diversity of the city's economy and by concentrating the new base on unstable industries.

Moreover, the approach to conventioneering and tourism embodied in the Yerba Buena project and similar centers across the country—creation of a special, protected zone unrelated to the rest of the city—

suggests a set of values that ignores the area's most pressing problems. Yerba Buena Center means expenditure of renewal funds on a self-contained convention-tourist complex within which the representatives of the business and professional community can convene—safe from the dangers and problems of the urban society outside, which continues to deteriorate precisely because of that pattern of expenditure and building by the city which favors a haven for conventioneers over much-needed housing and services for its own citizens.

SOME BLIND SPOTS IN RENEWAL THEORY

One of the central canons of urban renewal is that, in addition to being a program to revitalize the city through new development, it is also a program to clear slums and thereby reduce or eliminate the costs associated with slums. A basic aim of Yerba Buena Center is to "cure" the "social maladjustment" and "undesirable environment" through clearance of the area and relocation of the residents (S.F. Redevelopment Agency, 1965). It should be obvious that the social problems that produce and are produced by "slum environments" (apart from the issue of how that term may legitimately be defined) do not disappear with the destruction of the physical site labeled "slum" or "blighted."[19] The larger effect of such displacement may be merely to shift or actually increase the costs of public services. Because neighborhoods like the South of Market area that offer low-rent housing and accessibility to supportive facilities are in short and diminishing supply in the city, dispersal of displacees (which might conceivably have reduced the strain on public services and hence costs) did not occur. Instead, the Yerba Buena project has merely moved the bump along the carpet by creating conditions of overcrowding and deterioration in two adjacent low-rent areas. The various public costs for welfare and social services may actually increase with forced relocation—which disrupts social networks, mutual-assistance patterns, and support systems, particularly among the elderly.[20]

Many of the financial and social costs of slum clearance are borne privately by displacees. Rent increases for persons displaced between December, 1969, and December, 1972, averaged $36 per month.[21] If these figures are true for the displaced population as a whole, the total added rent bill caused by the Yerba Buena Center relocation will be around $1 million per year.[22] Although a portion of this amount is off-set by the short-term relocation payments which some displacees receive (these last four years after which the displacee is left to fend for himself), the private bill being borne by this segment of the population that can least afford such costs is immense. Other costs include moving expenses that are not reimbursed, furnishings, and opportunity costs involved in finding a new place to live. The overall housing conditions of the relocated population doubtless improved, but the costs of these improvements were borne by people whose inability to afford higher rents was demonstrated by their previous housing conditions. And these improved housing conditions may not last long, since one of the likely effects of the project is the "probable future displacement of some South of Market residents [those relocated from the Yerba Buena area, as well as Filipino and Black families living in adjacent areas] as a result of private development stimulated by the project and as a result chiefly of parking-lot construction where older housing now exists outside the project area" ("Yerba Buena Center," 1973, p. S-21).

A second unquestioned assumption of renewal theory is that improvement in the tax base generally benefits the city's population as a whole. In order for increased tax revenues to benefit the average person, taxes would have to be lowered or the quality of city services improved. Neither of these is a likely outcome from the Yerba Buena project. The rest of the city's population derives no benefit if the increased taxes from Yerba Buena Center are used to pay off the Yerba Buena Center bonds and cover increased costs of servicing the population it will generate. But a further issue relates to the changes in assessed valuations, which usually are designated as a benefit in most cost-benefit analyses of redevelopment. It is assumed by proponents of redevelopment that any increase in land value benefits the community as a whole because it indicates that the land is being put to a higher or more efficient use. San Francisco Redevelopment Agency reports highlighted the fact that the YBC project would increase the assessed value of improvements for every dollar of assessed value of land from $1.24 to $10–$12 (1965, p. 26). For commercial enterprises and speculative landholders, such increases are welcome. New and bigger buildings imply more profits even if they also involve increased real estate taxes. But for users and owners of residential land, as well as small businesses, these value increases tend to be harmful, because they lead to higher rents and taxes. As land values rise, the possibility of constructing and rehabilitating low- and moderate-income housing is further dimmed. High land values lead to intensive, highrise development and the destruction of existing uses. For example, in the Mission District, a low-to-moderate-rent Latino area, land value increases precipitated by construction of the Bay Area Rapid Transit line and stations in the neighborhood are resulting in replacement of existing homes, stores, and community institutions with more profitable uses and consequent destruction of a cohesive ethnic neighborhood (Heins, pp. 73–84).

"THE BOTTOM LINE"

Public intervention of the type represented by the urban-renewal program can be seen simplistically as a measure to "improve" the usage of land; it forcibly acts to change use from one class of users and beneficiaries to another. The Yerba Buena story suggests that besides intensifying the roots of urban conflict, this type of change is detrimental to the vast majority of the city's inhabitants.

The Yerba Buena project originated with and has been supported by certain well-defined segments within the city's business community, those parts of the ruling class whose aim is the rapid development of San Francisco as the financial and commercial center for the western United States and the Pacific Basin. The San Francisco Redevelopment Agency is carrying out the plan in part as a representative of this community, in part because the Agency assumes that the goals it is fostering represent the interests of the city as a whole.[23] The Agency believes without question that projects beneficial to business interests benefit the whole economy of San Francisco and therefore all the people of San Francisco. In reality, however, the aggregate benefits are private benefits, reaped by a small segment of the "public," while the vast majority of the public—the working class and most of the middle class—either benefits only marginally from the project or is actually hurt by it, either through increased taxes or more directly by incurring displacement and relocation costs.

The method the Agency and city use to calculate and advertise the potential results of Yerba Buena Center represents a peculiar form of cost-benefit analysis. The criterion for project approval is usually whether or not the project's aggregate benefits—narrowly defined, pre-

cisely quantified, and confidently predicted—are greater than the bud-
geted costs; the methodology represents a comparison of revenues and
expenditures rather than of real benefits and costs. Costs that are difficult to calculate or express in quantitative terms (e.g., social costs) are
simply ignored. Benefits are calculated through long-term projections
based on inadequate or tenuous premises. Despite the tentative nature
of these projections, they are offered to the public and to the public's
elected representatives as if the predicted future were guaranteed. The
Agency and the city consciously suppressed known or likely negative
effects and the tenuous quality of their projections.

The Board of Supervisors, which is elected to represent the public and must pass on the renewal plan and its financing scheme, in
large part agrees with the assumptions and reflect the interests of the
elite who are behind the Yerba Buena project. The Board also tends to
entrust "technical details" to the Redevelopment Agency, the city administration, and others presumed to have the necessary technical
skills. The word of high-powered bureaucrats, backed by consultants'
reports, is accepted at face value in the confusing world of financing
and planning projections. One Supervisor expressed his great skepti-
cism about the financing plan and the Yerba Buena project as a whole:
"When the financing plan came up before the Board, I asked for a
two-week delay because we had no time to study the proposal. But I
voted yes on the plan finally because of the recommendation of the
Finance Committee. But I really had no idea what was in the plan.
. . . Once a project reaches the financial stage it becomes almost unstoppable. . . . I am not at all confident in the projections he [the
city's Chief Administrative Officer] gave us." Another Supervisor remarked: "If you really want me to tell you, we have very little control
over the Redevelopment Agency. . . . Most people in this city don't
know much about Yerba Buena Center. . . . I am disturbed something
this big is not going on the ballot." Because the financing scheme allegedly does not require a public vote on the bond issue (this was the
principal reason underlying its design), the necessity to explain and
support the financial projections and the consequences of any errors
was substantially diminished. Because the interests of the average taxpayer and those immediately affected by the demolition and displacement are unrepresented in this process, it is not surprising that the
costs and benefits of Yerba Buena Center are skewed in the manner
we have shown.

The issue is not "rational" or "efficient" land-use planning. The process used in planning Yerba Buena Center was highly rational from the point of view of its ruling-class supporters, and the only inefficiencies were the roadblocks unexpectedly thrown in the project's path by several groups of outside opponents. From the point of view of the working class and large segments of the middle class, the problem with the planning of YBC was not its irrationality but that it was planned by those whose interests are fundamentally in opposition to their interests.

NOTES

1. For a more complete discussion of the economic theory of redevelopment, see Rothenberg (1967) and Edel (1971).
2. See Hartman *et al.* (1974). More recent moves by YBC supporters and opponents, some of which are discussed in this article, have been regularly reported in *Common Sense*, a San Francisco newsmonthly. See the following articles by Chester Hartman and/or Mike Davis: "Yerba Buena: Survival of the Fattest," April, 1974; "Green Light for Yerba Buena Center?" November, 1974; "Yerba Buena: Blank Check at the End of the Tunnel," April, 1975; "Yerba Buena: The Crunch Is On," May, 1975; "Sports Arena Swindle," September, 1975; "Making Sport with Our Money," December, 1975–January, 1976; "YBC: A New Ballgame," April, 1976; "Mayor's Committee on YBC: People's Politics—or Another Sham?" May, 1976; "Mayor's Comm. Halts YBC Arena," June, 1976; "Yerba Buena Center: It's Now or Never," July–August, 1976; "Yerba Buena Hoax," September, 1976; "The $207 Million Question," October, 1976; "Yerba Buendoggle Wins" and "YBC Foes Sue Supervisors: Voters' Handbook Censored," November, 1976.
3. "Yerba Buena Center" (1972), pp. H-1 to H-7 and Table, "Sources of Direct Income," p. H-10.
4. The Cow Palace, however, benefits from a $300,000 annual state subsidy.
5. Assumptions and "promises" of this nature are promiscuously made. In the November, 1972, elections the voters of Santa Clara County, forty miles south of San Francisco, approved a general-obligation bond issue for construction of a sports arena. One of the arguments used by supporters of the bond issue was that the Warriors and Seals would play many of their home games in the new facility.
6. See San Francisco Redevelopment Agency (1971), Exhibit II, Attachment A.
7. For a general description of the economic and other effects of intensive development in downtown San Francisco, see Brugmann and Sletteland.
8. The report attributes to Yerba Buena Center development all property taxes from hotel construction (anywhere in the city) built in anticipa-

tion of YBC becoming a reality. See "Yerba Buena Center" (1973), Table C-17.

9. This calculation is based on the difference between (a) actual revenues, as determined by the actual annual amount of revenue from land and improvements in the Yerba Buena area from 1965 to 1972 and the Redevelopment Agency's figures on what these amounts will be for 1973–1976, minus whatever tax-increment revenue over the 1965 base figure is estimated; and (b) projected revenues, as determined by utilizing the 1965 base figure and projecting a minimal growth rate for assessed valuations in the area equal to the citywide rate (1 percent per year). The method of tax-loss calculation is adopted from Ford (1971).

The urban renewal financing formula allows the city credit for foregone tax revenues in paying back the federal loan, but the amount of this credit for the Yerba Buena project, some $1.2 million, is considerably smaller than the city's actual loss, and one-third of this credit is paid for by the city through its local contribution. The tax credit is based solely on the value of the structure and ends when the structure is torn down; no credit is given for the value of the land.

10. "Yerba Buena Center" (1973), Tables A-42, A-43.

11. "Already there are indications that vacancies are on the rise, especially in older buildings. This could result in financial distress for older buildings and, carried to the extreme, eventual abandonment." *Ibid.*, p. V-B-27.

12. This last-named suit was decided against the plaintiffs in late 1975 and is now before the California Court of Appeals. This issue may become moot if the city rescinds the lease agreement that triggered the suit.

13. For a good treatment of the dynamics and effects of intercity competition in the world of professional sports, see Sethi (1971).

14. "Yerba Buena Center" (1973), p. S-17, Table A-61.

15. See Branaman, p. 6.

16. A sample of sixty relocated businesses was surveyed and interviewed for this study, under the direction of Prof. Roger Crawford, Department of Geography, San Francisco State University. For a review of business relocation experience, see Zimmer.

17. Wells Fargo Bank, p. 11, Table I.

18. In March, 1973, the Federal Equal Employment Opportunity Commission brought suit in federal court against the San Francisco and East Bay locals of the Bartenders International Union for alleged racial discrimination, charges brought by the Commission as far back as 1967. And in the same month a federal suit was brought by the Employment Law Center against the Waiters' and Dairy Lunchmen's Union and several hotels and restaurants, charging racial discrimination in the hiring and assignment of waiters; the local named as defendant has only 25 Blacks among its 3,000 members. As of this writing (1977), a consent decree requiring affirmative action and back pay had been written and was expected to be signed, ending the suit against the bartenders' union; a similar settlement was expected in the suit against the waiters' union.

19. "Slum clearance projects themselves generates effects that are adding impetus to a process that results in the cumulative development of blight in the older, low-rent neighborhoods outside clearance areas" (Gruen).

20. For one attempt at an evaluation of the full costs and benefits associated

with an urban renewal project, see Ford; on the social and personal impacts, see Fried.

21. This dollar figure was included in a first-draft copy of the Environmental Impact Report but was dropped from the published version in favor a more general statement about rent changes.

22. Study of Boston's West End urban renewal project suggests that the increased housing costs for relocatees may have been as much as $2,000 per family (Ford, p. 85). Downs (p. 223) has made the following calculation regarding privately borne costs of displacement: "Present practices regarding residential households displaced by highways and urban renewal projects will unfairly impose uncompensated costs . . . averaging from $812 to $1,194 per household for each of the estimated 192,800 households involved. The median income of these households is probably around $4,000 per year. Therefore *the average uncompensated loss which each is compelled to suffer amounts to confiscation of from 20 to 30 percent of one year's income.*" (Emphasis in original.)

23. According to a US Dept. of Housing and Urban Development official, "[Justin] Herman [the Redevelopment Agency's high-powered executive director from 1959 until his death in 1971] could move rapidly on renewal—demolition or construction—because he was absolutely confident that he was doing what the power structure wanted insofar as the poor and minorities were concerned. . . . That's why San Francisco has mostly luxury housing and business district projects—that's what middle-class planners and businessmen envision as ideal urban renewal" (Lilley).

REFERENCES

Branaman, Marybeth, *South of Market Commercial and Industrial Survey* (San Francisco: San Francisco Redevelopment Agency, July 1963).

Brugmann, Bruce, and Greggar Sletteland, eds., *The Ultimate Highrise: San Francisco's Mad Rush Toward the Sky* (San Francisco: San Francisco Bay Guardian Books, 1971).

Burck, Charles G., "The Superstadium Game," *Fortune,* March 1973.

Development Research Associates, *Transient Housing Study* (Prepared for San Francisco Redevelopment Agency, 1970).

Downs, Anthony, *Urban Problems and Prospects* (Chicago: Markham Publishing Co., 1970).

Edel, Matthew, "Urban Renewal and Land Use Conflicts," *Review of Radical Political Economics,* Summer 1971.

Ford, Edward J., Jr., "Benefit-Cost Analysis and Urban Renewal in the West End of Boston," (Doctoral dissertation, Boston College, 1971).

Fried, Marc, "Grieving for a Lost Home," in L. J. Duhl, ed., *The Urban Condition* (New York: Basic Books, 1963).

Gruen, Claude, "Urban Renewal's Role in the Genesis of Tomorrow's Slums," *Land Economics,* Aug. 1963.

Hartman, Chester, *et al., Yerba Buena: Land Grab and Community Resistance in San Francisco* (San Franciso: Glide Publications, 1974).

Heins, Marjorie, *Strictly Ghetto Property* (Berkeley: Ramparts Press, 1972).

Lilley, William, III, "Herman Death Ends an Era," *National Journal,* Sept. 18, 1971.

Memorandum to George Moscone, Mayor, from James P. Jaquet, Director, Office of Community Development. Subject: Options for Yerba Buena Center, January 13, 1976.

Rothenberg, Jerome, *Economic Evaluation of Urban Renewal* (Washington, D.C.: Brookings Institution, 1967).

San Francisco Convention and Visitors Bureau *Annual Reports* (1965–1975).

San Francisco Redevelopment Agency, *Redevelopment Plan for Yerba Buena Area Project D-1,* Dec. 1965.

San Francisco Redevelopment Agency, "Presentation to the San Francisco Board of Supervisors," Feb. 18, 1971.

Sethi, S. Prakash, "Corporate Decisions and Their Effects on Urban Communities—The Milwaukee Braves, Atlanta: Indiscriminate Moving of Sports Franchises," in *Up Against the Corporate Wall* (Englewood Cliffs, N.J.: Prentice-Hall, 1971).

Wells Fargo Bank, N. A., *San Francisco Central Business District: A Growth Study,* Feb. 1970.

"Yerba Buena Center Public Facilities: A Description of the Scope, Character, Financing, and Leasing Plans for the Public Facilities," submitted by Thomas J. Mellon, Chief Administrative Officer, March 6, 1972.

"Yerba Buena Center Public Facilities and Private Development, Environmental Impact Report," draft submitted to the City and County of San Francisco by Arthur D. Little, Inc. and URS Research Co., May 1973.

Zimmer, Basil, *Rebuilding Cities: The Effects of Displacement and Relocation on Small Business* (Chicago: Quadrangle Books, 1964).

Housing, Mortgage Lending, and the Contradictions of Capitalism

MICHAEL E. STONE

This paper focuses on the relationship between housing costs and incomes in the United States, and the consequences of the particular ways that capitalism has tried to cope with this problem. Despite the tremendous growth of the forces of production in the United States, an extremely large proportion of the population is still unable to afford "a decent home and a suitable living environment."[1] The problem is partly caused by the extremely high cost of housing, which is generated by the various elements of the housing market. But it is also the result of the extremely unequal distribution of income produced by the labor market.

Capitalism cannot solve the problem of incomes and housing costs because the required redistribution of income would lead to the collapse of the labor market, while the required reduction of housing costs would lead to the collapse of the housing market. The housing problem is thus due to an inherent contradiction between the requirements of these two basic institutions. The evolution of the housing sector in the twentieth century—particularly the growth of the mort-

* This paper is a revised version of Stone (1975), containing both more historical and more recent data and analysis, while excluding some material on the role of the state. Copyright © 1977 by Michael E. Stone.

gage system and the extensive intervention of the government—can be understood as attempts to manage this contradiction in the interests of capital.

In the long run these attempts have not only failed to solve the housing problem, but have actually generated some very serious economic and political problems. The stability of the entire financial structure has become interwoven with the stability of the huge residential mortgage debt created by the evolution of the mortgage system. Since the mortgage payments on this debt constitute the biggest single component of most families' housing costs, the increasing difficulty in paying for the high cost of housing threatens the mortgage system—and the rest of the financial system—with collapse. This linkage has made housing a significant contributor to the crisis of capitalism in the 1970s, and also has made the housing sector especially vulnerable to the crisis. The growing dependence of capitalism on the ability and willingness of people to continue to pay the mortgage debt-service costs—directly as homeowners and through rents as tenants—has given housing unprecedented significance.

THE HOUSING PROBLEM

In broad terms, the housing problem can be described as follows: there are not enough dwelling units in decent condition, at bearable prices, with required amenities and secure tenure, at accessible locations, in safe and congenial communities with adequate services and facilities. Some quantitative sense of the depth and scope of the problem is also needed, though, to guide the search for causes and the definition of a solution. For if the problem is found to be pervasive and persistent, then its sources will have to be sought within the very institutional structure of the society and not in some aberration or maladjustment in the normal functioning of the system.

Quantitative measurements of the housing problem, such as those derived by the Joint Center for Urban Studies, inevitably ignore certain aspects of the problem which are too hard to measure, but these figures provide at least a starting point for analysis. The Joint Center study, carried out under contract with the federal government, found that in 1970 a total of 13.1 million U.S. households—more than 20 percent of all households in the country—were suffering from one or more forms of "housing deprivation." This total included households in three partially overlapping categories, as follows: 6.9 million in "physically inadequate" housing units; 1.2 million "overcrowded" households; and 6.9 million renter households with a "high rent burden."

As extensive as the problem appears from this study, the definitions used for the categories of "housing deprivation"—conventional definitions used in other studies as well—actually tend to understate the extent of the problem. Most significantly, the official and generally accepted standard for determining "high rent burden"—or more broadly "shelter poverty" to cover homeowners as well as tenants— is that any household paying over 25 percent of its income for shelter is spending more than it should (U.S., Congress, 1971). This standard is completely unrealistic for millions of working-class families, whether they are considered poor or middle-income. Quite apart from variations in individual situations, it is apparent that, in general, the lower the income and the greater the number of people in a household, the smaller the proportion of income they can afford for housing. For some families, 15 percent of their income is too much to have to spend for housing. For some, even 5 percent is too much if they are to meet their other needs out of their meager incomes.

Shelter costs are the most rigid and inflexible of all consumption expenditures. Sudden changes in the income of a family, especially downward changes, are generally reflected immediately in adjustments of the amount spent for other items, including food, but not in the amount spent for housing. When shelter costs go up, it is not easy to reduce or substitute the housing services consumed—at least in the short run—so other expenditures have to be reduced: when the rent or property taxes go up, a family cannot, for example, readily give up its living room or switch to a cheaper brand of bathroom.

Furthermore, the amount a household can and does pay for shelter is strongly correlated with where it lives geographically. This relationship affects not only the quality of the housing people occupy, but also access to jobs, to commercial facilities, the quality of schools and other public services, and the character of the physical and social environment. The squeeze between shelter costs and incomes is thus central not only to the housing problem, but to working-class living standards in general.

Defining and Measuring Shelter Poverty

As the previous discussion implies, a rational standard for determining how much a household can afford for shelter needs to reflect differences in income, on the one hand, and variations in expenditures for nonshelter necessities, like food, clothing, and medical care, plus taxes, on the other. Although every household has its own unique expenses and conditions of life, the standard budgets computed periodically by the U.S. Bureau of Labor Statistics (BLS) provide a set of typical living costs for households of various sizes and composition. The "lower budget" in this series defines a minimum adequate standard of living.

The BLS lower budget can be used to determine the maximum amount, on average, a household of a given income and size can afford for shelter and still meet its other needs at this minimum adequate level. For each household size and level of income, the calculation involves subtracting from income the sum of all nonshelter consumption expenditures in the BLS lower budget plus personal taxes corresponding to that income and household size.

This approach reveals that in 1970, for example, a family of four would have needed an income of nearly $8,500 to be able to afford 25 percent of its income for shelter. Indeed, if their income was $5,500 or less, they could not have afforded to pay anything for shelter. By 1975, prices had gone up so much that no four-person household with an income of $11,500 or less could have afforded to spend 25 percent of its income for shelter and still meet its other needs at the BLS minimum level. Four-person households under $8,000 could not have afforded anything for shelter in 1975 if they were to meet their other needs at a minimally adequate level. Clearly the conventional standard of 25 percent of income hides the actual hardship faced by low and even middle-income households that may be paying less than 25 percent of their income for shelter, but which still are "shelter poor" because their housing costs leave them insufficient resources for meeting their other needs at even a minimum level of adequacy.

The extent of shelter poverty, based on the income-dependent standard just described, has been estimated from 1970 Census data. In 1970 over 16 million households—8 million renter households and over 8 million homeowner households—were paying more for shelter than they could afford. This was more than one-fourth of all households in the United States and more than 40 percent of all households with incomes of under $10,000 during the previous year. Over one-third of all renter households—nearly half of all renter households under $10,000— were shelter-poor in 1970. Since 1970 shelter poverty has become even more pervasive because of unprecedented inflation and the worst depression since the 1930s.

Shelter Poverty and Capitalist Institutions

The problem of shelter poverty cannot be separated from the problem of income distribution. The forces of production in the United States have developed to the point where the level of personal income is, on average, more than $20,000 a year for every family of four in the country. Of course most families are far below this average because the structure of the labor market distributes the total income of the nation very unequally.

Under capitalism human labor power is a commodity. Most people need to sell their labor power for a wage in order to be able to obtain housing and other necessities. Clearly it is in the immediate interests of capitalists to have wages at the lowest possible level that will maintain the quantity and quality of workers they seek to employ. In the long run, the minimum level of wages certainly must be at least at the level of subsistence that will maintain and reproduce the working class. The capitalist is indifferent, though, about whether these wages are adequate for his or her workers to purchase the necessities of life at a level equivalent, for example, to the BLS lower budget. Class struggle and the demand for various kinds of skilled labor have certainly enabled many workers to achieve incomes above the bare subsistence level, but the labor market still tends to keep the incomes of most families as low as possible.

On the other side, under capitalism the price of housing is determined by the structure of the housing market. Since housing is both a commodity and a necessity, its price is basically determined by the relationship between people's ability to pay and investors' expectation of profits. That is, if the price of housing rises, people generally have to pay, but they obviously cannot pay more than they have. If the market price of existing housing is much lower than the cost of producing new housing, it is not profitable for capitalists to produce new housing. Indeed it may not be profitable to keep some existing housing on the market. The shortage may force some people to double up and may drive the price of existing housing up toward the cost of new housing, but the price is ultimately limited by people's incomes.

While the conflict between high housing costs and inadequate incomes has a depressing effect on the quantity and quality of housing, it also exerts an upward pressure on wages. Capitalists in the housing sector may be indifferent about whether the price of housing leaves households with enough income to pay for other necessities, but they do want buyers who can pay their price. Workers, in turn, struggle for higher wages to pay the price required to produce and provide their shelter and also to meet their families' other needs.

There is no way that capitalism can resolve the conflict between the labor market and housing market. In order to eliminate shelter poverty and prop up the housing market, every household would have to be guaranteed an income at least equal to the BLS lower budget. For a family of four this was $7,000 in 1970 and about $10,000 in 1975 (U.S. Bureau of Labor Statistics, 1972 and 1976). Labor would then take a bigger share of the nation's productive output; profits would decline, leading to reduced investment and reduced production. At least as importantly, with no unemployment and no low-wage jobs, capital would lose its power over labor. The working class could no longer be maintained in a subordinate position by job competition and insecurity. This solution would thus lead to the collapse of the labor market, the central institution of capitalism.

On the other hand, if a large proportion of American families continue to have insufficient incomes, the housing market will collapse, as it already has in many urban neighborhoods where housing stands abandoned. More generally, to eliminate shelter poverty without disturbing the labor market, the price of housing would have to be set at a level the occupants realistically can afford after paying for their other necessities. Housing prices would be driven down, in many cases to zero. Property values would collapse, and private investment in housing would cease. Mortgage payments would stop on many buildings, leading to collapse of the mortgage system, and with it much of the financial structure of capitalism. While such a collapse would wipe out a portion of real estate values and mortgage debt, as it did in the 1930s, for example, it would also bring production to a halt. Vast unemployment would not resolve the conflict between incomes and housing costs.

Shelter poverty is thus more than a social problem incidental to the basic functioning of the economic system. It will not be eliminated simply through growth in the capitalist economy or modest government assistance. Rather, it must be recognized as the result of an inherent contradiction between some of the most basic institutions of capitalism —a contradiction which the system cannot resolve without bringing about the demise of capitalism itself.

THE STATE AND THE HOUSING SYSTEM

Although capitalism has not been able to resolve the contradiction between labor and housing markets, it has not been able to ignore the problem either, because it undermines the housing market, adds to the wage costs of employers, and is a potential political threat to the orderly functioning of the system. Thus, over the past half century it has become increasingly necessary for the capitalist state—particularly the federal government—to intervene in the housing sector to try to manage the conflict in the interests of capital.

On the one hand, this intervention has been defensive. The state has attempted to relieve some of the economic pressure on the housing and labor markets and defuse the contradiction socially and ideologically so that it will not become a source of political consciousness and action. At the same time, state action has also sought to serve the interests of capitalist offensively—stimulating profits and capital accumulation in housing and related sectors of the economy, in order to counteract the depressing effect of inadequate incomes on the housing market.

Defending the System

The principal element in capitalism's defensive strategy has been the promotion of mortgaged homeownership through the development of the long-term, low-down-payment mortgage loan. The U.S. National Commission on Urban Problems has clearly stated the ideological objective: "Homeownership encourages social stability and financial responsibility. It gives the homeowner a financial stake in society. . . . It helps eliminate the 'alienated tenant' psychology" (p. 401). The way in which the long-term mortgage has furthered this goal within the constraints of the income–housing cost problem is explained below in the section on the mortgage system. This strategy could never have been implemented, though, without substantial state support. Mortgage guarantees through the Federal Housing Administration (FHA) and Veterans Administration (VA) have promoted easy lending for and massive construction of housing for owner-occupants. Federal income-tax benefits available to owners but not renters have served in part to reduce housing costs while promoting homeownership.

The success of this strategy is well known. In 1940 only 44 percent of all housing units were owner-occupied; by 1974 the proportion had increased to 65 percent. The number of owner-occupied units increased from 15 million in 1940 to 46 million in 1974, while the number of renter-occupied units increased only from 20 million in 1940 to 25 million in 1974 (U.S. Bureau of the Census, 1975c, Table 1225; 1976b, Table A-1).

The tremendous insecurity of renting, plus the apparent economic and social benefits of ownership, have made homeownership the desired goal of most families. State intervention has made this goal realizable for the majority of people, even as it mitigated the benefits and served the larger interests of capital. Homeowners' interests have become tied to those of landlords and lenders. They tend to become concerned about property values, hoping they will rise indefinitely, and resenting the intrusion of "undesirable" neighbors. Homeowners become tied to a location, not able to move freely and negotiate most powerfully their conditions of employment. They become reluctant to jeopardize the stability of their incomes through strikes or other militant actions, fearing foreclosure and consequent loss of both their shelter and their investment.

Mortgaged ownership could not, however, be a viable strategy for families with incomes so unstable or marginal that they could not be expected to support or be constrained by a large, long-term debt. Some defensive action by the state has therefore been necessary to cope with the threat of the housing problem among those who continue to be "alienated tenants." Public housing has been a major part of the response. Following its initial creation as an employment program in 1937, public housing has actually served in the postwar years as an important device for regulating the poor, often in close conjunction with the welfare system (Piven and Cloward). Large and depressing projects, patronizing and authoritarian management practices, and the threat of eviction into the costly private housing market have made public housing an effective tool for social control.

Public housing and other subsidy programs for "low-income" families generally require tenants to pay about 25 percent of their adjusted incomes for shelter, even though a realistic cost standard, such as that described above, would have them paying little or no rent at all. Thus these programs by no means free the recipients from shelter poverty and often leave the tenants in substandard housing because the public agencies do not use the subsidies to ensure adequate maintenance. Nonetheless, the fear that they will lose their subsidies often provides a remarkably effective damper to tenant action against these oppressive conditions.

Faced with the spread of shelter poverty among "moderate-income" families, who have too much income to qualify for public housing and other "low-income" programs but not enough to be able to buy a house, further defensive action began in the 1960s. The federal government devised programs which subsidize private developers and financiers who provide housing at below market rents. Under these programs, people do not pay shelter costs pegged to their incomes, but instead benefit from the general subsidy to the development. The tenants have thus faced severe rent increases when costs have risen but subsidies have not. In response, they have become some of the best-organized, most militant and politically conscious tenants in the country (Achtenberg and Stone; Brodsky). This situation reveals the danger of a state response which promises to relieve the income–housing-cost problem but cannot in fact do so.

It should not be concluded, though, that the kinds of strategies used to defend capitalism against the housing problem can ever be fully successful. As the discussion below of housing and the crisis of capitalism will show, the opportunities for achieving homeownership are rapidly being narrowed to the rich, and many who bought in the past are losing their illusions and even their homes.

As for the rental strategy, for fiscal year 1976 the U.S. Congress authorized $625 million to subsidize 400,000 families (U.S. Congress, 1975, p. 8). To reach all eligible tenants the program would cost at least $10 billion to $15 billion at current rent levels. Including low-income homeowners under such a housing allowance would bring the annual cost to $25 billion to $35 billion (Cochran and Rucker; Gans). And a program that would go beyond conventional standards of acceptable shelter expenditures toward the elimination of shelter poverty would at least double this figure. Apart from the political impossibility of this government enacting a program of the required magnitude, the fiscal problems of the state will foreclose any remaining dreams of an adequate response. Capitalism is not only unable to resolve the housing contradiction. It is increasingly less able even to defend itself against the problem.

Advancing the Interests of Capital

State intervention in the housing problem has also aided capitalists by stimulating demand, creating investment opportunities, and providing protection against risk, as well as bestowing actual financial assistance.[2] The objective has not only been to aid individual capitalists. The most important goal has been to restore, sustain, and enhance the process of capital accumulation in response to the tendency toward declining profits and depression in the housing sector—a tendency generated by the income–housing-cost conflict.

The capitalist class is, of course, not monolithic or homogeneous. State action thus has not uniformly served the interests of all the types of capitalists in the housing sector. Rather, the patterns of intervention reflect the hierarchy of power within the sector, the power of housing capitalists vis-à-vis other capitalists and the system-preserving goals of the class as a whole.

Within the housing sector, the major beneficiaries of government intervention have been banks and other mortgage lenders, followed by developers, and then landlords and other equity investors. The power, profits, and size of the mortgage-lending industry have grown with the spread of the long-term, low-down-payment mortgage. In addition to FHA and VA mortgage guarantees, the government has created a series of other agencies to channel funds into the housing sector via the mortgage lenders. The Federal Home Loan Bank System (FHLBS), created in the early 1930s, insures savings accounts and provides backup funds to lending institutions. The Federal National Mortgage Association (FNMA), created in the late 1930s, was designed to facilitate the free flow of mortgage money throughout the country and attract additional funds in this way.

The results of state intervention inevitably were contradictory. While the mortgage system grew tremendously, it also generated additional problems, as described in subsequent sections, and made housing especially vulnerable to state actions aimed at stabilizing the capitalist system as a whole. For example, periodically the state acts to cause the overall economy to contract in order to eliminate "imbalances" which develop during the expansionary part of the business cycle. Housing has been forced to bear a disproportionate share of the restraint on capital during these system-preserving contractions, because of the relatively greater power of industrial capital and commercial banks.

Housing capitalists have sought to overcome this relative weakness with the assistance of their segments of the state apparatus. The Government National Mortgage Association (GNMA), the Federal Home Loan Mortgage Corporation (FHLMC), and state housing finance and development agencies have all been created since the 1960s to channel more funds into housing in reaction to this contradiction. In addition to these public agencies, changes in the federal tax laws in the 1960s stimulated private creation of real-estate investment trusts (REITs) and housing partnerships, which also attracted funds by making housing investment more profitable. Ultimately, these efforts by the state have spawned further contradictions, which have contributed significantly to the crisis of capitalism and the depression of the housing industry in the mid-1970s, as explained in the final section.

THE MORTGAGE SYSTEM

Although massive state intervention in housing began in the Great Depression of the 1930s, the need for intervention, and its emphasis on homeownership and mortgages, was more than just a response to the general crisis of the Depression. Since the end of the nineteenth century, the housing system had been evolving rapidly in response to the problem of incomes and housing costs, on the one hand, and certain aspects of the development of modern capitalism, on the other. Most significant was the growth of mortgage lending, which in turn became a major contributor to the collapse into the Depression and to the devastation of the housing market.

Since the 1930s, the mortgage system has become even more crucial in the dynamics of both the housing and financial markets. Mortgage loans are now used to finance the construction of most new housing and the purchase of virtually all new and used housing in this country. The loans must be repaid—with interest—by the residents. Mortgage payments are generally the biggest single element of occupancy costs, accounting for about 30–70 percent of the cost of housing for both tenants and homeowners. The mortgage system exerts a decisive influence over who lives where, how much new housing gets built, and whether neighborhoods survive. Mortgage lending has also been the largest and one of the fastest-growing parts of the entire credit system. It has contributed to economic growth, but also to the increasing problems of housing and the economy.

The Rise of Institutional Mortgage Lending

Between the end of the Civil War and the Great Depression of the 1930s, industrial capitalism brought about a tremendous increase in the forces of production. In 1900 the gross national product was two-and-a-half times what it had been thirty years earlier.[3] By 1929 the economy had grown to five-and-a-half times what it had been in 1900. The tremendous amount of surplus value created could not be absorbed entirely through profitable investment in additional productive capacity. New investment outlets had to be found.

Some of the surplus of course went into imperialist expansion in foreign countries. Some went into speculation—buying and selling existing businesses and real estate. New opportunities were also created, though, by the demographic and social changes created by industrial capitalism. Specifically, the growing urban population created the need for and possibility of profitable investment in housing and public works. All that was required was institutions to assemble and channel the available capital.

One element in the ongoing economic and social process was the growth of managerial, technical, and professional employment. The salaries of these workers provided them with the possibility of some personal savings. Rather than investing directly in capitalist enterprise, they put their money primarily into savings accounts in commercial banks, mutual savings banks, and savings-and-loan associations. In 1867, savings and other time deposits in these types of institutions totaled $300 million. By 1900 they had increased to $3.4 billion, and by 1929 to nearly $35 billion. Savings in financial institutions thus grew at ? much faster rate than the overall economy.

Around the turn of the century, the financial institutions began to invest these growing funds in housing, both the construction of new housing and the buying and selling of existing housing. They did not make equity investments, though, which would have involved part ownership and acceptance of whatever rate of return the real estate market offered. Instead they *lent* money for housing, demanding a specific interest rate and specific term in which the loan had to be repaid. As security for their investments, the lenders required that the real estate itself be pledged as collateral. Since the pledge of property as security for a loan is called a "mortgage," this type of real estate investment is known as mortgage lending.

Mortgage lending had certainly existed prior to the twentieth century, but until then it was not widespread, and most of the loans were made not by financial institutions, but by individuals and nonfinancial businesses. In 1890 less than 30 percent of nonfarm, owner-occupied housing units were mortgaged, and the typical loan was for less than 40 percent of the value of the property.

Between 1900 and 1929, residential, nonfarm mortgage debt grew from $2.9 billion to more than $29 billion. The financial institutions had accounted for just $1.4 billion in 1900, but held $17 billion by 1929. The housing industry and housing market had come to depend vitally on mortgage credit. Mortgage payments had become an integral and rigid part of the cost of occupying most housing. And financial institutions had become the dominant force in housing.

During this period, institutional lenders would generally make loans for no more than 50 percent of the value of a piece of property, so that if they had to foreclose on the mortgage they could be sure of recovering their money by selling the property. The large down payment or "initial equity" needed to obtain a mortgage loan and buy a piece of residential real estate meant that most borrowers were middle-class families with sufficient savings for the down payment and landlords with other sources of equity capital. Most of the urban population thus remained tenants without a vested interest in property and without the great burdens of personal debt.

In addition, most mortgage loans were for terms of just three to five years. During the term the borrower made interest payments to the lender, but usually did not repay any of the loan itself. At the end of the term, the entire loan was due for repayment. Normally the lender would just refinance the loan for another term—perhaps at a higher rate of interest—if he believed that the economic situation of the borrower and the housing market would ensure continued interest payments and maintain the value of the property.

The mortgage system thus came to depend for its survival on continuous economic growth and prosperity. Indeed, the rapid expansion of mortgage credit was a way lenders could contribute to the prosperity they needed to protect their investments. But this was also their undoing. Between 1900 and 1929, residential mortgage debt grew nearly twice as fast as the overall economy. During the 1920s, housing debt grew more than four times as fast as the economy. A larger and larger proportion of the nation's income therefore went to mortgage payments. The potential squeeze between incomes and housing costs was developing into an actual tension between incomes and mortgage payments—and between past debts and future prosperity.

When the economy collapsed at the end of the 1920s, the mortgage system collapsed as well, adding significantly to the speed and depth of the plunge into the Depression. Out of work, residents no longer had the incomes to sustain the same level of housing costs. Homeowners could not keep up their mortgage payments; landlords could not collect enough rent to pay their mortgages. People went to the banks to withdraw their savings, but the banks could not give them the money because it had been invested in mortgages.

The banks foreclosed on about 1.5 million nonfarm properties by the mid-1930s, evicted the residents, but were then unable to sell much of it. Some banks decided not to foreclose, figuring they would eventually be bailed out by the government or by improvement in the economy. Total nonfarm residential debt declined from its peak of about $30 billion in 1930 to about $24 billion in 1935, and increased very little thereafter until the end of World War II. With no funds, residential construction practically came to a halt, and the buying and selling of houses nearly ceased.

The Modern Mortgage System

In order to encourage financial institutions to make loans with low down payments and long terms, indeed to stimulate almost any lending in the 1930s, the federal government had to provide protection and assistance. This included Federal Housing Administration (FHA) mortgage insurance so that the banks would not lose money if borrowers could not pay. It also included the Federal National Mortgage Assocation (FNMA) secondary mortgage market, where lenders could sell some of their FHA-insured mortgages and obtain additional investment funds. To undertake any lending at all, though, the financial institutions needed to obtain savings deposits again. The federal government therefore created deposit insurance in the early 1930s to encourage people to put money into savings accounts. Deposit insurance could not generate savings, though, when people did not have sufficient income to save. Thus savings and other time deposits in 1940 were more than $4 billion below their 1930 peak of over $35 billion.

It took World War II to restart the economy and generate the savings needed to set the restructured mortgage system in motion. By 1946, savings deposits were nearly twice their 1940 level. These new funds, plus housing needs that had been unmet since the Depression began, provided the impetus for the postwar housing and mortgage boom, facilitated by the low-down-payment, long-term, federally backed loan.

The modern mortgage loan typically covers 70–100 percent of the price of the house or apartment building and is for a term of 20 to 40 years. Interest rates are usually fixed for the life of the mortgage, ranging from about 4–6 percent for loans made before the late 1960s to 8–10 percent or more since then (U.S. President, Table B-57). Monthly payments are computed so that the loan will be fully paid off by the end of the term and so that payments will be constant from month to month, with a declining proportion of each payment going for interest as the unpaid balance decreases.

The development of high-ratio (i.e., low-down-payment) loans has made it easier to buy residential real estate by reducing the amount of cash needed for a house of a given price. However, for a given price, higher loan-to-value ratios obviously result in larger monthly mortgage payments unless the repayment term is stretched out. Longer loan terms offset higher loan ratios and substantially increase the sum a borrower's income can support. For example, at the interest rates that prevailed until the late 1960s, a $100 monthly payment would pay for a ten-year loan of only about $9,000–$10,000, but would cover a twenty-year loan for about $14,000–$17,000, or a thirty-year loan for about $17,000–$21,000.

The long-term, low-down-payment mortgage thus undercut the income–housing-cost problem in several ways: economically by both lessening monthly payments for a loan of a given size and reducing the personal savings needed to buy; politically by promoting the illusion of ownership through the reality of debt. In so doing it of course also stimulated the demand for houses and mortgages, which in the post-war period contributed substantially to overall economic growth as well as benefiting the construction and lending industries (Harvey; Stone and Achtenberg, Chap. 3).

The fundamental change in mortgage lending led to the rapid growth of residential mortgage debt on the national balance sheet. Between 1946 and 1965, total debt in the economy more than tripled—from about $400 billion to over $1.2 trillion. Residential mortgage debt was by far the biggest single component of the increase—growing by 760 percent. The dollar increase in residential debt during this period was more than double the dollar increase in federal, state and local, or consumer credit, and nearly twice as great as the total growth of long-term and short-term debt of nonfinancial corporations. In the nine years after 1965, total debt in the economy more than doubled again, and housing continued to be the largest segment of the increase. Over the entire 1946–1974 period, housing debt grew two-and-a-half times as fast as the overall economy, while total private debt grew twice as fast as the gross national product.[4]

The rapid increase in debt was induced in several ways by the change in mortgage-loan ratios and terms. First, higher-ratio loans create more debt even if house prices and market activity do not increase. Second, longer loan terms mean lower rates of repayment in the early years of the loans. For example, at the interest rates that were common until the late 1960s, after five years of amortization 40–45 percent of a ten-year loan had been repaid, but only 15–20 percent of a twenty-year loan, and only 7–9 percent of a thirty-year loan. Thus lenders had to place more and more reliance on new funds, instead of being able to finance new loans primarily out of repayments on old loans. And as interest rates have risen, the rate of repayment has become even lower, thereby accelerating the need for more mortgage money.

The growth of mortgage debt is also attributable to the rapid increase in the demand for housing following World War II. Rising demand was due to economic growth and the rapid increase in the population of metropolitan areas, but was also the result of the easier availability of mortgage credit. Between 1946 and 1974, nearly 44 million new housing units were started (U.S. Bureau of the Census, 1975b, Series N 156, and 1975c, Table 1212). Over 60 percent of the existing stock of housing has been built since World War II, and nearly all of it has been financed with mortgage loans.

The Housing Market and Mortgage Payments

Although mortgage payments are very sensitive to the characteristics of the loan—the interest rate, repayment term, and loan-to-value ratio—they also reflect the high cost of producing housing. Housing is costly to build in any society because of the large quantity of labor and materials required. Under capitalism, the cost is even higher because of private ownership and control of the necessary money, land, and industry. For example, the median cost of a new single-family house has been about three times median family income for at least the past generation. The median price increased from $19,300 in 1963 to $26,600 in 1970 and then soared to $44,300 by 1975 (U.S. Bureau of the Census, 1976a). Because houses are commodities that are produced to be sold, these development costs must be repaid by the buyers. Although mortgage loans permit the costs to be repaid incrementally as part of ongoing occupancy costs, the rapid inflation in the cost of new housing has been translated directly into larger mortgage payments.

In addition, since housing is not only a commodity but also is quite durable, used houses are generally sold many times during their lifetimes and are quite competitive with new houses. Their prices reflect the slow rate of depreciation, plus possible land appreciation and rising costs for new housing. Since mortgage loans finance the transfer of used houses, the mortgage payments endured by families in older buildings correspond to property values that prevailed the last time the buildings were sold or refinanced, not the original cost, which may have been much lower and may have been paid off many years ago.

Apart from simply transforming the high price of residential buildings into monthly mortgage payments, the mortgage system also more directly influences the actual selling prices of houses. More than 75 percent of the funds for housing development (including land costs) are provided by short-term (1 to 2 years) construction mortgage loans. Lenders' profits on these loans are included in the total development cost of new housing. At the end of 1974, construction financing charges amounted to about 10 percent of the total cost. During the 1970s they have been by far the fastest-growing cost component, increasing 148

percent between 1970 and 1974, compared with 62 percent for land
and 37 percent for labor and materials (National Association of Home
Builders).

Mortgage Lending and the Housing Shortage

The price of existing housing, as suggested above, is driven up by rising costs for new housing. In addition, the price of existing housing,
even poorly built or poorly maintained buildings, is driven up by the
scarcity of housing. In the long run, the housing shortage is due to the
failure to resolve the conflict between incomes and housing costs: a
growing proportion of the population simply cannot afford new housing, despite the changes in mortgage loans and the direct and indirect
government subsidies. The most immediate determinant of the amount
of new housing produced, though, is the availability of mortgage funds.

The need for housing to accommodate new households, replace lost
units, and rehabilitate or replace substandard units has been quantified.
Official goals have been set for meeting the need, but they have not
been achieved even with 44 million new units since World War II.[5]
The shortage is not due to lack of potential: in most years residential
construction has accounted for only about 3–5 percent of GNP; in 1972,
housing starts reached the unprecedented level of 2.4 million units,
very nearly meeting the official annual goal (U.S. League of Savings
Associations, 1975, Tables 55 and 56, p. 102). Rather, the shortage is
the result of dependence on the mortgage system for financing housing.

First of all, nearly half the funds that mortgage lenders have available to invest is used to finance the transfer or refinancing of existing
housing, rather than construction of new and rehabilitated housing
(Stone, 1975, footnote 32, p. 36). In addition, even though new construction falls short of the actual need, there may be no market for new
houses if people cannot obtain loans to buy them. Thus the relatively
high rates of construction in the early 1970s left builders and construction lenders with an inventory of nearly 500,000 new, single-family
houses they could not sell (MBA Economics and Research Dept., 1974,
p. 84). For these reasons it is clearly not in the interest of lenders to
direct all, or even most, of their available funds into production of new
housing.

Although the increasing shortage is partly the result of lenders'
failure to use their funds entirely productively, the gap between need

and production has not increased at a uniform rate. Housing production demonstrates cyclical fluctuations, which are the result of the effects of the business cycle on the total amount of credit in the economy and on the allocation of available funds to various uses including housing. Three times since the mid-1960s—in 1966, in 1969–1970, and again in 1974–1975—the inherent and increasing instability of the economy required the government to impose a policy of "tight money" in an effort to restore equilibrium and preserve the system. Interest rates soared, and money flowed out of housing into other, more profitable investments. The incredible shift of funds brought housing starts from the highest level in history in January 1973, to the lowest level in almost 30 years by December 1974 (U.S. Bureau of the Census, 1975a, Table 5). Dependence on the mortgage system has made housing especially vulnerable to the crisis of capitalism as a whole.

HOUSING AND THE CRISIS OF CAPITALISM

During the 1960s the postwar prosperity began to crumble. U.S. imperialism was challenged at home and abroad. Resistance of the Third World to U.S. domination, especially in Southeast Asia, forced the government to increase military spending. Urban riots plus domestic opposition to the war forced increases in spending for social programs while restricting tax increases. The federal budget thus had a growing deficit in the late 1960s, which had to be financed by borrowing in competition with other users of credit.

At the same time that Third World insurgency was beginning to threaten foreign investments of U.S. firms, growing competition from Europe and Japan posed an additional challenge. These foreign pressures, along with decreasing unemployment and rising wages at home resulted in a sharp decline in corporate profits in the late 1960s. In response, the corporations began to borrow more money to finance moveouts and mergers, which they hoped would restore profits.

The new demands for credit have come on top of the continuing needs of other sectors of the economy, including housing. This process has increasingly exposed a fundamental contradiction in the whole system of debt financing—a contradiction that capitalism cannot ultimately resolve. On the one hand, if the federal government allows the money supply to increase to meet all the needs for borrowed funds, it sets off price increases in the economy, since the amount of money being spent goes up faster than the amount of goods and services being produced. Inflation leads to higher interest rates and more borrowing in anticipation of further price increases. Debt accelerates far ahead of the ability to repay it, leading toward a financial crisis.

On the other hand, if the government tries to restrict the growth of credit to prevent or limit inflation, then some borrowers get squeezed out. Previously accumulated debts eventually have to be paid, and many individuals and businesses are totally dependent on new loans to pay off the old ones. Without continued access to credit to pay their bills, they may go bankrupt. Since the banks and other creditors have also borrowed heavily to expand their lending and stimulate the economy, when they do not get paid, a chain of defaults can ensue. Thus a credit squeeze can also bring the financial system to the brink of collapse.[6]

As the corporations and the government have tried with increasing desperation to reverse the decline in profits and decay of the empire, the economy has swung more and more violently between the poles of this contradiction. Housing has been at the center of the crisis because of the problems arising from the spread of long-term mortgages and the associated growth of mortgage debt.

Long-Term Mortgages and Short-Term Savings

Residential mortgages have been financed primarily by so-called thrift institutions—savings-and-loan associations and mutual-savings banks. At the end of 1974 they held 56 percent of all residential mortgages (U.S. League of Savings Associations, 1975, Table 19, p. 87). These institutions have tended to specialize in residential lending: at the end of 1974, mortgages accounted for over 86 percent of the assets of savings-and-loan associations and over 68 percent of the assets of mutual-savings banks (U.S. League of Savings Associations, 1975, Table 52, p. 106; National Associations of Mutual Savings Banks, Table 1, p. 6). Most of the residential mortgages not financed by thrift institutions are held by commercial banks and life-insurance companies, which have not specialized in housing finance: mortgages comprise only about 10 percent of their assets.

Long-term, fixed-interest-rate mortgages provide lenders with the same rate of return year after year regardless of what has happened to interest rates since the loan was made. This is not a problem for diversified lenders, such as commercial banks, which do not have most of their funds tied up in such long-term loans. Nor would it be a problem for thrift institutions if they obtained their funds on a long-term, fixed-interest-rate basis. The potential difficulty arises because thrift institutions have obtained money almost entirely from savings accounts, which have been attractive investments for families because they have offered liquidity, as well as security and geographical convenience. That is, savers want to be able to withdraw their funds quickly—small savers in order to meet large expenditures or emergencies, and wealthier savers in order to shift their money into more profitable investments.

Thrift institutions cannot easily or quickly raise the interest rates they pay on savings accounts because most of their income is from long-term, fixed-interest-rate mortgages. Until the mid-1960s, interest rates on savings accounts were generally competitive with other investments and were substantially higher than the rate of inflation, so this rigidity was not a problem. Thrift institutions were thus fairly successful at sustaining a steady inflow of funds and using them to support their own growth and finance a large fraction of the expansion of mortgage credit. Housing funds were restricted in periods of tight money, but primarily because corporations and the federal government could compete more successfully for the funds of commercial banks and insurance companies, not because of significant changes in savings deposits and mortgage lending at thrift institutions. As the major suppliers of housing credit, thrift institutions were relatively insulated from the rest of the capital markets, and the risk in "borrowing short and lending long" did not manifest itself as a contradiction.

Since 1966, increasing competition for borrowed funds has caused a steady, long-term rise in the general level of interest rates on top of the short-term fluctuations. Periods of tight money have been increasingly severe, with interest rates soaring higher each time and housing credit being restricted ever more sharply. As interest rates on savings accounts have become less competitive, wealthier depositors have withdrawn savings to invest in more profitable instruments offered by commercial banks, the federal government, and industrial corporations. For example, in 1966 households diverted $14.5 billion of their savings into open-market paper. Mortgage repayments and new savings deposits barely offset this loss, leaving thrift institutions with little money to lend for housing. In the summer of 1969 and again in the summer of 1974, savings withdrawals at savings-and-loan associations actually exceeded new deposits by more than $1 billion (Commission on Mortgage Interest Rates, p. 312; U.S. Savings and Loan League, Table 64, p. 70, and Table 66, p. 72; MBA Economics and Research Dept., 1975, p. 26).

In response to the restricted supply of funds, and in order to raise interest rates at all on savings accounts, lenders have offset the low returns they receive on older mortgages with higher interest rates on new mortgages. Continuing demand for mortgage credit and housing has generally sustained higher mortgage-interest rates. Higher interest rates have encouraged investors other than thrift institutions to put some of their funds into residential mortgages, but have also contributed to the overall rise in interest rates. The unpredictable and volatile flows of savings have made it harder for smaller and weaker thrift institutions to survive, so that in some communities they are being absorbed by larger ones.

Rising interest rates have also led to reduced rates of repayment on loans. For example, a thirty-year mortgage at 5 percent interest is 8 percent repaid after five years and 19 percent repaid after ten years; at 10 percent interest only 3 percent has been repaid after five years and only 9 percent after ten years. Lower repayment rates only add to the need for new funds to finance additional mortgages, increasing competition for funds even more, adding to interest rates, in a self-reinforcing cycle.

Interest Rates and Housing Costs

Between 1950 and 1975 the price of a new single-family house more than tripled. Median family income also almost tripled. However, rising interest rates caused the monthly mortgage payments for a new median-priced single-family house with a thirty-year mortgage to increase by a factor of six. In 1950 about two-thirds of all families could have afforded the payments on a new house. By the mid-1970s less than one-third could afford a new house. While this trend will gradually result in production of smaller and cheaper houses—as many as one-third of all new single-family houses are now mobile homes—the political value of the long-term mortgage as the facilitator of home-ownership is clearly being undermined.

Ironically, the lengthening of mortgage terms, which was intended to reduce the monthly cost of mortgage payments, has made the payments much more sensitive to interest rates. When interest rates double from 5 percent to 10 percent, the monthly payments on a ten-year loan increase by only 32 percent, but payments on a twenty-year loan go up by 46 percent and on a thirty-year loan by 64 percent. This effect is then piggy-backed onto rising prices for houses, causing mortgage payments to rise faster than incomes.

As more families are priced out of the housing market, the effective demand for new houses and mortgage credit is reduced despite the growing housing shortage. While this eases slightly the pressure on interest rates, declining demand is not an appealing prospect to the mortgage and homebuilding industries. The increasing tendency for developers primarily to produce luxury housing, the shift toward mobile homes, the rapid growth of cluster developments and condominiums, and the bankruptcy of many homebuilders are all primarily a response to the squeeze of high interest rates on the market for new housing. Indeed, the virtual collapse of the real estate investment trust (REIT) industry, the default and near-default of a number of state housing-and-development agencies, and even the terrifying number of bank failures in 1974–1976 occurred largely because high interest rates, scarce credit, and runaway inflation in the real estate market undermined effective demand for housing.[7]

Response and Contradiction

Attempts to deal with the weakening financial structure of the mortgage industry have only exacerbated the inherent instability of the economy and made housing more significant strategically.

Mortgage lending has traditionally been a rather localized and specialized business, involving investors who could directly evaluate and monitor both the properties and the borrowers. Mortgage insurance, the gradual standardization of mortgages, and government-sponsored agencies that buy and sell mortgages were supposed to open up this market by making mortgages more attractive and less risky to investors who might be far away from a property or might not have invested extensively in mortgages before. Local thrift institutions or mortgage companies still originate the loans, but they then can sell the mortgages to other investors—life-insurance companies, pension funds, banks, or even thrift institutions in other parts of the country. The local lenders act as collectors of the monthly payments and receive a fee for this service.

In this so-called secondary mortgage market—originally created just for FHA and VA loans, but expanded in 1970 to privately insured loans as well—mortgages are traded much like bonds. Sales-price discounts or premiums make up the difference between the interest rate paid by the residents of the housing and the prevailing interest rate in the capital markets. In this manner local originators of mortgages are not locked into a loan until the borrower pays it off, and funds are attracted from more sources and directed to local areas with high demand.

The secondary mortgage markets have never fully worked as intended. Large private investors such as pension funds have still regarded mortgages as too risky and unfamiliar. So government-backed agencies have become the principal investors in the secondary mortgage market as the economic crisis struck the traditional mortgage industry. In the tight-money period of 1966, the Federal National Mortgage Association (FNMA) went to Wall Street, raised $2.2 billion, and used the money to buy mortgages from thrift institutions and mortgage companies. In 1969–1970, FNMA and the newly-created Government National Mortgage Association (GNMA) and Federal Home Loan Mortgage Corporation (FHLMC) raised $9.6 billion in the capital markets to buy mortgages. Finally, during the massive inflation and depression of 1973–1975, these three agencies borrowed $17.5 billion to pump into residential mortgages (U.S. League of Savings Associations, 1976, Table 26, p. 34).

In addition to these secondary mortgage-market activities by federal agencies, the Federal Home Loan Bank Board also raised money to prop up thrift institutions that were losing savings deposits. They provided nearly $1 billion in 1966, another $4.3 billion in 1969–1970, and $13.8 billion in 1973–1974 (U.S. League of Savings Associations, 1976, Table 26, p. 34). In 1969 and in 1974, more than 40 percent of all the new money for residential mortgages came from federal agencies. This money came not from traditional savings accounts, but from the national capital markets.

State and local finance-and-development agencies also mushroomed since the late 1960s to raise more money for residential mortgages. By the middle of 1975 they had $10.6 billion in housing loans outstanding (U.S. Dept. of Housing and Urban Development, 1975, Table 8). They obtain funds by selling tax-exempt notes and bonds in the national financial markets.

Real estate investment trusts, which are private companies with special federal tax advantages, also became a new force in the mortgage industry. Between the late 1960s and the mid-1970s their assets grew from almost nothing to nearly $21 billion. About $6.7 billion of their assets were in residential mortgages in 1974, primarily construction loans for luxury apartments and condominiums (Securities and Exchange Commission). They have obtained money partly by selling shares in the stock market, but mostly by borrowing at high interest rates from big commercial banks.

The development of new instruments to raise and allocate mortgage credit has not been entirely successful, as the growing housing shortage reveals. It has, however, had two very significant consequences for the stability of capitalism.

First, the new devices increase competition for borrowed funds just at the points when government monetary policy is seeking to reduce the supply of credit. This has caused even higher interest rates, leading to further withdrawals of savings deposits as savers have pursued the higher returns. Increased withdrawals from thrift institutions have substantially offset the additional funds for housing raised through the capital markets. If the mortgage system, and housing capitalists generally, are ever able to compete more successfully for funds, there will be even higher mortgage interest rates and higher interest rates throughout the economy, adding further to the instability of the system. If housing financiers are not able to compete, the housing shortage will worsen.

Second, residential finance is no longer a relatively separate and insulated component of the credit system. Many investors other than thrift institutions and small savers now have billions of dollars tied up with the mortgage system. The stability of the structure of residential debt is thus increasingly vital for the stability of the entire financial structure of capitalism. But the stability of the housing-debt system depends upon continued mortgage payments from people in existing housing and sufficient demand for new housing being built with short-term construction loans. In the mid-1960s and again in 1975, more than 1 percent of all homeowers were over sixty days behind on their mortgage payments. During the 1960s the number of foreclosures per year doubled from about 50,000 to about 100,000, and by 1974 had increased to about 147,000, which was 0.4 percent of all mortgaged structures ("More Mortgages Said Delinquent"; U.S. Bureau of the Census, 1975c, Table 1237, p. 723). The spread of defaults on real estate construction loans in 1974 and 1975 triggered the biggest bank failures in U.S. history. The collapse of the mortgage system was a major factor in the onset, the speed, and the depth of the plunge into the Depression of the 1930s. How much more profound would be the effects of its collapse today!

In the face of rising housing costs and decreasing homeownership opportunities, younger families can expect smaller houses and more debt. However, even new home ownership is unlikely on a significant scale, since industrial and financial corporations are trying to capture all available sources of capital in order to modernize and expand to halt the downward tendency of profits. Moreover, rapid expansion of debt on top of existing debt would just increase the risk of financial collapse. Thus there will be a worsening housing shortage and acceleration of housing costs beyond the ability of working-class people to pay.

NOTES

1. This declaration of National Housing Policy was first made in the Housing Act of 1949.
2. For more detailed analyses of the forms and consequences of state intervention in housing see Aaron; Achtenberg and Stone; Harvey; Sawers and Wachtel; Stone (1973 and 1975); Stone and Achtenberg; U.S. Department of Housing and Urban Development (1974).
3. The quantitative historical data not otherwise referenced in this and the next sections are from U.S. Bureau of the Census (1975b), Series F1, N262, N265, N301, N305, N307, X689.
4. Figures on debt outstanding and the growth of debt in the U.S. economy from 1946 to 1974 are summarized in Stone and Achtenberg (Table 10, p. 18, and Table 12, p. 19) and have been obtained from U.S. President (Table B-60, and Table B-62), and from "Flow of Funds."
5. See Stone (1975, Table 4 and footnote 30) for a year-by-year comparison of National Housing Goals with actual production from 1968 to 1975.
6. For an excellent analysis of the unfolding of the economic crisis, with particular emphasis on the credit system, see Editors of *Monthly Review* (1970, 1974, 1975, 1976).
7. This analysis is developed more fully in Stone and Achtenberg, chapter 3.

REFERENCES

Aaron, Henry J., *Shelter and Subsidies: Who Benefits from Federal Housing Policies?* (Washington, D.C.: Brookings Institution, 1972).

Achtenberg, Emily, and Michael E. Stone, *Tenants First: A Research and Organizing Guide to FHA Housing* (Cambridge, Mass.: Urban Planning Aid, 1974).

Brodsky, Barry, "Tenants First: FHA Tenants Organize in Massachusetts," *Radical America*, Mar.–Apr. 1975.

Cochran, Clay, and George Rucker, "Every American Family: Housing Need and Non-Response," in Donald J. Reeb and James T. Kird, eds., *Housing the Poor* (New York: Praeger, 1973).

Commission on Mortgage Interest Rates, "Mortgage Market Developments in the Postwar Period," in Jon Pynoos, Robert Schafer, and Chester Hartman, eds., *Housing Urban America* (Chicago: Aldine, 1973).

Editors of *Monthly Review*, "The Long-Run Decline in Liquidity," *Monthly Review*, Sept. 1970.

———, "Keynesian Chickens Come Home to Roost," *Monthly Review*, Apr. 1974.

———, "Banks: Skating on Thin Ice," *Monthly Review*, Feb. 1975.

———, "Capital Shortage: Fact and Fancy," *Monthly Review*, Apr. 1976.

"Flow of Funds," *Federal Reserve Bulletin*, various issues, Table A56.

Gans, Herbert J., "A Poor Man's Home Is His Poorhouse," *New York Times Magazine*, Mar. 31, 1974.

Harvey, David, "The Political Economy of Urbanization in Advanced Capitalist Countries: The Case of the United States," in Gary Gappert and Harold M. Rose, eds., *The Social Economy of Cities*. Sage Urban Affairs Annual, Vol. 9 (Beverly Hills: Sage Publications, 1975).

U.S. Congress, House, Committee on Banking, Currency, and Housing, Housing Act of 1949, 42 *U.S.C.*, 1441, as excerpted in *Basic Laws and Authorities on Housing and Community Development, Revised through July 31, 1975* (94th Cong., 1st sess., 1975).

Joint Center for Urban Studies of the Massachusetts Institute of Technology and Harvard University, *America's Housing Needs: 1970 to 1980* (Cambridge, Mass.: Joint Center for Urban Studies of the Massachusetts Institute of Technology and Harvard University, 1973).

MBA Economics and Research Department, "Mortgage Market Trends," *Mortgage Banker*, Oct. 1974.

———, "Mortgage Market Trends," *Mortgage Banker*, July 1975.

"More Mortgages Said Delinquent," *Boston Sunday Globe*, July 20, 1975.

National Association of Home Builders, *Economic News Notes*, May 1975.

National Association of Mutual Savings Banks, *1975 National Fact Book of Mutual Savings Banking* (New York: National Association of Mutual Savings Banks, 1975).

Piven, Frances Fox, and Richard A. Cloward, *Regulating the Poor: The Functions of Public Welfare* (New York: Pantheon Books, 1971).

Sawers, Larry, and Howard M. Wachtel, "The Distributional Impact of Federal Government Subsidies in the United States," *Kapitalistate*, Spring 1975.

Securities and Exchange Commission, *Real Estate Investment Trusts: A Background Analysis and Recent Industry Developments 1961–1973*, Economic Staff Paper 75-No. 1.

Stone, Michael E., "Federal Housing Policy: A Political Economic Analysis," in Jon Pynoos, Robert Schafer, and Chester Hartman, eds., *Housing Urban America* (Chicago: Aldine, 1973).

————, "The Housing Crisis, Mortgage Lending, and Class Struggle," *Antipode*, Sept. 1975.

————, and Emily Achtenberg, *Hostage! Housing and the Massachusetts Fiscal Crisis* (Boston: Boston Community School, 1977).

U.S., Bureau of the Census. *Census of Housing: 1970, Metropolitan Housing Characteristics*, Final Report HC(2)-1, *United States and Regions* (Washington, D.C.: U.S. Government Printing Office, 1972).

————, *Construction Reports*, Report C20-75-1, *Housing Starts: January 1975* (Washington, D.C.: U.S. Government Printing Office, 1975a).

————, *Historical Statistics of the United States, Colonial Times to 1970*. Bicentennial Edition (Washington, D.C.: U.S. Government Printing Office, 1975b).

————, *Statistical Abstract of the United States: 1975*, 96th ed. (Washington, D.C.: U.S. Government Printing Office, 1975c).

————, *Construction Reports*, Report C27-75-Q4, *Price Index of New One-Family Houses Sold: Fourth Quarter 1975* (Washington, D.C.: Social and Economic Statistics Administration, 1976a).

————, *Current Housing Reports*, Advance Report H-150-74, *Annual Housing Survey: 1974, Part A, General Housing Characteristics for the United States and Regions* (Washington, D.C.: U.S. Government Printing Office, 1976b).

U.S., Bureau of Labor Statistics, *City Worker's Family Budget for a Moderate Standard of Living: Autumn 1966*, Bulletin 1570-1 (Washington, D.C.: U.S. Government Printing Office, 1967).

————, *3 Budgets for an Urban Family of Four Persons 1969–70*, Supplement to Bulletin 1570-5 (Washington, D.C.: U.S. Department of Labor, 1972).

————, *BLS Revises Estimates for Urban Family Budgets and Comparative Indexes for Selected Urban Areas Autumn 1975*, Press release USDL: 76-759, May 5, 1976.

————, "Housing the Poor and the Shelter to Income Ratio," in *Papers Submitted to Subcommittee on Housing Panels*, prepared for the Committee on Banking and Currency by Dorothy K. Newman (92nd Cong., 1st sess., 1971, Part 2).

U.S., Congress, House, Committee on Appropriations, *Department of Housing and Urban Development—Independent Agencies Appropriations for 1976, Hearings Before a Subcommittee of the Housing Committee on Appropriations, Part 5: Department of Housing and Urban Development* (94th Cong., 1st sess., 1975).

U.S., Department of Housing and Urban Development, *Housing in the Seventies: Report of the National Housing Policy Review* (Washington, D.C.: U.S. Government Printing Office, 1974).

————, *HUD News*, Press release HUD-No. 75-361, September 10, 1975.

U.S. League of Savings Associations, *Savings and Loan Fact Book: 1975* (Chicago: U.S. League of Savings Associations, 1975).

————, *Savings and Loan Fact Book: 1976* (Chicago: U.S. League of Savings Associations, 1976).

U.S. National Commission on Urban Problems, *Building the American City* (Washington, D.C.: U.S. Government Printing Office, 1968).

U.S. President, *Economic Report of the President* (Washington, D.C.: U.S. Government Printing Office, 1976).

U.S. Savings and Loan League, *Savings and Loan Fact Book: 1970* (Chicago: U.S. Savings and Loan League, 1970).

three

THE BUCK
STOPS HERE

New York City's fiscal problems are indicative of the problems facing almost all older cities in the United States. By "older" we mean those that reached their maximum population before 1940. These cities were formed under one set of historical conditions as Gordon explained in Part I, and are today confronted with a crisis of function as the process of capital accumulation on a world-wide scale no longer integrates such cities in the old ways. This tension between the processes of capital accumulation and urbanization are described by Hill. He roots present-day political struggles in the larger process of capital accumulation and the demands it places on the state.

Tabb looks at the particulars of the New York City situation, finding that the general patterns described by Hill are at work in the case of New York City, but that the nation's largest city also faces unique circumstances which, while consistent with the situation in other older and larger cities, is conditioned by its leading role as headquarters of the global-oriented giant corporations.

The juxtapositioning of the Hill and Tabb papers highlights the emerging methodology that runs as a constant thread through the papers in this volume. Hill discusses the structure of municipal production and the revenue distribution that results from the patterns of capital accumulation over time. Tabb discusses the particular case of one city, showing how changes in production relations interact with political scapegoating in order to blame the victims of the crisis rather than the class forces which dominate the transformation process.

Fiscal Collapse
and Political Struggle
in Decaying Central Cities
in the United States

RICHARD CHILD HILL

My purpose in this essay is to explore the interconnections between the fiscal crisis facing many central cities, corresponding political struggles, and possible trajectories of urban change in the United States. At the outset the relationships between capital accumulation, urbanization, and the expansion of the state are briefly investigated. This provides a foundation for an exploration of the sources of the fiscal crisis facing many central cities and the relationship between the fiscal crisis and urban political struggle. I conclude the analysis by sketching out three alternative scenarios of the future of decaying central cities in the United States.

CAPITAL ACCUMULATION AND URBANIZATION

The city is forged upon the hearth of a given mode of production and is shaped with a given set of technological instruments. In a capitalist

* This is a revised and greatly condensed version of a paper originally prepared for presentation at the Conference on Urban Political Economy, New School for Social Research, New York City, February 15, 1975. It has appeared in somewhat different form in *Kapitalistate*, Summer, 1976.

society, urbanization and the structure and functioning of cities are rooted in the production, reproduction, circulation, and overall organization of the capital accumulation process. Since the process of capital accumulation unfolds in a spatially structured environment, urbanism may be viewed as the particular geographical form and spatial patterning of the relationships taken by the process of capital accumulation.

Capital accumulation requires (1) fixed investment of part of the surplus product in new means of production; (2) production and distribution of articles of consumption to sustain and reproduce the labor force; (3) stimulation of an effective demand for the surplus product produced; and thus (4) additional capital formation through ever-increasing product innovation, market penetration, and economic expansion. Correspondingly, the capitalist city is a production site, a locale for the reproduction of the labor force, a market for the circulation of commodities and the realization of profit, and a control center for these complex relationships (Castells, 1969, p. 423).

In all of this the notion of an urban *system* must be emphasized. A particular city cannot be divorced from the encompassing political economy within which it is embedded and through which it manifests its particular functions and form. As David Harvey has argued, in a capitalist society the circulation of surplus is constantly shifting to new channels as new opportunities are explored, new technologies achieved, and new resources and productive capacities are opened up. Correspondingly, the prestige and vitality of individual cities come to rest largely upon their location with respect to the geographical circulation of the surplus. Therefore, according to Harvey,

> the geographical pattern in the circulation of surplus can be conceived only as a moment in a process. In terms of that moment, particular cities attain positions with respect to the circulation of surplus which, at the next moment in the process, are changed. Urbanism, as a general phenomenon, should not be viewed as the history of particular cities, but as the history of the system of cities within, between, and around which the surplus circulates. . . . The history of particular cities is best understood in terms of the circulation of surplus value at a moment of history within a system of cities (p. 250).

Periods of urbanization in the United States correspond to phases in the process of capital accumulation. Each period is characterized by a dominant type of city and a particular pattern of relationships among cities within the evolving urban system (Hill, 1976). Of particular salience here is the urban transformation corresponding to the monopoly stage of capital accumulation—the rise and development of national and multinational business enterprises and the increasing concentration, centralization, and global extension of capital. The contemporary urbanization process is characterized by the dialectical interaction between the centralization of corporate control over capital, technology, and organization and the decentralization of production, employment, and commerce facilitated by advances in the productive forces (particularly transportation and communication) through the metropolitan domain. Dominant metropolitan centers become the locus of corporate administration and control; product innovation, development, and diffusion; service; and quaternary employment. The rural and urban periphery become more differentiated and stratified as they provide the agricultural and industrial products necessary for the maintenance and expansion of metropolitan regions (Berry; Hymer).

Patterns of uneven development rooted in the evolving system of capitalist production correspond to patterns of uneven urban development—simultaneous urban growth and decay—in the evolving urban system.[1] Cities in the urban hierarchy in the United States are integrated through spatial relationships along three axes that correspond to trajectories of uneven urban development: (1) between metropolises and regional hinterlands; (2) between higher and lower metropolitan centers in the hierarchy; and (3) between each metropolitan center and its surrounding urban field (Hill, 1976). The underdevelopment of regional hinterlands, the de-development of aging central cities, and the expansion of suburbs and new metropolitan "growth centers" are all interrelated manifestations of the evolving political economy of late capitalism in the United States.

CAPITAL ACCUMULATION, URBANIZATION, AND THE STATE

Crucial to understanding the urban fiscal crisis is awareness of the role the city plays as a form of government, a vital component of the capitalist state. As such, the city has increasingly been delegated managerial responsibility for facilitating the process of capital accumulation and mitigating the contradictions emanating from the unremitting quest for private profit.

With the emergence and growth of monopoly capitalism, the state takes on an active, rapidly expanding, and increasingly central role in the economy and society. Following the seminal work of James O'Connor, we can view state expenditures as having a dual character corresponding to the state's two basic and frequently contradictory functions in a capitalist society. On the one hand, *social capital outlays* are state expenditures required for capital *accumulation* and are indirectly productive of private profit. There are two kinds of social capital: (1) social investment (social-constant capital) which consists of projects and services that increase labor productivity and therefore the rate of profit; and (2) social-consumption expenditures (social-variable capital) consisting of projects and services that lower the reproduction costs of labor, and other things being equal, also increase the rate of profit. On the other hand, *social expenses,* the second category of state expenditures, consist of projects and services which are required to maintain *social order.* Social expenses are not even indirectly productive of capital accumulation.

O'Connor has persuasively argued that there is a reciprocal relationship between the expansion of the capitalist state and growth in the monopoly sector and total production. And there also seems to be a direct connection between the process of urbanization under monopoly capitalism and expansion in state investment, consumption, and expense outlays.

Urban infrastructure is ever more capital-intensive and indivisible in nature. Advances in science, technology, and specialized knowledge and skills embodied in the urban labor force can neither be funded nor monopolized by any one firm or few firms. Consequently, in the United States and other advanced capitalist countries, monopoly capital has socialized an increasingly large share of the costs of planning, constructing, and revamping urban social-investment projects aimed at increasing the productivity of labor power (e.g. transportation, R&D facilities, and utility and urban-renewal projects).

With the urbanization and proletarianization of labor, the costs of reproducing the labor force also rise enormously as the market penetrates every sphere of family activity. Modern capitalist societies are compelled to allocate an increasing share of the social product to social-consumption spending, including elementary and secondary schools, recreational facilities, and hospital and medical complexes. Social-consumption expenditures also include social insurance against economic insecurity (e.g., workmen's compensation, old-age and survivors insurance, unemployment and health insurance).

There is also a tendency for social expenses of production to rise over time, and the state is increasingly compelled to socialize these expenses. Monopoly-sector productivity and productive capacity tend to expand more rapidly than the demand for labor. Unable to gain employment in monoply industries, and frequently facing race and sex discrimination, the unemployed, underemployed, and those at low wages in competitive industries progressively concentrate in aging central cities and become full or partial dependents on the state. In the process, the state, in order to ensure order and maintain legitimacy, faces mounting pressures to meet the various demands of those who must bear the costs of capital accumulation.

In sum, with the development of late capitalism, O'Connor argues that

> the growth of the state sector is indispensable to the expansion of private industry . . . particularly monopoly industries . . . and the growth of monopoly capital generates increased expansion of social expenses. The greater the growth of social capital, the greater the growth of the monopoly sector. And the greater the growth of the monopoly sector, the greater the state's expenditures on the social expenses of production (pp. 8–9).

THE URBAN FISCAL CRISIS

As the capitalist state becomes increasingly responsible for the capital investment requisite to private accumulation and for the expense outlays necessary to maintain social order in a class society, the contradictions inherent in capitalist development are increasingly played out in the arena of the state. Although the state has socialized more and more capital costs and absorbs more and more expenses of production, the social surplus continues to be appropriated privately. The increasing socialization of costs and the continued private appropriation of profits creates a fiscal crisis: a "structural gap" between state expenditures and state revenues. The result is a tendency for state expenditures and expenditure demands to increase more rapidly than the means of financing them, resulting in economic, social, and political crises (O'Connor, p. 9). Fiscal crisis becomes the state budgetary expression of class struggle in a monopoly capitalist society.

The form taken by the fiscal crisis, as well as the intensity with which it is expressed, is heavily influenced by the structure of the capitalist state as an instrument for producing the goods and services requisite to maintaining private accumulation and social order. There are three basic elements of the structure of the state in the United States that are fundamental to understanding the dynamics of the urban fiscal crisis and its long-range implications for social change: (1) federalism; (2) the fragmentation of local government in metropolitan areas; and (3) the nature of central-city government as a structure for accumulating revenue and for producing and distributing goods and services.

Federalism

In the United States, the level of state expenditures, the trends in state outlays, the distribution of state expenditures by function, and the methods of obtaining state revenue, vary among federal, state, and local governments and between relatively autonomous units within levels of government. The largest share of the federal budget goes to outlays on social expenses in the form of military expenditures, direct money payments to the indigent, the aged, and the infirm, and provision of welfare services. The federal government takes in about two-thirds of all tax dollars and retains a virtual monopoly over the more "progressive" tax sources: individual and corporate income taxes and wealth and inheritance taxes (Netzer, p. 80; U.S. Bureau of the Census, 1972, p. 87).

While state and local governments foot a large share of the welfare bill and have developed an extensive social-control apparatus, their budgets are largely devoted to social capital expenditures. In particular, local governments assume major responsibility for social-capital and social-consumption outlays in urban areas including schools, fire protection, sanitation, transportation facilities, industrial parks, and so on. State and local governments gain the major share of their revenues from the most regressive taxes. Sales taxes are the major source of revenue for states. The property tax is the major indigenous source of revenue for local governments (Netzer, p. 81; U.S. Bureau of the Census, p. 87).

Given the dynamic connection between monopoly capital accumulation, urbanization, and the expansion of the state, the heaviest demands for new government spending are currently being made on state, and particularly on local governments (Fleming, pp. 33–39). But while the federal government has relatively great tax-raising capabilities but only limited responsibility for civilian expenditures, local governments have more circumscribed tax-raising capabilities to match their increasingly heavy expenditure demands. The result is a large and growing fiscal "imbalance" between levels of government in the United States.

Fragmentation of Local Government

The U.S. Constitution not only divides governing responsibility among federal, state, and local governments, but also between relatively autonomous units within levels—particularly at the local level of government. Metropolitan landscapes are dotted with hundreds of municipalities, school districts, and other types of single- and multi-purpose units of local government. The fragmented system of government at the local level, and the heavy responsibility assumed by local governments for providing social capital outlays, generate contradictions within the heart of the urbanization process itself.

First, uneven economic development among geographical areas interacts with a politically fragmented metropolis to produce uneven fiscal development among local government jurisdictions. In particular, aging central-city and inner-ring suburban municipalities and school districts simultaneously experience an expansion in the relative size of their resident surplus labor force and a capital and tax base outflow to the expanding suburban fringe and to metropolitan centers in more dynamic regions of the country.[2] As the tax base becomes separated from social needs, older central cities are increasingly unable to generate the revenue required to meet rapidly increasing expenditure demands (Advisory Commission on Intergovernmental Relations; Muller).

Second, externalities—where the activity of any one element in an urban system generates unpriced costs or benefits upon other elements in the system—increase geometrically with the size and complexity of the urban system. Central-city government investments in "human capital" spill over their boundaries as the middle class and those with specialized skills migrate in large numbers to suburbs and other metropolitan areas. Central cities also foot the bill for numerous investments in physical capital and social-consumption facilities in which the technology of the service itself makes it impossible to confine the benefits within their borders. Aging central cities also confront increasing demands for social expenses as the result of the "spill-in" of the relative surplus population from declining rural areas and the obsolescence of an increasing share of their local labor force due to technological change and the international expansion of capital. These expenditures are frequently funded from taxes on central-city property and labor force but redound to the benefit of the suburban fringe and the nation as a whole.

In sum, the dynamics of capital accumulation and urbanization require expanded social-investment, social-consumption, and social-expense outlays resulting in a striking increase in the role of local governments in the U.S. economy. But the geographical circulation of surplus value according to the criterion of profitability, within a state structure characterized by federalism and a fragmented system of local governments, has meant the divorce of tax base from social needs, exploitation through fiscal mercantilism, and fiscal crisis in aging central cities in the United States.

The Structure of Municipal Production

Since the process of capital accumulation in a monopoly capitalist society is increasingly a function of state social-capital expenditures, and since local governments bear primary responsibility for these outlays, it follows that the geographical circulation of the surplus as well as the quality of life and prestige of individual cities increasingly become a function of the pattern and composition of city-government (municipal, school district, special district) outlays (Berry, pp. 17–21). Today, aging central cities in the United States find themselves confronted with increasing demands for social-expense outlays which are not even indirectly productive of private accumulation. They simultaneously experience fundamental barriers to accumulating revenue for social-capital outlays requisite to transforming the resident labor force to labor productive of private capital accumulation. This is the general contradiction underpinning the fiscal crisis of central cities today.

This contradiction results in economic, political, and social crises and the development of increasingly intense struggles among groups in the central-city political arena. The form that these struggles takes is shaped by the way in which the central city government is organized to produce goods and services to meet the contradictory requirements of capital accumulation. There are three dimensions of central-city production that are crucial here: (1) relations of revenue accumulation, (2) relations of production of goods and services, and (3) relations of circulation or distribution of goods and services in the city.

Each element in the structure of central-city production underlines a basic issue and axis of struggle in contemporary urban politics. Revenue accumulation refers to the class relations and class distribution of the means of financing city government expenditures (i.e., who pays for what is produced). Goods-and-services production denotes the class relations of setting budget priorities and producing goods and services (i.e., who determines what goods and services are produced and how they are produced). Circulation points to the social relations between city bureaucracies and residents and the class distribution of city expenditures (i.e., who benefits from what is produced).

Revenue Accumulation

A city has to accumulate revenue in order to produce goods and services. But since the city is a component of the capitalist state, its method of generating revenue is subject to three basic rules governing the relationship between the state and the accumulation process in a capitalist society. (1) Capital accumulation takes place only in private enterprises. The state cannot appropriate a surplus to reinvest in its own enterprises to produce a further surplus. However, (2) the state has both the authority and the mandate to create and sustain conditions of private accumulation. Therefore, (3) the state's ability to produce goods and services depends upon the presence and continuity of private accumulation. In the absence of private accumulation, state revenues dry up and the power of the state disintegrates (Offe).

Secondly, not only must local governments operate within the parameters of capitalist accumulation, but within the U.S. federalist system they have only those rights of self-government explicitly granted them by state governments. This subordinate relationship between city and state governments places added constraints over municipal revenue accumulation since many state constitutions limit the scope of local fiscal authority with respect to both taxable sources and tax rates (Friedman, p. 5). And given the fragmented, competitive structure of government within the metropolitan area as a whole, local jurisdictions are pressured to grant tax concessions to attract job-producing firms.

Financing current expenditures through deficit financing, the hallmark of the federal government, is prohibited to local governments. Municipalities and school districts finance the bulk of their operating expenditures from regressive property, sales, and flat-rate income taxes. The rapidly mounting tax burden experienced by an increasingly impoverished central-city population and the seeming lack of effectiveness and efficiency of city programs have resulted in an intensifying tax revolt among local residents (Reischauer and Hartman, p. 21).

Central-city fixed-capital outlays, on the other hand, are usually financed through bond issues (i.e., through deficit financing). Legally prescribed debt limits are generally tied to the total assessed value of property, which is open to political manipulation. Also, state laws frequently exempt social-capital projects, like pollution-control, job-development, housing, water, and sewage facilities, from constitutionally prescribed limits. Under increasing fiscal pressure, and without a rigid definition of capital-expenditure ceilings, governments of big cities like New York began transferring operating expenses into the capital budget. But the result was to shift the form of the fiscal crisis to increasingly large interest charges that must be paid out of operating expenses. As a result, the city's credit rating by leading bond agencies drops and the interest rate on new bond issues increases, further exacerbating the fiscal dilemma (Stern, p. 60; Friedman, pp. 29–30).

In sum, as central cities deteriorate, their bond ratings fall, interest charges rise, interest payments as a percentage of current operating expenses escalate upward, and they find it increasingly expensive and difficult to borrow to finance social-capital demands. At the same time, an intensifying taxpayer revolt poses stiff barriers to increasing, or at times even maintaining, current operating expenditures through tax increases. The result is an increasing inability on the part of aging central cities to generate social-capital outlays to upgrade their resident labor force, to attract private capital and tax base, or to meet the intensifying demands for social expenses generated by an increasingly impoverished resident population.

Relations of Production

Because U.S. cities operate within the parameters governing the relationship between the state and private capital accumulation in a capitalist society, forces "external" to the city have a marked influence on the central city's budget. But within this set of parameters, the internal decision-making structure of central-city governments operates to exacerbate the urban fiscal crisis. There are two elements of the relations of central-city production which deserve brief consideration: (1) the process of setting budget priorities, and (2) the relations between city management and city workers. Both elements exert strong pressure for expansion in central-city expenditures.

City production of goods and services, in contrast to private capitalist enterprise, is not directly governed by market profitability criteria. Rather, "budget-making is a political process conducted in the political arena for political advantage" (Friedman, p. 4). From the perspective of the city council, the most important budgetary decisions involve the construction or acquisition of new social-capital facilities (capital budget) rather than the annual expenditures required to maintain these facilities once in operation (operating budget). Legislators generally have pragmatic, short-range interests; capital budgets are politically manipulable; and new social-capital projects are visible and yield immediate political payoff. Local capital budgeting, most research reveals, is governed less by long-range planning than by traditional pork-barrel, logrolling legislative politics with a built-in tendency to proliferate projects in wasteful and inefficient ways (McConnell).

The municipal operating budget, on the other hand, tends to be governed by "incrementalism" (Wildavsky). Decision-making tends to be partial, short-range, and pragmatic. The politics of the operating budget primarily reflect the concerns of city agencies and a few key elected officials. Public participation is generally "too little, too late" and frequently represents little more than "democratic ritual." Existing appropriations are the basis for future funding and generally are presided over by city bureaus. Previous decisions are reexamined infrequently. Budget decisions are tentative adjustments to an existing situation based on past experience and are made along the margins. All but the most immediately identifiable alternatives tend to be neglected, and all but the most visible consequences tend to be ignored (Alford; Friedman, p. 18).

However, since most local government spending goes toward the salaries and the benefits of the municipal labor force, well-organized and knowledgeable city employee unions can exert direct and significant influence over the municipal budgetary process. During the 1960s and early 1970s, municipal collective bargaining and negotiated wage agreements became the rule in cities in most parts of the country, and municipal employee strikes to achieve demands increased rapidly (Spero and Capozzola, Chap. 1). In the past few years, city-employee groups have more vigorously demanded improved working conditions and wage increases to advance their level of living and protect against inflation. At the same time, local governments have been pressured by rising prices in goods and services purchased from the private sector and by growing resistance to tax increases by local residents. The result has been a collision between rising employee demands and a tightening vise on city management's ability to fund such settlements.

Union justification for wage increases and improved working conditions in state-sector collective-bargaining sessions has been switching from comparability data based on private-sector conditions and compensation to comparability data based on conditions negotiated in local governments in other areas, threatening city management with the specter of a "limitless" spiral in the cost of municipal settlements (Zack, pp. 38–40). And class conflict in the state sector has yet to be institutionalized. Most states still outlaw strikes by municipal employees. Binding arbitration is anathema to city management and unions alike, since it shifts responsibility for settlements outside the city political arena. City unions do not as yet play a regulating role in production relations because, in contrast to capital-intensive private enterprises, labor-intensive city services are not conducive to productivity increases to offset wage increases. In the absence of marked increases in productivity, and in the face of declining sources of revenue, the wage-and-benefit demands of municipal employees threaten to bankrupt the city.

Relations of Distribution

The residential location of a social group, relative to the distribution of city investments, carries with it more or fewer city services, better or worse schools, more or less access to commercial activities, employment opportunities, and so on. With increasing urbanization, social investment, social consumption, and social expenses mount rapidly. As the city government's share of the total production of goods and services increases, inequality in real income among social groups in the city increases, and political struggles over the distribution of public goods and services intensifies.

Moreover, as the size of the state sector in central cities expands, the question of who gets the action becomes increasingly important and divisive as it engages the class interests of more and more people. Expansion in central-city government has been, among other things, a safety valve. It has been a sponge absorbing part of the relative surplus population fostered by the dynamics of monopoly capital accumulation. A large share of the dwindling number of *new* employment opportunities in aging central cities has been in municipal and school-district government. This has fostered an intensifying struggle among local residents for access to municipal employment (Hill, 1977).

Thus central-city relations of revenue accumulation, production, and distribution increasingly foster an urban politics characterized by an intensifying triadic struggle between (1) outraged taxpayers, (2) increasingly militant municipal unions, and (3) insurgent community groups. At present these segments of the urban working class are largely locked into a mutually antagonistic set of social relationships. Taxpayers rebel against the lack of efficiency and effectiveness of municipal expenditures, the service claims of the relative surplus population, and the wage-and-benefit demands of municipal unions. Insurgent community groups attack budget priorities, the lack of accountability of service bureaucracies and municipal unions, and the unequal distribution of city services and employment opportunities. Municipal unions castigate "community witch-hunters" and "tightfisted" taxpayers alike. Central-city politics, one observer has recently noted, is akin to a bucket of crabs (Baker, p. 27).

In summary, there seems to be a general contradiction between capital accumulation and urbanization in the United States. Capital accumulation requires urbanization but urbanization requires investment, consumption, and expense outlays that market exchange cannot handle. This dramatically increases the role of state enterprise in the economy. But the structure of state production, particularly at the level of local government, is only partially complementary to private accumulation. Federalism, the fragmented system of local governments, and the structure of city-government production increasingly prevent decaying central cities from accommodating themselves to the requisites of monopoly capital accumulation or the social needs of central-city residents. The result is fiscal crisis and intensifying political struggle.

BLACK STRUGGLE AND THE URBAN FISCAL CRISIS

The interpenetration of black urbanization, central-city stagnation, and the urban fiscal crisis sets the tone and shapes much of the character of political struggle in decaying central cities in the contemporary United States. The massive migration of Blacks to central cities over the past three decades has shifted the locus of black-liberation struggles from regional and national civil-rights strategies to political mobilization in the arena of central-city government. Since a large share of the black urbanization stream has been absorbed by declining central cities, the pattern of black urban politics is intimately bound up with the dynamics of the urban fiscal crisis.[3] Black political struggle in central cities has surged forward along three fronts: (1) escalating demands to improve the level and quality of city facilities and services in black neighborhoods; (2) an intensifying struggle to capture a larger share of the supply of jobs in city government; (3) a simultaneous drive to obtain power in City Hall—the necessary prerequisite to changing budget priorities, upgrading the quality of city services in black communities, and providing black access to municipal employment.

Blacks constitute the largest share of the relative surplus population in many stagnating central cities, and black urbanization has gone hand in hand with deterioration in the level and quality of city facilities and services in inner-city neighborhoods. Central-city social-capital and social-expense outlays have neither sufficed to transform the relative surplus population to labor productive of large-scale private accumulation nor have they served to guarantee black acquiescence to the urban political system.

Expansion in the relative size of the black population in central cities, and growth in expenditures and employment in municipal government at a time when private employment opportunities were dwindling, convinced a large share of the black community that capturing control over central-city government was likely to be the most effective instrument to advance the black-liberation struggle. Black power in city hall is a necessary prerequisite to changing budget priorities, redressing the imbalance in the provision of city facilities and services among neighborhoods, and providing large-scale black access to municipal employment opportunities. But this struggle met with intense resistance from central-city service bureaucracies, municipal unions, and professional associations.

Political struggle by the black community erupted in the central-city political arena several decades after the city experienced fundamental political reform. Urban reform shifted the center of the central-city political system away from a ward-level patronage-based system to that of centralized governance, based upon presumed dedication to rational, merit-based rules of procedure. Municipal bureaucracies became the new urban machines. Monolithic, entrenched in law and tradition, and supported by the local press, middle-class civic groups, and an organized clientele enjoying access under existing arrangements, this new machine structure has posed resilient barriers to black acquisition of power by traditional means.

As central cities experienced a substantial shift in the residential population from white to black, black demands that the allocation of jobs in areas of local government reflect the racial composition of the resident population have escalated. Blacks have asserted that the needs of the black community that must be met through local government services include dimensions of the black experience that can be understood and dealt with only by other Blacks. This political strategy includes a denouncement of "absentee" bureau heads, city professionals, and unionized employees as outsiders, as suburbanites exploiting the central city. In a racially changing central city, territorial claims based upon the right to self-rule have constituted a political stance that whites have had a difficult time circumventing (Conforti).

Black political struggle has produced important gains in many central cities. Recent research reveals that Blacks continue disproportionately to occupy the lower ladders of local government employment, but they have also gained entry into higher-level jobs in large numbers in many agencies and tend to be more heavily represented in municipal employment than in the private sector (U.S. Commission on Civil Rights). Moreover, as central cities approach black majority status, black mayors, Congressional representatives, officials, and commissioners are being elected in large numbers. A recent estimate suggests that some 2,600 Blacks hold office across the nation. Black mayors currently preside over ninety-six cities. And it has been estimated that within a decade, black administrations will head the majority of the country's ten largest cities and that one in three Blacks are likely to live in cities with black administrations (Greer).

TRAJECTORIES OF URBAN CHANGE

The aging central city has become the repository of intensifying contradictions engendered by the process of monopoly capital accumulation—contradictions best revealed in an escalating urban fiscal crisis. These central cities may well constitute the birthplace of new economic and political forms of organizing social life. The extent to which transformations in the structure of urban life correspond to the needs of the masses of currently deprived central-city residents will depend, to an important extent, upon how the interconnections between political struggle and the urban fiscal crisis work themselves out. While the future of decaying central cities is uncertain, three trajectories of urban change *are currently reflected in embryo* in the political economies of aging central cities. All aging central cities embody each of the three tendencies toward change in varying proportions and degrees. Each embryonic tendency, when worked through to its logical conclusion, constitutes a scenario—a relatively distinct image of the future of decaying central cities in the United States. Since all three tendencies are present in aging central cities, each scenario should also be viewed as constituting a political agenda for antagonistic groups locked in political struggle to shape the future of urban life in the United States.

The Pariah City

The Pariah City is a form of geographical and political apartheid—a "reservation" for the economically disenfranchised labor force in a monopoly capitalist society (Long). Once the central location for the concentration of cheap labor in great volume, the aging central city now finds that competition from welfare payments and other social expenses keeps its labor force far from cheap. In the context of a global capitalist system, the central city's traditional jobs are being absorbed by labor-repressive, low-wage regimes in the Third World. Those in the current group of immigrants fortunate enough to "make it" soon move to the suburbs that have reached a level of population and purchasing power sufficient to the provision of amenities that only the central city was formerly capable of sustaining. The city emigrés leave behind the "poor, the deviant, the unwanted and those who make a business or career of managing them for the rest of society" (Sternlieb, p. 16).

Revenue-sharing constitutes the social-expense payment by the outside society to the Pariah City's bureaucracies and politicians to maintain the reservation. Part of this payment goes for the subsistence of the natives, another part to the keepers, and the rest to those who manage to make a profit from the reservation. Government expenditures on welfare, housing, food stamps, medical payments, and the like serve as indirect subsidies to local businesses. The relative surplus population, the underemployed, and the working poor become a "conduit" for the transfer of state revenues to inner-city slumlords, merchants, loan sharks, service professionals, and the like, who in turn transmit the surplus outside of the city (Hamilton, pp. 40–45).

Professional "keeping" associations make containment a business with little more concern for those confined to the reservation than is common among security guards in a prison. Social-expense outlays give birth to a growing municipal bureaucracy, which is sustained by the plight and misery of the poor but which yields little in the way of productive resources to the oppressed. Rather, these increasingly expensive programs are placebos, forms of symbolic action, which "provide psychic satisfaction to the patrons of the poor, convince outsiders, especially the media, that something is being done, and indicate to the urban poor that some one up there cares" (Sternlieb, p. 18).

The Pariah City portends dismal prospects for the black-liberation struggle. Black control of the Pariah City is a "hollow prize" indicating little more than political control over an economically sterile environment. With capital outflow and deteriorating tax base, central-city black leaders experience ever-increasing dependence on state and federal funds, coupled with rising indifference to the problems of the Pariah City by white-dominated state and national legislative bodies. Coopted, locked into visible public positions, but without resources to substantially alter the condition of their constituents' lives, black urban leaders "dangle on white men's strings while receiving little more than crumbs" (Friesema, p. 77). The cumulative effect is to convince potential voters and political leaders that the game is not worth the toll in personal dignity. Despair and apathy define the political culture of the Pariah City.

Such seems to be the trajectory of change in many decaying central cities in the United States. But the Pariah City is a house of cards whose imagery is created from a number of shaky assumptions. For one thing, the Pariah City is not an isolated reservation in Arizona or New Mexico. It is at the core of an increasingly complex and interdependent metropolitan system. Even as they stagnate, central cities remain important control centers housing major economic and political institutions, the mass media, and key transportation nodes. In a metropolitan society, the possibility of widespread, violent, mass rebellion by impoverished and desperate inner-city residents convinced that they are inheriting the wind threatens the system at its foundations.

Moreover, the fiscal crisis of aging central cities not only augurs decay in several large urban centers, but also portends strong disaccumulation tendencies in the capitalist system itself. Decaying central cities are absorbing an ever-larger share of the capitalist state's revenue and using this capital in ways that are both wasteful and unproductive of large-scale private accumulation. Central-city fixed investments, which still constitute a sizeable share of the holdings of urban financial institutions, are threatened as well. The Pariah City is an inherently volatile form of urban organization that confronts the capitalist system with disaccumulation and mass rebellion. It is doubtful that the metropolitan apple can long flourish while its core rots.

The State Capitalist City

The State Capitalist City is an integral unit of corporate state capitalism. It combines state, metropolitan, municipal, and special-district forms of organization into an urban political system governed according to principles of corporate planning. In the process the central city is integrated into a geographically, politically, and economically efficient space economy.

The State Capitalist City, and the social-industrial complex of which it is a part, alleviate the fiscal crisis by generating rapid and sustained productivity throughout the economy.[4] It increases productivity both by increasing government efficiency and by using the budget as an instrument to improve productivity and raise profits in the private sector—particularly in monopoly industries. Social expenses are transformed into social capital through massive social-investment subsidies to monopoly industries. This ameliorates the material impoverishment of the relative surplus population by incorporating it into "a new stratum of indirectly productive workers: technologists, administrators, paraprofessionals, factory and office workers, and others who plan, implement and control the new programs in education, health, housing, science and other spheres" (O'Connor, p. 116). In sum, the State Capitalist City is a highly tuned "feedback mechanism" that continuously transforms the surplus labor force generated by monopoly capital accumulation into labor productive of further monopoly capital accumulation.

The emergence of the State Capitalist City is associated with a fundamental alteration in the relations of revenue accumulation, production, and distribution of goods and services in the central city and metropolis as a whole. The inadequate handling of spillovers, inequities in service and tax levels among local governments, and the fiscal imbalance among levels of government are alleviated by shifting the fiscal burden and overall coordination and control of service production to higher levels of government. The property tax is largely replaced by flat-rate income, sales, and value-added taxes levied by metropolitan and state governments. Continuously ongoing research projects and conferences are directed to the development and refinement of techniques (e.g., program-performance-budgeting systems, operations research, cost accounting) to turn the budget into an instrument to improve efficiency and evaluate the relationship between social-capital outlays and private accumulation.

The development of centralized administrative control, budgetary planning, and technocratic procedures provides the organizational means to adjust city budgetary priorities in favor of monopoly capital accumulation. Billions of dollars of state revenues flow into subsidies for new corporate "solutions" to problems of transportation, labor-force development, pollution control, crime prevention, administration of prisons, and the like. Social tensions in the inner city, especially among oppressed minorities, are reduced by creating jobs in the new social-capital projects. Blacks are integrated into a hierarchically ordered class structure. The price of social integration is political impotence—a condition that Blacks share with their white counterparts in office, factory, and neighborhood.

The State Capitalist City is a top priority on the agenda of the class-conscious wing of monopoly capital. It holds out the potential for reversing the strong tendencies toward disaccumulation and urban rebellion underpinning the current urban fiscal crisis. However, divisions within the capitalist class, the power of organized labor and the professional associations, the symbiotic relationship between local businesses and City Hall, and the structure of the state, including federalism and a fragmented system of local government, pose formidable obstacles to the realization of the State Capitalist City.

The transfer of fiscal responsibility and managerial initiative to state and metropolitan forms implies the wholesale destruction of the autonomy and privileged status of suburban fiefdoms. But the fragmented system of local government is entrenched in law and tradition, and powerful suburban-rural coalitions dominate the legislatures of most state governments. Monopoly capital, in combination with the executive wing of federal and state governments, has taken steps towards regional government and metropolitan planning. But the history of comprehensive reform attempts to date has largely been one of failure (Bollens and Schmandt, Chap. 11).

The massive revenue accumulation required by the State Capitalist City entails a considerable increase in the tax exploitation of the organized working class and suburban white-collar and professional groups. The rationalization of the relations of production and distribution of city goods and services portends the end of pork-barrel, logrolling local politics. "Scientific Management" also rationalizes and routinizes the city's production and delivery systems at the expense of worker discretion and prerogative.

In sum, whether the fiscal crisis will be ameliorated by the State Capitalist City depends upon the extent to which enduring political coalitions can be forged between monopoly capital, the relative surplus population, and the federal and state governments—all at the expense of the organized working class, competitive capital, the professions, and the suburbs.

The Socialist City

The Socialist City forms the core of a socialist society.[5] In the short run the development of the Socialist City involves a politics of emancipation, self-help, and the development of a viable local economy. The problem for the emerging Socialist City is to devise alternatives to the market mechanism that allow for the transfer of productive power and the distribution of surplus to areas where the unfulfilled needs of its deprived and impoverished residents are so starkly apparent. Over the long haul, it involves the redefinition of social needs and the concept of surplus itself. In the *mature* Socialist City, socially necessary labor produces socially beneficial use values for present and future residents. The surplus arises out of unalienated labor and loses its class content as city residents yield their surplus labor for socially defined and agreed-upon purposes (Harvey, p. 235).

The transition to the Socialist City portends radical transformations in the relations of revenue accumulation and the production and distribution of public goods and services. Revenue accumulation is governed according to the principle of community ownership of the community's wealth. When a city owns and develops itself, the surplus produced goes to the residents. Residents come to realize that if part of the wealth created by economic activity can be channeled directly to the city treasury, the city is able to markedly expand public services and facilities (Kirshner and Morey). Emergent socialist relations of revenue accumulation are forged out of a series of "nonreformist reforms" generating cumulative pressure against the parameters governing the capitalist state (Gorz, pp. 7–8).

Municipal ownership of selected businesses and the generation of a city surplus through user charges on selected social-capital investments help underpin the development of the Socialist City. Through eminent domain, tax foreclosure, or outright purchase the emerging Socialist City acquires property in areas surrounding its social-capital investments, leases it out to private business, and captures the increment in value. Pension and accrual funds provide blocks of capital for investment in community-owned ventures. Public-assistance recipients are encouraged to pool their money, and with the aid of low-interest city loans to develop housing, food, and credit cooperatives. Jobs in the community cooperatives are created and the money stays in the community (Kirshner and Morey).

In the Socialist City, the relations of production and distribution are governed by the principle of social production to meet social needs. The long-term interests of the city and the visible and compelling short-term interests of its residents coincide. Community ownership of the community's wealth, and social production to meet social needs, imply massive investments of resources in public-sector activities and employment to revitalize the city and improve the quality of urban life. The *emerging* Socialist City implies a large-scale redistribution of wealth. But the *mature* Socialist City implies much more. It implies stability in the material standard of living coupled with continuous improvements in the quality of urban life—in the way in which people relate to one another and their environment through earth-preserving and life-sustaining forms of work and play.

In the Socialist City, the market is replaced by a decentralized planning process. Citywide hearings provide continuous community representation throughout the year. Neighborhoods have the independent sources of information, staff, and other resources necessary to play an autonomous part in the decision-making process. With the maturation of the Socialist City, technology is demystified, all claimed economies of scale are challenged, and science and technology are put in the direct service of human needs, aspirations, and imagination. Various forms of "soft" technology are developed whereby people in neighborhoods can feed, heat, and transport themselves on a community basis. Soft technology "reduces stress on the environment, is low in capital demands, frugal in its use of resources and decentralizing in its social impact" (Morris and Hess).

The creation of the Socialist City obviously faces formidable barriers. Capitalist parameters governing the state tend to limit redistribution and city production of goods and services to the point at which they seriously threaten the production and circulation of private profit. The mutually antagonistic relations between city workers, community groups, and private-sector workers (in their role as taxpayers) have confounded the mobilization of the central-city labor force into a political coalition capable of transforming the character of city and society. Clearly a scenario of the Socialist City that remains unconnected to concrete political struggles pressuring urban administrations in a socialist direction, and that fails to confront the central problem of how public control over production and distribution of surplus in the private sector is to be achieved, represents little more than a utopian pipe dream.

At the same time, however, it would be a serious error to overlook the socialist undercurrent emerging in local and state politics in the United States today. Over the past fifteen years a plethora of "grass-roots" direct-action, electoral, and alternative-institution groups have emerged out of the civil-rights, antiwar, women's, welfare-rights, consumer, and ecology struggles (Perlman). These movements have catapulted representatives into political office who in turn have begun to place public ownership and control over some forms of capital on legislative agendas in cities and states across the country.

In June, 1975, the first "National Conference on Alternative State and Local Public Policies," sponsored by the Institute for Policy Studies, brought together more than 150 officials—mayors, judges, state legislators, city-council members, state and city department heads, school-board members—from state and local governments throughout the United States. The more than twenty conference workshops, ranging from land-use planning and comprehensive tax reform to job creation and housing cooperatives, revolved around one overriding theme: public control over capital (Rowen). One particularly significant product of the conference was a sourcebook of policy proposals, legal initiatives, and legislative enactments on alternative institutional arrangements in state and local government (Institute for Policy Studies). At subsequent regional conferences, and at the second National Conference held in Austin, Texas, in June, 1976, detailed proposals, legislative initiatives, and already-enacted bills on public ownership of banks, insurance companies, lotteries, liquor stores, and electric power companies, as well as mechanisms for citizen participation and government accountability, served as a focus for critical discussion and debate.[6] The Institute for Policy Studies has set up a national legislative clearinghouse and coordinates a network for the communication of shared experiences among state and local political activists around the country.

It would be foolish, of course, to suggest that a Socialist City could be nurtured in the soil of a capitalist society. Rather, political struggles directed toward constructing and implementing socialist urban institutions are best viewed as primitive, yet dynamic and evolving, local foundations for the construction of a socialist society. Sequentially induced, nonreformist reforms can pressure capitalist parameters but can be successful only to the extent that they emanate from the midst of an organically developing mass socialist movement. Powerful political organization cannot be based solely on the control of City Hall, but must be wedded to vertically integrated organizations that are influential from the neighborhood through the state into the houses of Congress. The city must be the base for a system of political power that is mutually reinforcing and supportive. It is as important to have allies in the state legislature and Congress as it is to have effective organization in the city itself. This is all the more crucial due to the commanding role played by state and federal governments in the allocation of resources and programs. Without this type of vertical political integration, political and economic development of the central city will be constrained. The blackening of municipal power and the development of a continuous planning and coordinating network between political officials in aging central cities, urban state legislators, and the Black Congression Caucus in Washington may lay part of the foundation for the multilevel political apparatus needed to support the central city and move in the direction of an urban-based national party.

Alternative state and local policies geared to the creation of cooperative forms of social production to meet social needs are currently being hammered out in the areas of energy, housing, public employment, and so on. But these policies and this vision are unlikely to be effective unless formulated in such a way as to *unite rather than divide* key segments of the working class in our declining urban areas. The absence of a broad and united labor constituency leaves left-oriented officials vulnerable to conservative attack by a state capitalist urban-reform movement riding the whimsical crest of shifting electoral mood. Nonetheless, there are elements within the central-city political arena that suggest that current divisions between overtaxed private-sector workers, the municipal labor force, and insurgent community groups may be overcome in the future.

Unions and associations of municipal employees have a strategic importance in central-city politics. There are strong pressures moving municipal workers toward an understanding of their own interest in the transformation of the central city.[7] For one thing, there is an increasingly glaring contradiction between the ideology of "public service" that informs the functions of city administration and municipal employment and the increasing rationalization of the municipal labor process wrought by State Capitalist urban reforms (O'Connor, p. 241). As resources decline, and as city workers become proletarianized and threatened with unemployment, pressures mount for a coalition between municipal unions and neighborhood activists around a program of upgrading the quality of urban services through expanding and decentralizing municipal employment.

Black political struggle has a potentially powerful role to play in the development of the Socialist City. In almost every declining central city, Blacks and other oppressed minorities constitute an increasingly large share of both the municipal labor force and the relative surplus population. Black leaders are coming to power in central cities. Issues of economic impoverishment, on the one hand, and race and sex oppression on the other, may serve as another basis for cementing a coalition between city workers and insurgent community groups (O'Connor, p. 244).

At the same time, the dependence of municipal workers on the city's budget to meet their own material needs means that the demands of organized city workers encounter increasing hostility from an overtaxed central-city working class. Union demands for improved wages and working conditions, if they are to be realized, will at some point have to be tied to changes in methods of revenue accumulation and overall city budget priorities. To the extent that city workers begin demanding that their material needs and conditions of work be met by reallocating available resources and not by increasing taxes, and to the extent that they begin to challenge the priorities of State Capitalist reforms, the present divisions between private and state workers and the relative surplus population will begin to narrow. Demands for public-service jobs to meet community needs, supported by changes in budget priorities and the tax structure in favor of the working population, are potentially powerful instruments for uniting the fragmented urban working class.

CONCLUSION

All three trajectories of urban change—Pariah, State Capitalist, and emergent Socialist—are currently reflected in the political maelstrom of decaying central cities in the United States. The extent to which contemporary transformations in the structure of urban life will correspond to the needs of the majority of central-city residents will ultimately depend upon how the dynamic relations between the urban fiscal crisis and concrete political struggles work themselves out. At present, deeply distressed Northern cities like Newark and St. Louis most closely approximate the Pariah scenario of urban change. But the dominant tendency in most central cities in the United States is toward State Capitalist urban institutional arrangements (Hill, 1977). The emerging Socialist alternative to State Capitalist urban reform will be effective only to the extent that programmatic policy alternatives are tied to the concrete needs and interests of all three segments of the working population in a manner that unites rather than divides us. To serve this aim, alternative policies must be a vehicle for clarifying the class character of current government arrangements and be explicitly linked to a vision of a better social order. The unifying theme must be community ownership of a community's wealth and social production to meet social needs. What remains unalterably clear at this point is that "unless a vision of a better social order can be made concrete and related to present possibilities, people will struggle for what they can get within the existing system" (Kirshner and Morey, p. 19).

NOTES

1. It is possible to take a snapshot of the process of simultaneous urban expansion and decay by looking at the percentage change in the size of the employed resident labor force in the fifty largest cities in the United States between 1960 and 1970. The results of one study of this type (Hill, 1977) revealed that twenty-one cities experienced declines in the size of their resident employed population. St. Louis ranked at the top of this index of urban stagnation with a 21 percent decline in resident employed labor force, followed by Newark (−16%) and Cleveland (−15%). At the same time, twenty-eight of the fifty largest cities expanded, with Nashville (+174%), Jacksonville (+144%), and San Jose (+118%) leading the list. The urban fiscal crisis tends to be concentrated in the declining central cities; these cities constitute the subject matter of this essay.

2. The geographical distribution of federal expenditures over the past several years has heavily favored urban "growth centers" in the Southern Rim of the United States at the expense of aging cities in the Northeast (Fainstein and Fainstein, pp. 27–32).

3. For example, of the twenty cities in the United States with the largest black populations, thirteen experienced declines in resident employed labor force, ranging from −21 percent in St. Louis to −2 percent in Washington, D.C., between 1960 and 1970. All five of the cities containing the largest number of Blacks (New York, Chicago, Detroit, Philadelphia, and Washington, D.C.) experienced declines in employed resident population during this period (Hill, 1977, Table 3).

4. My portrayal of the contours and implications of the State Capitalist City is deeply indebted to O'Connor's analysis of the social-industrial complex (pp. 51–58).

5. To avoid misinterpretation, let me emphasize that I *am not* arguing that socialism can be constructed on an urban island amidst a capitalist sea. What I am suggesting is that there is a pressing need for a theory of socialist transition in late capitalist societies like the United States and

that a theory of this nature must afford a central role to the dynamics of urban political struggles. This is a point that has been stressed by Marxian political economists in France (Castells, 1977; Lojkine, 1977).
6. For a review of a number of these proposals refer to Shearer; Case, et al.
7. For example, the American Federation of State, County and Municipal Employees representatives have actively participated in the alternative state and local policy conferences and workshops.

REFERENCES

Advisory Commission on Intergovernmental Relations, *City Financial Emergencies: The Intergovernmental Dimension* (Washington, D.C.: U.S. Government Printing Office, 1973).

Alford, Robert, "The Limits of Urban Reform" (Paper presented at the Annual Meeting of the American History Association, San Francisco, 1973).

Baker, Ross, "The Ghetto Writ Large: The Future of the American City," *Social Policy*, Jan.-Feb. 1974.

Berry, Brian J. L., *Growth Centers in the American Urban System*, Vol. 1. (Cambridge, Mass.: Ballinger Publishing Co., 1973).

Bollens, John C., and Henry J. Schmandt, *The Metropolis* (New York: Harper and Row, 1970).

Case, John; Leonard Goldberg; and Derek Shearer, "State Business," *Working Papers for a New Society*, Spring, 1976.

Castells, Manuel, "Vers une théorie sociologique de la planification urbaine," *Sociologie du travail* (Paris), 1969.

————, "Les conditions sociales d'émergence des mouvements sociaux urbains," *International Journal of Urban and Regional Research* (Paris), 1977.

Conforti, Joseph, "Racial Conflict in Central Cities," *Society*, Nov.-Dec. 1974.

Fainstein, Susan S., and Norman I. Fainstein, "The Federally Inspired Fiscal Crisis," *Society*, May-June 1976.

Friedman, Lewis, "City Budgets," *Municipal Performance Report*, Aug. 1974.

Friesema, H. Paul, "Black Control of Central Cities: The Hollow Prize," *Journal of the American Institute of Planners*, March 1969.

Greer, Ed, "The 'Blackening' of Urban America," *New American Movement Newsletter*, June 1974.

Gorz, Andre, *Strategy for Labor* (Boston: Beacon Press, 1968).

Hamilton, Charles, "Urban Economics, Conduit-Colonialism and Public Policy," *Black World*, Oct. 1972.

Harvey, David, *Social Justice and the City* (Baltimore; Johns Hopkins University Press, 1973).

Hill, Richard Child, "Capital Accumulation and Urbanization in the United States," *Comparative Urban Research*, forthcoming.

————, "State Capitalism and the Urban Fiscal Crisis in the United States," *International Journal of Urban and Regional Research*, 1977.

Hymer, Stephen, "The Multinational Corporation and the Law of Uneven

Development," in J. W. Bhagvati, ed., *Economics and the World Order* (New York: World Law Fund, 1971).

Institute for Policy Studies, *"What Do I Do Now?: A Reader on Public Policy* (Washington, D.C.: Institute for Policy Studies, 1975).

Kirshner, Edward M., and James Morey, "Controlling a City's Wealth," *Working Papers for a New Society*, Spring 1973.

Lojkine, Jean, "L'analyse Marxiste de l'état," *International Journal of Urban and Regional Research* (Paris), 1977.

Long, Norton, "The City as Reservation," *The Public Interest*, Fall 1971.

McConnell, Grant, *Private Power and American Democracy* (New York: Alfred A. Knopf, 1967).

Morris, David, and Karl Hess, *Neighborhood Power: The New Localism* (Boston: Beacon Press, 1975).

Muller, Thomas, *Growing and Declining Urban Areas: A Fiscal Comparison* (Washington, D.C.: Urban Institute, 1975).

Netzer, Dick, *Economics and Urban Problems* (New York: Basic Books, 1970).

O'Connor, James R., *The Fiscal Crisis of the State* (New York: St. Martin's Press, 1973).

Offe, Claus, "The Theory of the Capitalist State and the Problem of Policy Formation" (Paper presented at the Eighth World Congress of Sociology, Toronto, Canada, 1974).

Perlman, Janice, "Grassrooting the System," *Social Policy*, Sept.-Oct. 1976.

Reischauer, Robert, and Robert Hartman, *Reforming School Finance* (Washington, D.C.: Brookings Institution, 1973).

Rowen, James, "The Office-Holding Activists," *The Nation*, July 5, 1975.

Shearer, Derek, "Dreams and Schemes: A Catalogue of Proposals," *Working Papers for a New Society*, Fall 1975.

Spero, Sterling, and John M. Capozzola, *The Urban Community and Its Unionized Bureaucracies* (New York: Dunellen Publishing Co., 1973).

Stern, Michael, "Fiscal Experts See the City in Severe Financial Crisis," *New York Times*, October 27, 1974.

Sternlieb, George, "The City as Sandbox," *The Public Interest*, Fall 1971.

U.S. Bureau of the Census, *Pocket Data Book, 1971* (Washington, D.C.: U.S. Government Printing Office, 1972).

U.S. Commission on Civil Rights, *For All the People . . . By All the People: A Report on Equal Opportunity in State and Local Government Employment* (Washington, D.C.: U.S. Government Printing Office, 1969).

Wildavsky, Aaron, *The Politics of the Budgetary Process* (Boston: Little, Brown and Co., 1973).

Zack, Arnold M., "Meeting the Rising Cost of Public Sector Settlements," *Monthly Labor Review*, May 1973.

The New York City Fiscal Crisis

WILLIAM K. TABB

The New York City fiscal crisis of the mid-1970s is conventionally attributed to greedy bankers, corrupt politicians, selfish municipal unions, and malingering welfare recipients. Such explanations of social causation are essentially misleading. They personalize and, in so doing, seriously obscure the larger social processes at work. They do not help us formulate meaningful solutions.

A careful look at the data shows New York City's municipal unions and its welfare population are not the "cause" of the city's problems. Compared with those in other large cities in the United States, such costs are not out of line. These costs appear sizable against the background of a severe overall economic downturn and a long-term loss of employment that is found not only in New York City but also in much of the Northeast, Mid-Atlantic, and industrial Midwest. The movement of capital, and thus of jobs, lies at the heart of the crisis of most older industrial cities. Finally, the attempt to transform New York City into the world corporate capital has imposed a higher cost structure on the city. Overextension of borrowing by shortsighted and opportunistic

* The author is exceedingly grateful for assistance from a number of people, especially Ann Fisher, Matthew Edel, Raymond Franklin, David Gordon, Elizabeth Roistacher, Larry Sawers and Margaret Tabb.

politicians was the immediate trigger to the crisis, but the extent of city borrowing itself cannot be explained without full consideration of this restructuring process.

The crisis is caused by decisions based on private profit calculations and the failure of society through the political process to place social needs ahead of the imperatives of the market. The present trend is not inevitable but results from forces that can be subject to conscious democratic control.

Incorrect explanations act as the rationale for centralization of decision-making and the seizure of power by the city's financial community, which has been instrumental in causing the crisis and has taken control of administering its own solution. Their "solution," however, is iatrogenic, i.e., the very "cure" creates the disease. When this is understood, far different cures are called for, and indeed the dismissal of the discredited "doctors" is demanded.

The traditional "explanations" are dealt with in the first section of this paper. Considering them in some detail is important because they are the rationales for the usurpation of power by the bankers. The data that will be presented is now familiar to most close observers —but unfortunately only after they have been used with great effect to blame the wrong people. Almost all analysts are now willing to admit that New York City's fiscal problem is rooted in the loss of jobs and the failure to generate sufficient new ones to employ the city's work force and support its municipal services.[1] The tasks then are to explain the erosion of the city's economic base and to discuss the issue of whether New York is unique, and if not, as I shall argue, then why has the city's crisis been so dramatic? In a final section, policy options will be discussed.

BLAMING THE VICTIM

The conventional explanations for the New York City fiscal crisis assert that excessive municipal wages and exorbitant welfare payments caused the increased tax squeeze; that the proper solution was to "bite the bullet" by reducing these expenditures. But does the hard data really proclaim the guilt of city workers and welfare recipients? The answer depends, of course, on how comparisons are made.[2]

Arguing against assisting New York City, then–Treasury Secretary

William Simon said: "New York spends in excess of three times more per capita than any [other] city with a population over 1,000,000." He proffered a comparison that turns out to be exceedingly misleading: "Looking at the payroll, Census Bureau data shows that New York employs some 49 employees per 1,000 residents. The payrolls of most other major cities range from 30 to 35 employees per 1,000 inhabitants." The fault lies in Simon's comparing apples and oranges.

The U.S. Congressional Budget Office, a high-caliber nonpartisan agency, made a serious effort to calculate comparative costs. It found that New York City has *not* spent far more. Many of the services that in New York are provided by the city government are in other cities provided by state, county, school-board, special-district, and other non-municipal jurisdictions. A truly comparable estimate must be based only on standard city functions: i.e., elementary and secondary education, roads, police, fire, sanitation, parks, and general and financial administration. New York's actual per capita expenditure for *all* city functions is $1,224 a year as compared with the highs of $858 for Boston and $806 for Baltimore, and with the lows of $248 for Los Angeles and $267 for Chicago. But when we compare *standard* city functions only, the figure for New York City is less than that for many large older cities (New York, $435; Boston, $441; Baltimore, $470; San Francisco, $488), and only slightly higher than that for Los Angeles ($408). From this view it is clear that New York's per capita expenditures are not out of line (p. 146).

When the same standard-functions adjustment is made for comparability with other older cities, we find that Philadelphia, Newark, and Baltimore each has more employees per capita. The Scott Commission study found that expenditures by the New York City government for "common municipal functions" during the precrisis period (1965–1972), measured by both per capita level and growth rate, appear relatively "normal" (pp. III-ii)

> Labor costs, a focus of growing concern in all cities, also do not appear "abnormal" in New York City as compared with these other cities. Both the rates of city government employees per city resident and the average level of wages appear well within the range experienced by most large cities (p. 37).

In another careful study of the data, Professor Charles Brecher concluded:

Once allowance is made for the variations in functions, New York's rate of increase in expenditure is typical of large cities. Among the 10 largest cities, New York ranked seventh in rate of increase in per capita expenditures for functions common to all cities, and for those cities with responsibilities similar to New York's, there was little variation in rate of expenditure growth (p. 3).

Between 1965 and 1972, 31 percent of the city's increased labor cost was due to increased work force, 46 percent to increased prices, and 23 percent represented higher real wages for city employees. Interestingly, with respect to increases in retirement costs, a third was due to more workers covered, 50 percent to price increases, 4 percent to increases in contribution rates, and only 12 percent to real wage increase. While city expenditures in this period had increased by over 150 percent, labor costs rose by about 90 percent and retirement costs even less. These were the years of the alleged "giveaways" (see Scott Commission).

Similarly, while New York City's welfare levels are said to be "generous," in real terms they are *lower* than those of Chicago, Detroit, Philadelphia, and even Milwaukee. In February, 1975, average monthly public-assistance payments per person in the city were $94 (hardly a munificent sum). The 973,000 persons receiving such payments constituted 12.6 percent of the population. New York City was far from having the highest incidence of welfare recipients. In Baltimore the proportion of the population on welfare was 16.8 percent, in St. Louis 16.4 percent, Philadelphia 16.4 percent, Boston 17.0 percent, Washington, D.C., 14.9 percent—all for the same February, 1975, payment month.

Of New York City's city and state welfare expenditures, two-thirds are Medicaid payments to doctors, pharmacists, nursing homes, and hospitals—not cash payments to the poor. A proper investigation of where the welfare dollar goes, of who benefits from "welfare abuse," of who the "chiselers" are, would not focus on the poor. Almost 10 percent of the city's population receive Medicaid benefits, at an average cost per recipient of $2,000 per year. The city, with its large share of the aged poor, pays one-fourth of these staggering costs. Indeed, the fastest-growing cost in city government is not wages or welfare; it is the costs of Medicaid. Medicaid costs have risen by 25 percent *each year* between 1971 and 1976.

Furthermore, far more recipients are harassed off welfare or have their cases closed by fiat than cheat the government. This is evidenced by the findings that half the appeals brought by recipients against city agency actions are accepted by the state, and that in another 30 percent of the cases appealed, the city concedes prior to decision. Clearly, thousands of recipients do not contest unfair decisions. Many do not know they can appeal, and others believe they cannot "fight City Hall."

The New York City crisis was so dramatic because of the extensive debt, and its increasingly short-term nature. This overextension was encouraged by the New York banks in the 1960s for two reasons. First, such loans were a safe, profitable source of tax-free income. Second, the loans went not to help the poor as is frequently alleged, but to finance the costs of transforming New York City to better serve as the headquarters city of the giant U.S.-based international corporations.

Interestingly, the two other older large U.S. cities that seem closest to New York in contracting debt are San Francisco and Washington, D.C. The former is being transformed into "Wall Street West" through a costly renewal program (described by Kessler and Hartman in this book) and the latter is, of course, the administrative capital of the U.S. government. Robert Fitch, after examining the components of New York City's debt, asserts:

> We can understand the financial collapse of the City and its failure to participate in the modest national recovery of 1976 as a consequence of the peculiar role that the City has sought to play over the last fifty years or so. The National Center strategy pushes out industry, requires an enormous infrastructure and generates very heavy debt (p. 257).

This, of course, is not all there is to explaining New York City's debt, as we shall see below, but it is important to make the key connection between overextension of debt and the transformation of the city.

The difficulties engendered by changes in the economic base, as David Gordon has shown (in an earlier essay in this book), place strains on older cities, which cannot easily adjust to their new functional role. The New York City fiscal crisis is a reflection of true transformational costs of the banks' efforts to remake the city. This argument is to be made in a number of steps: first, it is shown that job loss has been the cause of the fiscal crisis; second, that the situation is as serious in many other older cities (except that because they have not borrowed as much, their crisis does not outwardly appear as dramatic), and that a larger process of regional stagnation in the old industrial heartland of the nation is advancing at an alarming rate; third, that the solutions being offered by most politicians and urban experts are iatrogenic, that is, the "solution" is responsible for the disease; and finally, the problems of older cities and regional strife are reflective of an underlying contradiction between the interests of our giant corporations and the nation's citizens, both in their role as taxpayers and as workers.

THE MATERIAL BASE OF THE CRISIS

New York City's loss of 542,000 jobs between 1969 and 1976 lies at the root of the city's fiscal crisis. In 1975 the rate of job loss was twice the average for the preceding seven-year period. The city lost 61,000 public-sector jobs in 1975, bringing the number of government employees to the lowest level since 1966. In addition, another 25,000 manufacturing jobs were lost. That was nothing new: close to half the jobs lost since 1969 had been in factory employment, making the factory work force nearly a third lower at the end of the period than at the beginning. These figures can also be compared with 1950–1969, when the city lost an average of 11,000 factory jobs a year, and for 1969–1975, when losses averaged 43,000 a year. The city has lost 40,000 more manufacturing jobs in the most recent five years than it had in the preceding twenty years! (U.S. Bureau of Labor Statistics)

Job loss is inevitably followed by tax-revenue loss. Economists at the Maxwell School, Syracuse University, estimate that the city loses from $651 to $1,035 in tax revenues, depending on wage level and job category, for each job lost. The city's Finance Administration estimates are lower but still sizable: the loss of a $6,500 blue-collar job results in a loss in sales- and income-tax collection of $320 a year; a $10,500 clerical job, of $532; and a $15,500 professional job, of $950. If the half million jobs that disappeared between 1969 and 1975 were today providing income for New Yorkers, the city would be receiving $1.5 billion more in tax revenues and there would be no crisis.

The dramatic job loss is itself an effect, not a basic cause. The origin of the problem lies in the cyclical nature of our economy and in secular trends brought about by private and public decision structures, which minimize private costs and ignore externalities, specifically the social costs of development patterns. The results are, of course, felt not only in New York City. Geographic mobility of capital and privatized decision-making result in the growth and then the decay of cities and, increasingly, in their troubled older suburbs. It can be predicted that the same pattern will take place in the now-growing parts of the country, the so-called "Sunbelt" in the South and Southwest, in the decades to come.

NEW YORK IS NOT ALONE

New York City's problems are part of a larger trend. In almost all of the older manufacturing cities, the same problems are encountered. To avoid the burdens imposed by the decline in central cities that are occasioned by corporate investment policies, upper-income residents move to exclusive and excluding suburbs. Free choice in the private sector leads mobile capital to move to low-wage areas, leaving behind urban social problems requiring increased taxation from a dwindling tax base.

If, as headline writers suggest, the New York economy is crumbling, then the city is not going downhill alone. Between 1965 and 1972, while New York City lost nearly 16 percent of its jobs, Philadelphia lost 17 percent and New Orleans nearly 20 percent. The recessions of recent years have had dire effects on most of the nation's older cities, particularly on those in the New England and the Middle Atlantic regions. In long-run terms, the economic epidemic has been characterized by a decline in the old manufacturing areas, and by growth in the Sunbelt and in parts of the Northwest. The decline in the quality of life in the older central cities is spreading to their newer suburbs; the rot of a deteriorating infrastructure and housing stock and the curtailment of public services are metastasizing.

In July, 1973, the Advisory Commission on Intergovernmental Relations had issued a report entitled "City Financial Emergencies." Two years before the highly publicized fiscal crisis in New York, the commission had focused on the "incredible and seemingly insoluble array of financial difficulties" facing urban governments due to a wide spectrum of deep structural problems: outmoded capital facilities, inability to increase the tax base, and irreversibly soaring demands of public services. Debt ceilings, taxpayer rebellion, and competition with other jurisdictions placed limits on the cities' ability to raise funds—despite the fact that the basic needs of the citizenry were not even then being adequately met. The "general inability to make the revenue sources stretch to fit the expenditures mandated by the state and demanded by the people" had reached, in the commission's view, emergency proportions (pp. 2–4).

In the cities of almost all of the older industrial states of the northern Midwest and Northeast, stringent cutbacks in municipal services were made. A national survey in 1975 by the Joint Economic Committee found state and local governments eliminating some 140,000 jobs, raising taxes by $3.6 billion, cutting services by $3.3 billion, and canceling or deferring some $1 billion in construction projects.

In Chicago, Cook County Hospital has to borrow $1.5 million every two weeks in order to meet its $4 million payroll; in 1975, the County Board decreased the hospital allocation by $8.8 million and, as a result, matching funds were lost. In Detroit, some museums are open only on alternate weekends. Police are forced to take off two weeks without pay. When Detroit firemen refused a similar package, hundreds were laid off. Bumper stickers and billboards sprouted with pictures of Detroit burning, captioned "What if you had a fire and nobody came?" Small businessmen in the northwest, a middle-class part of the city, are talking of seceding from Detroit on the grounds that the city has failed to meet its obligations to the community. There is a petition drive to recall the mayor. It would be difficult to find a city in the Northeast or the industrial Midwest that is not experiencing serious financial problems and cutting service levels.

CAPITALISTS, WORKERS, AND REGIONAL GROWTH

As the Northeast suffers from decline—in population growth, tax base, jobs, credit rating—the Sunbelt is being touted as the New Frontier of economic development and political power. Many of the reasons traditionally offered for the region's present growth—climate and natural amenities, inexpensive land, low cost of living, and weak unions—are not new factors. What is new is that as the cost of doing business in older "worn-out" cities increases, comparative costs of production in the older areas and the "newer" ones have prompted many decision-makers to relocate. Retired workers, armed-forces bases, and military contractors have provided a critical mass for new growth poles throughout the South and West. The increased profitability in oil and agribusiness has helped these regions. Federal expenditure patterns have also been important: current rough estimates show the Sunbelt states to be collecting some $13 billion more in grants and expenditures (especially military) than they paid in federal taxes, while the Northeast and Mid-Atlantic regions received some $20 billion less (Fainstein and Fainstein).

The South and Southwest are expected to grow due to their lower cost of living, and especially their lower wage rates, which attract northern firms with the lure of advantageous tax treatment and of a productive, difficult-to-unionize work force. By combining tax incentives, antiunion policies, and low social-service expenditures, these states are able to attract corporations to relocate. As *Business Week* tells it:

> When companies go south, they often hire labor relations consultants— "union busters," as the unions brand them—to advise them on how to keep unions out. Another popular tactic is to take a very hard line in bargaining if the union does get in. Typically, a company will reject demands for dues checkoff, arbitration of unresolved grievances, and a seniority system—the very core of a union's strength. "You can strike the company over these issues," says a Southern union official, "but the people just can't hold out long enough" (p. 111).

Employers who cooperate with the union in the Northern strongholds, and indeed use the union to control rank-and-file insurgency, fight the unions tooth-and-nail in their new plants in the South and Southwest. Where unions have been invited in, it has seldom been to the advantage of workers.

Economic and political struggles, not merely some sort of technological or climatic imperative, explain both the pull of the Sunbelt and the push from the Northeast. These struggles are not, in origin, regional ones. The attempt of workers to better their conditions, and of capital to improve its profits by cutting costs, has, as one of its aspects, geographic mobility—a weapon workers are finding their employers more and more willing to use.

INTERESTS IN CONFLICT

Capital's dominance has not gone unchallenged. In fact, a case can be made for the thesis that it was the victories in the 1960s by some of the most oppressed segments of society that set the stage for the current situation; the real crisis today has been precipitated by the business-government counteroffensive.

One of the major accomplishments of the civil-rights movement—especially in its later phase, which moved from the 1964 March for "Freedom Now" to a demand for "Jobs and Income"—was its relative success in bringing economic issues to the fore. The War on Poverty was a recognition that these issues could no longer be avoided. The National Welfare Rights Organization's demand for an adequate standard of living for all, regardless of their attachment to the job market, was a major challenge to the system. It resulted in some reform of the welfare system and in serious consideration by Congress of a Family Assistance Plan that would establish an income floor for all Americans. The black liberation movement's demand for community control led to the creation of economic-development corporations (though these brought few new jobs). The demands for jobs-or-income were made with increasing frequency. At the ideological level, there was a growing consensus that individuals had a legitimate claim on society's resources, a right to protection from oppressive conditions. Direct action—from rent strikes to sit-ins in government offices—were seen as legitimate responses to government failures in countering abuses of greedy landlords, merchants, employers, and public-sector bureaucrats. In auto plants and the U.S. Post Office, for instance, through wildcat strikes and slowdowns, black workers often spearheaded direct action. These activities had a wide impact in at least three major areas.

First: Day-to-day struggle on the job over control of the workplace—always a factor in antagonistic production relations—was accentuated. These struggles were escalated most impressively in the older industrial areas. The difference in the cost of labor between the older industrial cities and the Sunbelt widened both quantitatively and, more important, qualitatively. Class-conscious actions of the more sophisticated and militant workers in the old industrial Northeast, through resistance and sabotage in response to speedups and work stretch-outs, meant rising costs of production. Productivity is a matter of work attitude, and companies found worker discontent on the rise, labor discipline eroding; they sought more docile workers in the South and Southwest.

Second: Public-service recipients became increasingly militant, demanding more responsive and higher-quality services from hospitals, schools, and welfare agencies—all of which were overcrowded and offered services far inferior to the official, though still inadequate, standards.

Third: Urban dwellers in older cities grew resistant to urban-renewal efforts that destroyed ethnic neighborhoods. They also fought highway construction that tore up communities and displaced families and small businesses without proper compensation.

In short, urban resistance, first reaching "crisis" proportions in the racial riots of the 1960s, was part of a larger crisis that pervaded older industrial cities, whose residents were growing politically more sophisticated and whose demands were being met by capital flight. The welfare state, in addition to "cooling" worker resistance as some analysts maintained, was also creating a rising expectation of rights—rights that the system was not willing to grant. Instead, in the worst economic crisis since the Great Depression, the counterdemand has been for reduced wages and fringe benefits, fewer public services, and less mass participation in decision-making.

This analysis of the New York City fiscal crisis is consonant with what we know about the triggering causes, that is, the overextension of credit and the role of the banks. During the economic expansion of the 1960s, the banks lent money to the city, the same way they extended loans on supertankers, jumbo jets, and real estate—as if the boom would go on forever. As long as the economy was growing there was little danger in such loans. When the downturn came, the city was overextended. The timing was doubly bad because it coincided with the new Nixon policy of fiscal federalism, which sharply curtailed aid to the city, and with reduced aid from the state as well. Between 1965 and 1973, state and federal aid grew by an average of more than 50 percent a year. For 1973–1975, the growth rate was 8 percent. In a highly inflationary period, real aid failed to increase. This is the period of increased reliance on trick budgets.

The problem created by an economy incapable of producing anything approaching full employment except in rare peak periods (usually associated with a war) also has a geographical dimension. Upper-income suburbs are created to escape the social costs associated with the production of an urban poverty community. The better-off insulate themselves from the central city, sheltering their money and their persons from the urban problems created by production decisions which ignore social cost in the pursuit of better balance-sheet reports.

In the late 1960s Dick Netzer, who later was to join the Municipal Assistance Corporation (MAC) board, wrote of the city's fiscal problem: "The City on its own has a very limited ability to solve the problem. The City government must devise a program which will maximize the probability that the fiscal problem will in fact be solved from without, by higher levels of government" (p. 653). New York, like almost all older industrial cities, was in a no-growth situation. Its aging physical plant housed a growing lower-income population. Job loss was a serious problem, and tax revenues lagged behind rising expenditure levels. Urban financial experts had come to the decision that "there are few, if any, untapped revenue sources of any quantitative consequence" (Netzer, p. 673). Since taxes on New Yorkers were already "higher than elsewhere in the nation by wide margins" (p. 673), and since there were "few business activities indeed that would not substantially reduce their total tax liabilities by leaving New York City" (p. 674), increasing taxes seemed to make little sense. New York's higher personal tax levels also offered and offer incentives to individuals to migrate to suburbia. The only way it could increase its expenditures was through outside aid. When the additional revenue-sharing stopped, the city floundered; not wishing to make the heartless cuts that it eventually was forced to make anyway, it temporized still further.

INCREASING DEBT

In the spring of 1974, Mayor Abraham Beame presented the usual city budget—one that mislabeled nearly three-quarters of a billion dollars in expenditures so that they could be construed to be part of the capital budget. (The cost of constructing schools and bridges may be amortized through *capital budget* bond issues; toilet paper and other day-to-day purchases should go in the *expense budget,* paid out of current tax revenue.) Thus he could borrow still more and add to the overburdened debt structure in order to pay for the $722 million in expenditures that should either have been paid for out of current revenues or not have been committed. Beame created a Stability Reserve Corporation to facilitate borrowing a half billion to be repaid over the years. In an intricate juggling of books, he arranged the estimates of anticipated revenues, dates of tax collections, and expenditures so as to "balance the city's budget." In the previous year, the last Lindsay budget had done much the same. In it, $564 million of current expenditures had been placed into the capital budget (double the amount for the previous year). By postponing payment on previous debts, still newer obligations could be and were contracted.

The city budget was widely considered by those with even a casual acquaintance with such matters as nigh unto fraud. To those who prepared the budget, the use of such gimmicks had an internal logic.

In the late 1960s, the city extended its borrowing against an anticipated increase in revenues from projected real estate taxes and from federal and state aid. Federal aid under President Nixon had failed to keep pace with expectations. With the severe downturn in 1973 real estate, tax receipts failed to grow. Short-term borrowing was the easy way out for hard-pressed politicians.

Answering the charge before a Senate Committee that New York's fiscal crisis was "caused" by the irresponsible borrowing of irresponsible politicians, Mayor Beame excused his own actions, saying:

> I have long acknowledged that the City was resorting to undesirable budgeting practices to meet its responsibilities to the public—practices which have already been known to the underwriters. But, those sophisticated in city finances recognized that the borrowing and the gimmickry were the product of common consent of all concerned—by all political leaders—and by all levels of government, and with the full knowledge of the financial community, in recognition of the very special and enormous burdens which the City of New York must bear.
>
> When I assumed office in January 1974, I publicly recommended programs to eliminate it. Yet, financial institutions which had provided the City with credit when they knew of this large gap have become reluctant to loan money in the very face of reforms and economies already underway (U.S. Senate, p. 5).

The Mayor's statement is, I submit, essentially correct. The question then becomes: Why was such a course taken? And did everyone "cooperate"?

Interestingly, those who would now scapegoat the mayor had as much to do with bringing the present situation into being as he did.

The city's overborrowing legally required the state's approval. The man who extended this permission through his hold on the legislature was former New York State Governor Nelson Rockefeller. Under his aegis, the state itself went heavily into debt. To exceed constitutional borrowing limits, Mr. Rockefeller asked the help of a friend, a Wall Street lawyer and expert on bonds, later to become the law-and-order Attorney General indicted in the Watergate burglaries. John Mitchell is the man who dreamed up the "moral-obligation bond," which allowed New York State to borrow beyond constitutional limits (and to avoid voter rejection on public referenda). The legality of these bonds —certainly their financial soundness—has been questioned by many, including Secretary of the Treasury William Simon, who, in refusing help to New York, said its own irresponsible borrowing was to blame. But when Simon was the ace bond salesperson for Salomon Brothers, who sold many of these very questionable debt instruments, he was more enthusiastic. These "innocents" very clearly knew what they were doing. Indeed, one might argue that the city overborrowed because of —not in spite of—these men.

But it was not just a matter of selfish or venal individuals. There is no claim here that there was a bankers' conspiracy to "get the city," to milk it and bleed it and profit from its misery. Bankers as people are not any more venal than others. As bankers, however, they act by bankers' logic. For those who suffer as a result of this logic, the consequences can be harsh indeed.

In the six-month period between October, 1974, and March, 1975, the city's large banks bailed out of the New York bond market, selling $2.3 billion in city securities. Realizing that their loans in the past had so overextended New York's obligations, they rushed to pull out fast, before others saw how serious the situation was becoming. In so doing, they pulled the rug out from under the city, which was in that very time period attempting to roll over $3 billion of its short-term debt. As one press report recounts, "This sudden avalanche of New York City bonds and notes set off a panic among municipal investors. As a result, the City was barred from capital markets—perhaps for decades. New York City didn't jump; it was pushed" (Newfield and DuBrul, p. 11).

The New York bankers sold heavily, dumping city obligations, and then claimed, after they themselves had saturated the market by unloading their portfolios, that the city could no longer borrow and that first MAC and then the EFCB (Emergency Financial Control Board) needed to be created to run the city. Once the market for New York securities collapsed and interest rates rose to record levels, they returned to the market themselves. This led many close observers to blame the banks for the city's painful suffering, for they caused the panic and then took control of the city to ensure they would profit from the solution of the crisis.

In acting like bankers, it made sense, for example, to keep rolling over the billions upon billions in real estate loans. New York City's six largest banks held $3.6 billion in face-value loans backed by bankrupt condominiums, hotel developments, and unsold second-home and retirement villages. This $3.6 billion is far less secure in a real sense than the $1.7 billion these banks held in city securities. The city is an amateur in shoddy budgeting and gimmickry compared with the Real Estate Investment Trust entrepreneurs who pyramid loans and leverage their accounts to four dollars for every dollar they may have. Cases abound such as the one in which, in a declining market, an $8.5 million hotel is magically (and for a mere $50,000 fee) revalued at $26 million. As President Ford was giving his "Drop Dead" speech (from the *Daily News* headline of October 30, 1975: "FORD TO CITY: DROP DEAD") Chase Manhattan Mortgage and Realty Trust was negotiating with its forty-one creditor banks to reduce interest on its more than three-quarters-billion-dollar debt—from 9.75 percent to 2 percent. The banks did not scale down their loans to the city; indeed they raised the interest rates. By 1977, 20 percent of New York's budget went to interest payments—the largest and fastest-growing single item. (The city's MAC bonds were paying 10 percent interest in late 1976.)

Since the bankers have some influence on making the rules and the ways they are enforced, "suffering" has not been spread evenly. The key bankers' meetings to decide whether to extend the city credit were held in bank offices at 23 Wall Street, a building on which real estate taxes were reduced that year by a quarter of a million dollars. The Stock Exchange building's taxes were reduced by a similar amount (on top of other reductions the two previous years). When Dun and Bradstreet pondered the rating to be given the "irresponsible" city, they themselves pled poverty and obtained a $200,000 reduction in the property-tax assessment for their building at 99 Church Street. Nearby stood the tax-exempt World Trade Center, so called so the Port Authority could build this mammoth office complex by dubbing it a "port facility." If they were private buildings, the city would receive about

$50 million in taxes from the towers. Instead, taxpayers were (1) paying interest to the banks for the money lent to build the structure, (2) paying its operating deficit, (3) paying higher taxes to the state, which are turned over to the World Trade Center for the high-cost office facilities, and (4) making up the tax reductions granted to other office buildings with vacant space due to offices moving to the World Trade Center. The details of how David Rockefeller as head of the Lower Manhattan Association prevailed upon the then–Governor Nelson Rockefeller to appropriate the taxpayers' money in the four ways mentioned above would only be the beginning of the story of how banks both cause fiscal problems and profit from their "resolution."

The key point here is that the interests of most New Yorkers and those of the banks are in sharp conflict. The banks have always reaped windfall profits from the city. When the New York subways were being built, the city was stuck with 60 percent of the construction cost—money it did not have and had to borrow from the banks. By 1940, when the subways had finally been run into bankruptcy, the city's initial $355 million debt owed to the banks stood at $1.8 billion—the original debt had not been paid off, and interest had continued compounding. The city then borrowed another $1.5 billion to buy the bankrupt lines of the IRT. New York is still paying off the debt on the subway system.

The incompetent political hacks who are blamed for the city's problems have worked closely with the banks and real estate speculators. Indeed, the relationship between the city's bankers and its politicians has been a symbiotic one. Conflict breaks out only in time of crisis; then, if the politicians don't cooperate with the bankers' solutions, they are replaced.

In periods of financial stress (there have been twenty such business cycles in the United States since the Civil War), restructuring is carried out by the largest banking houses and corporations at the expense of smaller firms and of workers, who have less bargaining power at the trough of the cycle. In the cities, this takes the form of an unwillingness to reinvest and the intensification of the search for new low-wage areas at home and abroad upon which to base the next period of growth. In the twentieth century, these cycles create a surplus work force in the older centers, and deprive the cities of the tax revenues needed to meet the cost of maintaining this swollen reserve army of now-redundant workers—workers who will be absorbed only at the peak of the cycle.

In the history of New York City, there have been many essentially similar cycles. In an expanding economy, expenditures rise to meet the needs of citizens for services as well as the needs of politicians for patronage jobs, contractor contributions, and votes at election time. Special-interest groups swarm, each trying to get as much of the pork barrel as possible. In a larger economy prone to business cycles, optimistic projections of growth give way (after overexpansion in the downturn) to talk of the need for austerity and responsible government (Boss Tweed was elected to throw the rascals out). If the crisis is a severe one, a coalition of "good-government" activists backed by the banks, large real estate interests, and major downtown retailers may take a very direct role in guiding local politics. In the two most recent disaster periods—the Great Depression and the current period (the worst economic debacle since the 1930s)—bankers may directly assume management of the city over the opposition of elected officials.

In 1933 the state legislature set up a Mutual Economic Commission ("Big MEC"?), which was able to fend off day-to-day disasters. By juggling accounts it managed to pay the bills and meet the reduced payroll. The crisis continued until 1935, when a sort of Emergency Financial Control Board was set up with minimal pretense concerning democratic accountability. The new state legislation was called the "Bankers Economy Act." A new auditing and bookkeeping system was established under the direction of the banks, and sound management practices were introduced.

The extent of the economic upswing of the 1960s is a rare occurrence in U.S. history. The most recent parallel to it is the 1920s. In both of these decades of sustained expansion, New York City experienced a major boom in office construction. Each ended with a glutted market. In both instances, the city optimistically projected growth rates in a period of affluence, then became overextended and went into receivership. The 1935 Bankers Agreement abdicating power to the financiers was a less euphemistic transfer of power than the creation of the Emergency Financial Control Board.[3]

Unless the current New York City fiscal situation is seen in the historical context of cyclical crises and structural transformation, the role of the bankers can be given too volunteerist a cast. While the names and faces change, the process is part of the normal way the system works. To obscure this central reality, the victims of the crisis are blamed—workers, city employees, and service recipients.

THE CONTINUING CRISIS

"Solving" New York City's fiscal crisis is relatively easy. Someone must pay. If the poor, the unionized workers, and the neighborhoods accept mammoth reductions of all kinds, the problem is "solved."

Because U.S. capital does not care about the social costs of its investment decisions, welfare costs rise, surplus labor has no place to go, real wages are forced down. Increased tax burdens (thanks to the substantial erosion of the tax base in favor of the giant corporations) and inflation are the most powerful ways of redistributing income away from those who work as well as those who have no work.

Under this "solution," what is in store for the city? Not one set of sacrifices, but continuing severe cutbacks in service and a cycling downward into further decay are to be expected—to be ended only when "planned shrinkage" gets rid of enough of the poor, and unionization among municipal workers has been adequately beaten back.

American social scientists are fond of denying that there is such a thing as class struggle. In the case of the New York fiscal crisis, they speak in value-neutral terms of increasing efficiency. Politicians urge us all to pull together, share the burden, bite the bullet. The perspective offered in the present analysis suggests that class conflict in fact lies at the heart of the problem—it explains why the crisis exists, why those in power choose the scapegoats they do, why they seek to impose the "solutions" they do. Alternative answers that do not require the poor and the workers to bear the burden of the crisis must begin with an analysis that does not blame them for the existence of the crisis. The conventional analyses, when subjected to scrutiny, have been found to be incorrect, misleading. The simplest of class analyses is strongly suggestive of which forces are, in fact, to blame and of how to conceptualize alternative answers to the crisis.

We can trace the problem "back" then—from welfare and wages, corruption and overborrowing, to the loss of jobs and taxable resources, to the workings of the profit motive and the political system that has "solved" our economic problems by creating even more severe ones.[4]

The increased mobility of capital, along with its ability to plan on a global basis, undercuts the power of workers as individuals, and to the extent that the latter have access to institutional representation in unions and local governments, the possibility of defensive action there, too, is undercut. The effect of workers in one area having to compete for jobs with those in another, and of jurisdictions' being able to encourage plant location through tax giveaways and free services, mean lower wages and higher tax levels for working people in all areas.

The real answer, then, is in the social control of investment. In the absence of some sort of planned development, even the areas of the United States that are now more favored, the South and the West, will find their amenities increasingly vandalized. Ecological ruin, after all, is a manmade disaster, and pollution and congestion are already prevalent in much of the Sunbelt. It is almost surely in the interest of both the rapidly growing and the contracting regions to slow down this process. The New York crisis will spread, not just to other older cities (it is there already), but also to newer ones and their more affluent suburbs. As the Gross National Product rises, we become poorer in our quality of life. Instead of helping to offset social costs through progressive social programs—in health, housing, mass transit, income maintenance, and job creation—a "planned-shrinkage" policy is being advocated. We Americans are asked to be "realistic" about what government can do, and told that we should not throw money at problems. It is time to face up to this long-term trend and to discuss the alternative to perpetual deterioration. That alternative is the social control of investment, which of necessity would include planned full employment and price controls. The distribution of jobs and resources is already a political issue. The central question is whether it will be decided under democratic control by consumers and workers, or by corporations and their politician friends who claim there is little they can do to meet social needs.

The issue can perhaps be addressed in a somewhat different manner by asking the question: If someone must be brought in to centralize the running of the city and work out a coherent policy, why the banks? Why not the best technical experts? Why not professionals in government, trained at the best schools, paid salaries commensurate with their responsibilities? New York City has the second largest government budget in the United States and would be the fourth largest corporation if it were privately owned. Shouldn't an operation that size be run on the same basis as General Motors or Chase Manhattan Bank, with the best talent unlimited money can buy? Certainly a good data system and stringent cost-benefit techniques could save the city millions, easily paying for such salaries.

Why is it that the banks and giant corporations are allowed to hire the best talent money can buy in profusion, while government agencies are kept to a poor make-do level of staffing at less than competitive salaries? Is it because corporations prefer to face such amateurish competition when they are challenged in governmental actions? A bumbling, inefficient government is in the best interests of the corporate sector's freedom to do as it likes with minimal interference. And when government, which after all must work within the very limited constraints of our free-enterprise system, fails to solve economic problems, politicians are discredited. But replacing them does little good. The problem is with the way the whole system works, not the mistakes of the individual inept or corrupt politicians. We seem very far indeed from having any kind of vision of a decentralized, participatory sort of democracy that would encompass control of economic and political decision-making.

In the light of the analysis of New York City that has been presented, what is the future likely to hold? The emerging strategy is that of *"planned shrinkage"*—the dismantling of services to lower-income communities with the goal of pushing their residents out of the city. This is an integral part of the *transformation strategy*—get rid of the poor, break the power of the municipal unions and reduce services, except to the business community and upper-income areas.

PLANNED SHRINKAGE

Jay Forrester, a Massachusetts Institute of Technology professor, has used a computer-simulation "urban dynamics" model to work out the likely effect of various city policy options. The one that maximized a city's well-being called for tearing down poor people's homes. It is very simple. The computer coldly and logically spewed out its conclusion: if we destroy people's homes and they have nowhere to live in the city, they will have to leave. As a result, the average income of the city rises and the city's well-being increases. By concerning itself with the *city* instead of with its *people,* computers can come to such conclusions.

Not only computers but also flesh-and-blood people can think this way. A most important recent development in the New York City fiscal crisis has been the public surfacing of just such a policy formulation. Roger Starr, the City's Housing and Development Administrator in early February, 1976, sent up a trial balloon. He suggested, as an alternative to continued across-the-board cuts in city services, that the city "thin out services" in certain slum areas: that the city close fire and police stations and curtail public education as a way of accelerating population decline. Such action would make whole areas of the city uninhabitable, and then the land could be bulldozed. By offering "inducements" for people to move elsewhere (hopefully out of the city?), the "city" could be saved. The acceleration of housing abandonment emerges as a major strategy proposal by some conservative thinkers for solving the city's crisis. "We should not encourage people to stay where their job possibilities are daily becoming more remote," he asserts (Starr, especially p. 104).

Many urban experts—"the new pragmatists"—endorse these policies as inevitable and also as finally in the "best interests of the poor themselves." Thus one of the leading urban economists in the country, George Sternlieb, asks whether the city "has the political courage to realize you won't be able to support the poor unless Manhattan is a refuge for the rich." His answer to his own question: "You can't support the poor without the rich, and every time someone rich stays in Manhattan it's a triumph for the poor—but that's very hard to sell in New York" (quoted in Kaiser, p. 23).

The transformational strategy did not prove as easy to implement as the financiers at first thought. For one thing, the wrong people started leaving as the budget cuts began to have painful effects on the city's quality of life. Second, the municipal workers had become so demoralized by the wholesale firings, the loss of real income for those who remained, the powerlessness of their unions, and the chaos resulting from the budget cuts that efficiency fell. Not only did workers no longer have the supplies and equipment to do the job, but work loads had increased so that any pride in doing a job well was impossible to maintain. Third, as interest group was played against interest group to the disadvantage of all, the delicate social fabric was rent.

The debate among those who make policy for New York City is how far they can go with planned shrinkage, what to do with the surplus people, how to overcome resistance to the transformation strategy by those who suffer from it. Are there any other choices?

A second approach, and one that has a great deal of appeal to many New Yorkers, is to resist massive cuts in municipal services, and instead to tax the banks, the corporations, and the rich who earn their income in the city. If taken in isolation, a comparative-statistics approach declares this second choice to be self-defeating. It would contribute to, rather than stem, the exodus of the city's tax base.

A third approach would be to recognize that the city's problems cannot be solved within its own borders and that a supportive national urban policy is called for, which at the barest minimum would consist of a liberalizing set of reforms—nationalized health care, welfare reform, and a fairer expenditure pattern of federal largesse—and which, as its ultimate goal, would seek to socialize the investment decision-making processes.

The second and third approaches can be seen in dialectical relation. By pushing for adequate services, even in the face of a shrinking local tax base, pressure is placed on all levels of decision-making to modify the rules of the game. The city's interests lie in a sensible national urban policy. Its tools include persuasion, to be sure, but also required are militant political actions and a broad-based movement willing to face up to the seriousness of our problems and willing to consider radical ideas on how best to solve them.

NOTES

1. The conventional wisdom seems ever to lag behind changing reality. The best expert opinion of the early 1970s was that New York was alive and well, and that it really had no serious problems. Consider the following:

   "The City's funded debt has not been increasing at all rapidly in recent years, as debt repayment more or less matches new borrowing. If this policy persists, debt service costs will grow only slowly in the years immediately ahead. There is no reason to expect the policy to change, unless the capacity of city agencies to actually consume larger Capital Budget allocations improves rapidly; even so, until the market for municipal bonds eases substantially, it is improbable that any administration would feel comfortable about an aggressively expanded new borrowing program" (Dick Netzer, in Fitch, 1970, pp. 664–65).

Of the commonly accepted proposition that "New York City's economy is shrinking, the facts do not support this view of the local labor market." Another "currently accepted proposition is that the unique role of New York City as a stronghold of corporate headquarters is being eroded and that it is only a matter of time before this trend will lead to the decline of the City's economy. Again, a look at the facts will help set the record straight" (Eli Ginsburg, 1973, pp. 70–71).

"Predictions of rapid decay for New York's economy are likely to be proved wrong. The City's employment base grew substantially over the last decade and at a rate equivalent to that of most similarities. Although the manufacturing sector has declined somewhat, this is true of manufacturing relative to total employment in every large city" (1973) (Stanley Friedlander and Charles Brecher, p. 28).

2. Professor Terry W. Clark and associates of the University of Chicago have sought to put the New York fiscal crisis in perspective through a comparison with a representative sample of places of residence of the U.S. urban population. Leading newspapers popularized their contention that "population size is associated with many variables affecting fiscal matters but has minimal direct effect on fiscal strain" (p. 5). This may be a misleading generalization, since it is drawn from an analysis of a sample of fifty-one cities that range in population from 50,000 to only 750,000, with which New York City, Chicago, and Los Angeles are compared.

Thomas Muller, comparing U.S. cities with populations of half a million or more, comes to somewhat different conclusions. The choice of samples reflects an underlying difference in approach. The Clark study sees the crucial comparison to be the amount New York spends per capita compared with the average of American cities. In a competitive economy, in this view, the relevant comparison is the urban average, for given freedom of movement, the affluent will relocate to avoid taxation.

Muller, on the other hand, is interested in comparing the fiscal status of growing and declining larger cities. Interestingly, public spending per capita in U.S. cities, arranged by population size, does not increase markedly up to cities of a half million (see table reproduced below). This is of significance in comparing the findings of the two studies.

Expenditure for Common Services Per Capita for U.S. Cities by Population Size

City Size	Dollars per Capita
50,000 to 99,999	129
100,000 to 199,999	157
200,000 to 299,999	180
300,000 to 499,999	177
500,000 to 999,999	232
1,00,000 +	283

Source: City Government Finances in 1972–73 (Washington, D.C.: Bureau of the Census, 1974).

Muller's conclusion (that declining large cities in the North and industrial Midwest are in trouble compared with "Sunbelt" cities) is in
Clark's view oversimplified. "The stereotypes," Clark writes, "are false,
or at least misleading" (p. 5). Clark's more limited sample, weighted as
it is to smaller cities, does not find the trend Muller observes. However,
the expanded sample, and the more representative one, does in fact
show the "stereotype" view to be supported. The excellent statistical
work of both studies forms the basis of very different policy emphases.

Most decision-makers and the general public are exposed to such
scholarly studies only in the simplified form in which they appear in
newspaper accounts. The public may reach opinions, and decision-
makers may act on the views, formed in this manner. It is important to
explain why these different results come about—in this case because of
different sample cities used for comparison.

3. The press for the most part treated the transfer of power with awe and
respect for the banks, generally praising their willingness to get involved. The takeover was greeted with editorial assurance by the *New
York Times*:

The intricate series of maneuvers, commitments, and legislative action
through which New York City has been rescued from the disaster of
default provides much needed reassurance of democratic society's capacity to overcome partisanship and selfish interest in the face of crisis.

The *Times* sees not disenfranchisement, but a boon to democracy. It
also characterized the teachers' strike to preserve past gains in working
conditions as a "shameful desertion" by teachers of their classrooms—
while the governor and Big MAC are praised for their stand in opposition.

The only New York newspaper with any significant circulation to print
a different position was the *Village Voice*. In its pages, Pete Hamill
wrote of the banks:

They managed their coup d'état with an extraordinary gift for the
Big Con. They gave the impression that only New York was profligate,
that only New York had trouble paying for its paper, that only New
York was wasting money.

The junta's bankers did not mention their own responsibilities in reducing New York to panhandler status: how they manipulated the huge
office building boom of the '60s that has left us with 32 million empty
feet of office space; redlined marginal neighborhoods that could have
been saved with an infusion of private capital; recklessly shot craps
in the stock market; and exported New York capital to distant parts of
the United States and the world.

The central tactic of the Big Con is to place the blame elsewhere.
The bankers have placed the blame for their own bottomless greed on
New York. It is like the mugger blaming the victim for not having
money" (1975, p. 7).

4. The inability of the U.S. capitalist economy to create full employment
and the phenomenon of manufacturing leaving the industrial Northeast, on the one hand, and the militance of the working class poor in
the 1960s demanding humane levels of social-service benefits, on the
other, set the terms of the urban fiscal crisis of the 1970s. The reformist

achievements of the 1960s did not address the causes of the problem but rather sought to ameliorate conditions through expanded welfare measures. These benefits, while far from adequate, look relatively over-generous in a period of economic crisis and retrenchment. The "right" to such services in a market economy can never be absolute, since it violates the very logic of the allocation process. Welfare in a market society is demeaning because it must be extended in a manner that does not interefre excessively with work incentives. It must perpetuate stratification and hierarchy by characterizing recipients not as victims of the economic system but as parasites on the social order. The demand for minimal income for the nonworking drives a wedge between them and overtaxed workers.

Similarly, the demands of municipal workers are portrayed as coming at the expense of these same taxpayers. Price increases in the private sector, a far more important source of declining living standards, while disliked, are taken as inevitable. Further, the argument that unless profits are protected, "they" will not be able to create jobs for us, reflects an acceptance that the key decisions that affect our lives are beyond our control. The function of government may be to promote full employment, but the only acceptable way to do so is to bribe the corporations through higher profits. Textbook notions that ours is a pluralistic society in which contending interest groups vie for influence seem naive in the face of the power of capital.

REFERENCES

Advisory Commission on Intergovernmental Relations. *City Financial Emergencies: The Intergovernmental Dimension* (Washington, D.C.: U.S. Government Printing Office, 1973).

Auletta, Ken, "An Agenda to Save Our City," *New York*, March 22, 1976.

Brecher, Charles, *Where Have All the Dollars Gone? Public Expenditures for Human Resource Development in New York City, 1961–1971* (New York: Praeger, 1974).

Business Week, "The Second War Between the States," May 17, 1976.

Clark, Terry Nichols; Irene Sharp Rubin; Lynne C. Pettler; and Erwin Zimmerman, "How Many New Yorks?: The New York Fiscal Crisis in Comparative Perspective," draft of a study in progress; September 15, 1976, version, University of Chicago, Department of Sociology. Also see Terry Nichols Clark, "Fiscal Strain in New York and Elsewhere—Is New York Still First?" *New York Affairs*, in press.

Fainstein, Susan S., and Norman I. Fainstein, "The Federally Inspired Fiscal Crisis," *Society*, May-June, 1976.

Fitch, Robert, "Planning New York," in Roger E. Alcaly and David Mermelstein, eds., *The Fiscal Crisis of American Cities* (New York: Vintage Books, 1977).

Forrester, Jay W., *Urban Dynamics* (Cambridge, Mass.: MIT Press, 1969).

Friedlander, Stanley, and Charles Brecher, "A Comparative View," in Eli Ginzburg, ed., *New York Is Very Much Alive* (New York: McGraw-Hill Book Co., 1973).

Ginzburg, Eli, "The Manpower Record," in Eli Ginzburg, ed., *New York Is Very Much Alive* (New York: McGraw-Hill Book Co., 1973).

Hamill, Peter, "Welfare Must Be Abolished," *Village Voice*, Sept. 29, 1975.

Kaiser, Charles, "Black and Puerto Ricans—a Bronx Majority," *New York Times*, Apr. 19, 1976.

Muller, Thomas, "Growing and Declining Urban Areas: A Fiscal Comparison," (Washington, D.C.: Urban Institute, Nov. 1975, with minor revisions Mar. 1976).

Netzer, Dick, "The Budget: Trends and Prospects," in Lyle C. Fitch and Annmarie Hauck Walsh, eds., *Agenda for a City: Issues Confronting New York* (Beverly Hills: Sage Publications, 1970).

New York Times, "State of the City: Industry and Labor," May 13, 1975.

Newfield, Jack, and Paul DuBrul, "Banks to City: Drop Dead," *Village Voice*, Nov. 22, 1976.

(Scott Commission) Maxwell Research Project in the Public Finances of New York City, *New York City: Economic Base and Fiscal Capacity* (New York: State Study Commission for New York City, 1973).

Starr, Roger, "Making New York Smaller," *New York Times Sunday Magazine*, Nov. 14, 1976.

U.S. Bureau of the Census, "Population Estimates and Projections," *Current Population Reports*, Series P-25, number 615 (Washington, D.C.: U.S. Government Printing Office, 1976).

U.S. Bureau of Labor Statistics, Middle Atlantic Region "1975 Year End Report on Employment, Prices and Earnings in New York City." *Regional Labor Statistics Bulletin*, Number 39, Jan. 1976.

U.S. Congressional Budget Office, *New York City's Fiscal Problems: Its Origins, Potential Repercussions and Some Alternative Policy Responses* (Washington, D.C.: U.S. Government Printing Office, 1975).

U.S. Senate, Committee on Government Operations, *Federal Response to Financial Emergencies of Cities* (Washington, D.C.: U.S. Government Printing Office, 1975).

four

ORGANIZING TO
MEET THE CHALLENGE

The papers in this part analyze two very different attempts to organize for social change. Jim Green and Allen Hunter describe how Black people and their white allies in Boston have struggled against racial segregation and its adverse impact on the quality of education. The broader issue in Boston is racism and how it divides the working class, preventing unity in its struggle for common goals against common enemies. Their paper places the material base of racism in the material insecurity of white workers and the usefulness to the ruling class of divisions within the working class. The paper describes the fifteen-year struggle by the Black community to end de facto segregation in Boston schools. The story is one of a patient, grass-roots organizing campaign as a part of a national civil-rights movement.

Katharine Coit analyzed recent struggles for social change in Italy. She first establishes that citizen participation in the U.S. War on Poverty in the late 1960s was an exercise in cooptation rather than a true incorporation of a working-class point of view into the program. Then she describes the way that militant organizers, often associated with trade unions, have launched campaigns to occupy housing, to stop paying telephone-rate and transit-fare increases, and to reduce rental payments. These methods have exposed the contradictions in the system, have given the masses a sense of their power and their opponents' vulnerability, have offered participants a taste of self-direction, and by involving millions in illegal activity have exposed the way the legal system and the politicians protect property before people. The cases Coit discusses present a very different political and economic philosophy—that people's needs come before profits—a very subversive idea in a capitalist economy.

The involvement of large numbers of ordinary people in acting to change the rules—rules that are given to them by those in power in a society's key political and economic institutions—is what we mean by the term *mass movement*. The ideology of a mass movement reflects the perceptions of such a grouping—who their friends are, who their enemies are, what needs to be changed, and the way they justify such actions with recourse to some set of principles. In the case of busing in Boston in the 1970s, Green and Hunter explain the struggle against busing by militant whites, and for quality education by committed Blacks, in a way that gets at some of the causes of racism. Coit discusses a different set of problems in another national context. Both, however, are relevant to the experience of rent strikers and local parent-controlled school boards struggling to control their community institutions in cities throughout the United States.

Racism and Busing in Boston

JIM GREEN and ALLEN HUNTER

"Don't Blame Me, I'm from Massachusetts" was a bumper sticker that appeared in the only state that voted for McGovern in 1972. That slogan has an ironic ring now, because some of the people who voted against Nixon are engaging in organized and sustained racist attacks on Boston's black people. Since the opening day of school on September 12, 1974, racist attacks have come in several forms, including the stoning of buses carrying black students and the beating of two Blacks by mobs in South Boston. In the large black housing project at Columbia Point, tenants responded to violent white attacks by arming and organizing for self-defense. To counter this, the police occupied Columbia Point.

The busing of black and white children to relieve racial imbalance in the Boston schools has finally been won after a decade of concerted School Committee opposition to improvements in the education of

* We wrote this article in November, 1974, as a collective editorial statement for *Radical America,* a Boston-based socialist journal. At that time it was important to take a strong stand against racist violence and against primarily racist opposition to busing. The polemical purpose of the article flowed from the political urgency of the busing crisis that erupted in Boston in 1974. There was no time to produce a documented history, but two years of further study and reflection on events have convinced us that our analysis was fundamentally correct.

black children. Now, in addition to continued obstruction by the School Committee, a serious problem is developing in the form of organized opposition to busing in many of Boston's predominantly white working-class neighborhoods.

Although Democratic Party demagogues like City Councilor Louise Day Hicks and School Committee Chairman John Kerrigan have promoted racist politics, we cannot underestimate the deep-seated, well-organized quality of racism among large numbers of white working-class people in Boston. Unlike other cities where whites launched violent but rather short-lived demonstrations against busing, the opposition to desegregation in Boston has been mobilized for several years on a block-by-block basis in predominantly Irish South Boston and other sections. It will be a dangerous force to contend with for some time to come. Ku Klux Klan and Nazi Party organizers have come to South Boston, sensing the potential for a turn toward fascism.

Because white working-class people have been prominent in the racist attacks, it has been difficult for some socialists to explain racism without reducing the problem to one in which either the corporate elite is manipulating working-class people by provoking racism, or to one in which the race-baiting politicians of the old Democratic machine are whipping up racism to advance their own political fortunes. While both of these are partial explanations, they miss the real point. White working-class racism is not simply a question of bad ideas being put into people's heads by racist demagogues, nor is it simply a question of the ruling class manipulating workers into racist positions. There is a material basis to white working-class racism in Boston and elsewhere.

White working-class people oppose integrated education as a way of defending their material advantage over Blacks. Most white working-class people are against busing white children to black schools because in a racist society, black schools are poorer schools. Many white working-class people are against even voluntary busing of black children to white schools because they fear that if black students come in, their "neighborhood" schools will be allowed to deteriorate in various ways. Some people in Boston's white working class have chosen to help Blacks fight discrimination by joining the struggle of Blacks for equality. Many others have chosen to defend segregation by attacking the black struggle for equality in education. The thrust of the racist movement that has crystallized this fall is to keep black people in their place—in segregated schools, in ghetto housing, and in the lowest-paying jobs.

The question of neighborhood schools is not the main issue in Boston. White working-class parents have in some cases chosen to send their children some distance to attend predominantly white parochial schools, or even to special Boston-wide public high schools. Busing is not really the issue, because schoolchildren have been bused back and forth across the city for some time. Nor is the issue one of compulsion. School itself is compulsory, regular attendance is compulsory, a certain curriculum is compulsory. Busing is no more forced than any of these other aspects of schooling.

The issue is racism, and it is wrong to shift the debate away from it at this time. To argue now about the educational value of busing or of community-controlled schools versus integrated schools would be to equivocate. It is wrong to avoid the issue by arguing about the merits of various hypothetical alternatives: alternatives to the current busing plans do not now exist for most black parents in Boston. While we do not call for integration, we do oppose forced exclusion and segregation of Blacks and other minorities; we support their right to integration either as a goal or as a tactic to secure equality. It is also wrong to avoid the issue by emphasizing the poor quality of white schools in Boston. However poor their quality, there has been an organized racist attempt to attack black children attending these schools.

While the serious problems with this particular busing plan are the fault of the court and the obstructionist School Committee, we think it is wrong to see busing as a ruling-class plot. The achievement of busing is, in fact, the result of a long struggle Boston Blacks have waged against segregation. We oppose those Left groups that attack the plan because it seems to be dividing workers at the present time. Most black people in Boston, whatever their initial assessments of the busing plan, now support busing as one way of achieving better education for their children. In this case, we support the right of black students to be bused in safety. We also believe white children need to be bused because, unless there is a two-way busing, the black schools will be allowed to deteriorate further. In fact, some black schools have already been repaired in anticipation of the arrival of white students.

To waver on the issue of busing is to play into the hands of those racists who know that the defeat of busing (which is possible) would greatly strengthen the racist status quo. If the racists succeed in stopping busing, they will have gained a victory and set a dangerous precedent; they will also have inflicted a real defeat on black people and the movement for working-class unity. Conversely, a black victory will be a working-class victory. As black people demand and achieve democratic rights and equality, they are transforming the structure of the working class. In doing so, they narrow the differences between Blacks and whites, erode the material base of racism, and create greater opportunity for class unity. In this sense, we see this black demand for equality as a class demand.

In short, we are arguing that racism is at the center of the conflict in Boston. We see racist divisions within the working class as one of the mainstays of capitalist domination. Since our political focus is on racism and its origins and development, we are less concerned here with important questions about quality education or the history of the Garrity busing decision.

Given this emphasis on the problem of racism, our argument proceeds as follows: (1) we look at how the political economy of metropolitan Boston structures the situation within which the black struggle and the white reaction have developed; (2) we present the recent history of attempts by Boston black people to improve educational opportunities as one way of decreasing the material differences between Blacks and whites; and (3) we then show how white racist organizations—led by the School Committee—have fought to retain their material privileges.

THE POLITICAL ECONOMY OF RACISM IN BOSTON

The development of black support for busing and the strength of the opposition to busing in white working-class areas must be seen in the context of an evolving struggle over scarce resources not only in education, but in the job and housing markets as well. The bigger struggle being waged over desegregation is clearly part of a larger and longer struggle that has taken place within Boston's troubled political economy.

Although New England led the nation in industrialization during the early nineteenth century, Boston remained largely a commercial and financial center. Since it was not primarily an industrial city, the first immigrants sought jobs in the public sector through the Democratic patronage machine that developed in the early twentieth century, and clung tenaciously to craft jobs in the building trades and light industries through exclusionary AFL unions.

Because Boston did not become a major industrial center, the black migration to the North during World War I was much smaller than it was in other cities. Although the rate of post–World War II black migration to Boston has been comparable to that of other Northern cities, Blacks still constitute a relatively small proportion of the population (18 percent). And of course Blacks have suffered in Boston's severely limited job market. Lacking industrial jobs and lacking access to jobs in unionized sectors, black migrants were stuck for years in service occupations and other menial jobs. Unlike earlier immigrants, notably the Irish, they were not able to secure government jobs, which still occupy a large percentage of the city's work force. However, in the post–World War II era, Boston Blacks have slowly improved their occupational position by gaining federal and state jobs, by commuting to the new suburban jobs in light industry, and by gaining a foothold in Boston's enormous private institutional sector. Black women are increasingly important in the city's hospitals and, to a lesser extent, in its large clerical labor force.

Blacks have even worked their way into some of the better-paying industrial jobs traditionally dominated by whites, notably in meatpacking, where one of the city's few CIO unions developed in the 1930s. Although building-trade unions were still officially segregated through the 1960s, a few Blacks worked their way into some crafts.

This black progress, though rather limited, has nevertheless frightened many white workers who maintain their jobs through the old patronage machine (city workers, white-collar and blue-collar) or the old exclusionary AFL unions, especially in the building trades. White workers still enjoy important advantages over black workers. Although the proportion of Blacks increased in many occupations between 1950 and 1970, the black-white wage differential did not change over these years. In 1970, as in 1950, black workers earned only about two-thirds what their white counterparts earned. Furthermore, many jobs remained closed to Blacks, including most of the best-paid construction jobs, jobs as policemen and firemen, and upper-level white-collar positions.

White working-class people in Boston's most segregated areas have also maintained a relative advantage over Blacks in the housing market. Racist real estate agents and discriminatory bankers that "redline" ghetto districts have prevented Blacks from moving into areas like South Boston, Hyde Park, and West Roxbury, where many working-class people own their own homes. Blacks have also been kept out of the poorer white working-class sections where most people rent rooms in three-decker apartment buildings or projects. Although the white tenants in these poorer sections suffer from rent-gouging landlords and poor city services, they have not suffered nearly as much as Blacks.

Tenants in the worst white housing projects have used violence to keep Blacks out, because they believe that the presence of Blacks or Puerto Ricans will cause housing to be neglected even further. For example, last year white youths in South Boston's D Street Project shot and killed a black teen-ager who lived with the only black family in the project. Subsequently, the several Puerto Rican families in the project were literally driven out. As bad as the D Street project is, its white residents believe that it could get worse if black or Spanish-speaking tenants move in.

The racism of these white tenants does not result simply from a hatred of nonwhites; there is also a material basis to this racism. These poor whites are making last-ditch efforts to defend their relative advantages over Blacks and to prevent the spread of ghettolike housing conditions in their neighborhoods. This directly parallels their defense of white "neighborhood schools" and their opposition to busing white students to black ghetto schools that have been deliberately neglected over the years.

The bad housing situation in Boston has been worsened by the urban-renewal demolition that began in the 1950s. It destroyed all of the multi-ethnic West End and most of the racially mixed South End, both low-rent districts, and it wiped out nearly all of Lower Roxbury, which used to be the center of the black community. Urban renewal occurred when the old patronage machine was deposed and new "good-government" politicians appeared who would assist big capital, instead of trying to bleed it for taxes as James Michael Curley did during his mayoralty. The old machine lost out to the new politicians, who today are represented by Mayor White on the city level, but the machine saved its Irish and Italian neighborhood strongholds from urban renewal. It also preserved some relatively low-rent housing in these neighborhoods while similar housing was being destroyed in more mixed sections of the city where the machine no longer had political power.

The post–World War II suburbanization intensified the segregation of the housing market in the area. The GI Bill opened the suburbs to many white workers, but racist real estate companies and banks helped these working-class suburbs remain as lily white as the wealthy suburbs. Over 90% of the black population in the metropolitan region lives in Boston and Cambridge.

Working-class movement to the suburbs accelerated in the 1940s and then again in the 1960s with the development of light industries and research outfits along Route 128, the new peripheral interstate highway around Boston. But a large number of white working-class people have remained within the city limits of Boston to compete with growing numbers of Blacks and Spanish-speaking people for scarce jobs, poor housing, and limited school facilities.

Boston has never had a significant tax base. Old industries—textiles and shoes—developed outside Boston, while private, tax-free institutions multipled within the city. When the Irish political machine took over the city during World War I, Yankee finance capitalists responded with a freeze on large-scale building that lasted until urban renewal began in the 1960s. However, urban renewal failed to increase the city's tax base enough for city services to be improved substantially. Meanwhile, suburbanization drew more taxpayers out of the city. Today, Boston's metropolitan area has a much larger percentage of suburban dwellers than any other major city in the country. So Boston's hard-pressed taxpayers, including many working-class homeowners who have remained in sections like Hyde Park and West Roxbury, support city services that are exploited by an increasing number of suburban commuters.

Inner-city whites resent middle-class suburbanites who use the city's services but escape its frustrations, notably busing. However, this resentment of the suburbanites' class privileges has not diminished their hostility toward the city's black people. Instead of really attacking the many obvious privileges suburbanites enjoy, many white working-class people insist on attacking the favors Blacks have allegedly received from the government and private institutions of various kinds.

While it is true that Blacks have fought for federal and state jobs with increasing success and that some Blacks were able to set up their own forms of patronage through a few of the federal poverty programs in the 1960s, these developments failed to compensate for the exclusion of Blacks from the best-paying blue-collar and white-collar jobs in the city. Furthermore, Blacks have certainly not displaced any white workers on the federal or state level, let alone on the city level where black people are all but excluded from the thousands of jobs still dispensed by the old patronage machine. As a result, Blacks get much worse treatment than whites when it comes to city services, partly as a result of the fact that the police, fire, sanitation, and street-repair departments, as well as other agencies, are still staffed almost exclusively by whites.

But it is no easier to convince white working-class people that Blacks get poorer city services than it is to convince them that Blacks are not taking any more advantage of welfare than poor whites. In an economy of scarce jobs; rising taxes, rents, and food prices; declining city services; and deteriorating schools, any gains made by black people, no matter how limited, are viewed as a threat by most white working-class people. When only exclusionary craft unions and demagogic patronage politicians represent white working-class people, their fears and frustrations can be turned into organized racism. While the racist mobilization led by machine politicians uses code words like "forced busing" and "neighborhood schools," it is clear that more is involved than school desegregation. The racist mobilization developing in Boston is also a defense of important material advantages white workers still enjoy over black workers in the crippled political economy of Boston.

THE BLACK STRUGGLE AGAINST SEGREGATION

Racism emerged as a major force in the politics of education in Boston in the early 1960s. In 1960 a number of people upset with the worsening conditions of the Boston schools formed "Citizens for Boston Schools." Primarily a white group with an elite professional membership, the group did involve some younger leaders of the black community. The Citizens group ran four candidates for the School Committee in the fall of 1961. Its two white candidates won, and its two black candidates lost. Neither before nor since has there been a black member of the School Committee. Also in the early 1960s, the Education Committee of the NAACP tried to get the Massachusetts Commission against Discrimination (MCAD) to both recognize and criticize the existence of de facto segregation in the Boston schools. But the MCAD refused to do so; in fact, it said that racial segregation was not a problem in the schools. The NAACP continued to push for the recognition of de facto segregation. In the fall of 1962 it tried unsuccessfully to discuss the problem with the Superintendent of Schools.

In the spring of 1963, the Citizens group, the NAACP, and CORE all completed studies of the Boston schools that were critical of the de facto segregation in the city. The three groups began to support each other's work. Then in May, the NAACP came out with a more detailed report, which requested a public hearing before the School Committee. The Committee—including Louise Day Hicks, first elected in 1961 to "keep politics out of education" and not yet identified as a foe of desegregation—was conciliatory and set up a hearing for June.

At about the same time, a group of black and white civil-rights activists, the Massachusetts Freedom Movement, was organizing a demonstration in support of civil-rights workers in Birmingham who were being brutalized by Birmingham Police Chief "Bull" Connor. Composed of young liberals and radicals who had organized picket lines against Woolworth's as part of a national boycott, the Massachusetts Freedom Movement called for a one-day boycott of the schools to protest the poor education that black children were receiving. But as word got around about their plans, Edward Brooke, then State Attorney General, and Governor Endicott Peabody intervened to stop the demonstration. They won a promise that the boycott would not be held if the School Committee was responsive at the hearing.

The hearing was held June 11, 1963, and different groups were able to present their criticisms of the schools. The prepared reports and the comments documented the inequities of de facto segregation. CORE and the Citizens group emphasized differences in expenditures for predominantly black and predominantly white schools, and documented discrimination against black teachers and administrators. Six of the nine predominantly black elementary schools were overcrowded; for instance, one school with a capacity of 690 had an enrollment of 1,043, and another with a capacity of 300 had an enrollment of 634. The average cost per pupil in Boston's elementary schools was $275.47, but in one largely black district the average was $238.05, and in another it was $228.98. As of 1963, there had never been a black principal in Boston, and there had been only one black administrator. Only 40 of the 2,000 teachers were black.

The NAACP presented fourteen demands. The first one called for "immediate public acknowledgment of the existence of de facto segregation." While the School Committee acknowledged some problems resulting from de facto segregation, a majority refused to agree with the bald statement itself. Because of the unwillingness of the School Committee to acknowledge de facto segregation, the boycott took place on June 19, 1963. About a quarter of the black students stayed out; over half of the junior and senior high school students boycotted. Following the boycott there were attempts to confront the School Committee at its meeting, and there was picketing at the Committee headquarters. The response of the School Committee was to propose that a committee more representative of the black community be set up to study the question. A biracial committee was set up, but before long its black members quit, saying they did not want to be Uncle Toms. As a result, the School Committee was forced to call another meeting, but within minutes it was gaveled to a close by Hicks because a majority of the BSC refused to discuss de facto segregation. Picketing continued throughout the fall.

The summer of 1963 saw the development of clear intransigence on the part of the majority of the School Committee. During this time Hicks changed her line and used latent racism in conducting a victorious reelection campaign that fall. Of all the candidates, she received the most votes. Since 1963, race has been the primary political issue in the Boston schools.

The Racial-Imbalance Law

In February 1964, there were nationwide one-day boycotts of the schools to protest the poor quality of education for black students. In New York and other cities, hundreds of thousands of students stayed out for the day. Over 20,000 supported the boycott in Boston, and many of them attended freedom schools that had been set up for the day. This boycott, along with more informal pressure, led Governor Peabody to call for a blue-ribbon committee to study discrimination in the state's schools. This study was presented in April 1965. It found that of fifty-five schools in the state that were predominantly black,

forty-five were in Boston. It also stated that racial imbalance was harmful to both black and white children. The findings were accepted by
the succeeding Governor John Volpe, the Greater Boston Chamber of
Commerce, and the Catholic Archdiocese of Boston (Cardinal Cushing
had been a member of the committee). Its recommendations included
two-way busing of both black and white students, and suggested that
there be legislative action.

Volpe proposed legislation to deal with de facto segregation, and
the Racial-Imbalance Law was enacted in August 1965. Racial imbalance was defined as a "ratio between nonwhite and other students
in public schools which is sharply out of balance with the racial composition of the society in which nonwhite children study, serve, and
work." The law gave the state the power to direct school committees
to come up with plans for desegregation, to review and revise those
plans, and to withhold state funds if necessary to enforce its decisions.
The law specifically stated, however, that desegregation plans could
not involve busing students outside of their school districts if their
parents objected. In other words, the law demanded desegregation,
but undercut the most effective short-term solution.

Black Parents Create New Programs

After the passage of the Racial-Imbalance Law, there was a lull in
activities directed against the Boston School Committee. In part there
was a wait-and-see attitude, given that the state now had the legal
power to move. In part there was a lull because of the declining
strength of the NAACP after the early 1960s. But there was not a lull
in activity dealing with education within the black community itself.
As early as 1962, the Northern Student Movement (NSM) and a number of churches in the Roxbury area set up after-school tutorial programs. These programs were begun in a number of Northern cities in
the early 1960s by the NSM, a group that formed to support black
civil-rights activities in the South and to deal with the problems of
segregation and inequality in the North. In the space of two years,
about two thousand students made use of the programs set up by NSM
and the churches. Beyond the help that the students received, these
activities provided an arena within which some of the NSM leaders
gained skills and recognition; today many of the former leaders of

NSM in Boston have become leaders of Boston's black community. Another result of the tutorial programs was that they provided a place for parents to get together, to meet one another, and to discuss the educational alternatives open to them.

In the fall of 1965, Operation Exodus began. Ellen Jackson, a parent at the Gibson School, organized a boycott of classes to protest conditions in the school. This was the school described in *Death at an Early Age* by Jonathan Kozol, who had been fired the previous spring. To dramatize their boycott, the parents took advantage of a recent decision by the School Committee. The School Committee had instituted a new program called the "Open Enrollment Policy," whereby parents could send their children to a school outside their home district if there was space for them in another school. Subsequently, the courts have recognized that this does not work to relieve school segregation: even if a large number of black parents make use of it, white parents do also, taking their children out of black schools and sending them to white schools, thus increasing segregation. But whatever the larger results of open enrollment, the parents who were boycotting the Gibson School soon found that their children were going to better schools. Taking advantage of the new policy, they decided to continue sending their children to the other schools. Out of this grew Operation Exodus, a privately organized busing plan that involved, in its first year, over four hundred black students going to schools outside their own districts. The schools did not pay for this; hence the primary activity of the parents in Operation Exodus became that of fund-raising. They held bake sales, made contact with suburban liberals, and in one way or another raised the $1,200 to $1,400 needed every week to keep their children going to better schools.

After much work, the parents won public funding to cover transportation costs. This permitted further expansion, peaking with about 1,100 students in 1969–1970. The following year Operation Exodus dropped to about 170 students as other options became available.

Busing alone was not enough. The students involved encountered various kinds of discrimination. Some school administrators removed desks and chairs so they could argue that there was no room for a black student, but would have them replaced when a white student applied. There was some physical segregation of Blacks within the schools, and at times they were stuck in the backs of classrooms. However, despite discrimination in the receiving schools, the general success of Operation Exodus—parents felt their children were in smaller classes and learning better—increased the pressure for more busing.

The following year (1966), another volunteer busing program was begun by older established liberals in the black community working with suburban liberals on the various school committees. Known as the Metropolitan Council for Educational Opportunities (METCO), it bused black students—elementary through high school—from the city to the wealthier suburban schools. Today there are about 2,500 students involved, and there are ten applications for every opening in METCO. Like Operation Exodus, METCO won federal funding and a foundation grant, so that neither the parents nor the suburban communities have to bear the costs of the program. The Boston School Committee did not attack the program because it did not affect Boston's white schools.

In the winter of 1965–1966, some parents with children in tutoring programs at Roxbury's St. Ann's Church began discussing the possibility of starting their own school. They were soon joined by some parents from the Gibson School. The group split over the role of outside professionals and whether the school was to be for the neighborhood or for the larger community. The split followed class lines, with the slightly poorer parents from St. Ann's in favor of less professional influence and more local emphasis. The Gibson School parents opened the New School for Children with a professional staff earning good salaries; the St. Ann's parents opened the Roxbury Community School with fewer outside experts, parents sometimes serving as teachers, and more of a neighborhood flavor. Both of them have raised thousands of dollars. They, along with Roxbury's third black community free school—the Highland Park Free School, started in 1968—got a Ford Foundation grant of $500,000 and $175,000 from a group of local foundations. Together these three schools have been important in Boston as a focus of support, and beyond Roxbury have been able to attract liberals and innovative educators because the teaching and learning styles encouraged there are seen as models.

Operation Exodus, METCO, and the free schools provided several alternatives to the neighborhood public schools for a number of black students. But the overwhelming majority of black students remained in schools that were run-down, poorly maintained, understaffed, and undersupplied. The next wave of protests came from within these schools.

Parents and Students Organize School Boycotts

Between the fall of 1968 and the spring of 1971, parents or students organized boycotts or walkouts in a number of schools. For instance, on the first day of school in the fall of 1968, a group of parents at the Gibson School demanded that the newly appointed principal resign. She refused, and parents claimed the school as their own and installed their own principal. When the parents were locked out of school the next day, they took their children to a nearby community center and were joined by several teachers who had helped to start the group. The teachers were fired; but they and the parents ran a liberation school that lasted a couple of months. It started with all six hundred of the students in the school, and even after two months of harassment by the school officials, welfare department, etc., there were still eighty-five children whose parents refused to let them go back to Gibson. Some of them went to the New School for Children, some went into METCO or Operation Exodus. The Gibson School has generated so much parent involvement because it is one of the worst schools in Boston. But there were boycotts and pressures from parents at other schools as well. For instance, at two of the junior highs in Roxbury, parents got together to demand that black headmasters be appointed. They were successful, even though the appointments took place only at the last moment, right before the beginning of school in the fall of 1968.

These pressure groups and boycotts were not organized by existing groups in the Boston community. The NAACP was weak in Boston at this time, and the Urban League also lacked a base. Rather, these boycotts were organized by indigenous groups, and influenced by the national growth of black-liberation and black-nationalist groups and ideologies.

High-School Boycott

In the high schools, the initiative was taken by the black students themselves, not by their parents. From 1968 through 1971 there were sporadic boycotts of schools by black high-school students. They formed black student groups within the high schools, and slowly organized a loosely structured union of black students, the Black Student Union. These boycotts were like the earlier ones: started by a few students, but once under way, gaining wider support. In 1968, for example, a student was suspended from high school by the principal for wearing a dashiki, a violation of the dress code. Black students walked out, joined by some white students. Similar boycotts occurred sporadically for the next two years.

In February 1971, the Black Student Union organized a citywide boycott to protest racial segregation in the schools. They walked out and presented five demands to the School Committee: (1) recruit black teachers; (2) recruit black guidance counselors; (3) commission an independent study of racial patterns in the city's schools; (4) end harassment of black students; and (5) grant amnesty to all striking students. John Craven, Chairman of the School Committee, called the BSU statement "outlandish," and as usual the BSC made no concessions. The strike failed to attain its demands, but in other ways it clearly won a great deal. Many black students got experience in organizing; they allied with and got support from the Student Mobilization Committee (a campus antiwar group led by the Young Socialist Alliance). They held public hearings; and they even got support from white students who went out on strike. From April until the end of school in June, it was a black-led student boycott with Blacks and whites protesting the racism and poor conditions of the schools.

Community Control of the Schools

Out of the community schools, the parent boycotts, and the student boycotts—and out of the national interest in community control—community control of schools became an issue in Boston. In the 1971 and 1973 School Committee election campaigns, a black woman and member of the Communist Party, Patricia Bonner-Lyons, ran on a community-control platform. Although the CP did not have a sizable following in Boston generally or in Roxbury in particular, Bonner-Lyons did well. In the first election she polled over 50,000 votes and almost won; in the second she ran less successfully, but still did well in Roxbury. At first, members of the BSU were not active in her campaign; but as their strike ended, and since she was clearly a better alternative than any of the others, some people in the BSU worked for her.

The unsuccessful Bonner-Lyons campaigns did not spell the end of concern for community control. From the early 1970s through to the election of November 1974, it was one way that black parents sought to change the schools. Community control has also been sup-

ported by Mayor Kevin White, a liberal Democrat, and many of the
white professionals who are also eager to take power away from the
School Committee. A variety of community-control plans were voted
on in the 1974 primary elections. In the November elections, the voters
were given a choice of continuing with the School Committee or doing
away with it, creating several community committees, and giving
power to the Mayor's office. The Mayor's plan was defeated overwhelmingly, and the BSC was retained.

In March of 1972, while some Blacks were working on community
control, a group of black parents supported by the NAACP Legal Defense and Education Fund brought a case against the BSC in Federal
District Court to challenge the continued and increasing segregation
of the schools. It was this case that finally resulted in the June 21, 1974,
decision by Judge W. Arthur Garrity, Jr., in which he ordered that the
School Committee begin the first stage of school desegregation in September 1974. It had been clear for at least two years that Garrity would
decide in favor of the plaintiffs, and that he would order desegregation.
In doing so he was not taking a particularly courageous stance, but was
following the logic of Northern school-desegregation cases that has
been established in the past few years.

THE BOSTON SCHOOL COMMITTEE

Even after the Boston School Committee lost in the courts, it continued
to act in a high-handed racist way, and it continues in its efforts to foil
parents and state and federal officials in developing a good plan.

Why has the School Committee played this role for the past decade? What are the sources of its power? We will consider these points
as well as how it has perpetuated and deepened the patterns of racial
segregation in the city and how it has worked in every way it could to
frustrate the plan being implemented.

The present organization of the Boston School Committee dates
back to 1949, when it was reorganized by the state legislature, controlled by Yankees. The Constitution of the Commonwealth of Massachusetts—as with all states—gives the state the power to grant charters
to cities; it also gives the state the right to review and annul local laws.
The legislature ruled that there be five at-large members, all of whom
serve two-year terms, and that they run as nonpartisan candidates in
elections held in odd-numbered years. Whatever the original thoughts

of the Yankees in the State Legislature, the citywide elections have helped the Irish and other white candidates, and prevented any Black from ever being elected.

In its heyday, the Irish machine could mobilize support through its patronage power, and the schools were and are part of this. There are managerial, teaching, and janitorial jobs within the schools; there are the contracts for building and repairs in the schools. Over the years, members of the School Committee have had relatives and in-laws who worked as teachers or administrators in the schools. There is evidence that the School Committee has raised the salaries for certain jobs and then received large campaign pledges from people in those jobs. Testimonial dinners are given for Committee members, and teachers are pressured into buying costly tickets. Thus, even with one-third of the students of the city in parochial schools, the school system had an importance far beyond its educational function. Despite the general decline of the machine it has been able to retain control of the School Committee.

In a larger context, the School Committee represents "local" capitalists in their resistance to "national" capitalists. The Committee, through such current and past members as Hicks and Kerrigan, has links to local real estate and banking interests. As small owners, they, and the people they represent, do not have the capital for urban-renewal schemes, and they have opposed the attempts of the larger banks, the insurance companies, and the university and state managers to restructure the city. On the other hand, they use racism—as do the big banks when useful—to keep housing patterns clearly delineated by race. Because of the two-way relationship between school integration and housing integration, they have used the schools to keep Blacks not only out of the schools, but out of certain sections of the city as well.

The Boston School Committee grasped the issue of race in the spring and summer of 1963 as a political rallying point. Since then the opposition to black demands for better schools has been, in part, a ploy on the part of demagogic politicians to hold on to their political strength through racist populism. The School Committee and its supporters—particularly homeowners—have fought against desegregating the schools because of the fear of "white flight." Time and again the BSC and its supporters have scored points in blasting the suburban liberals, who urge integration while not experiencing it themselves.

Recent marches and demonstrations have also gotten support from white working-class suburbanites who want to defeat busing now to prevent the possibility of metropolitan busing, and also to keep Blacks down in the ghetto and out of the suburbs.

How the School Committee Fights Desegregation

The School Committee has gone about its racist business in a number of different ways. Its members have used racial slurs in their electoral campaigns. For instance, in 1965, Committee member Joseph Lee—who happens to come from an upper-class Yankee background—said that "white children do not want to be transported into schools with a large portion of backward pupils from unprospering Negro families who will slow down their education. . . . White children do not want large numbers of Negro pupils from unprospering Negro families shipped into their mainly white schools. . . ." And in the same year, Louise Day Hicks said, "We have in our midst today a small band of racial agitators, non-native to Boston, and a few college radicals who have joined in the conspiracy to tell the people of Boston how to run their schools, their city, and their lives."

Since 1965, when the Racial Imbalance Law was being considered, the School Committee has used its opposition to the threat of busing as a political weapon. At first the NAACP and the Citizens for Boston Schools denied that they were for busing either. But Hicks and the others kept denouncing busing as they sensed the growing political support for that issue. When the school superintendent wanted a minor busing program in the fall of 1965 to relieve overcrowding in a black school by transferring some students to a white school with room, the School Committee rejected the proposal, even though busing had been used in the past to deal with overcrowding. Furthermore, the School Committee had used busing to *maintain* segregation. In 1972 it was revealed that black children were being bused past white schools with room for them, and white students were being bused past black schools with room for them.

In hiding these facts, the School Committee, along with many others, has helped to foster myths about busing. In fact, nationwide there has been a steady increase in the number and percentage of students bused to and from school. With the rise of larger schools with more varied curricula, more and more students have ridden buses to school. Presently in the United States, about 43 percent of all school children go to school on buses, but only 3 percent of students are bused to relieve racial imbalance. In Boston, about one-third of the students in public schools are already bused or are using public transportation to go to special high schools or to new "magnet" schools that are meant to attract students from throughout the city. Similarly, the Boston School Committee has harped on about the sanctity of neighborhood schools when, in fact, many of the district boundaries are drawn, not along natural boundaries, but artificially so as to maintain racial segregation in the schools.

The School Committee has consistently furthered racial segregation in the Boston schools. In 1965 there were forty-five racially imbalanced schools. By 1973 there were sixty-eight. In part this increase is due to the growth of the black population within the context of segregated housing. This results in de facto segregation. But Judge Garrity—following recent court decisions about similar situations in other large cities—agreed that there was de jure segregation as well. For example, he found that the BSC intentionally furthered racial segregation by allowing some schools to become overcrowded while leaving others with extra space; by making use of portable-classroom facilities to avoid transferring students; and by opening new schools in such a way as to further racial segregation. He found that the BSC drew school district lines in such a way as to perpetuate racial segregation. He found that the patterns of feeding students from the junior highs into the high schools were developed with the intent of maintaining segregation. Open enrollment and transfer policies were managed with a "singular intention to discriminate on the basis of race." Staff and faculty were distributed in the school system in such a way that the predominantly black schools had the less-qualified people.

The School Committee has also fought desegregation in other ways. It has withheld information and released it only under threat of a court order. For example, the State Board of Education, in drawing up the current desegregation plan, was not able to get the school-related demographic statistics it needed, and the BSC had to be forced to release them. Even then they did not provide all that was needed. The BSC has also prepared "desegregation" plans that wouldn't alter racial patterns. It has even tried to resubmit such plans after they have been rejected by the state. It has tried to count as part of its "desegregation effort" the independent actions of black parents in Operation Exodus and METCO. As a consequence of this intransigence, the city has lost millions of dollars because state and federal governments determined that the School Committee was in violation of the law.

By December 1973—half a year before the Garrity decision—forces were converging on the School Committee in such a way that it was obvious it would lose its court cases. The BSC's attorney, James St. Clair—before going on to represent Nixon—told them that "all legal avenues had been exhausted" and that further appeals would be "frivolous." The Committee, never having made any preparations for school integration, then began to stall and ask that the implementation date be put forward to September 1975. Over the summer of 1974, the School Committee did nothing to prepare the school administrators, teachers, or parents for the desegregation plan that fall. It held no public meeting to explain how the plan would work; it held no workshops for administrators or teachers or students on how to deal with the upcoming situation.

One of the consequences of the BSC's racist intransigence is that the plan drawn up by the State Board of Education and ordered to be implemented by Garrity is a very poor one. In the first stage of the integration plan, not all students in all parts of the city are involved, and this has caused a lot of bitterness on the part of many white parents who are now involved. The plan has also faltered because Garrity has not become involved in the intricacies of the plan, and it often appears to concerned parents and teachers that he is making decisions by fiat.

There is also considerable opposition to this particular busing plan among Blacks, because of the dangers it presents for many black students and teachers. But since school started, most Blacks have rallied to defend the rights of black students to be bused safely. There are various groups and individuals—in and out of government positions—who have monitored buses, bus routes, and schools. The Black Caucus (of state legislators) led a black demonstration in 1974 demanding protection for black students. In the 1974 primary elections, the one black politician who endorsed Governor Sargent's compromise voluntary busing plan was soundly defeated for the State Senate nomination by Representative Bill Owens, a supporter of mandatory busing and an outspoken critic of the racists in Boston city government.

The Home and School Association

The School Committee has worked to mobilize support for its racist policies in a number of ways. Its members have continually spoken out in a variety of forums in which they could whip up racist sentiments and opposition to busing. But they have also organized support for their position, and have stifled opposition. In Boston there is no PTA. Instead there is a "Home and School Association," whose bylaws prohibit it from criticizing the School Committee or the School Department.

The Home and School Association acts as a front organization for the School Committee. For the past several years it has not really concerned itself with any educational issues beyond the maintenance of segregation. The Home and School Associations exist only in white or partly white areas. Liberals who have tried to raise educational issues or have questioned racist orthodoxy have found their attendance at meetings discouraged. In some areas, the school principal has even appointed the parent head of the organization.

With this close relationship to the school administration, the Home and School Association has used school supplies, duplicating machines, mailing lists, and other material and information to publicize antibusing demonstrations. Furthermore, the School Committee has directed principals to use the teachers, through their homeroom classes, to act as conduits for informing parents of antibusing rallies and demonstrations. In at least one instance the students were supposed to return notes from their parents if they wanted rides. These notes were then passed from the teachers' hands back to the principal, who would see to it that parents got rides to the demonstration.

The Home and School Association is now entrenched in block-by-block organizations in several white sections of the city. Using phone chains and word of mouth, the Home and School Associations act as the organizational base through which hundreds of people can be turned out to demonstrate within hours. Like most community-based organizations and like most organizations concerned with schools and children, the Home and School Associations are predominantly controlled and run by women in the neighborhood.

In media coverage, we have mostly heard about the Irish stronghold of South Boston. South Boston is a virtually all-white area: it can have a good block organization without having to skip over or worry about the presence of black families in the area. In Hyde Park, another area with a lot of racial violence in the fall of 1974, and where the white homeowners have voted overwhelmingly for the racist candidates, the Association is strong, even though there are black families in the area. With the decision by Garrity that in the fall of 1975 all of Boston will be involved in the integration plan, the Home and School Association began organizing in other sections. There are now eight antibusing information centers operating in areas of Boston and nearby suburbs. These centers are part of the effort to defeat integration, and provide little other "information." For instance, when parents phone with a question about occurrences in the schools, they are told that they were warned that integration would not work and they should keep their children at home until the busing plan has been defeated.

During 1974, an umbrella organization known as ROAR (Restore Our Alienated Rights) has emerged. ROAR puts forward the calls for motorcades, rallies, demonstrations, boycotts, etc. This group holds its weekly meetings in the city council chambers, and may have been organized by Louise Day Hicks, now a City Councilor, to replace the School Committee as the organizational center of antibusing activity in case the BSC was enjoined from taking part in these racist mobilizations.

The strategy of the School Committee, the Home and School Association, and ROAR is to defeat the busing plan, and they think they can win. There have been antibusing rallies and demonstrations for years, but since last spring there has been a marked increase in activity. In February and March, 1974, there were large meetings to protest the busing plan and to organize protests against the Racial-Imbalance Law. Hicks spoke at a meeting in South Boston, and Kerrigan spoke in Hyde Park. In April thousands demonstrated against busing in front of the state capitol.

One of the few groups that gave concrete support to the desegregation plan was the Boston Teachers Union. While it did not do much, its leadership supports the plan. The current leadership of the union, in fact, is a reform group that organized in the fall of 1968 when the BTU did not support the teachers fired from the Gibson School. Now more liberal than many of the members of the union, the BTU leadership has been cautious about confronting the racist sentiments of the teachers.

With only a modest effort by the BTU and the concerned but minor efforts of a black and white reform group called City-Wide Education Coalition, the racists were the main force in the fall of 1974. The antibusing forces began the school year with a boycott of the schools which kept overall school attendance down in the whole city for several weeks. By mid-November 1974, attendance was normal at most schools, especially at the elementary level, but at several high schools, not many white students were attending. Beyond the boycott, there were weekly Sunday rallies with ROAR speakers, local state representatives, and a popular radio talk-show host sympathetic to ROAR. Some rallies were planned to draw in support from sections of the city to be affected in 1975. They also drew support from white working-class suburbs, many of whose residents have only recently moved out of South Boston or some other white or transitional area.

CONCLUSION

In short, the issue in Boston today is racism. It is not only the institutional racism of capitalist job and housing markets and the hypocritical racism of the suburban liberals who control the state government, but it is also the well-organized racism of the Boston School Committee and its white petit-bourgeois and working-class supporters throughout the city. We have tried to point out that the racism of the School Committee is produced in part by threats to an old patronage machine which, through various exclusionary methods, is attempting to preserve the relative advantage of white workers over black workers in Boston's shrinking economy.

We are not simply describing racist attitudes among white workers, but rather are analyzing an organized racist movement that has appeared in several of Boston's white working-class neighborhoods. Because these neighborhoods suffer from high unemployment, poor housing, and lousy schooling, it has been tempting for liberal journalists and leftist groups alike to explain away white working-class racism as a product of "lower-class frustration," "backlash" or "manipulation" of various kinds. But it is wrong to explain racism away by ro-

manticizing the ethnic pride and community solidarity of neighborhoods like South Boston (which in fact contain real divisions), or by
resorting to a conspiracy theory that explains away racism as a frustrated response to a ruling-class plot in the form of busing.

We have tried to show that busing is, in fact, the result of a determined civil-rights drive fought on a national level and a determined
drive which Boston Blacks have launched for better education on a
local level. The racist resistance to the black battle against school
segregation is linked to the ongoing fight to keep Blacks out of white
neighborhoods with decent housing or to keep Third-World workers
out of high-level white-collar and blue-collar jobs.

In Boston, this resistance has been mobilized largely through the
remnants of the old patronage machine, represented by appendages
like the Boston School Committee and allies like the exclusionary AFL
craft unions. It is part of a hard-fought defense of the relative privileges
of white workers over black workers. These privileges are more significant in the areas of jobs and housing than in education, but racist leaders realize that if schools are desegregated, the Blacks will have won
an important victory against institutionalized racism and will have
set a dangerous precedent.

Although the old patronage machine has lost much of its power
since Curley's time, it still represents the last line of defense against
black encroachments into the white world of Boston, into its segregated schools, jobs, and housing facilities. The Yankee capitalist class
has seriously undercut the economic power of the old machine over
the years, and the liberal Kennedy wing of the Democratic Party has
deprived it of considerable power in the city, state, and federal government. As a result, the old machine controls fewer jobs than ever before.
In a metropolitan area with high unemployment and in a period of
high inflation, the various leaders of the old machine, notably the Boston School Committee pols, have resorted more and more openly to
organized racism as a means of intimidating Blacks who challenge
what control the old machine still has over jobs and public facilities in
the city of Boston.

Busing has of course been a boon to these demagogic leaders of
the old machine; it has enabled them to unite the white petite bourgeoisie of the city with large sections of its white working class around
a defense of the various material benefits segregation has preserved for
them. These racist politicians know that the desegregation of schools is

but the first battle in a full-scale assault working-class Blacks will wage for equality in jobs and housing.

As long as these racist politicians control the School Committee, they will be able to maintain considerable working-class support by dispensing patronage jobs and by favoring predominantly white schools, but the very existence of the School Committee is being threatened by various black groups that have the support of liberal political leaders in City Hall and the State House. In fact, the total domination of the Democratic Party by the liberal wing led by White in City Hall, Governor Dukakis in the State House, and Kennedy in Washington, may force the old-line machine politicians to make some kind of formal split.

In any case, the defeat of busing would strengthen the beleaguered School Committee and its racist leaders immensely and would therefore prolong the existence of the old patronage machine in many white working-class communities. The Left in Boston, though not large, has made some inroads in working-class communities where the power of the old patronage machine has broken down. But the Left has been totally insignificant in segregated areas like South Boston where the machine is still strong and helps to mute class antagonisms.

The defeat of busing would be much more than a defeat of the latest thrust black people have made to improve education; it would also be a serious setback to the general struggle against the kind of racism that divides the working class. Furthermore, the implementation of busing, as one means of breaking down an important form of segregation, is a victory not only for the black struggle for equality but also for the working-class struggle for unity.

First of all, the breakdown of segregation raises the possibility of black-white cooperation for better education, a phenomenon that has already occurred in more integrated sections of the city. In fact, there is already tangible evidence to show that the busing of white children to poor black ghetto schools has resulted in improvements within these schools which black parents were never able to achieve in the past. In other words, despite the obvious problems with this busing plan, it does create some limited possibilities for improving educational facilities for both black and white students.

The blow busing strikes at Boston's dual system of education also raises the possibility of the ultimate defeat of the old patronage machine and its overtly racist leadership. Although Hicks and Kerrigan, and others of their ilk, received much national publicity (some of it quite favorable), they have failed to fulfill their promise to stop busing. This promise alone has accounted for much of their political appeal in recent years. And their political fortunes will probably suffer in the long run because of their failure to keep this promise. In fact, Hicks, Kerrigan, and other political leaders of the old machine have recently suffered defeat in their campaigns for higher office.

Although it is difficult to be optimistic about the short-term effects of the busing crisis in Boston, the following points should be noted: the racist defenders of segregation have suffered a major defeat; the powerful Democratic Party has been seriously divided and disrupted; and, most importantly, the solidarity of the black community in Boston has forced predominantly white community organizing groups to deal seriously with the issue of racism for the first time and has encouraged some segments of the Left to organize what should be an important national mobilization and demonstration against racism in Boston.

Nevertheless, the immediate effect of the busing crisis has been to increase tension between black and white workers in this city. There is no way to deny this. No rhetorical calls for black-white unity around educational demands or broader political demands will erase this fact. White racism in Boston is a deep-seated and well-organized phenomenon, and it will not be uprooted easily. The only hope for working-class unity in Boston and other segregated cities lies in a direct assault on segregation in all its forms and in an organized defense against the racist attacks which segregation fosters.

Local Action, Not Citizen Participation

KATHARINE COIT

Citizen participation has been a part of American politics from New England town meetings to the Community Action Program of the War on Poverty. However, it has also been true that unless special provisions are made, those citizens who tend to participate are the more prominent members of the society: representatives of business, banks, industry, churches, and labor unions. Their participation is used to give legitimacy to, and so gain acceptability for, decisions of the administrative unit. Since the basic goals of these citizens and those of the administration tend to be similar, their participation can be both non-antagonistic and influential.

Participation of low-income groups presents greater difficulty than that of middle- and upper-strata groups. The poor lack time, organizational skills, and well-placed connections in the power structure. Clearly, they also lack economic clout. In a struggle, for example, between a low-income neighborhood and a powerful vested interest eager to speculate in a neighborhood to renovate it for luxury apartments, the advantage often lies with those financially in control of the situation. Furthermore, local officials traditionally tend to favor those elements that they feel will "do something" for the town. Indeed, the question arises whether the goals of citizen participation are compatible with the fundamental need of low-income groups, the elimination of poverty.

The history of the War on Poverty offers ground for extreme pessimism about the possibilities of successful intervention by low-income urban dwellers led by government-financed organizations. The premises behind citizen participation in the Community Action Program were that low-income groups do not have the same possibility of influencing decision-makers as middle- and upper-income groups. The stated goals of the program were to "attack poverty" and to provide assistance and services, to give a "promise of progress" towards the elimination of poverty through improving "human performance, motivation and productivity." To attain these goals, the poverty program provided for the maximum feasible participation of the poor in the local programs, *yet no real resources were offered them.* In short, the poor, once given the impetus, were to pull themselves up by their own bootstraps. In addition, the War on Poverty was waged primarily against the symptoms of poverty rather than its fundamental causes, which are rooted in the economic system. A second conceptual error arose in the failure to make a clear-cut distinction between local action and citizen participation. This was never established in the minds either of administrators or of most participants. It is this latter error that is central to the present discussion.

The fundamental difference between citizen participation and local action is that the former is organized from above, is the emanation of some local or federal organ of the state, while the latter is organized autonomously at the grass-roots level. It does occasionally happen that some citizen-participation organizations develop a political consciousness and truly conflictual strategies; however, the vast majority fall into the category that I call *participationist* because their lack of independence, their basic ideology, and the limited scope of their action prevent them from having more than token power. On the other hand, I would argue that local action organized at a grass-roots level with *no* official ties offers *more* possibility for meaningful social change. Because of the confusion between the two, it is important to emphasize how "participationism" can reinforce the status quo by coopting people into pseudo-conflicts rather than engaging them in effective struggle.

THE CONSERVATIVE USES OF CITIZEN PARTICIPATION

By the end of the 1960s, the citizen participation within the federal War on Poverty was under fire from all sides. Some criticism from the established local and central administration was aimed at the groups that appeared radical and seemed to be getting out of hand (Moynihan, 1969). Many articles in the Left-liberal press, however, were devoted to demonstrating that participation has not worked as it should. Sherry Arnstein, for instance, demonstrates how very often participation is manipulation or therapy, how occasionally it involves informing, consulting, and placating (which she categorizes as tokenism), and how it only rarely reaches the stage where citizens can be said to have attained a degree of power. Arnstein and the other liberal critics indicate clearly that participation does not work, but they stop short of suggesting that the root cause is in what I will call, for lack of a better term, *the ideology of participationism*. For even if the citizen participation of Arnstein worked and became what she calls "citizen control," without other fundamental changes in the political and economic system, the results would be the reintegration of marginal elements and the bolstering of the status quo.

A closer analysis of citizen participation imposed from above suggests five ways in which this action is conservative rather than radical.

1. For one thing, "participationism" tends to eliminate the notion of antagonism between the working and ruling classes. Participation emphasizes the community of interest within a *territorially determined* group. It emphasizes the cooperation of these groups with the administration. Furthermore, experience has shown that in the United States the most vocal elements of a community, those most organized, those most prepared to dominate a local movement are very often the middle-class members, or more rarely, the upwardly mobile members of the working class. In the Community Action Agencies and in the Model Cities Program, we can observe this phenomenon. These groups, if not dominated by the members of the staff, are dominated by the upwardly mobile poor and the middle-class people in the area.

2. Participation encourages compromise and conciliation in order

to obtain minimal concessions. The attitude is often, "We'll go along with urban renewal if in return we get some low-income housing so that at least a few members of the neighborhood will be able to move back in."

3. In other cases, participation is used to keep troublemakers off the streets and put them to less threatening occupations (Piven).

4. Participation creates one more hierarchy, one more elite, rather than encouraging each individual to contribute to a collective decision. The paid staff members, because of their position and because they have their entire day to devote to the community, have a great deal of power in these local agencies. It is inevitable that the residents will leave most of the work to the staff, who in turn can use their position to manipulate the residents. Furthermore, the staff is nearly always mainly made up of members of the middle class, in spite of "maximum feasible participation."

5. Participatory agencies tend to skim off the local leadership from the community by employing them. With its leaders employed by the administration, any effective opposition by the community to administrative proposals is rendered leaderless.

These criticisms of participationism view the phenomenon as part of a larger process—the ideological assault on the poor, not a war on poverty. Participation has been one means of giving middle-class attitudes, middle-class values, to the working class and to the very poor. This can be seen as a bad thing in that, in the absence of other leverage, once the poor accept middle-class "decorum," they may become less rather than more effective.

When one examines the literature on the War on Poverty, it becomes very obvious that one of the prime goals was to give the lower classes, and particularly the ethnic minorities, a middle-class *mentality* rather than middle-class *resources*. Daniel P. Moynihan makes it clear in his Report on the Negro Family that, in his view, the deterioration of the Black family is at the root of their problems. In the 1960s, thousands of pages were devoted to the "culture of poverty" and how to break the "cycle of poverty." The argument ran: people can make their way out of poverty through changes in attitude, motivation, and willingness to make sacrifices. Policy was aimed more at changing the attitudes of mind than at offering material help. It was a psychological assault to give the poor the motivation to work their own way out of poverty. As Charles Valentine has so ably shown, this was only a subtle way of blaming their poverty on the poor.

Case studies of Community Action Programs lead to the conclusion that the types of programs that were encouraged with more funds and a minimum of bureaucratic harassment were those in which there was a strong tendency to emulate the middle classes. For instance, one of the examples often cited as "good" citizen participation is a group in East Harlem that included a variety of programs designed to give the people of the neighborhood middle-class behavior. The programs offered classes in "poise" for teen-age girls, and scholarships to white middle-class summer camps for the children, who are obliged to adapt to being a tiny Black or Puerto Rican minority in a group of rich white suburban children. This group desired a high mix of middle-income residents with the low-income residents in its housing corporation.

Those groups that were vociferous, that encouraged disruptive behavior, that had a radically new approach—such as the Blackstone Rangers in Chicago, the Area Wide Council in Philadelphia, Mobilization for Youth and the Real Great Society in New York—all ran into difficulty. They were either reorganized, defunded, harassed by the Internal Revenue Service, or eliminated in one way or another. There were hardly any groups that managed to continue to be funded for a long period while still functioning in a way that I call *conflictual* rather than *pseudoconflictual*.

The whole liberal ideology that refuses to recognize even the existence, or in any case the significance, of conflicting interests between middle- and low-income groups cannot see the fundamental error of organizing citizen participation from the top down. The authors of the poverty program believed that poverty could be eliminated within the existing social structure. Encouraging the poor to participate in programs that are to eliminate poverty within the capitalist system is in fact misleading them. This becomes obvious if one believes that poverty is necessary to capitalism, as David Gordon has suggested. While these programs may have helped some poor to "break the poverty cycle," the nature of the system pushed others back into poverty.

By permitting some of those at the bottom of the social and economic ladder to participate or even merely to air their hostility toward some of the most obvious injustices relating to urban life and urban space—through demonstrations and other forms of protest—by permitting this *but at the same time keeping a lever on these groups, a participation that is reinforcing rather than undermining the present system of domination* is being legitimized in the eyes of the poor and the working-class groups. The lowest echelons of society are given false hopes that there will be justice and equality for their class if they just learn to participate.

LOCAL ACTION

To say that these officially organized community-action programs simply coopt and disarm militance is not to say that autonomous local-action groups must inevitably reinforce the present social system. How can this be avoided?

To make a tentative beginning, there would seem to be three directions in which local action groups can and should direct their attention.

> *1.* Local action groups should work to develop a class consciousness and critical analysis of capitalism by starting with a particular issue leading to a more global analysis of the system of private enterprise. In other words, they should relate the privations of daily life to some of their fundamental causes, such as the priority given private property over human rights and the predominance of the profit motive in real estate markets.
>
> *2.* To work out methods of self-management in associations or groups where leadership is shared rather than hierarchical and elitist; and where directions are not parachuted from above. On a larger scale, to develop methods whereby inhabitants can creatively take part in making the decisions concerning their neighborhood and homes.
>
> *3.* To develop a strategy that is truly conflictual rather than pseudo-conflictual.

The development of a critical analysis requires an overview of the working of the political, social, and economic system. It must convey an understanding of how the particular problem to which the group addresses itself is part of a much broader issue. This has been achieved with only limited success in the United States.

The single issue approach is generally used by local action groups. Focusing all action on one problem such as high rents without developing a further analysis leads to an incomplete response on the part of the community group. Such an approach does not develop political consciousness, nor is it as likely to win even limited gains as a more broadly based movement.

Recently in Italy there have been examples of local action which have not only succeeded in improving local conditions for the working class but have also been successful at linking local action to the broader issues at stake. Even though conditions in Italy are very different, a study of some of these groups is helpful in showing some of the radical potential of local action.

LOCAL ACTION IN ITALY

Local action in Italy, or "le lotte sociale," is not only a recognized strategy of the Left but it is, as this is written, also being debated in all the major unions (and being used by a few of them). Most important, such actions are rapidly being taken up on a massive scale. Their relative success in Italy can be attributed to the fact that the industrial cities of northern Italy offer particularly flagrant examples of the contradictions inherent in highly urbanized centers under a capitalist mode of production. Due to particular circumstances in Italy, these contradictions are felt as much or even more by the working class as consumers than as producers. To the majority—recent immigrants from the agricultural south or small towns—while their wages are not high, they do represent an increase over the purchasing power they had formerly as peasants or agricultural wage workers. There is clearly a desire to put this increased purchasing power into better living conditions. However, the housing crisis is such in Italy that even public housing costs often one-half of the salary of the worker who is lucky enough to get such housing. Their only other choice is to live in shantytowns on the edge of town or in the dilapidated and unsanitary slums of the older sections of the city. There is thus widespread dissatisfaction over housing conditions. At the same time, the Italian Left is probably the most vigorous in Western Europe. The Communist Party is considered unusually broad-minded. The extreme Left is not overly sectarian. Frequently, the different ideological groups work side by side in a local struggle.

These three factors—the massive immigration to the northern urban centers, the dissatisfaction over specific local issues such as the housing problem, and a large and vigorous Left—contribute to the development of local action. When there is a spark of protest over intolerable living conditions or high prices, the situation is ready for this spark to ignite a fire. Unlike the situation in the United States, a large percentage of the Italian working class is aware of its exploitation. There are active militant groups ready to channel and encourage the protest. If the leaders of the unions and the political parties of the Left do not outwardly back these conflicts, they do nothing to prevent the rank and file from taking them up.

Militant Squatting

One of the most widespread types of action has been the occupation of newly built public housing. Over the last five years all the major industrial cities and many smaller ones have had hundreds and even thousands of units of housing taken over by squatters. There have been two phases to the squatting movement. In the first phase, the squatting was done by impoverished working-class people who had no adequate housing and often no permanent employment. Their first motive was a need for a decent place to live. Their second was a will to force a reflection on the housing question and particularly on the scandalous way in which public housing is assigned. Often organized by workers in the building trades who would spread the word as soon as new apartments were built, the squatters would move in. If at first there were only twenty families or so, very rapidly the news would get around and overnight all the units would be full. Negotiations would then begin, the squatters agreeing to move out only if they were promised decent housing elsewhere. Sometimes they were successful and sometimes they were driven out by the police, but usually not until three or four months later. The most successful struggles were those where the workers who had been assigned the new units, and who were waiting to move in, rallied to the side of the squatters and refused to move in until the squatters had been promised housing elsewhere. Such cases occurred in numerous cities of Northern Italy. There were also more unfortunate cases where the authorities were able to pit the workers assigned to the housing against the squatters.

In the more recent phase, the primary reasons for squatting have been political. The majority of the squatters have been union delegates and union members. As far as housing is concerned, individual needs for shelter, in their view, though important, are secondary to exposing the contradictions of the capitalist mode of production. Therefore, the demands they have put forth are: (1) Rents proportional to income. A worker's rent should be 10 percent of his wage. (2) An end to evictions of those who cannot pay their rent. (3) An end to the corrupt methods of assigning public housing.

New strategies have been evolved, such as symbolic squatting. In Rome, in the space of one night, 10,000 squatters occupied public housing in symbolic protest. Thousands of tenants in all the large cities have unilaterally reduced their own rent. They pay what they can, or what they feel the just rent should be. Because of the sensitivity of public opinion and the militancy of local groups, the authorities do not respond by evicting those paying only part of the legal rent.

Accompanying this political action, a large number of books and articles written in Italy in the recent years have been devoted to a consideration of urban conflicts. In these works and in the left-wing parties, a critical analysis is being developed of (a) the building industry, (b) land speculation and the role of promoters and banks, (c) the role of the government in relation to urban-land use and the housing question, and (d) the extraordinary expansion of the northern cities at the expense of the rural south and the social consequences of this growth.

In many instances these occupations have also been the occasion for experiments in self-management on a local level. The organization and the contacts with the authorities are done by those occupying and not by the political groups that back the movements. To a greater or lesser extent, depending upon their political orientation, the backers confine their role to sparking off the movement, giving it publicity and material help, and supplying personnel for nightwatches, day-care centers, and the like. The occupiers themselves hold daily committee meetings and weekly general assemblies to make the decisions concerning the occupation.

Another important aspect of these occupations has been the collective action necessary for their survival. Vigils are necessary to warn the occupiers of police attacks. Often, a certain amount of work has to be done, such as connecting electricity lines and water mains, in order to make the apartments inhabitable. Other collective arrangements have been made to improve living conditions. Parents get together to set up day-care programs for children and sometimes even schooling for those prevented by the move from going to regular schools. In the evenings, various types of entertainment have been devised. Many observers have noted a strong sense of solidarity among the squatters. Their experience, in which their whole way of life is radically changed for a period of three to four months, is bound to have profound influences on the participants.

"Autoreducing" Public-Utility Rates

The other strategy that has often been successfully used locally in all large cities has been the "autoreduction" of the cost of public utilities, transportation, telephones, and rents. The "autoreduction" of rents is thought to be extremely widespread, but it has not proved the best strategy for collective action. For in spite of the efforts of militant groups to persuade tenants that "autoreduction" is a militant act, many are still ashamed to make public the fact that they pay only part of the legal rent. Furthermore, only the local housing authorities, which keep the information secret, have the exact statistics as to how many tenants do not pay the full rent.

On the other hand, the "autoreduction" of the cost of bus services between Turin and surrounding suburbs and villages met with definite success (Cherki). When the bus companies in the area raised the rates from between 20 percent and 50 percent, according to the distance, there was a swift reaction among the workers, for they are entirely dependent on the buses to get to work.

Before this increase, the left-wing metal worker's union, Federazione dei Lavoratori Metallurgi (FLM), had formulated, though in vain, certain demands concerning transportation, including its nationalization and the gradual establishment of free transportation. The FLM, helped by local groups in each village or suburb, then organized the struggle against the rise in the rates. Rather than a boycott, which would cause serious difficulties for the workers, it was decided to "autoreduce" the fares. By means of the distribution of leaflets from booths set up in front of the local ticket offices, it was explained to riders that they were to pay the former price of the ticket. The money was collected from the workers and handed over to the bus companies. The workers were given receipts to use as tickets. Once they had accepted the money, the bus companies were obliged to run the buses at the former rate. This action spread from company to company and resulted in widespread victories. Within a month the regional government withdrew its approval of the higher rates, permitting instead a much smaller increase. At the same time they made the decision to nationalize half of the private bus lines within a few years.

The victory goes far deeper than winning these concessions. What was proved was that innovative types of action can be successful. This action was a break from tradition for the unions in that it took place outside the factory; it involved the collaboration of local groups and unions; it was direct; it was illegal; and it received the cooperation of the large majority of workers concerned.

The government-owned telephone company, the SIP, was also the target for a successful campaign throughout Italy to "autoreduce" the cost of the telephone. In July, 1975, the telephone company decided to raise the price of phone calls and also made it obligatory for the user to pay for two hundred calls per three months, regardless of whether that number of calls had been reached. Those who use the phone rarely, generally in the lower-income brackets, were severely hit, particularly the elderly who have a phone to receive calls from their children and to make emergency calls to the doctor.

In many cities the left-wing groups started campaigns to "autoreduce" the telephone bill by encouraging users to pay only what they had paid the previous quarter. At the same time the Communist Party and the unions organized the signing of a petition demanding the revision of the increase. Of the two campaigns, the former was far more effective. The events in the city of Bologna illustrate how this strategy was used.

In Bologna, which has had a Communist government since the war, the first step taken was to collect signatures for a petition. However, one day three elderly women, who did not feel that it was enough to sign a petition, went to the telephone company extremely incensed and determined not to pay a cent. One of the telephone-company employees explained that if they did not pay, they would lose their phone, and he advised them to pay a small amount. This incident was taken up by the local papers. Seeing the extent of public furor on the subject, the left-wing groups got together to organize a campaign to show the telephone users how to pay only part of the bill. Tables were set up in strategic places in the city, with one in front of the telephone company. Within a week, six thousand users had "autoreduced" their bills. Others who had already paid signed a petition threatening to "autoreduce" their next bill if it were not revised. Several meetings were held, attended by many elderly and representatives of all the left-wing groups. Not only was the telephone company denounced, but so too were the maneuvers of the government and their attempts to make the working class bear the brunt of the economic crisis. An effort was made to form permanent grass-roots committees to continue actions of the sort.

The unions kept on with their petition, since that was the official tactic; however, it was made very clear that signing the petition did not prevent people from "autoreducing" their bills as well. Many did both. For many, it may have been the first time that they stood up for their own rights by going further than merely signing their names to a petition.

These new forms of strategy, both squatting and the "autoreduction" campaigns, are still in the experimental stage. Because of their unusual success and mass backing, they play a greater role each year in Italy. While one cannot claim for sure that the recent gains of the Italian Left are due to these new forms of conflict, it is fair to say that the simultaneous marked increase in local action is not merely coincidental.

CONCLUSION

To briefly sum up, several hypotheses can be inferred from the situation in Italy:

1. The successes of these actions constitute both concrete achievements for the workers and at the same time political victories. The authorities have had to make considerable concessions when faced with massive but "illegal" action. The message is clear. The right of the users to housing and services they can afford is a more fundamental right than that of the public or private companies to make a profit.

2. The effective weakening of the target companies is proof that

positive action can be carried beyond the area of production. The extension of the workers' struggle to questions concerning consumption (or to be more precise, concerning the conditions of their environment) has been particularly successful when there is collaboration between the unions and the local groups.

3. The merit of being able to combine the use of imagination in devising new forms of conflict and sensitivity to the concrete needs of the locality has contributed greatly to their success.

4. Without minimizing the role of the "extreme Left," which has been vital, its insistence that the conflict be carried out by those directly concerned rather than by a small political elite has borne fruit in some, if not all, cases.

These examples of local action in Italy are by no means exhaustive, but suggest some of the possibilities local action holds.

There are many examples in the United States of local action or grass-roots action, but the economical, political, and particularly the ideological situation is radically different. In the United States there is less unity within the working class, less solidarity, and very little belief in the necessity of a class struggle. In fact, much of the working class and most of their spokespersons partake of the high American standard of living and show little interest in fundamental social change. There are also virtually no large Socialist or Communist parties or unions.

Local action, even when it does not have the inherent limits of citizen participation, thus tends to be limited to the attainment of immediate results. Action that is clumsily linked to "ideological" or "socialist" goals is rapidly discredited. One cannot hope to obtain the same radical action as in Italy all at once.

In some cases, however, actions carried out in the United States aim at immediate results but also aim at developing a critical analysis and class consciousness. For example, when a local group assumes the right to decide how best to develop a neighboring lot owned by a private trust and it involves the whole neighborhood in doing so, it is not only trying to improve neighborhood conditions but is making a fundamental attack on private property. When tenants go on rent strike, it can be to demonstrate that they believe in the right for all to a comfortable home at a reasonable rate. Not all the participants may see it this way, but local action creates the context where new possibilities are created, and consciousness changes in action.

Rather than to act for the sake of action or to condemn this sort of action for not being truly radical, one should understand both the pitfalls and the potential in order that a radical praxis be developed that holds within it the seeds of fundamental social change. The ambiguity of local action is inevitable in that it seeks to do two things at the same time—obtain reforms and change political consciousness. Once this ambiguity is understood, the potential of this type of action is unleashed. Local action is like a tool, in that what results depends less on the tool than the user. Reflection is thus necessary, experimentation essential. Given the fiscal crisis of many cities in the United States, such movements here may in fact be far closer than anyone now thinks.

REFERENCES

United States

Arnstein, Sherry, "A Ladder of Citizen Participation," *American Institute of Planners Journal*, July 1969.

Fenn, Richard K., "The Community Action Program: An American Gospel," *Science and Society*, Spring 1969.

Gordon, David M., "American Poverty: Function Mechanisms and Contradictions," *Monthly Review*, June 1972.

Krause, Elliott, "Functions of a Bureaucratic Ideology: Citizen Participation," *Social Problems*, Fall 1968.

Moynihan, Daniel P., *Maximum Feasible Misunderstanding* (New York: Free Press, 1969).

———, *The Negro Family; The Case for National Action*. Washington: U.S. Department of Labor, 1965.

Piven, Frances Fox. "Whom Does the Advocacy Planner Serve?" *Social Policy*, May-June 1970.

———, and Richard A. Cloward, *Regulating the Poor: The Functions of Public Welfare* (New York: Vintage Books, 1971).

Stoloff, David, "Model Cities, Model for Failure," *Architectural Forum*, Jan.-Feb. 1970.

Valentine, Charles A., *Culture and Poverty* (Chicago: University of Chicago Press, 1968).

Local Action in Italy

di Alemanni, *et al.*, eds., *Autoreduzione* (Milano: Sapere, 1975).

Cherki, Eddy, "Luttes sociales en Italie," *Les temps moderne* (Paris), June 1975.

di Ciaccia, Francesco, *La condizione urbana* (Milano: Feltrinelli, 1974).

Daolio, Andreina, "Les luttes urbaines en Italie," *Espaces et société*, (Paris), April 1975.

———, ed., *Le lotte per la casa in Italia* (Milano: Feltrinelli, 1974).

Della Pergola, Giuliano, *La conflittualita urbana* (Milano: Feltrinelli, 1972).

Roscelli, Ricardo, ed., *Edili senza lavoro operai senza casa* (Torino: Einaudi, 1975).

five

LEARNING
FROM OTHERS:
CITIES AND SOCIALISM

Most of the papers in this collection have stressed the material basis of the urban crisis in the way the process of capital accumulation has taken place in the historical conditions of U.S. economic development. But what of other countries that are no longer capitalist? Have they done any better? Do not their cities have the same problems of congestion and bad housing as we have? Are there important differences in approach to urban problems among socialist societies? These are the questions dealt with in the two final papers by David Barkin and Larry Sawers.

Geographically, at least, the closest socialist country to the United States is Cuba; it lies but ninety miles off our shores. But since its revolution in 1959, its social, political, and economic organization has moved dramatically and decisively away from our system to its own brand of socialism. Barkin describes what this has meant for its people living in cities and in the countryside. Cuban urbanization policy, unlike our own, includes a planned development of both city and country within a single framework.

Barkin stresses the process of socialist revolution in which "urban" questions are seen as only one aspect of social transformation. Thus the integration of town and countryside, the location of schools, and maximal participation in decision-making have a great deal to do with the spatial ordering of residential and productive units. Barkin's treatment of Cuban cities thus contrasts markedly in this respect with Hill's analysis above in that it is not a discussion of simply urban policy questions, but is an analysis of a total social transformation.

The two largest socialist nations, China and the Soviet Union, are discussed by Sawers. While neither has yet approached the United States in per capita income—indeed China even today ranks among the world's poorer nations in per capita income—both are often designated as superpowers. They and the United States contend for leadership in the world. One arena of this competition is surely how well each has done in building livable cities. What lessons can be learned from each? While both are socialist nations, China and the Soviet Union organize their economies and their urban policies quite differently, as Sawers demonstrates.

Clearly the level of economic development, national culture, and institutions in the United States are nothing like those in these two nations. What then can we learn from the Soviet Union's and China's urban policies? One thing that can be said with confidence is that socialism in the United States would not be like the socialisms that we see in the world today. Not only is the United States a far richer country with a unique historical tradition, but it can also learn from the mistakes of pioneering socialist countries. Furthermore, a socialist United States would not face hostile and more powerful capitalist countries. Even though the United States is different from other countries, we have much to learn from the very different ways other countries have met the challenge of creating a humane urban environment.

Confronting the Separation of Town and Country in Cuba

DAVID BARKIN

The growth of socialism in Cuba has been marked by a profound restructuring of its cities and their relationship to the rural areas, reflecting the need to harmonize the imperatives of economic growth with human needs. In this article the relation of changes in the productive and political structure of Cuba and its evolving spatial organization are examined. Cuba has made a deliberate decision to avoid the "growth pole" strategy of regional development in favor of a more even pattern of urban settlements. Two specific programs—greenbelts around the principal cities and the placing of the entire junior high school system in the countryside—illustrate the specific geographic impact of overall social and economic planning. A new local administrative structure was created to increase and institutionalize popular participation in national policy formation and economic planning. Most importantly, urban development and planning efforts led to the relative de-emphasis of the Havana metropolitan area.

By focusing on the historical evolution of the forms that have contributed to changing the country's spatial structure, this article shows how the Cuban planners have tried to integrate economic factors into the broader context of desired social policies. Unlike alternative approaches that use the more mechanistic tools of location theory, developed within the context of neoclassical economics, the Cuban analysis not only focuses on the efficient allocation of resources but also on an evolving sense of what is desirable from a social point of view. The striking thing about Cuba's urbanization policies is that while spatial reorganization has increased productivity it has also reinforced the process of constructing socialist values and practices in that society.

THE PREREVOLUTIONARY DISTRIBUTION
OF PRODUCTION AND POPULATION

Prerevolutionary Cuba's spatial structure reflected the country's sub-jugation, first by Spanish and then by North American imperialism (22, 24). Monoculture led to the misuse of the land, destructive harvest cycles, disastrous economic cycles determined by the "free-market" price of sugar, a rigidly stratified social structure that set people strug-gling against one another, and an administrative apparatus riddled by graft. Manufacturing production was rudimentary, and three-quarters of it (excluding sugar) was concentrated in Havana. Nine-tenths of all shipping went through the capital city's port. As might be expected, cultural life was also concentrated in Havana along with political and administrative control. But even within the city, wealth was concen-trated in the hands of a small group of people: 94 percent of the popu-lation had no saving capacity at all, spending as much as one-half of their incomes on food for an inadequate diet. In the rural areas back-wardness and poverty reigned; a growing landless rural proletariat was plagued by unemployment. Those who fled to the cities in search of work found poor housing and the absence of basic public services (13, 26).

Under these circumstances, it is no wonder that Havana continued to grow in an uncontrolled fashion, and through its parasitic growth to impoverish the rest of the country. Poverty-stricken areas and urban slums remained because of the pattern of uneven development; the wealth of rich areas attracted even more investment and further im-poverished the poor regions by siphoning off financial and human re-sources. The state's development policies exacerbated these problems by encouraging additional investment in a few key sectors and regions.

Havana's growth was accompanied by a deteriorating quality of life. The cost of basic necessities and the pressures to consume forced people into debt, because their wages were insufficient to maintain even a minimum standard of living. Internal migration, fed by cycles of unemployment and discriminatory hiring practices, heightened the problem of inadequate education, medical care, and cultural offerings, because those with money were unwilling to pay for an expansion or improvement of services for the working class. Land speculation made things worse by raising the cost of housing and making it even more inaccessible for most of the population.

Thus, on the eve of the revolution Havana was systematically draining the rest of the country of people and resources. Just as it had been doing since its foundation as a Spanish colonial city, the Cuban capital was the beneficiary of monopoly restrictions, which guaranteed that the small number of wealthy people in the city enjoyed the benefits of trade. They shared their profits with their North American "patrons," who enjoyed Cuba's casinos, beaches, and flourishing brothels. The few Cubans who graduated from the nation's inadequate school system or from foreign schools were forced to move to Havana where all administrative and economic control was centered; job opportunities were unavailable elsewhere for all but the eccentric person who was willing to cope with the sacrifices rural life entailed (1).

A SOCIALIST APPROACH TO SPATIAL DEVELOPMENT: THE REVOLUTIONARY PROGRAM

Havana's exploitative role was obvious to all in the 1950s: the city produced very little for the rest of the country but demanded food from the hinterland for survival. The revolutionary struggle was directed against this reality, and those leaders knew that the peasants and rural workers would play an active role in transforming society. History forced the Cubans to redesign the use of their territory (19), and socialism provided the basis for avoiding the oppressive pressures of concentration and competition that make regional planning difficult under capitalism.

As early as 1953, Fidel Castro, in his famous self-defense following the unsuccessful attack on the Moncada Barracks, declared that the economic program of the new government would include important measures that would benefit the rural population (9). The guerrillas began to implement them during the struggle itself by setting up rural

schools and medical outposts in liberated areas. The proposed measures can be divided into two groups:

1. The *redistributive*, which includes agrarian reform, profit shar-
   ing, Cubanization of land and utilities, enforcement of tax laws,
   recovery of ill-gotten wealth, massive housing programs, and
   the expansion of education and health services; and
2. the *developmental*, which includes diversified growth through
   import substitution and agricultural diversification, use of inac-
   tive capital, expansion of agriculture, and the creation of full
   employment.

While agriculture was not the only sector that would be affected,
it was to be the target of important efforts from the very beginning.
Within five months of coming to power, the new government enacted
an Agrarian Reform Law, which expropriated all large estates but
guaranteed the integrity of smaller farms. The law eliminated rents for
small tenant farmers and encouraged the establishment of cooperatives. Rural areas were integrated into the revolutionary program
through a series of measures aimed at improving the well-being of the
farm population. "People's stores" provided basic foods, medicines, and
other items at low prices. Medical facilities were improved, and the
number of rural primary schools was doubled in the first two years.
Electricity and telephone rates were reduced.

Changes were also taking place in the urban areas. The Urban Reform Law of 1960 prohibited a family from having more than one
home and put a ceiling on rents of about 10 percent of family income.
It also guaranteed everyone the right to decent housing, a promise yet
to be fulfilled because of inadequate resources. Changes in prices and
social services also benefited the poorer groups from the first days of
the new government (3, 7, 11).

These measures contributed to the decentralization of the population and of economic activity and to the urbanization of rural areas.
Important new spatial development policies are promoting rather than
competing with overall growth policies. They economize on the heavy
initial investments in infrastructure, permitting a broader and more
intensive use of existing roads and other facilities for education, medical care, and culture. These policies permit people to shift their tasks
on a seasonal or even on a daily basis between industrial or urban

jobs and agricultural needs so that maximal effort can be made at crucial harvest periods. The obvious need to promote agricultural growth made rural development important. It had to be complemented by industrialization to increase the productivity of the land and the work force and to free resources for continued expansion (4, 6). There was little opposition from urban interests to the redistribution of power and resources back to the previously exploited rural areas as it became clear that agricultural development would accelerate the whole country's material and social progress. Finally, the commitment to the development of the "new socialist person"—a person conscious of collective development, of the need to combine manual labor with intellectual tasks as part of the overall process of revolution, and of the need to subordinate individual desires to social needs—underlined the importance of a massive restructuring of Cuba to integrate rural and urban life into a more coherent and unified environment in which everyone would participate more fully in the country's social, economic, and political life.

CHANGES IN THE PRODUCTIVE
AND GEOGRAPHIC STRUCTURE

Along with these changes in distribution, more fundamental alterations of the country's productive structure were undertaken. A new emphasis on cultivating idle land and diversifying agricultural production led to the creation of eighty-three new rural towns between 1959 and 1962. These new settlements served several purposes: they provided a means of delivering better public services to agricultural areas, they provided better housing to isolated peasants, whose homes were replaced by more permanent structures, and they formed the basis for the gradual restructuring of the rural economy so that it might better respond to the needs of a longer-term development program. Furthermore, by bringing together groups of previously isolated people, it was easier to mobilize and train them for new occupations and to integrate them into the process of socialist transformation. The new towns were only the beginning of a very ambitious program that strengthened rural society by initiating a process of "rural urbanization" and reduced rural-urban migration to the cities.

Other measures were taken to remove the pressure from Havana and to help decentralize population and production. Two new ports were constructed at Cienfuegos and Nuevitas; fertilizer manufacture, electricity generation, and oil refining are the principal activities in the former city, which is also an important tourist site and sugar-loading port. The other port, on the north coast, is principally a loading center for the country's major export, sugar. New manufacturing facilities for domestic appliances in Santa Clara and agricultural processing plants in a number of smaller cities where specialized agricultural programs were begun further accelerated the decentralization process.

The development of Oriente Province, on the extreme eastern end of the island, however, was the most ambitious of the long-range development policies. It reflected the 1963 commitment to a long-range strategy of economic growth, on the one hand, and to geographic decentralization and the integration of rural and urban activities, on the other. A program for the development of the nation's rich nonferrous mineral resources in the northeastern part of the island was conceived as part of the second stage of development during the 1970s, once agricultural growth and diversification had proceeded sufficiently to assure adequate domestic supplies of food and financing for the needed imports of equipment and technology. In addition, Santiago—the country's second largest city—is being reshaped as an important center for industrial production, university education, and tourism. Further, other cities in the province are being developed to support a fishing center, rice cultivation, a dairy program, and tanning, textile, refrigeration and light metals industries.

Agricultural programs throughout the country are part of the plan to increase sugar production and establish a firm basis for diversified agricultural production. For the most part, the largest sugar mills that existed before the Revolution have been enlarged while the economic base of the surrounding communities has been broadened. Large new areas have been planted in citrus fruits, which are rapidly becoming a large Cuban export; rice cultivation also expanded rapidly, as have dairy production and processing facilities. A gradual change in settlement patterns has accompanied agricultural development: isolated peasant homes are being exchanged for newly constructed facilities in small rural communities to facilitate the more efficient cultivation of lands and reduce rural-urban differences. The social reality dictates, for example, that rural clinics and schools can be most effective in improving conditions if people live in communities rather than in widely separated homes. More important, perhaps, is the process of active cooperation among people, which can be stimulated more readily when people are in close and constant contact with each other. Productive work can also be more easily scheduled when people are able to make collective decisions about how to accomplish given goals. These changes in production were not the simple result of decisions by a small group of people to move in this direction, but rather the direct consequence of the struggle to create a socialist society; they have not been easy to implement and in the process have created new problems and contradictions (5, 8, 23). The changes have been possible because large numbers of people have begun to participate actively in formulating and implementing national programs and policies.

URBAN DEVELOPMENT AND PLANNING

The Cubans are highly conscious of the need to consider the spatial effects of their development program (15). Once they chose agriculture as their key development sector, they moved to concentrate specific crops in the most propitious areas for highest yields, taking advantage of natural conditions and existing productive systems. This decision then paved the way for complementary programs of industrialization, construction, and training. These programs led to complex spatial changes. Among the factors which affect and weld this process into a unified whole and which relate to the harmonizing of urban and rural life, and of manufacturing and agricultural activities, are:

1. the technification and industrialization of agriculture,
2. an emphasis on the direct connection between study and production for workers and students,
3. the universalization of university education and the direct tie between work, research, and training,
4. the new forms of social organization of work, which bring people together in larger communities in both the planning and control stages,
5. the dispersion of industrialization along with the limitation of new activities in the Havana area,
6. the decentralization and industrialization of construction activity,

7. the redesign and expansion of the transportation system, including a high-speed railroad system, new ports, and better
mass transport,

8. the conservation and better use of natural resources for rest
and recreation, and,

9. the equitable distribution of a system of social services, including specialized facilities.

Urban planning is integrally tied in to the national planning
process. The National Planning Council (JUCEPLAN) was created
in 1960, and shortly thereafter (1964) the Institute for Physical Planning began to move toward the design of a long-term land use plan.
It was clear that Havana's growth would have to be slowed apprecia-
bly, and during the 1960s, very little new construction took place except for essential port-expansion programs. New industrial projects
were located in the other principal cities with ready access to the sea
or transport networks, and agricultural programs were planned in conjunction with the new cities that were being built or projected.

In the context of most of the rest of the hemisphere, Havana
stands as an exception to the general pattern of overdeveloped capital
cities. By having slightly reduced the proportion of the total population living and working there, the Cubans seek to reduce congestion
and other problems due to unplanned and unlimited growth. Since
1958, other notable changes in urban settlement patterns have also
occurred. The small towns (from 50,000 to 100,000 people) have increased in number and population while attracting rural migrants
(24.2 percent of the total migration as compared with 13.3 percent
previously). In addition, the smallest villages (from 2,000 to 5,000
residents) have greatly expanded in number and play an increasing
role in capturing part of the rural exodus (7.6 percent in the 1960–
1975 period compared with 4.4 percent of all migrants before 1958
[12, p. 54]). Thus, although the rural population (communities of less
than 2,000 people) has declined from 47 percent to 40 percent of the
population since 1958, this has not led to growth of slums in the largest cities but rather to a redistribution of the population in new urban
structures (26). Smaller towns are growing all over the island and becoming integrated into a national network (17, 20). (The definition of
"urban" itself was changed to include communities of 500 people or

more who enjoyed four or more of the following services: electric lighting, paved streets, running water, a sewage system, medical facilities, and a school [14].)

New Communities

By 1975, almost 350 small communities had been created throughout the island to bring the rural population together. Special preference was given to the less densely populated areas in the east, and most of these communities were directly related to a specific productive plan; the largest number (122) were tied to sugar-cane production, while livestock development ranked second with 88 new towns. Of the others, 21 communities are tied to rice, 20 to citrus fruits, 15 to industrial plants, 10 to coffee, 9 to tobacco, and 4 to fishing. Others were built to handle several activities (12, p. 53). It is important to note that each of these "new-town" communities was constructed with basic housing facilities—usually apartment buildings of four floors with twenty units each—a supermarket, primary school, and a day-care center. Almost 150,000 people live in these villages.

In the 448 communities with 1,000 people or more in them, special programs for urban development are advancing. Urban zoning plans provide the guidelines for future development in conjunction with the national annual and five-year plans (10). On a national scale these plans are part of a longer-term project to create another 390 urban centers by the mid-1980s. The basic criteria for urban planning are: (1) a gradual concentration of the rural population in new towns which, together with existing villages, will cover the totality of the agricultural and livestock-producing areas of the country; (2) the creation of a number of urban subsystems based around intermediate-sized urban centers in which diversified economic activities can be planned and combined with teaching functions, and where there are adequate weekend rest centers and vacation facilities, as well as other basic services to enrich the region's integration with other subsystems and with the total system. This policy, it is hoped, "will ensure easy access to the more specialized services and leave open the possibility of the total use of the territory" (15, p. 71); and (3) the gradual restructuring of existing urban centers in accordance with their new roles in the development process and in the transformation of the society.

The pattern of land use and the construction of socialist society go hand in hand (25).

In 1975, 537 urban centers were included in this planning process. These include most of the smaller centers built since 1971 (some 100) as well as 250 that are being built within already existing urban areas. Some 300,000 new housing units have been built in these communities along with complementary services. A key element in this program is the explicit rejection of the growth pole approach to regional planning. The Cubans conceive of their national territory as a continuous whole rather than as a collection of producing centers. Their planning process is designed to integrate the subsystems into a single national unit rather than into separate enclaves of economic and social activity.

The Housing Problem

This planning process is also directly tied to the development of industrial systems for new construction. The Cubans inherited a huge housing deficit, which was heightened by many substandard units. The immediate response was to initiate the production of prefabricated elements that could be easily assembled by local self-help groups with little or no machinery. Other prefabricated approaches for building larger buildings were used in urban areas. During the 1959–1972 period some 560,000 new housing units were constructed, but since a large number of these were built by individuals with the simplest materials, it is estimated that only 295,000 of them can be considered adequate. This problem also had repercussions in the new towns that they formed. Many of these new towns were unplanned, without sufficient provision for basic urban services and adequate standards of hygiene. As a result, many of the early settlements, which were created in response to the people's most immediate needs, will have to be redesigned in the coming years.

To confront the great demand for housing the Cubans have adopted a new approach. Although initially faced with insufficient quantities of building materials, by 1971 the problem had become one of an inadequate number of construction workers. Since there were increasing supplies of cement and new plants making construction materials, the Cubans came up with the solution of trying to increase the labor force available for housing construction by relating higher productivity in agriculture and industry to an increased supply of housing. This would have the benefit of increasing productive efficiency while contributing toward the solution of a social problem and reinforcing the importance of collective consciousness. Workers in a given center were encouraged to find ways of increasing productivity and thus free workers for construction *microbrigadas* of 30 to 35 workers, each of which would build new housing near the plant. About 37,500 units were constructed in this way between 1971 and 1975. The Cubans hope that the accumulated deficit can be eliminated by about 1980.

The *microbrigadas* are an important adjunct to the whole urban development program. They symbolize the commitment to have people participate directly in the solution of their own problems. People—ordinary workers—are challenged to find ways to increase labor productivity and to find extra hours for voluntary work to meet their own needs and to solve a social problem of national magnitude. *Microbrigadas* also exemplify a pattern of urban expansion in which housing is coordinated closely with employment centers to ensure that schooling, medical facilities, and transportation are also available as part of a national program of human settlements.

Self-Sufficiency: A Physical and Intellectual Problem

One of the greatest barriers to the further development of Cuba's productive potential—other than the pressures of defense imposed by the omnipresent and oppressive nature of North American imperialism—was created by the achievement of full employment. It is a measure of the country's progress that Cuba now has insufficient people power to accomplish all the tasks that have been planned. The growing labor scarcity arose because of the expansion of productive activities in all areas and the difficulties experienced in raising labor productivity, given the limited capital equipment (4). As a consequence, the Cubans have been obliged to find new ways to increase labor productivity and to mobilize people who might not otherwise be in the labor force. This necessity has reinforced the efforts to accelerate the pace of socialist construction at all levels by encouraging all people to search for the solution to problems at a local level and to use resources that might otherwise be idle. Each town and workplace has countless success stories of creative ingenuity. Two examples of such new approaches, applied at a national level, are the greenbelt program for agricultural production in the principal metropolitan areas and the schools in the countryside.

The Greenbelts

One of the greatest problems in satisfying the minimum consumption needs of the population was the lack of adequate supplies of food, in part due to inadequate transportation facilities and the long distances food had to be brought to the major metropolitan areas. The "problem" was in part the result of the Revolution. With the redistribution of income, the demand for basic foods increased dramatically, and new solutions had to be found for the supply of many basic products.

Agricultural diversification on a national scale was one of the first responses. Idle land was cultivated with the basic products of the Cuban diet—rice, tubers, and some vegetables. Efforts were also made to increase food supplies by producing poultry on a large scale and investing heavily in fishing; on a longer-term basis, investment in cattle and pigs is expected to be important. These efforts, together with importing more food, ensured that the ration program was able to guarantee every person in Cuba an acceptable minimum basic diet for the first time in the nation's history. The Revolution has done away with malnutrition.

There were many problems, however, with the planning of food production on a national level. It became quickly apparent that provincial and regional programs had to be implemented and that special provisions had to be made for the large metropolitan areas. Around each of the large cities a substantial area was reserved for various types of agricultural and livestock production. On such land modern state farms were created and efficiently cultivated with machinery and modern irrigation systems. The farmers were given new housing and training to permit the introduction of new crops and farming techniques. The products grown in these regions were selected on the basis of ecological suitability, local needs, and national guidelines. The important considerations in this process were desire to avoid long-distance transport of perishable foods, to assure the basic supply of important foods for the local population, and to mobilize the existing urban population to assist in the various agricultural tasks requiring substantial numbers of people, especially at the critical harvest period (18).

The greenbelt program was part of the answer to these problems. It provides for the local needs of the population, to the extent that conditions permit, and allows people to offer many hours of volunteer work. Tubers, vegetables, and coffee are cultivated and harvested by volunteer workers and schoolchildren from the nearby cities. Cows, which supply the region's milk, pasture in the fields. Improvement of the local diet was the visible compensation for such volunteer efforts.

In addition to agricultural production, the greenbelt programs were integrated into the overall urban planning effort to provide environmental protection and recreational facilities for the urban population. These efforts were especially important in Havana and Santiago, because little effort had been directed toward a rational use of the nearby areas in conjunction with urban planning; as a result there were insufficient agricultural areas and recreational facilities. In Havana the most fully developed of the programs, a large recreational area (Lenin Park) makes use of the irrigation facilities and includes a zoo, games, and other activities as part of the greenbelt.

All in all, the greenbelts have proved to be an important part of urban planning and design. They are part of a broader program that has successfully controlled the physical expansion of the city and ensured adequate agricultural and recreational facilities for the city dwellers—bringing the country to the city.

The Schools in the Countryside

Education is particularly important in Cuba since increases in production and popular participation in decision making require more schooling. But Cuba, like most countries, was faced with the problem of how to expand its school system to accommodate all children. The traditional answer of going slowly and waiting until resources became available was not acceptable in the context of the egalitarianism characteristic of the Cuban Revolution. At the same time, however, it was clear that new ways would have to be found to confront old problems—ways which would free resources for education, on the one hand, and which would not retard agricultural and industrial progress, on the other.

The first step was to eradicate illiteracy by a massive mobilization of the whole population in 1961. Students and teachers sought out virtually all illiterates and traveled to the mountains and rural farming communities to teach them to read and write. The goal was literacy as a means of participating more fully in the Revolution. Another measure, adopted during the 1960s, was to take schoolchildren to the fields where they would assist in cutting cane, and to teach them to cultivate gardens and perform other chores as part of the changing concept of education. Instead of separating agricultural and urban activities, the Cubans attempted to integrate them. The combination of school work with regular agricultural work was seen as a way of bridging the chasm that had traditionally existed between town and country.

In Cuba, this program was conducted within the context of a growing labor scarcity and the need for increasing supplies of virtually every kind of merchandise. Every contribution schoolchildren could make—no matter how small—would either free people for other tasks or increase the quantity of goods available. To the extent that it was successful, such a program would facilitate a greater expansion of the school system than might otherwise have been possible.

Thus, once begun, the schools in the countryside were quickly recognized as an important step in moving Cuba's youth ahead toward the goal of forging the new socialist person in a socially practicable manner. They also had an important impact on the country's pattern of urban development.

The typical school in the countryside had full boarding facilities for 500 students and staff people. Classroom and auxiliary facilities necessary for a complete junior-high-school education are located next to productive lands the students cultivate. The school complex includes dormitories for teachers, staff, and students, classrooms, laboratories, workshops, meeting rooms, a library, a barbershop, an infirmary, a movie theater, a school store, and, more recently, a swimming pool (16).

The academic program is combined with productive work: while 250 students are in class the other 250 are doing agricultural work. Fidel Castro, an enthusiastic supporter of the program, has said of the new system: "The students begin to create material goods with their own hands. That is to say, they begin to learn and to know how the material goods that people need are produced. They begin to acquire the habits of work as the most natural and most elementary duty of every citizen, *together* with the habits of study. . . !" (2)

This program is expanding rapidly. Each school is given responsibility for a particular area of the countryside. Higher productivity and technical knowledge are important, as specific goals are set as part of the national and regional plans for agricultural production and school finance. The schools not only are expected to supply their own needs but also are integrated into regional programs for supplying the local population with basic foods. To resolve the problem posed by school vacations, the parents of the students and other workers are invited to stay at the boarding schools for their vacations, work three hours, and then have the rest of the day to themselves to take special hikes or use the athletic facilities. In this way the Cubans are also resolving the problem of inadequate hotel facilities for summer vacations and reinforcing the spirit of collective work as an ever-present part of life.

Just as important, however, during the four hours a day of work during the school year, the students are expected to produce more than enough to cover the costs of their education. Thus, involving the schools in the countryside program was more than just a way to socialize students—it was guided also by economic necessity. These schools are being located within the new agricultural areas, which facilitates the application of modern technology to increase productivity.

The government plans to expand this approach to education to include all junior-high students by 1980. This means that enrollments in these schools will grow from about 100,000 in 200 schools in 1975 to 1 million students incorporated into the program of work and study in 1980. The main constraint on expanding this program now—and it has a very high priority—is the lack of sufficient building capacity. (One note, which is not quite beside the point: The students in these new schools are doing substantially better in academic terms than other Cuban junior-high-school students.)

The schools in the countryside are an excellent illustration of the new approach toward urbanization. The students live in rural areas and are responsible for agricultural work as part of a broader program to integrate work and study for everybody. They are usually near a village from which some workers are drawn for supervisory and specialized tasks at the school and on the farm. The school and the village form part of a regional subsystem joined together with a local urban area. In this subsystem there are a number of these schools in the countryside as well as a senior high school at which many of the junior high school teachers are attending classes. There are also a regional medical facility and other urban services and amenities shared by a network of smaller villages. University students and faculty often work in some of the local factories and agricultural programs as part of their regular course work and in turn give classes to the workers with whom they are living and working. In this way the students, many of whom come from urban areas, have regular contact with the "urbanized" rural population and are directly involved in productive work while advancing in their own studies. This intermixing is an important element in training. It reduces the social barriers between town and village.

Like the greenbelt program, the schools in the countryside are an integral part of the Cuban effort to restructure their society and prepare the people to participate actively in productive tasks and decision making. The Cubans developed both programs as part of their Revolution. They have consciously designed them to improve social relations in production. They had to take the pre-revolutionary conditions and mold them into a new egalitarian order—a slow, painful process that cannot be accomplished by abstractions, but rather by changing given, concrete conditions. The schools are particularly significant because they are helping to resolve many problems: they contribute in breaking down the barriers between mental and physical labor, in reintegrating the conception and execution of work into a single process, in bridging the gap between city and country, in providing an environment conducive to the training of people for socialism, and in providing ways to support the schools while mobilizing people for productive work.

A New Structure for Controlling the Means of Production

As new urban centers and regional subsystems were created, it became clear that the inherited structure of centralized administration and jurisdictional boundaries was quickly becoming outdated. People were being encouraged to participate in decision making at all levels, and new institutions were needed to stimulate the process; economic activity and social services were expanding and being decentralized rapidly, and this called for a reshaping of provincial and municipal boundaries to create more manageable administrative units.

The new administrative boundaries were only a prelude to more fundamental changes in the process of public administration. In June 1974, Cuba conducted its first elections for administrative officers since the Revolution. These took place in Matanzas Province on an experimental basis. Since the elections, the new system has proved very effective in permitting the local solution of many problems and in overseeing the implementation of national programs in the province. These elections created and staffed the new "Organs of Popular Power" at the municipal level; the elected official then selected regional and provincial officials who coordinate interjurisdictional relations. Although relatively little time has passed since its creation, the Popular Power system has already proved very effective in the process of institutionalizing the Cuban Revolution—that is, in developing structures that will strengthen the several directions in which people must simultaneously move in order to build socialism (21).

This new administrative structure is part of an important new thrust in Cuba since 1970—a democratization and institutionalization of the governmental structure. To prepare for this, most Cubans participated in discussions of many important policy proposals conducted by the several mass organizations. The largest of these is the group of Committees for the Defense of the Revolution, to which most Cubans belong and which are organized on a neighborhood basis throughout the country. Others are the Federation of Cuban Women, also organized on a community basis; the Confederation of Cuban Workers; the National Association of Small Farmers; and the several student and youth organizations. All of these were reorganized to facilitate communication and to provide a more effective channel through which the masses of people could have a clear voice in what was happening (8).

The need for better communication became apparent in 1970 as a result of many of the production and coordination problems that arose during the effort to produce 10 million tons of sugar. It was clear that without better mechanisms for communication and response by the leadership, a growing chasm between the central authorities and the people was going to create additional problems of mismatched production in the various regions; new mechanisms were needed to move the nation closer to socialism. Proposals for regional reorganization and greater popular participation were made after a period of reevaluation. These were implemented along with measures to relate wages more directly to individual productivity in an effort to combat the problems of absenteeism and declining production that arose in the 1960s (5).

As a result, the Cubans have strengthened the basis for their further development. A five-year development plan was formulated, and national elections for local officials of Popular Power were held in October 1976. These elections, based on the new regional structure, were the culmination of a process by which control over local public services and production was vested in the people living within the area. The people, through meetings convened by their officials, could begin to participate directly in the implementation of programs to improve local conditions and to resolve local problems. They work strictly within the guidelines established by the national plan and by the production goals established for local work centers, and they do not have jurisdiction over plants that produce for the nation as a whole, as is the case with most heavy industry; these guidelines themselves were established after extensive consultation with the people. But they are working to resolve basic problems which often have an immediate impact on local conditions: transportation schedules, garbage collection, maintenance, food distribution, school and hospital services, cultural and sports activities, and the like. The Popular Power Organization also works directly with the trade unions to improve working conditions and to increase production, as well as to improve communication between the workers and the national planning board (JUCEPLAN) in the design of the annual programs to implement the five-year plan.

The Popular Power structure is still in its infancy. Its greatest challenge is to establish a workable balance between decentralized administration with popular participation and central direction of the society by the Communist Party; the process of stimulating popular participation in local administration will also lead to greater participation in the planning and direction of the society at all levels. The party is encouraging this movement as a way to break down many of the divisions that formerly existed in Cuba and to build a firmer base for socialism. In the process, a new geographic structure of rural towns and related urban systems is being forged into a single socialist country.

URBAN GROWTH AND SOCIALIST TRANSFORMATION: A CONCLUSION

The Cuban experience demonstrates that geographic development cannot be separated from the development of the social and productive forces. The history of capitalist societies is of a growing chasm between town and country, between mental and manual labor, and between classes. The Cubans attacked this problem frontally from the very beginning. The earliest redistributive measures forced a reallocation of resources from the urban areas to the countryside. Since then, Cuba has moved much further in the direction of directly attacking the causes for these divisions.

A new productive structure was necessary to support the changing social structure. Material and human limitations dictated an initial emphasis on agriculture. Now that agriculture has been restructured to supply food and exports, Cuba has moved to a second stage of development, in which industrialization is receiving primary emphasis. These stages are part of a broader program of socialist construction in which new political and social demands have also made their impact.

The residential structure of the population is gradually changing with the creation of a large number of smaller cities. Havana's population is growing only as fast as that of the country as a whole. Geographical decentralization is part of the industrialization plan and of programs to modernize agriculture. These efforts are being joined in new cities and towns where the population is mobilized for various tasks in a variety of sectors. The schools are being constructed in the countryside as part of these new regional development programs. Cultural offerings are widely available all over the island. And, significantly, the administrative structure has been altered to respond to the new requirements of the people and the possibilities of the evolving productive apparatus. Just as important, the "social 'disorganization' so characteristic of cities in capitalist countries" is no longer a problem, and "Cuban streets are clean and safe, and rarely populated by drunkards" (17, p. 27).

It seems significant that in the process of creating these changes, the Cubans have also been successful in opening channels of communication and in creating flexible administrative structures responsive to criticism. They have increased their ability to deal with problems through popular participation. In this way, Cubans also suggest that the transition to socialism is only a way station on the road to communism.

NOTES AND REFERENCES

1. Acosta, M., and J. Hardoy, *Urban Reform in Revolutionary Cuba*, Occasional Papers No. 1 (Antilles Research Program, Yale University, 1973).

2. Aguilera Macias, J., "El plan 'La escuela al campo': Un logro de la educación en Cuba," *Educación* (Habana) October 1971.

3. Bambirra, V., *La revolución cubana: Una reinterpretación* (México: Nuestro Tiempo, 1974).

4. Barkin, David, "Cuban Agriculture: A Strategy of Economic Development," in D. Barkin and N. Manitzas, eds., *Cuba: The Logic of the Revolution* (Andover, Mass.: Warner Modular Publications, 1973).

5. ———, "Popular Participation and the Dialectics of Cuban Development," *Latin American Perspectives,* December 1975.

6. ———, "The Redistribution of Consumption in Cuba," in D. Barkin and N. Manitzas, eds., *Cuba: The Logic of the Revolution, op. cit.*

7. Boorstein, Edward, *The Economic Transformation of Cuba* (New York: Monthly Review Press, 1968).

8. Casal, L., "On Popular Power: The Organization of the Cuban State During the Period of Transition," *Latin American Perspectives,* December 1975.

9. Castro, Fidel, *History Will Absolve Me* (New York: Grossman Publishers, 1969).

10. ———, Speech to the First Congress of the Cuban Communist Party, *Granma Weekly Summary,* December 28, 1975 and January 4, 1976.

11. Center for Cuban Studies, *Urban Reform Law* (New York: Center for Cuban Studies. n.d.).

12. Comité Cubano de Asentamientos Humanos, *Los asentamientos humanos en Cuba* (Habana: Editorial de Ciencias Sociales, Instituto Cubano del Libro, 1976).

13. Cuba, Consejo Nacional de Economía, *El presupuesto familiar cubano: Muestreo estadístico en el capital de la República,* Documento 162/EI/1 (Habana: August 13, 1951).

14. Cuba, Junta Central de Planificación, *Boletín Estadístico 1970* (Habana: 1970).

15. Cuba, Ministerio de Desarrollo de Edificaciones Sociales y Agropecuarias, *Cuba: La Vivienda/Desarrollo Urbano* (Habana: 1974).

16. ———, *La arquitectura escolar de la revolución cubana* (Habana: 1973).

17. Eckstein, Susan, "The Debourgeoisement of Cuban Cities" (Typescript, Boston University, 1976).

18. Edel, Matthew, "An Experiment in Growth with Social Justice: Thoughts on the 1970 Cuban Harvest," *Economic and Political Weekly* (India), July 1970.

19. Garnier, J.-P., *Une ville, une révolution: La Havana* (Paris: Editiones Anthropos, 1973).

20. Hardoy, J., "Spatial Structures and Society in Revolutionary Cuba," in D. Barkin and N. Manitzas, eds., *Cuba: The Logic of the Revolution, op. cit.*

21. Harnecker, M., *Cuba, ¿Dictadura o Democracia?* (México: Siglo XXI editores, 1975).

22. López Segrera, F., *Cuba: Capitalismo dependiente y subdesarrollo* (Habana: Casa de las Américas, 1972).

23. Pérez-Stable, M., "Whither the Cuban Working Class?," *Latin American Perspectives,* December 1975.

24. Pierre-Charles, G., *La genesis de la revolución cubana* (México: Siglo XXI editores, 1976).
25. Serge, R., *Cuba, Arquitectura de la Revolución* (Barcelona: Editorial Gustavo Gili, 1970).
26. Universidad Católica de Cuba, "¿Porqué Reforma Agraria?" (1957; rpt. in *Economía y Desarrollo* [Habana], No. 12, 1972).

Cities and Countryside
in the
Soviet Union and China

LARRY SAWERS

The purpose of this paper is to contrast regional and urban planning in the Soviet Union and China. Planners in the two countries have attempted to shape the regional distribution of economic activity and population and thereby to eliminate the "contradiction between town and countryside." Soviet efforts, which are discussed first, have focused primarily on preventing the growth of large cities and encouraging the growth of smaller cities. They have found this goal more difficult than anticipated and now appear to be abandoning it. In China, attempts to eliminate the town-countryside contradiction have revolved around developing small-scale industry in small towns and on the communes while preventing population movements into the large cities. Indications are that they have achieved considerable success. The second section of this paper examines urban planning or the design of spatial form within cities. The Soviets have designed cities with imposing centers and new housing arranged in neighborhoods, each with services supplied according to plan. Planners, however, do not believe that these neighborhood units should be any more than effi-

* The second part of this paper is a revised version of "Urban Planning in the Soviet Union and China," *Monthly Review*, January 1977; © 1977. Monthly Review, Inc. Reprinted by permission.

cient arrangements for delivering services. The Chinese, on the other hand, are building cities without dominant central districts. Neighborhoods are organized around productive activities, and a wide variety of formal and informal organizations promote, in contrast to Soviet neighborhoods, a sense of engagement and community on the part of residents.

CITY AND COUNTRYSIDE

Preventing Big Cities in the Soviet Union

After the 1917 revolution and ensuing civil war, Soviet cities lay in ruins, with much of their populations scattered to the countryside. The 1920s were crisis years of difficult rebuilding. In 1928, when the Soviet leaders began their first attempts to plan the entire economy, a vigorous debate began on how to resolve the contradiction between town and countryside (Goodman and Goodman, pp. 95ff.). One proposal was to develop "strip cities" or narrow bands of urban development stretching across the countryside, which would give the entire population access to urban amenities as well as fresh air and open space. Another proposal was simply to lower urban population densities (Lynd). Other ideas were to build satellite cities around the major urban centers. These communities, based on the writings of Howard and similar to the New Towns of Britain, the United States, and elsewhere, were to be self-contained settlements of several tens of thousands of inhabitants. Residents would largely work and shop within their communities but would be within convenient commuting distance (no more than fifty to sixty miles) of the metropolitan area in order to take advantage of cultural and entertainment resources which could be supported only in the large city. Most planners argued that these proposals should be supplemented by turning the countryside into a large agricultural factory, with a rural proletariat having access to urban amenities. All but the first of these proposals have played a significant role in Soviet spatial planning, but its primary theme has been the attempt to limit the growth of large urban concentrations. In 1931 a ceiling was placed on the population of Moscow; soon other large cities were assigned maximum populations. These targets have been frequently revised upward, but as late as 1958, Khrushchev stated flatly that large cities' growth must end (Osborn 1970, p. 203).

When one moves into a Soviet city, registration with the police is required, thus giving the authorities a device to control migration. Either the controls are not vigorously used to limit migration or migrants have found ways to circumvent them, since limits on population growth of larger cities have been consistently exceeded. Population has tended to crowd into existing urban centers where housing and urban services, though inadequate, do exist, rather than settling in new centers where such services are extremely scarce. The large cities have grown rapidly, surpassing growth limits soon after their promulgation. In spite of the fact that more than 800 new settlements have been built, the smaller urban places have grown more slowly than the larger ones (Svetlichnyi, p. 30). Between 1929 and 1969, the proportion of the urban population living in cities smaller than 100,000 fell from 64.9 percent to 48.2 percent (derived from Ruzavina, p. 82). The cities with the highest rate of population growth have been those with a half million or more inhabitants (Frolic, p. 677). Pioneers sometimes fail— the Soviet Union is the first country ever to attempt to limit big-city growth. Without the controls that they have exercised, it is probable that Soviet metropolises would be even larger than we now find them. Population ceilings are quickly exceeded, but one cannot demonstrate that Soviet attempts to limit the growth of big cities are without any effect.

Another way in which Soviet planners have attempted to limit the growth of large cities has been the restriction of urban spatial development. Beginning in the 1930s in Moscow and later in other cities, greenbelts were established surrounding the cities. In Moscow, the belt is about six miles wide and begins from eight to ten miles from the city center. Originally, the greenbelt was meant to be used solely as a recreation resource. Parks, zoos, sports fields, and lakes would provide Moscow's citizens with evening and weekend recreation. However, the intentions of the planners of the 1930s have not been fully met. Nearly one million persons live within the greenbelt, and the half million who live in the suburban zone beyond commute through the greenbelt to work in the city (Osborn, 1970, p. 213). Several important suburban communities lie within the greenbelt, and already about half of it is built up with industrial and residential development. Thus the Soviets have been only partially successful in limiting the spread of their larger cities.

The reason for the failure of administrative attempts to restrict migration and spatial growth relates to the inability of industrial-location planning to prevent new industrial growth in the existing urban centers. Soviet authorities have attempted to limit the growth of large cities through efforts to channel the location of new industrial enterprises into smaller cities. There is widespread agreement in the literature on Soviet urban planning that this goal has been only partially fulfilled. Economic planning has maintained its dominance over spatial planning from the beginning. This is reflected in the absence of effective measures to punish those who violate spatial plans (Kucherenko, p. 31). The reasons commonly given can be summed up by saying that industrial plants and the ministries that operate them, when faced with extremely ambitious growth targets, find that locating in existing urban centers enables the enterprise to appropriate what the Western economist calls external economies of scale (e.g., Simon, p. 311; Osborn, 1966, pp. 28–29). Industries can increase output faster if they locate near a preexisting infrastructure, a skilled labor force, suppliers, and customers. The geographical concentration of industry in the Soviet Union has increased for the same reasons that it did during a comparable period in the development of the United States and other capitalist countries. Other reasons for industrial concentration include the Soviet emphasis on building very large-scale plants in order to wring every last internal scale economy possible out of the technology being used. A few very large plants by themselves can together form the basis for a city. Furthermore, the pricing system does not discourage urban concentration. With wage rates, freight rates, and utility charges uniform across the country and rents nonexistent, enterprises have not been forced to pay for the external diseconomies associated with locating in large urban centers (Fallenbuchl). Thus, industrial development could be most easily encouraged in already-existing population centers. Since most housing has in the past been built by industrial enterprises, new housing grew up around the new and expanding industries. Attempts to limit population growth and the spatial spread of the city have been swamped by the overriding wish to increase production.[1]

One must remain, however, sympathetic to the Soviet desire for rapid growth. Much of what little urban and industrial wealth was in the country in 1914 was destroyed by World War I and the civil war. Long before World War II, the Soviets foresaw an invasion from Germany and began desperate preparations for war. The war itself devastated the western part of the country and killed a tenth of its population. As soon as that war was over, a cold war began, requiring still more resources to be devoted to military preparations. Given the obstacles the Soviet Union faced, it is not surprising that economic growth became its foremost priority. This emphasis on growth has had an obvious effect on Soviet cities.

The realization that limiting urban growth is far more difficult than originally conceived has led to much rethinking about the issue in the 1960s. Perevedentsev, a prestigious expert on migration policy from the Academy of Science's Institute of Economics, has argued that large cities are more efficient than small, that administrative costs are cheaper in larger cities, and that attempts to limit population growth run counter to the "natural process of urbanization," which is seen as a universal process quite independent of the prevailing mode of production (cited in Frolic, p. 685). O. S. Pchelintsev describes urban development largely in terms of the external scale economies that form the basis of capitalist cities and the bourgeois analysis of them. The object of planning, he argues, should be to resolve the contradictions of urban development by encouraging further growth rather than by limiting city size. These articles and others have stirred up much debate. Perevedentsev, for example, has been specifically criticized for his fascination with bourgeois ideas (Frolic, p. 685). But one high official of Gosstroi (the State Construction Committee), P. Svetlichnyi, has published comments supporting these authors. The notion that "urbanism is a universal world process" is rapidly gaining ground in the Soviet Union (Frolic, p. 679). One very careful Western observer of Soviet city planning argued in 1966 that the "city planning profession may soon give up the whole idea of an 'optimal size' for cities as unfruitful and impossible to enforce" (Osborn, 1966, p. 29). Michael Frolic in 1970 indicates that the trend continues.

Some authors who have abandoned earlier allegiance to limiting big-city growth still argue that the contradiction between town and countryside must and can be eliminated. Pchelintsev, for example, asserts that the current optimal size is merely an historical stage, and that in the future the city as a social-spatial form will be eliminated. "The new, higher social-spatial form, based on unconstrained layout of extensive areas and upon specialization and spatial separation of functional zones, contrasts with the old urban form and constitutes a means of overcoming it and of resolving its contradictions" (p. 21). The entire country will become one suburbanized industrial region, and this "suburban regional form is a special sort of *synthesis of the classical forms of village and city*" (p. 22). The contradiction between town and countryside, according to this author, will be eliminated by transforming the country into an extended suburban region.

The experience of the Soviet Union (and Central Europe) shows that planning organized on efficiency criteria replicates the same uneven development as found in explicitly capitalist economies. The emphasis on the development of the forces of production and economic efficiency has overwhelmed earlier attempts to lessen the contradiction between town and countryside by limiting the growth of big cities. Attempts to arrest the growth of large cities has at best slowed their growth, and it now appears that Soviet planners are giving up the goal of limiting big city growth.

Walking on Two Legs in China

The Chinese, like the Soviets, have made the dispersion of industry the centerpiece of their regional economic planning. The decentralization of industry has occurred in two directions, away from the coastal provinces to the interior (comparable to the Soviet movement of industry away from the European regions) and away from the larger urban centers to smaller ones or to rural areas. Until 1958, it was the former type of decentralization that was stressed. At the time of the revolution, industry was located primarily in the coastal regions (eight major coastal cities accounted for three-quarters of all the modern-sector industrial production), but between 1949 and 1957 over half of all investment went to the inland regions (Roll and Yeh, pp. 82–84). By 1958, inland cities produced one-third of gross industrial product as compared with one-quarter a decade earlier (Richman, p. 565). The reasons given for the emphasis on the development of the interior were primarily military, but saving on transportation costs and the exploitation of as-yet-undeveloped natural resources in the interior have also been stressed. With the advent of the Great Leap Forward in 1958, the Chinese have shifted their focus away from development of the inland regions versus the coastal ones, and there has been little change in the relative share of gross industrial output from coastal and inland regions since that time (Roll and Yeh, p. 81; see also Buchanan, pp. 236–39).

The Great Leap Forward, 1958–1961, saw a new burst of energy aimed at redirecting regional economic patterns inherited from feudal and capitalist society (Wheelright and MacFarlane, Chap. 2). Industrial policy became one of "walking on two legs," i.e., development of medium and small industry in the small towns and on the communes, as well as continuing efforts to expand large-scale industry in the coastal centers, thereby taking advantage of both modern technology and indigenous methods. The reasons for this policy were given as follows:

1. Natural resources such as coal and iron-ore deposits were widely spread and easily mined. Other resources such as ashes were ubiquitous. Small-scale industry could tap these resources easily with minimum demands on the overstrained transportation network.
2. The indigenous technology was less demanding in quality of construction. Poorer quality of raw materials encouraged the development of new technologies that reduced costs.
3. Small-scale industry could often be constructed very quickly, leading to a rapid return on investment. For instance, in Wuhan, a small blast furnace with a capacity of 180 tons per year was constructed by twelve people in nine days.
4. In an economy where the means of production were extremely scarce, it was important to push small-scale industry, which was labor-intensive and used little equipment. For example, the above-mentioned blast furnace was built at an expense of only a few hundred dollars.
5. The modern industrial sector was most vulnerable to military attack; it was thus imperative that industry not be concentrated in a few big plants.
6. Small-scale industry, close to the farms, can employ labor that would otherwise be seasonally idle.

Perhaps the most important reason for emphasizing small-scale industry was what this policy did to people. "Walking on two legs" directly attacks the three great divisions among the people, between worker and peasant, between city and countryside, and between mental and manual labor. Small-scale industry calls upon the creative character of the masses in a way that leads to an enormous outburst of innovative energy; this contributed to many immediate technological improvements, but more importantly built the basis for further innovative efforts. Even a small success at solving a difficult problem of production yields not only knowledge and skills which can make further innovation easier, but it also builds the spirit of self-confidence, self-reliance, and powerfulness that is crucial in maintaining the momentum of the process. Allowing the masses to become involved in solving production problems breaks down the division between mental and manual labor. This involvement reduces alienation and unleashes enormous productive energies. The decentralization of industry is one part of a program to build a sense of involvement in the process of production quite unlike what is found in capitalist countries or the Soviet Union. The result is a rapid growth in the forces of production. The growth is not a quantitative increase in modern producers' goods as stressed by Soviet planners, but a qualitative shift; the forces of production grow because the energy of the people is freed from the fetters of the capitalist division of labor.

The Great Leap Forward developed an astounding number and variety of industrial enterprises. In 1958 alone, the communes constructed 200,000 small industrial plants. This number was in addition to 600,000 backyard steel furnaces and many thousands of plants that sprouted in the cities (CIA, p. 5). In 1960 the Soviets, disturbed about Chinese political and economic policies, abruptly withdrew their aid, even taking with them the blueprints of partially finished factories. About the same time, a severe drought struck the economy and agricultural production met severe difficulties. It is also clear that much of the production from the new factories was of poor quality. The Western press tends to emphasize the latter reason while the Chinese emphasize the former two, but whatever the proper balance, the Great Leap had to be abandoned.

As the economy recovered during the mid-1960s, a number of small plants, particularly for cement and chemical fertilizers, were constructed. During the Cultural Revolution, 1966 to 1968, the goals and perceptions of the Great Leap came once again to dominate industrial-location policy, but the massive campaign to build small plants that was launched during the Cultural Revolution never achieved the scope or intensity of the 1958 to 1960 period. After 1972, the pendulum appeared to swing once more, and the small-plants program was reduced (CIA, p. 6). One should note that the bulk of these small plants are under the control of the communes or provinces. The national planning agencies control only a portion of the modern sector, primarily producers' goods such as oil, steel, power, and transport, which amount to only 6.8 percent of the country's industrial production (Bettelheim, p. 46). This decentralization of industrial administration in China is in striking contrast to the centralization of economic-planning decisions in Moscow.

It is difficult to find numbers that indicate the extent of industrial decentralization in China today. Ever since 1960, the Chinese have published few statistics about their economy. Travelers repeatedly describe communes with a variety of small industrial plants. Wheelright and MacFarlane note a commune near Peking, for example, which has a powdered-milk factory, flour mill, soybean-oil mill, and seed-oil mill, in addition to small workshops producing parts of sewing machines, small cables and wire, and electrical accessories (p. 187; see also Buchanan, Chap. 7). But it is difficult to know how typical these communes, most of them near the larger cities, are of the entire country. The U.S. Central Intelligence Agency has published estimates of small-plant production. These plants are defined as ones that use simple technology, are located in rural areas, depend on local resources and administration, and directly or indirectly support agriculture. They currently produce almost all of the country's simple farm tools and a substantial portion of its basic farm machinery, more than 50 percent of its nitrogen fertilizer and 75 percent of its phosphate fertilizer, 50 percent of the country's cement, 5 percent of its electrical power, 30 percent of its coal, 20 percent of its iron, and 15 percent of its steel (p. 1). Another source indicates that the number of workers in rural industry is roughly equal to the number of urban industrial workers in mining and manufacturing (Sigurdson, p. 412). According to these statistics, however, workers are considered rural if they live in any town smaller than 20,000. We should further note that only about 5 percent of China's labor force is occupied in rural industry. China is still a largely agricultural economy, and the discussion of industrial location policy in these pages should not obscure that fact.

The obverse of the policy of industrializing the countryside has been one of agriculturalizing the cities. Self-reliance and self-sufficiency are goals throughout China. Where urban planners have been allowed to plan new construction rather than merely adapt to prerevolutionary structures, vegetable gardens are regularly a part of factory complexes. Even small enterprises are assigned plots. In Peking, self-sufficiency in apple production has been attained as several hundred thousand trees (not all apple) are planted each year within the city and its environs (CCAS, p. 146). As another example, of the forty-seven branches of the Kiangsi Communist Labor University, ten were self-sufficient in grain production (and eighteen were financially self-sufficient) (Gardner, p. 251). As cities expand, planners preserve cultivated land with high vegetable yield. In addition, thousands of city dwellers go to the countryside seasonally to assist with the harvest; in some cases as much as three-quarters of a town's population will go to the countryside (Karol, p. 203). Many thousands of party cadres and bureaucrats have spent months in rural areas in May 7 schools learning among other things the value of agricultural labor. To the Westerner, the industrialization of the countryside is perhaps the most striking aspect of the Chinese program to end the contradiction between town and countryside. But moving to urban self-sufficiency and changing urban attitudes toward the peasant by encouraging city dwellers to engage in agricultural production has been a crucial part of the Chinese strategy.

Clear differences between the Soviet Union and China are apparent with regard to the decentralization of industry and its administration, but there is another aspect of regional policy where differences between the two countries are much less clear. Both countries have attempted to reduce urban-rural distinctions in consumption patterns. Both have made dramatic strides toward eliminating illiteracy in the countryside and bringing at least a minimum level of medical services to rural areas. In both countries, aside from food consumption, standards of living remain higher in the cities than in rural areas. In the Soviet Union in recent years, farm income has risen more rapidly than urban (Bronson and Severin, 1973b, p. 380; Smith, p. 413). But significant differences persist; in 1964 rural workers earned only about 45 percent as much as urban workers (adjusted for income in kind but not for communal consumption) (derived from Bronson and Severin, 1966, p. 511). There are no systematic data for China which permit comparison with the Soviet Union.

There is some indication of significantly different access to higher education on the part of the peasants in the two countries. One observer of Soviet social programs remarks that realization of educational aspirations of university education were "drastically lower for farm children" (Osborn, 1970, p. 135). In China, on the other hand, vigorous efforts have been made to open up higher education to manual workers, particularly since the Cultural Revolution. Elitest entrance requirements that discriminated against peasants have been eliminated. Manual labor is required for a lengthy period before admission to higher education. Schools are expected to be productive, and many are self-sufficient in agricultural production. Thus there are clear differences between the Soviet Union and China with regard to peasants' access to higher education. Given the different stages of development of the two countries and their very different histories, it is quite difficult to evaluate the meager evidence available and arrive at any conclusive statements about rural-urban differences in consumption of education or other goods and services in the two countries.

Paralleling their efforts to decentralize industry, the Chinese have placed considerable energy into limiting the migration of peasants to the cities and have encouraged city dwellers to move to the countryside. Four basic commodities—rice, flour, plain cloth, and oil—are rationed in China's urban areas. Through a careful coordination of the issuance of ration cards and work permits, no one is allowed to come to the city without a job. Thus the growth of the urban population can be strictly controlled. Furthermore, many persons have been persuaded to move from the city to the countryside. "Workshops and entire departments are moved; the decisions are made after collective discussion in the factories about who is to leave, etc." (Bettelheim, p. 88). One observer reported that 8 million young people have left the city for the countryside since 1968 (Thompson, p. 600). The effect of all this on the over-all growth of cities in China is less than clear. During the 1950s, China's urban population as a whole doubled, with the medium-sized cities in the interior growing most rapidly (Thompson, p. 595). National data on the period since 1960 are unavailable, but there are a few clues that China's rapid urban growth is finished (Thompson, pp. 596–98). Several observers report that the central areas of Shanghai have not gained any population since Liberation. City planners in Changsa have reported that the population of that city has stabilized. A group of British city planners visited several Chinese cities recently and reported little sign of new construction on the periphery of the cities they visited. In short, there is little firm evidence, but what hints that do exist point in the direction of supporting the Chinese claim that they are conducting the first industrialization in history to be accompanied by disurbanization.

CITIES

The Rise and Fall of the Soviet Microdistrict

There have been two major concerns of Soviet urban planning since the 1930s: first, the overall geographical structure of the city or urban form, and second, the planning of individual neighborhoods.

The form and structure of Soviet cities is similar to that of capitalist cities, in that the center, with its multistoried buildings, dominates the city, while intensity of land use declines as one moves away from the center (Parkins, p. 67; Fisher, 1967, p. 1081). In Soviet cities, the central district was to be primarily administrative rather than commercial or industrial as in capitalist cities.[2] The 1935 plan for Moscow—which was to be a model for the rest of the country—mandated the construction of broad ceremonial avenues and an imposingly monumental center. Major thoroughfares were sometimes two and three hundred feet wide. One writer described the architectural style of the center as "grandiose and severe, dominating all other construction of the city" (Parkins, p. 67). Large, ornate buildings, skyscrapers, and enormous ceremonial squares were planned for the center. After World War II, this concept of planning continued to grow in importance (Parkins, p. 67). The University of Moscow is an example of the skyscrapers that punctuated Moscow's skyline between 1946 and 1952.

The ideological function of this style of design is supposedly to evoke solidarity through pride and grandeur. The danger is that instead of evoking a sense of socialist solidarity, the monumental center with its broad avenues radiating outward would become a visual symbol of hierarchical social structure and an expression not of socialist liberation but of repression (Goodman, Chap. V). The visual impact of the Moscow plan fosters a sense of personal triviality rather than political engagement with society. Many Western observers have commented that the Moscow plan of 1935 may have more to do with Russian nationalism than with socialism. Two years after Stalin's death, the heavily monumental style that flourished under his leadership was officially condemned by the Party (Osborn, 1970, pp. 249–50). However, the notion that the city center should dominate urban form remains an important principle of Soviet urban planning.

Beginning with the second five-year plan, the major tool of city planning in the Soviet Union has been the organization of residential apartment buildings into *mikrorayony*, or "microdistricts," which are neighborhoods grouped around locally needed services. First used in Moscow in 1935, the microdistrict ideally has 75 to 125 acres with a population of 5,000 to 15,000 (see Hall, pp. 170ff.). The ideal microdistrict had a child-care center, primary school, clinic, restaurant, library, clubroom, and park. Several microdistricts were grouped together to form residential districts, each of which had a higher level of services. The purpose of designing neighborhoods in this fashion has been primarily to organize the distribution of urban services. The use of microdistricts as a planning device gradually withered after their initial endorsement in the 1935 Moscow Plan. From the late 1930s to the mid 1950s, apartments were built along the broad, ceremonial avenues that were emphasized under Stalin's leadership, with architects often planning only the facades (Parkins, p. 46; Osborn, 1970, pp. 249–50). After Stalin's death the microdistrict regained favor, and by 1958 was the planning concept prescribed in the planning standards issued by Gosstroi, the state construction agency. During the 1960s, the use of the term and concept of the microdistrict once again appeared to wane, and is being supplanted by the term *kvartal*, which has a much more vague denotation, though it is generally smaller than a microdistrict. The planning of urban services in hierarchies of urban neighborhoods and districts, however, continues to dominate Soviet urban planning.

One should be aware that the planning of cities by neighborhoods is an ideal infrequently met in the past. During the later years of Stalin's leadership, even the ideal was put aside. After 1955, the planning of urban neighborhoods was often sacrificed to other goals. After the incredible destruction of Soviet cities during World War II, the meager resources that remained after industry and armaments were built were spent on desperately needed housing—other items were considered postponable luxuries.

> There has been a tendency to "save" the construction of service areas for the last, and then a hasty attempt has been made to provide them to people "stranded" in a serviceless area. Eventually these services will be provided, though there may be a considerable time lag. In fact, so great is the need to get people into new houses that families move before the pavements, gardens, and sometimes roads around the blocks are completed (Frolic, p. 301).

Hall has noted a "remarkable indifference to practical town planning in the Soviet Union itself, despite official enthusiasm and despite some notable pioneering examples" (p. 179). He goes on to say that as late as 1960, only 213 out of 875 cities had chief architects, and 600 had no approved plan. At present, however, most cities do have plans (Fromin, p. 51). The Soviets have not directed a great deal of energy toward urban planning or toward the implementation of the plans that have been made. At least part of the problem was the overwhelming emphasis on rapid industrialization. The Soviet Union devoted its scarce resources to factories and little was left over for housing, not to speak of the barest minimum of urban amenities.[3]

The concept that spatial arrangement of residences should be designed to foster interaction has been a recurrent theme in Soviet thinking about cities. The commune movement of the 1920s was one expression of this goal.[4] Some planners have believed that the microdistrict would also foster a sense of neighborliness. In the last decade, however, social interaction, as a goal of urban planning, has faded in the Soviet Union. The microdistricts are not devoid of social cooperation.

> Microdistricts are meant to provide the framework for a large array of community services. However, these are strictly voluntary. Volunteers staff kindergartens and libraries and help the police keep order. But neither the microdistricts nor the large residential districts into which they fit have any official function. Their boundaries do not coincide with administrative divisions, which are much larger (Osborn, 1966, p. 30).

The use of volunteers from the neighborhood to produce services for their neighbors has undoubtedly promoted a sense of community.

On balance, however, microdistricts in the Soviet Union appear to have done little to promote social interaction among their residents. One careful reviewer of Soviet urban sociology in the 1960s remarked that "Soviet sociologists have just published the results of a number of surveys showing that feelings of 'neighborliness' (sosedstra) have declined drastically in large cities. Social intercourse (obshcheenije) actually decreases in neighborhood units" (Frolic, pp. 681–82). Baranov has argued that "Based upon our research, inhabitants of apartment complexes in neighborhood units know only 5 to 10 of their neighbors by sight, 3 to 5 by name, and almost nothing about where they work or about their character" (cited in Frolic, p. 682). He concludes that the use of the microdistrict as a tool of organizing urban services rather than promoting social interaction is acceptable, since "the tyranny of neighborhood control and neighbor's opinion [is] one of the worst features of small town and rural life" (p. 684). One Soviet sociologist argues "that Soviet attempts to organize city life into a series of decentralized neighborhood units have failed because they 'contradict the very nature of the city with its basic tendencies of urbanization which require greater, rather than less, mobility'" (cited in Frolic, pp. 680–81). In the Soviet Union, one's primary identification is with one's fellow workers, not one's neighbors. The planning of cities in neighborhoods has apparently not encouraged social interaction, and planners are increasingly abandoning even the goal.

Even the notion that the microdistrict should be used as a tool for organizing the distribution of urban services is increasingly being disputed by planners and architects (Osborn, 1970, pp. 255–57). The issue as many see it is one of convenience; should shops and services be placed to serve only the residents of the microdistricts or to attract other clienteles? "In the terminology of Soviet planners this is the difference between 'closed' and 'open' forms of service and in the 1960s the advocates of the latter appear to be in the majority" (Osborn, 1970, p. 255). It is argued that much shopping is done on the way home from work and thus shops should be located along the thoroughfares. Shops in the microdistricts are patronized during the day primarily by the elderly who remain home in a society where most adults work. It is argued by many prominent planners that shops should be located to reflect these behaviors. The whole concept of organizing urban services, particularly commercial facilities, by neighborhoods may soon be abandoned in the Soviet Union.

An important strand in the Soviet analysis of cities that appears to underlie much of this current rethinking of urban policies deserves mention at this point. Robert Osborn observes:

> Urban planning in the Soviet Union has been left in the hands of professionals, who are not rigidly bound by political theory or unduly subject to party interference. . . . City planners in Russia seem at present to be less ideological, in the sense of pursuing a social ideal through planning, than their Western counterparts (1966, pp. 26–27).

This non-Marxist author sees a growing depoliticization of urban planning in the Soviet Union. It could be argued, on the contrary, that the politics of planning is not disappearing but rather shifting to a bourgeois perspective. Many careful analysts of the Soviet Union believe that it has come to resemble capitalist countries in a number of important respects (see, e.g., Sweezy). The Chinese and their followers even argue that capitalism has been literally restored in the Soviet Union. It does appear that many of the principles that previously guided Soviet spatial planning are fading out of use and being replaced by improvisation and pragmatism, but "being practical" is ideology, even though unexamined ideology.

An observer reports that during the last decade, social scientists in the Soviet Union have increasingly assumed that "an urban way of life exists in the USSR and that [this way] of life is part of a universal process" (Frolic, p. 678). Other authors speak of "urbanism as a universal world process," and of a "common metropolitan culture" (Frolic, p. 679). We have noted above the convergence of Soviet and Western thinking about optimal city size. The culmination of a half century of Soviet thinking about cities is the belief that the geographic structure of socialist cities is much the same as that of capitalist cities, though better managed because of central planning and the public ownership of land. Since the October Revolution, the dominant Soviet attitude has been that communism would be achieved by rapid quantitative growth in the forces of production. Adapting the spatial superstructure to the new mode of production has received steadily less and less emphasis over the decades. Some observers now argue that Soviet urbanologists have given up the belief that urban geography, which is part of society's superstructure, does or should differ between socialism and capitalism.

Communities within Chinese Cities

In contrast to the fitful and now virtually dormant view of the Soviets that city planning should be concerned with designing a physical environment that fosters social interaction, the major focus of literature on Chinese cities is the social and political engagement of city dwellers. This is apparent in the Chinese view of urban form, in the attempts to plan neighborhoods, and in the political organization of the city by neighborhoods.

In contrast to Soviet and Western cities, in China there is not a strong focus on the center of the city as the prime organizing core. There is, of course, much variation from one city to the next as the goals of Chinese city planning are applied flexibly in different contexts. Furthermore, some Chinese cities were built by Western imperialists, modeled after Western cities, and still bear the imprint of capitalist modes of constructing cities. Shanghai, for example, has a central business district dominated by many twenty-odd-story buildings. In addition, city planning in the 1950s followed the Soviet model; the city was the bureaucratic center of the economy and the city center was the dominant focus of the city. Large buildings were constructed in a ponderous style (CCAS, pp. 105, 107; Karol, p. 205). Where planners have not had to work with a city already constructed under capitalism, the center—at least since 1958—plays only a small role. The Committee of Concerned Asian Scholars describes Peking: "The impression is suburban, although the physical layout and land use are definitely urban" (p. 107). Canton is described as follows:

> Our first impression was of a continuous series of small towns. Each area had its own streets of shops, noodle stands, and playgrounds, with no apparent "center" of the city. From a rise looking out over the city, the rooftops seemed all of equal height, undulating with the curves of the land rather than jutting up from it. There were no skyscrapers. Because the city is spread out, as our bus rolled through the streets we saw only a gradual change from the more concentrated inner city to the suburbs (CCAS, pp. 107–8).[5]

Some Chinese cities have large central ceremonial squares like Soviet cities, but there is little evidence as to the current importance of these squares, whether they are seen as the pinnacle of the urban hierarchy or rather relics from an earlier age. In recent years the ceremonial role of the central square (Tienanmen Square) in Peking has been reduced, and National Day celebrations have been held in parks scattered throughout the city. (During the October 1st celebrations in 1975, Tienanmen Square was used as a vast parking lot. [*New York Times*, Oct. 2, 1975, p. 9; *Washington Post*, Oct. 1, 1975, p. A-1].) Since the Great Leap Forward, at any rate, the thrust of Chinese city planning has been the design of neighborhoods to promote social interaction. Planning an imposing center that dominates the entire city would, of course, detract from their emphasis on the neighborhood.

The city as a series of largely similar neighborhoods, as the CCAS describes Canton, contrasts sharply with the Soviet and capitalist city characterized by the sharp separation of land use into industrial, commercial, and residential districts (Parkins, p. 83). When efficiency is the goal, uneven development characterizes economic activity, and economic geography becomes highly differentiated. When "politics are in command," however, this as well as other divisions of labor can be eliminated.

The key organizing principle of current Chinese city planning is the attempt to plan neighborhoods around places of employment (CCAS, pp. 112–13). One such factory complex in Peking was described by the CCAS:

> The February 7 Rolling Stock Plant is essentially a self-sufficient unit; it conmbines both industry and agriculture in productive work and has integrated housing, schools, factory, health center, and farming into one area. . . . The main factory is surrounded by a number of subsidiary factories and cottage-type industries. These secondary production units are important, not only to ensure that all materials are used thoroughly . . . , but also to provide work for the residents of the complex who are not employed in the main factory. . . . The factory owns a large amount of farmland, also worked by residents of the complex (p. 139).

Self-reliant communes that combine industrial and agricultural production are being developed in the countryside. Corresponding structures are also being produced in the city.[6] In the Soviet Union, housing is often built by industrial ministries as part of the construction involved in putting a new factory into operation. But usually the housing is turned over to municipal authorities within six months after it is built; increasingly even the construction of housing is being overseen by the city rather than the factory. I have seen no mention in the literature of efforts to juxtapose the factories and "their" housing. The productive unit is not the focus of a neighborhood in the Soviet Union. In China, however, the factory complex is run by a revolutionary committee charged with overseeing both the factory and the surrounding neighborhood. The consequences of organizing the urban community around self-sufficient productive units includes not only economizing on critically scarce transportation services—in Shanghai, it is claimed, most workers live within ten minutes' walk of their jobs—but also the fostering of the social integration of neighborhoods (Towers, p. 125).

The ideal of living and working in the same small neighborhood with urban services supplied according to plan is not one that socialist city planners originated. Ebenezer Howard in the 1890s made such a proposal in his plan for "garden cities of tomorrow" (see Bookchin, Chap. 4, for an excellent discussion of Howard). Howard realized that the "idiocy" of rural life and the decay of urban life could not be eliminated without solving the contradiction between town and country. But he failed to see that this contradiction was insolubly exacerbated by bourgeois social relations. There were sweeping economic and social changes implied in his urban design, yet he focused solely on the physical layout of the urban area.

Later planners following in Howard's footsteps have repeated the same errors, ignoring the larger society and concentrating on the technical aspects of design. In so doing, they have been unable to realize that the "New Towns" they design (the modern version of Howard's garden cities) are not consonant with a capitalist society. Indeed, the so-called New Towns that have been built in the United States are primarily just expensive suburbs and do not meet the ideal of a community where people both live and work. In fact, most of their residents do not work in their community, and much shopping, recreational, and cultural activity takes place outside the New Town.

To the extent that actual New Towns approach the ideal of a self-contained community, they become increasingly unsatisfactory to their residents. In an affluent capitalist society, household choice is virtually the only area in which one can exercise any degree of personal autonomy. A community which greatly reduces the range of consumer choice is irrational in a capitalist society, since it removes the primary mechanism of motivation. In a socialist society, people can have a greater sense of involvement and participation in society; elaborate consumption choice is counterproductive since it fosters invidious comparisons between people, weakens moral incentives, and emphasizes the fetish of privatization. Whyte has written a delightful essay on the tendency of urban services in the new towns toward the median —the Sears, Roebucks and the Howard Johnsons. It is only in the cities that an extraordinary variety of goods and services can be found. Similarly, most New Towners work elsewhere because limiting one's employment choice to the neighborhood drastically limits the kinds of jobs one might hold. The ideal of integrating productive and community life that is impossible in capitalist cities is being attained in China.

Some cities of China, especially Shanghai, were largely developed by the time of the revolution. In neighborhoods with prerevolutionary housing, there are still attempts to integrate production and residence. These take the form of neighborhood factories, often begun and operated by women who were formerly not wage workers, the retired, and the handicapped. The "walking on two legs" policy applies to the cities as well as the countryside. Small-scale plants using traditional labor-intensive techniques are scattered throughout China's cities. They produce transistors, embroidery, machine parts, and so forth, and often utilize the waste products of nearby factories. Instead of residences being planned around production as with the factory complexes, here we find production growing out of the energy and creativity of neighborhood residents.

In cities where industry was already located in built-up areas, there was no room to build housing around the factory. In Shanghai, 1 million of the city's 6 million residents live in workers' villages built on the periphery of the city (CCAS, p. 113). The average workers' estate has about 70,000 residents who are housed normally in five-story apartments. Like the Soviet microdistricts, the workers' estates include shops, markets, clinics, schools, parks, and cultural facilities. The workers' estates as well as pre-Liberation housing are managed by housing boards.

One way of ensuring that the neighborhood will become a community of people engaged with each other is to center political organizations there (Sidel, Chap. 3). We have noted that in the Soviet Union, neither the microdistricts nor the larger residential districts serve any formal political or administrative function but are merely planning categories. On the other hand, neighborhood political organizations in China are elaborate. The public-security station represents the lowest level of municipal administration (Salaaf, p. 290). Its main tasks are to register the population, perform constabulary services, and administer the rationing system. Street offices normally have the same jurisdictional boundaries as public-security stations. "Their purpose [is] to mobilize the residents within the area for political activities and thus strengthen the party's political control at the basic level" (Salaaf,

p. 290). Under each street office are ten to twenty residents' committees, which routinely carry out essential day-to-day services. Functions include supervising social services and welfare tasks (e.g., employment offices, nurseries), transmitting governmental edicts, channeling complaints upward, mediating local disputes and family squabbles, reporting suspicious activity or persons, and especially to look after the welfare of the young, old, and non–wage workers who are not served by committees at their place of work. Residents are encouraged to participate in residents' committees, but street offices are staffed by paid cadres.

During the Cultural Revolution, street revolutionary committees were set up to conduct residential mass criticsm and repudiation meetings, operate study courses, and seize power in the residents' committees. Various forms of ad hoc citizens groups experimented with performing neighborhood constabulary functions. Thus the degree of grass-roots participation in the political process organized at the neighborhood level has been strengthened. The committees are heavily involved in the lives of the neighbors but the expectation is that family members will take care of each other; committee members do not rush in with each crisis (Sidel, p. 75). The revolutionary committees, however, play a crucial role in integrating neighborhoods into a common political outlook and mutually supportive behavior.[7]

Chinese neighborhoods are planned as much as possible to foster a sense of community, of people working and living together in an integrated whole. Even where this is not possible, considerable energy has been directed toward building neighborhood political involvement of the mass of city dwellers.[8] The result has been a striking "sense of commitment, of cooperation, of relatedness, evident in China's neighborhoods" (Sidel, p. 156). The social life of the neighborhood is organized around shared activity. This includes productive activity where the legacy of capitalist urban form does not prevent it, as well as a myriad of mutual-support functions such as preschool child care or health care, study groups, the resident's committee, and the informal interaction which the neighborhood architecture often favors. And it is this shared experience which makes Chinese neighborhoods come alive (Sidel, Chap. 7). One is struck by the repeated reference in the literature on China's cities to the warmth and intimacy of Chinese neighborhoods. An especially revealing anecdote related by Ruth Sidel concerns a crowd of children of a neighborhood in which she was visiting rushing out to greet the adults as they came home from work in the evening. Later she learned that the children were warmly embracing not their parents, but rather their neighbors.

The literature on Soviet cities cited above describes a growing lack of interaction and involvement among city dwellers, especially residents of the newer planned neighborhoods. The anomie and alienation of American cities is starkly apparent to all. This contrasts dramatically with Sidel's characterization of Chinese urban life: "The organization of life in China's neighborhoods can perhaps be best viewed as a total community support system, one fostered and maintained by the residents of the neighborhood themselves" (p. 147). Chinese neighbors are involved with each other. All acts, even self-destructive ones, are political acts in that they affect others; thus, where politics is in command, every action is of interest to one's neighbors. While Leningrad's chief planner rails against the "tyranny of neighborhood control . . . [as] one of the worst features of small town and rural life," the Chinese are putting bulletin boards in residents' committee offices with the name of every fertile woman in the neighborhood with information concerning family planning and birth-control for each woman. Chinese communities are characterized by concern with one's neighbors. One of the results of this is the astonishing lack of crime, venereal disease, and drug addiction in modern China.

The Chinese have set out to build a society where important distinctions between the masses of people are withering away and in which mass engagement of the population in managing their lives is possible. Rather than designing cities with important and imposing centers, the Chinese have focused on building neighborhoods that foster a sense of community and intimacy, both through the physical arrangement of neighborhoods around productive facilities, where possible, and through the vigorous development of neighborhood political and social-service organizations.

CONCLUDING REMARKS

Emerging over the decades, the goal of Soviet spatial planning has become *efficiency*. This can be seen in their debates over optimal city size and in their emerging consensus that large cities are efficient and therefore good. It can also be seen in the issues raised in debates about the internal structure of the city—whether or not the microdistrict is an efficient vehicle for delivering services. This stress on efficiency is quite in keeping with the broader notions of a development strategy and the transition toward communism that prevail in the Soviet Union. Since the first five-year plan was promulgated in 1928, the overriding concern of Soviet policies has been very rapid economic growth, led by the producers'-goods industries. The abundance thereby achieved, it was argued, would protect the Soviet Union from military conquest and lay the material basis for the development of communism. Other aspects of social change received progressively less emphasis over the years because it was believed that abundance by itself would inevitably lead to a thorough revolutionizing of society. Accordingly, spatial planning has been increasingly subordinated to industrial growth.

This is not to argue that the Soviets have not reduced or eliminated many of the problems endemic to capitalist cities in the West. The Soviets inherited a poor country, only to find much of the results of their first development efforts destroyed by war. This, coupled with the most rapid urbanization of any country ever, has forced the Soviets to cut out any unnecessary frills. Even so, urban life in the Soviet Union has amenities not found in Western cities. Quick, efficient mass transit, very little street crime, small amounts of environmental pollution, virtually free medical care, and the absence of racial ghettoes or fiscal crises are found in Soviet cities (Davidow). Social-welfare spending, the reduction of unemployment, and the public ownership of land has made this possible. But Soviet spatial planning, both in theory and practice, has come to resemble that of the West.

In contrast, the key theme of Chinese spatial planning is *engagement*—all of the Chinese policies are consistent with the goal of integrating disparate segments of society into a single community. Regional planning has attempted to merge the city with the countryside through a number of policies. Within the cities, planning has sought to build a sense of involvement within neighborhoods. The Chinese attitude toward spatial planning mirrors their analysis of the larger society. Liberation, they argue, was the seizure of state power by the laboring classes. The old ruling class was deposed, but a new aristocracy would arise and the old class relations would reappear unless a continuous battle against all forms of power and privilege, all distinctions of status and rank, was waged. In order for the laboring classes to maintain their control over society, their continuous political engagement must be fostered. The Chinese development strategy, therefore, has not relied on bureaucrats or experts, or the big cities and industries where they thrive, but rather has attempted to draw the broad masses of the population into the development effort. Their spatial planning has attempted to build a sense of community between peasant and city dweller and among those who live in the cities.

NOTES

1. It is interesting to note that other countries with planning systems and priorities similar to those in the Soviet Union have experienced a similar failure to limit urban growth of large cities (Fisher, 1967, p. 1080). Fallenbuchl, in analyzing Poland, argues that the Soviet model of development "tends . . . to induce unequal development of towns of different sizes and in different regions" (p. 315). This, he asserts, exacerbates the contradiction between town and countryside. In Hungary, even though postwar resource availability dictated industrializing the Great Panonian Plain, Budapest has grown rapidly and the eastern plain remains underdeveloped (Berend). In Yugoslavia, with regional decentralization and the return to the market economy, we not unexpectedly find the same uneven development that has characterized urban development in other market economies (Musič, p. 325).

2. Planners in other Central European socialist countries have also desired noncommercial city centers, but have been generally unsuccessful. Budapest and Belgrade, for example, have large commercial districts at their center that give them the appearance and ambience of Western cities.

3. A hierarchy of urban neighborhoods and urban services that has guided planners in the Soviet Union is also found in Western cities. Indeed, a rather elaborate economic theory, known as central-place theory, has been developed for explaining spatial hierarchies of urban services in cities and regions dominated by markets rather than planners (Berry and Garrison). N. V. Baranov, Leningrad's chief planner, argued that the ideal of organizing cities in microdistricts was nearly universally accepted by urban planners throughout the world. In the West, of course, very few neighborhoods are in fact actually planned; but as we have seen, the microdistrict concept has not been universally applied in the Soviet Union either.

4. During the first two decades after the revolution, Soviet urbanists focused on the communal apartment house as the principal means of redirecting the architecture that had been inherited from capitalism. The concept of the communal apartment house has also played an important role in the thinking of planners, architects, and social scientists since then, but in actual practice there cannot have been more than several dozen built since the Revolution.

5. In modern capitalism, spread-out, low-profile, centerless cities have been created by the automobile and are a sign of social fragmentation. In China, where there are few private automobiles, this type of urban

form was created by conscious planning for the purpose of fostering social integration. (See discussion of urban neighborhoods, pp. 353–59.)

6. It is instructive to note a contrast with Soviet planning: when agricultural land was left within cities as industry leapfrogged over farms, planners were severely criticized for allowing such irrationality to persist.
(Kucherenko, p. 30; Baranov, p. 40).

7. Cuba has also moved toward decentralizing political power. Neighborhoods are organized in Committees for the Defense of the Revolution,
which began with primarily military duties but later acquired a wide
variety of social-service functions. An urban neighborhood even has its
own judiciary system, with judges, lawyers, jurors, and defendants all
being neighbors of each other.

8. In the Soviet Union, the microdistrict is a tool for planning *new* neighborhoods. There is virtually no mention in the literature on Soviet cities
of communities in prerevolutionary neighborhoods.

REFERENCES

Baranov, N. V., "Regulating the Size of Cities, Buildings and Neighborhoods," *The Soviet Review*, Sept. 1960.

Barkin, David, "The Redistribution of Consumption in Socialist Cuba," *Review of Radical Political Economics*, Fall 1972.

Berend, Ivan T., "Development and Urbanization in Hungary," in Alan A.
Brown, *et al.*, eds., *Urban and Spatial Economics in Market and
Planned Economies*, Vol. 1 (New York: Praeger, 1974).

Berry, Brian, and William Garrison, "Recent Developments of Central Place
Theory," *Papers of the Regional Science Association*, 1958.

Bettelheim, Charles, *Cultural Revolution and Industrial Organization in
China* (New York: Monthly Review Press, 1974).

Bookchin, Murray, *The Limits of the City* (New York: Harper and Row,
1974).

Braverman, Harry, *Labor and Monopoly Capitalism: The Degradation of
Work in the Twentieth Century* (New York: Monthly Review Press,
1974).

Bronson, David W., and Barbara S. Severin, "Recent Trends in Consumption and Disposable Money Income in the USSR," in 89th Congress,
2nd Session, Joint Economic Committee, *New Directions in the Soviet
Economy* (Washington: U.S. Government Printing Office, 1966).

———, "Soviet Consumer Welfare: The Brezhnev Era," in 93rd Congress,
1st Session, Joint Economic Committee, *Soviet Economic Prospects for
the Seventies*, (Washington: U.S. Government Printing Office, 1973).

Buchanan, Keith, *The Transformation of the Chinese Earth* (New York:
Praeger, 1970).

Central Intelligence Agency, "China: Role of Small Plants in Economic
Development" (Washington, D.C.: May 1974).

Committee of Concerned Asian Scholars, *China: Inside the People's Republic*
(New York: Bantam Books, 1972).

Davidow, Mike, *Cities without Crisis* (New York: International Publishers,
1976).

Engels, Friedrich, *The Housing Question* (Moscow: Progress Publishers, 1935).

Fallenbuchl, Zbigniew M., "Development and Urbanization in Poland," in Alan A. Brown, *et al.*, eds., *Urban and Spatial Economics in Market and Planned Economies*, Vol. 1 (New York: Praeger, 1974).

Fisher, Jack, "Urban Planning in the Soviet Union and Eastern Europe," in H. Wentworth Eldredge, *Taming Megalopolis*, Vol. 2 (Garden City: Anchor Books, 1967).

――――, *Yugoslavia—A Multinational State: Regional Differences and Administrative Response* (San Francisco: Chandler, 1966).

Frolic, Michael, "The Soviet Study of Soviet Cities," *Journal of Politics*, Aug. 1970.

Fromin, G., "Soviet City Planning in a New Stage," *Problems of Economics*, Apr. 1974.

Gardner, John, "Educated Youth and Urban-Rural Inequalities," in John Lewis, ed., *The City in Communist China*, (Stanford, Calif.: Stanford University Press, 1971).

Goodman, Percival, and Paul Goodman, *Communitas*, 2nd ed. (New York: Vintage Books, 1960).

Goodman, Robert, *After the Planners* (New York: Simon and Schuster, 1971).

Hall, Peter, *The World Cities* (New York: McGraw-Hill Book Co., 1966).

Karol, K. S., *China: The Other Communism*, 2nd ed. (New York: Hill and Wang, 1968).

Kucherenko, V. A., "How Can Our Cities Be Improved?" *Soviet Review*, Sept. 1960.

Lynch, Kevin, *The Image of the City* (Cambridge, Mass.: MIT Press, 1960).

Lynd, Martin, "Planned Soviet Cities," *Soviet Russia Today*, April, May, and June 1941.

Marx, Karl, "The German Ideology," in Marx, Engels, and Lenin, *On Historical Materialism* (Moscow: Progress Publishers, 1972).

Music̆, Vladimir-Branco, "The Response of Yugoslav Urban Planning to the Development of the Country," in Alan A. Brown, *et al.*, eds., *Urban and Spatial Economics in Market and Planned Economies*, Vol. 1 (New York: Praeger, 1974).

Nikolayev, I., "Industry and the City," *Izvestia*, May 4, 1960, reprinted in *Current Digest of the Soviet Press*, Vol. XII, No. 8.

Osborn, Robert J., "How the Russians Plan Their Cities," *Trans-action*, Sept.-Oct. 1966.

――――, *Soviet Social Policies: Welfare, Equality and Community* (Homewood, Ill.: Dorsey Press, 1970).

Parkins, Maurice Frank, *City Planning in Soviet Russia* (Chicago: University of Chicago Press, 1953).

Pchelintsev, O. S., "Problems of the Development of Large Cities," *The Soviet Review*, Winter 1966–1967.

Richman, Barry M., *Industrial Society in Communist China* (New York: Random House, 1969).

Roll, Charles Robert, and Kung-Chia Yeh, "Balance in Inland and Coastal Industrial Development," in Joint Economic Committee, U.S. Congress, *China: A Reassessment of the Economy* (Washington, D.C.: U.S. Government Printing Office, July 10, 1975).

Ruzavina, E., "Economic Aspects of the Urbanization Process," *Soviet Review*, Sept. 1960.

Salaaf, Janet W., "Urban Residential Communities in the Wake of the Cultural Revolution," in John W. Lewis, ed., *The City in Communist China* (Stanford, Calif.: Stanford University Press, 1971).

Schroeder, Gertrude G., "Regional Differences in Incomes and Levels of Living in the USSR," in U. N. Bandera and Z. L. Melnyk, eds., *The Soviet Economy in Regional Perspective* (New York: Praeger, 1973).

Sidel, Ruth, *Families of Fengsheng: Urban Life in China* (Baltimore: Penguin Books, 1974).

Sigurdson, Jon, "Rural Industrialization in China," in Joint Economic Committee, U.S. Congress, *China: A Reassessment of the Economy* (Washington, D.C.: U.S. Government Printing Office, July 10, 1975).

Simon, Roger, and Maurice Hookham, "Moscow," in W. A. Robson, ed., *Great Cities of the World* (London: George Allen and Unwin: 1954).

Smith, Willard W., "Housing in the Soviet Union—Big Plans, Little Action," in 93rd Congress, 1st Session, Joint Economic Committee, *Soviet Economic Prospects for the Seventies* (Washington, D.C.: U.S. Government Printing Office, 1973).

Strumilim, S., "Family and Community in the Soviet of the Future," *Soviet Review*, Feb. 1961.

Svetlichnyi, P., "Soviet Town Planning Today," *Problems of Economics*, Dec. 1960.

Sweezy, Paul M., "The Nature of Soviet Society," *Monthly Review*, Nov. 1974 and Jan. 1975.

Thompson, Robin, "City Planning in China," *World Development*, July-Aug. 1975.

Torre, Susana, "Architecture and Revolution: Cuba 1959 to 1974," *Progressive Architecture*, Oct. 1974.

Towers, Graham, "City Planning in China," *Journal of the Royal Town Planning Institute*, March 1973.

Wheelright, E. L., and Bruce MacFarlane, *The Chinese Road to Socialism: The Economics of the Cultural Revolution* (New York: Monthly Review Press, 1970).

Whyte, William H., *The Last Landscape* (Garden City, N.Y.: Anchor Books, 1970).

Wu, Yuan-li, *The Spatial Economy of Communist China* (New York: Praeger, 1967).

Zeitlin, Morris, "A Tale of Two Cities," *New World Review*, Nov.-Dec. 1974.

Contributors

Patrick J. Ashton was born and raised in the city of Detroit. He currently lives in Lansing, Michigan, and is working on a Ph.D. in sociology at Michigan State University, where he also teaches. Pat is interested in urban political economy, the sociology of knowledge, and theories of the capitalist state. His current research focuses on the unionization of municipal workers.

David Barkin is a political economist who has visited Cuba a number of times since the revolution. He teaches Marxian political economy and development economics, and has specialized in Latin America. He is particularly interested in the transition to socialism and the contradictions provoked by the expansion of international capitalism in the Third World. He has taught at many institutions in North America and in Latin America.

Katharine Coit was brought up in Cambridge, Massachusetts. She studied political science, modern history, city planning, and urban sociology at McGill University, Montréal, at Newnham College, Cambridge, England, and at the University of Paris. Henri Lefebvre directed her doctoral dissertation, "Silences et revoltes des usagers" (a comparative study of local action in the United States, France, Great Britain, and Italy), just completed this year. Katharine is currently teaching a course in American Civilization at the University of Paris VII, and bringing up two French teen-agers. Her current research is on social control through the reproduction of hierarchical forms in community groups.

365

David M. Gordon teaches economics in the Graduate Faculty of the New School for Social Research. He has written *Theories of Poverty and Underemployment*, edited *Problems in Political Economy: An Urban Perspective*, and co-edited *Labor Market Segmentation*. He lives on the Lower East Side in New York City. He says he first knew he was a city kid when, as a young Californian, he preferred playground basketball to backpacking.

Jim Green is a member of the *Radical America* editorial collective and has taught urban and labor history at the university level.

Chester Hartman is an urban planner living in San Francisco. He holds a Ph.D. in city and regional planning from Harvard and has taught there. Currently, he is teaching at the University of California, Berkeley. His books include *Housing and Social Policy, Yerba Buena: Land Grab and Community Resistance in San Francisco*, and *Housing Urban America* (co-edited with Jon Pynoos and Robert Schafer).

Richard Child Hill teaches urban studies and political economy in the Department of Sociology at Michigan State University. He has published articles on patterns of social inequality in cities in the United States and is currently writing a book on the post–World War II political economy of Detroit.

Allen Hunter is a member of the *Radical America* editorial collective, has taught history and social sciences at the high-school level, and is now a graduate student in sociology.

Rob Kessler is currently a junior-high-school history teacher. He also works with Peoples Press, a nonprofit publishing collective that produces popular materials explaining the nature of U.S. imperialism. While at the Press, he has helped to write and produce *Children of the Dragon*, a children's story about Viet Nam, and *Angola, a Photo-Essay,* an introductory book about the recent successful independence struggle in Angola. Previously, Rob spent several years involved in tenant and community organizing in Berkeley and Oakland. During much of this time he was associated with the National Housing Law Project and worked on the case study of Yerba Buena Center and co-authored articles on the political economy of Yerba Buena and of municipal housing-code enforcement.

Ann Markusen is an assistant professor of city and regional planning at the University of California, Berkeley. She works actively with local women's, community, and labor groups. Currently she is working on a Brookings Public Policy fellowship studying regional economic development and the role of the state under capitalism.

John H. Mollenkopf lives in San Francisco and teaches urban politics and public policy at the Stanford Graduate School of Business. An expanded version of his paper is included in his forthcoming book, *Growth Defied: Community Organization and Political Conflict over Urban Development*. His current research focuses on urban service bureaucracies, particularly transit agencies, the comparative political economy of urban development, and the theory of the state.

Michael E. Stone teaches in the Center for Community Change and Housing, College of Public and Community Service, University of Massachusetts at Boston. He has worked with and for community groups in New Jersey and Massachusetts as an advocacy planner, researcher, technical assistant, trainer, and organizer. He is the author of *People Before Property: A Real Estate Primer and Research Guide*, and co-author of *Tenants First: A Research and Organizing Guide to FHA Housing* and *Hostage! Housing and the Massachusetts Fiscal Crisis*. He received his A.B. from UCLA and Ph.D. in astrophysics from Princeton.

Larry Sawers is an associate professor of economics at the American University in Washington, D.C. He joined the faculty there in 1969 and has helped to develop a graduate program in political economy at the university, one of only three in the country. He received his Ph.D. in economics from the University of Michigan and has since published in the fields of urban, labor, and public-finance economics. He likes wood carving, playing his guitar, and backpacking.

William K. Tabb was born in New York City, lives in a cooperative consisting of seven reconverted brownstones on Manhattan's Upper West Side, and teaches urban economics at Queens College, in the City University. For the academic year 1977–1978 he is Visiting Professor at the Department of Economics, University of California, Berkeley. He is the author of *The Political Economy of the Black Ghetto*. Having grown up playing stickball on city streets, he has recently discovered backpacking in the country. He likes it.

Index